Anime's Knowledge Cultures

Anime's Knowledge Cultures

Geek, Otaku, Zhai

JINYING LI

UNIVERSITY OF MINNESOTA PRESS

MINNEAPOLIS • LONDON

Portions of chapter 3 were previously published as "The Interface Affect of a Contact Zone: *Danmaku* on Video-Streaming Platforms," *Asiascape: Digital Asia* 4, no. 3 (2017): 233–56. Portions of chapter 6 were previously published in a different form in "From Superflat Windows to Facebook Walls: Mobility and Multiplicity of an Animated Shopping Gaze," *Mechademia* 7, no. 1 (2012): 203–21.

Published by the University of Minnesota Press
111 Third Avenue South, Suite 290
Minneapolis, MN 55401-2520
http://www.upress.umn.edu

ISBN 978-1-5179-1627-5 (hc)
ISBN 978-1-5179-1628-2 (pb)

A Cataloging-in-Publication record for this book is available from the Library of Congress.

Printed in the United States of America on acid-free paper

The University of Minnesota is an equal-opportunity educator and employer.

UMP BmB 2024

To G.

Contents

Introduction

The *otaku,* the passionate obsessive, the information age's embodiment of the connoisseur, more concerned with the accumulation of data than of objects, seems a natural crossover figure in today's interface of British and Japanese cultures. . . . Understanding otaku-hood, I think, is one of the keys to understanding the culture of the web.

—William Gibson, "Modern Boys and Mobile Girls"

In the first two decades of the twenty-first century, we witnessed a widespread cultural movement of geekdom that went global and mainstream simultaneously. While American media were announcing "it's hip to be square" and "geek is chic," their East Asian counterparts were embracing otaku and *zhai,* the Japanese and Chinese equivalents of geeks, as trendy labels to identify a new generation of pop culture heroes who thrived on the transmedia arenas of the digital era.[1] The worldwide rise of geeks and geek culture points to the emergence and significance of a new demographic of transnational knowledge workers in a global economy dominated by information networks. To a large extent, this knowledge class functions as a crucial yet often overlooked nexus in the ongoing transformations of information society that we are still trying to understand. These so-called geeks, otaku, and zhai are the active agents, as both consumers and producers, connecting techno-economic developments to sociocultural changes. Therefore, critically examining this social group and its cultural values, I believe, is the key to understanding our current information society at large.

This book is about the cultural values of geeks: how they emerged, why they matter, and what they mean in the historical moment of the early twenty-first century. Specifically, it investigates the historical and cultural formation of global geekdom through the lens of anime (Japanese animation) and its transnational fandom. As geek culture became trendy worldwide, so did anime. Usually sold and consumed together with comic books, science-fiction movies, and superhero toys, anime was a key element that played a crucial role in the transnational development and dissemination of geek cultures. The global spread of anime as a transmedial, transnational cultural form is thus closely tied to the historical emergence of those well-paid, tech-savvy, and cosmopolitan knowledge workers known as geeks. The key questions, therefore, are why anime appeals to this rapidly expanding social group and how anime constitutes a mediation environment that effectively translates between knowledge work and what Tiziana Terranova calls "knowledgeable consumption of culture."[2] These questions provide an important window to investigate the ways in which geek culture propagates, and is propagated by, certain modes of seeing, perceiving, interacting, consuming, and producing that are closely tied to the techno-cultural condition of informational knowledge work. Such geek sensibilities, which were established and articulated through the media environment of anime and its fandom, continue to be disseminated and gain ground today in a global context of information capitalisms.

Studying anime as the cultural nexus of global geekdom, this book shifts the center of knowledge culture from the computer boys in Silicon Valley to the anime fandom in East Asia.[3] It draws our attention to the ethnic and racial diversity and complexity in the sociocultural formation of geekdom by focusing on its East Asian counterparts in Japanese otaku and Chinese zhai cultures, problematizing the supposed American whiteness in the popular imagination of the knowledge class.[4] This shift from the techno-culture of computing to the transmedia system of anime also calls for a theoretical rethinking of how knowledge culture is mediated. In this book, I argue that the culturalization of informational knowledge work needs a media form, which is animation rather than computation. I illuminate how animation mediates knowledge culture by examining the forms, techniques, and aesthetics of anime, as well as the organization, practices, and sensibilities of its fandom. It is at once a historical and cultural study of transnational geekdom as a knowledge culture (Part I of the book, with a geocultural focus on China) as well as a theorization of anime as a media environment for knowledge work (Part II). The book begins to theorize the meanings and significance of anime geekdom as a cultural logic of information capitalism by first considering its global spread and diversity with a decentered media geography.

The Virtual Geography of Global Geekdom

The cultural turn at the new millennium began with a word. In December 2013, *Collins Dictionary* chose *geek* as the word of the year, reminding us how the meaning of the word had transformed dramatically from a slang of insult to a badge of honor. It highlighted the twice changed definition of the word, from "a boring and unattractive social misfit" to "a person who is preoccupied with or very knowledgeable about computing" and to "a person who is very knowledgeable and enthusiastic about a specific subject."[5] This transformation "from geek-as-sideshow-freak to geek-as-intelligent-expert," however, is not simply the redefinition of a word.[6] Instead, what we were witnessing is a radical social and cultural shift under the changing techno-economic conditions of information capitalism. And the impact of this shift is not limited to those "about computing" but had transformed a much broader cultural landscape in a global scale. In a *Time* magazine article titled "The Geek Shall Inherit the Earth," Lev Grossman observes: "What was once hopelessly geeky—video games, fantasy novels, science fiction, superheroes—has now, somehow, become cool."[7] Labeled as the postmillennial new cool, *geek* came to define one of the most dominant cultural directions at the beginning of the twenty-first century. In the North American context, one prominent example of this geek cultural turn is Hollywood, which took the lead with cinematic adaptations of fantasy fictions, role-playing games, and Marvel comics. Observing "how Hollywood's going geek and geek is going Hollywood," Ben Fritz, in an article for *Variety*, points out: "As fandom has become fashionable,

Hollywood has targeted and wooed geeks."[8] As a result, Comic-Con, which used to be a small, subculture gathering, has transformed to one of the most celebrated media events, with "studios, producers, directors and movie stars all fighting hard for geeks' attention."[9] In fact, Hollywood was so occupied by geeky blockbusters that the *Washington Post* journalist Ann Hornaday once bitterly complained that America's summer theaters were almost completely ruled by "teen boys at their pimpliest, stutteringest and downright geekiest."[10]

The scale of this geek cultural turn, however, is far beyond Hollywood. Its East Asian counterparts emerged with more prominent and far-reaching cultural influences under the banners of otaku in Japan and zhai in China. Derived from the Japanese greeting phrase "your house" (お宅), the term *otaku* had been popularized in Japan since the 1980s to describe subcultural fans who are obsessed with certain types of popular media such as anime, manga, games, science fiction, and special-effects movies, as well as those who hang out in Akihabara, a famous high-tech shopping district in Tokyo that sells electronics, computer parts, robotics, toy figures, and garage kits.[11] Although *otaku* and *geek* originated from different historical and cultural contexts, there are significant overlaps between these two terms that are often translated to each other. Like the English word *geek*, *otaku* in Japanese also used to carry negative connotations associated with pathological behaviors, but it later shifted to much more positive meanings. For instance, Toshio Okada, a Japanese producer, media specialist, and self-proclaimed "otaking" who once taught courses on the theory of otaku culture at the University of Tokyo, celebrated otaku as a new generation of Japanese youths who were attuned to Japan's highly consumerist society and thus were "the true heirs of Japanese culture."[12] If geeks are often imagined as the computer boys who shall "inherit the earth" with their expertise in digital technologies, then otaku are Japan's "database animals" who are believed to possess "an evolved vision" to redefine a postmodern subjectivity with an entirely different relationship to media and information.[13]

In China, where the world's second largest economy began its transition from massive industrial domination as the famous world factory to burgeoning postindustrial expansion with the rise of internet giants such as Baidu, Alibaba, and Tencent, geek and otaku, as global cultural references, had been taking the lead in defining the cultural sensibility of a whole generation of Chinese workers and consumers known as *zhai shidai*. The word *zhai* (宅) is a Chinese translation of *otaku*, as it takes the kanji (using Chinese characters in Japanese writing) 宅 (*zhai*) from the Japanese word お宅 (*otaku*). Although derived from the transnational dissemination of otaku culture from Japan to China, the term *zhai* had gained a much broader cultural currency and became a new vernacular to characterize the widespread penetration of geek cultural sensibility along with the rise of cosmopolitan knowledge workers in China's digital economy. As otaku culture centered on anime, comics, and games (labeled as "ACG culture" in China) began to dominate China's rapidly expanding digital media sphere, the phrase "wo hen zhai"—"I am so otaku"—became a popular motto among China's millennial youths. *Zhai* was thus chosen as the Chinese buzzword of the year in 2008 to celebrate the cultural prominence of China's zhai generation, which, according to the Chinese news media, not only defined the cultural meanings of the "Internet pop" (网络流行) but also characterized "a state of living and being" (生存状态) in the twenty-first century.[14] During the Covid-19 pandemic in 2020, zhai as "a state of living and being" was further embraced in China as a crucial cultural strategy to survive the pandemic quarantines and lockdowns, displacing the fear of an infectious disease with the obsession with spreadable media.[15]

From Marvel comics to Nintendo games, from Hollywood superhero movies in summer theaters to Chinese fan videos on the streaming platform Bilibili, the overwhelming cultural movement of global geekdom that emerged in the early 2000s continues today and is rapidly expanding and disseminating around world with varying forms and degrees in different geopolitical regions and sociocultural contexts. These diverse cultural forms are nevertheless united under the quasi-identifiable cultural marker of geekdom, though sometimes under different names, such as otaku and zhai. The book uses these three terms—*geek, otaku,* and *zhai*—interchangeably and unites them under the banner of geekdom to demonstrate their shared cultural practices and sensibilities, as well as to underline the global connections and movements among these diverse forms of knowledge culture, though it also emphasizes their different historical origins, meanings, and references in the different geocultural contexts of North America, Japan, and China. The purpose is to explore the transnational, transcultural connections among these three terms and to map a media geography that broadens and problematizes their supposed national and regional territories. The cultural identity of geekdom is not tied to any specific national identities or geographical locations; it is constituted by a deterritorialized mediascape of comics, games, and animations.[16] This deterritorialized and deterritorializing mediascape of geekdom, however, is not without a geographical configuration. The fact that popular discourses often associate geek cultures with the IT industry in Silicon Valley points to an imagined geography of global geekdom that is predominantly centered on California in the United States. This widely perceived, U.S.-centric geography, however, is problematized by the central role of anime, as well as its geocultural signification of East Asia, as a core element in the formation of geek culture identity in global arenas.

One of the goals of this book is to critically reconfigure the media geography of global geekdom, decentering it from computer culture in North America to anime culture in East Asia. I argue that geek culture is not a specifically Western phenomenon, and it has its cultural sources, inspirations, and implications in East Asia. By "East Asia," however, what I am referring to is less a physical territory than an imagined geocultural region that is constituted by the transnational, transmedial networks of anime. This geography of anime geekdom is not so much about fixed spatiality as it is about an expansive media sphere in perpetual motion, which is associated with but is not necessarily bound to the geographical region known as "Asia." It is what McKenzie Wark calls "virtual geography," the expanded terrain of global media vectors, "the experience of which doubles, troubles, and generally permeates our experience of the space we experience firsthand."[17] In this virtual geography of global geekdom, the shared cultural experiences of geeks, otaku, and zhai connected through transnational media flows generate an extraterritorial experience of coming together beyond spatial proximity or limitation, which is a renewed sense of media regionality that is not fixated to physical territories but is the result of the production and imagination of a malleable geocultural identity.[18] In other words, the experience of this virtual geography is less about the actual space (East Asia or beyond) than about belonging to a mediascape of anime that is identified with Asia, belonging to a "virtual region" of geeks. This book maps this virtual geography of global geekdom by examining how anime culture constitutes an expansive, extraterritorial media sphere of knowledge culture and how it functions as "vectors of movement, of information flow, [that] traverse any and every sphere of the world which knowledge may take as a separate object."[19] Mapping how anime geekdom moves as vectors of information flow is also to rethink the traditional notion of geographical territories in area studies, transforming them toward a virtual milieu of extraterritorial communities that are full of tension, unevenness, and contradictions. To study this dynamic sociocultural formation of geeks in a global media geography, we need to first understand who they are and why they matter.

From Knowledge Work to Knowledge Culture

What is it about geeks, otaku, and zhai that gave them such prominent positions as "heroes in movies and Man of the Year"?[20] The prevalent global geekdom movement points to the rising socioeconomic capital of the rapidly expanding demographic of knowledge workers who are demanded by the techno-economic system described as postindustrial or informational. As Lev Grossman observes: "It's as if the economic hegemony of the geek in the 1990s, when high tech and the Internet were driving the economy, has somehow been converted into a cultural hegemony."[21] As significant as they are, the socioeconomic capital of the knowledge workers do not automatically translate to cultural capital. As Pierre Bourdieu reminds us, between the economic capital and the cultural capital is a dynamic and complex process of mediation, whereby the social relations of power are intricate in the cultural judgment of taste.[22] At the center of this process is a social space that is closely tied to the material conditions and practices of labor and production. This space of workstyle and/as lifestyle is where cultural distinctions emerge. What remains to be examined is how the changing nature of work in postindustrial societies is articulated through and internalized in certain cultural forms and sensibilities and how these changing cultures further reinforce and influence the practices and conditions—in both technological and social terms—of the expanding labor force of knowledge work that is demanded by information capitalism. In other words, the key question is how geek cultures helped foster and propagate postindustrial knowledge work by internalizing its workstyle into a lifestyle with cultural forms and values.

The preeminence of a new class of knowledge workers has been observed by many. In his book *The Coming of Post-Industrial Society*, Daniel Bell characterizes the postindustrial society as essentially "a knowledge society" that relies on the expanding labor force of "professional and technical persons" who constitute a knowledge class. What Bell characterizes is not simply a change of occupational distributions but a social shift in which professional workers and their skills began to play an increasingly crucial role in the economy and politics of society. As Bell suggests:

> Post-industrial society is organized around knowledge for the purpose of social control and the directing of innovation and change; and this in turn gives rise to new social relationships and new structures which have to be managed politically.[23]

The formation of this "new social relationship" gave rise to the so-called New Class, which is "composed of intellectuals and technical intelligentsia."[24] Call them the "creative class" (Richard Florida), "knowledge workers" (Peter Drucker and Alan Liu), "informational labor" (Manuel Castells), or the "professional-managerial class" (Barbara and John Ehrenreich), this new group of white-collar workers are primarily those who are believed to possess the knowledge and skills to produce technological change, to generate economic value, and to manage societal control.[25]

It is certainly debatable whether these knowledge workers constitute a genuine sense of class formation with collective class consciousness in Marxist terms, because they do not share the same economic status or the ownership of production materials.[26] The question of class is also complicated by the shifting boundaries of economic inequalities—both within and without knowledge workers—between different genders, races, and educational levels, as well as between the developing and the developed economies. As Wark argues, these knowledge workers whom she calls "hackers" constitute an abstract class rather than an actual one, as they emerged out of the abstraction of class politics as such: "A class that makes abstractions, and a class made abstract. To abstract hackers as a class is to abstract the very concept of class itself."[27] But if not an actual class, does this "abstract class" constitute a social formation that is organized less by economic status than by shared occupation, profession, knowledge, and cultural practices? Is it the social field of what Bourdieu calls a "cultural class," which is formed with collective habitus as cultural capital?[28] Or the deterritorialized organization of a "multitude" that is celebrated by the Italian autonomist thinkers as a collective social subject that is formed by the productive force of "mass intellectuality"?[29] Or alternatively, do they simply represent a new kind of networked, posthuman subjectivity, as is often characterized by new media theories and digital culture studies, an identity that is defined less by gender, race, or ethnicity than by the changing technological conditions of information networks that mediate new modes of cultural communication, expression, and sensibilities?[30]

No matter if we call it a class, a social field, a multitude, or a cyberculture identity, the preeminence of a new body of knowledge workers—geeks, otaku, or zhai—had formed the social foundation of a prominent cultural shift that has often been studied in technological terms. Much work has been done to characterize the cultural transformations in the digital age under the rapid technological developments in the past decades. The focal point, however, often anchors on media technology itself. But technologies, as Gilles Deleuze tells us, "are always social before being technical."[31] If the technological "is in some sense isomorphic to the social and the political," there remains much to be learned about the concrete process of such isomorphic equations, in which the dynamic reactions between the techno-economic conditions, the changing relations of production, and the emerging cultural and ideological forms have to be closely examined in historically and socially specific contexts.[32] Because technologies do not change society automatically, the ongoing computerization or datafication of our lives is not directly a result of the implementation of information technology itself but rather is processed and mediated through social actors, such as geeks and otaku.

Nathan Ensmenger, in his book *The Computer Boys Take Over*, provides a detailed social history of how the profession of technical workers and their social role were assimilated into modern corporations as a productive and transformative force that not only changed the structure of economy but also shifted the cultural values of the society at large, "bringing about what is arguably the most profound social and technological development of our times."[33] Such a development, according to Wark, even allows geeks to "hack out a new politics," because this emerging "hacker class" that arises out of the transformation of information "has the capacity to create not only new kinds of object and subject . . . but new relations, with unforeseen properties, which question the property form itself."[34] With such productive potentials, these tech-savvy geeks were thus hailed by Richard Florida as a new "creative class" that is believed to be reshaping what is culturally meaningful and politically powerful. Although Florida's emphasis on creativeness is an investment and inflation of the cultural capital of knowledge workers, he is certainly right in arguing for the significance of this social group and their cultural values for "understanding the sweeping and seemingly disjointed changes in our society."[35] If we are to understand technology as primarily social (as Deleuze suggests), then we should start with understanding these technical geeks, because they are the ones who made technology social in the first place. Therefore, examining the cultural formations of geekdom, as well as its values and sensibilities, I believe, is the key to solving the equations that translate the material realities of information machines to the symbolic meaning of cultural changes.

The sociocultural significance of geeks also hinges upon the questions of power and identity, because the identity of geeks, as Ron Eglash points out, "has been a critical gateway to this technocultural access, mediating personal identities in ways that both maintain normative boundaries of power and offer sites for intervention."[36] Such geek identity as a "gatekeeper for technoscience" is often interrogated within the historical context of post–World War II America. Even in studies that address the racial and ethnic diversity of geeks as a contested ground between identity, power, and technology, geeks are primarily understood as an American cultural identity (though not necessarily a white male one).[37] This predominantly U.S.-centric approach to geek identity overshadows the diverse cultural roots and lineages of the global geekdom movement, which forms an expansive and malleable system of cultural reference that is far from an American one. Reexamining the identity and diversity of geeks from the lens of transnational anime culture, this book critically analyzes the cultural meanings of geekdom by broadening its scope beyond the context of the United States. It investigates the ways in which the historical rise of knowledge workers as a worldwide social force transformed a global cultural landscape—from East Asia to North America—through the dissemination and movement of geek, otaku, and zhai cultures with shared sensibilities.

But what exactly is geek culture? In an article published in *Science* magazine in 1998, Kevin Kelly, the founder of *Wired* magazine, claims that after the centuries-long rivalry between the two cultures of science and art, there has emerged a third culture: "It's a pop culture based in technology, for technology. Call it *nerd* culture. . . . For this current generation of Nintendo children, their technology is their culture."[38] The tendency Kelly describes, of technology becoming culture and culture becoming technology, is certainly not limited to those "Nintendo children," and neither does it describe anything particularly novel. But the key to Kelly's argument is rather the mediation process between technology and culture, the interface where geeks and otaku are uniquely positioned as the operators, producers, and consumers.

The mediation process in this pop culture in and for technology, the process of technology becoming culture and vice versa, operates through what Walter Benjamin calls "technological innervation." Benjamin borrowed the term *innervation* from Sigmund Freud to describe the mediation process between the external material conditions of technology and the internal neurophysiological reactions of human sensorium. For Benjamin, innervation is a transformative but nondestructive process that allows workers to internalize the physical realities of machinic encounter into their psychic and corporal behaviors as a "second nature" without the damaging effects of alienation, a process that is often mediated through pop culture entities such as cinema and animation (with Mickey Mouse being one of Benjamin's prime examples).[39] Call it "nerd culture" (Kevin Kelly), "network culture" (Tiziana Terranova), a "culture of real virtuality" (Manuel Castells), or a "culture of information" (Alan Liu), geek culture is essentially about the innervation of the technological conditions of postindustrial knowledge work into the cognitive, affective, and corporal capacities through a set of cultural logics as a transformative force.[40]

For postmillennial geeks, there are two major technological conditions that are to be internalized through this mediation process of innervation. First, information, the primary production material of knowledge work. Second, cybernetic systems, the primary infrastructure of postindustrialism. It is against this backdrop of the massive production and commodification of information and knowledge in the cybernetic systems of postindustrial societies that we are to make sense of geek culture, which is marked by the collective practices of obsessive (re)production, (re)distribution, and (re)consumption of certain kinds of information and knowledge that are closely associated with popular media. Therefore, geek culture is fundamentally about the innervation of the operating structures, materials, and principles of cybernetic information systems into cultural obsessions, a process of mediation between the material conditions of knowledge work and the symbolic forms of knowledge culture with a renewed sense of pleasure, desire, and belonging. It is as much the informationalization of culture as it is the culturalization of information. It is an innervation process that internalizes the technological conditions of cybernetic feedback loops—the machinic logic of the "if-then" iterations of computation—into popular cultural forms and practices that are marked by the psychic pleasure and obsession with endless cycles of trial and error, with a continuous search for information, and with a ceaseless quest for perpetual learning.

In sum, with the emergence of a social formation of knowledge workers, there developed a knowledge culture, whereby "knowledge" is equivalent with often-commodified data and information that is massively produced, managed, and consumed as cultural entities, and the cultural practice of knowledge cultivation is taken to be a lifelong process of perpetual learning that is performed as endless cybernetic feedback. This is a pop culture developed from and for postindustrial knowledge work, and it functions not only to articulate its ethos of informationalism but to reinforce the conditions and practices of its workstyle—that is, to foster more forms, techniques, and skills of such work. This knowledge culture—or, more precisely, the pop culture of knowledge work—defines what geekdom really means: it is a process of technological innervation that operates as a collective cultural obsession with excessively producing, sorting, and consuming information through cybernetic systems. To study geek culture, therefore, is to interrogate how the innervation process of technological conditions generates certain forms and aesthetics for the imaginations, desires, and practices of knowledge workers whose productivity and demand came to redefine the cultural logic of the digital era. In Alan Liu's words, our vital task is "to inquire into the aesthetic value" that is "now busily seeking new management amid the ceaseless creation and re-creation of the forms, styles, media, and institutions of postindustrial knowledge work."[41]

The core aesthetic value of knowledge culture, according to Liu, is the "laws of cool." Because of the historical connection and the continuous conflation between cyberculture and counterculture, the geek culture of knowledge work appears to be paradoxically both unique and universal, both alternative and normalized, both distinctive and omnipresent.[42] Equating the informational with the countercultural, geek culture is thus taken to be ubiquitously "different" (recalling Apple's famous advertising slogan "Think different")—that is, *cool*. Among the cool cultures of cool geeks, which are at once localized and global, subcultural and mainstream, there is probably nothing cooler than anime from Japan. Because Japan, according to many, is the postmillennial new cool.

Anime from "Cool Japan"

Long before geeks became cool, Japan—less a nation than a cultural signifier in the global popular—had already provided us with a fascinating imagination of what *cool* means and looks like in a fast-paced, superwired, and overdeveloped techno-future of informationalism. This imagined futuristic Japan was written into William Gibson's canonical cyberpunk novel *Neuromancer* (1984) and had been widely popularized by a variety of science fiction, films, animation, games, and television series since the 1980s, which all pictured Japan as both an exciting frontier of cybernetic technologies and an uncanny metaphor for posthuman dystopia.[43] In Gibson's own words: "Japan is the global imagination's default setting for the future."[44] At the center of this futuristic imagination of "cool Japan," which was quickly adopted and promoted by the Japanese government as a foreign policy for nation branding, was the tremendous success of Japanese cultural exports such as anime, manga, and games in the global market.[45] It was the international popularity of otaku culture with its newfound cachet among geeks worldwide, along with the rising cultural capital of these knowledge workers, that came to be celebrated as what Douglas McGray famously calls "Japan's gross national cool."[46]

The rise of anime as the cultural nexus of the millennial new cool decentered the global geekdom movement from North America to East Asia. Initially exported internationally as children's television programs in the 1960s, anime quickly became a cultural staple of global geekdom with the advent of computers and the internet since the 1980s.[47] J. A. McArthur highlights "anime geeks" as significant components of the digital subculture of geekdom.[48] Neil Feineman, in *Geek Chic: The Ultimate Guide to Geek Culture*, lists *Astro Boy* and *Akira* (two canonical anime texts), along with the Nintendo Game Boy, Capcom's *Street Fighter*, and the Sony PlayStation as the essential "geek items."[49] In a study of how American youth interacts with new media, popular anime such as *Pokémon* and *Yu-Gi-Oh!* are listed as the key items for "geeking out."[50] And anime fans throughout the world self-identify as geeks, nerds, or otaku. In an in-depth survey of anime fans conducted by Susan Napier in the early 2000s, one respondent "summed himself up as '*nerd, otaku, Trekkie, goth witch, net junkie.*'"[51] Anime also wielded tremendous influence on a wide variety of cultural products that are considered geeky. For instance, the famous cyberpunk film *The Matrix* (1999) is widely claimed to have been inspired by Mamoru Oshii's anime film *Ghost in the Shell* (1995) and Quentin Tarantino, who is often celebrated as a geek movie icon, blatantly incorporated anime sequences in his renowned postmodern cultural remix *Kill Bill* (2003).[52] Indeed, anime is an omnipresent element in the rapidly expanding terrain of geek culture. In a special issue of *Wired* magazine titled "Geekipedia," *anime* and *manga* were listed as the central geek terms that "you need to know *now.*"[53]

The worldwide popularity of anime and otaku culture went hand in hand with the global geekdom movement. If the market expansion of anime as a major cultural export provided the rising currency of "Cool Japan" in the global market, this currency is closely tied to the historical emergence of cosmopolitan knowledge workers with the advent of information technology. That is exactly how McGray explains the source of Japan's "gross national cool": "The geeks who read manga as children went on to become the millionaires of the 1990s. . . . They spread their interest in things Japanese."[54] It is not accidental that the geographical hotspots of anime geekdom are often located in high-tech centers: Akihabara in Tokyo, Silicon Valley in California, and Zhongguancun in Beijing.

Medium Cool: Anime as the
Media Environment for Knowledge Culture

At first glance, it may seem odd that anime assumes such a cutting-edge status in the high-tech world of the twenty-first century. After all, anime, or animation in general, is a century-old medium that dates back to the late nineteenth century. In much of its mode of production, anime, in Thomas Lamarre's words, is "unabashedly low tech."[55] Then why did anime, a low-tech medium from the last century, suddenly become the new cool in the information age? What can anime tell us about the cultural values of geeks? These questions point to the ethos of cool at the intersection between the media condition of anime and the knowledge culture of geekdom. Converging the notions of "cool culture," "cool media," and "cool Japan," I argue that the sense of cool in knowledge culture is fundamentally the effect of mediation. Anime functions as a cultural signature of cool Japan not because of its national origin but because of its operation as a cool media environment that is powerful for its decentering, distributive effect evoking transnational, transmedial participation and involvement. Examining anime as a media environment, I take an expanded definition of *media,* which is not simply a representational or communicative vehicle but is an immersive environment of material-symbolic milieu where human actors participate in and interact with information, ideas, and devices.[56] The book thus studies anime not merely as a (sub)cultural form or a media object but as a techno-aesthetic environment of mediation that is uniquely synergetic for knowledge culture.

To understand how anime provides a cool media environment for knowledge culture, let us first consider what it means to be cool. In his book *The Laws of Cool,* Alan Liu points out that "cool" becomes the cultural face of informational knowledge work because being cool—the aesthetic state of distance, remoteness, and nonidentity that is historically associated with racial minority and subcultures as being different or exiled from the dominant sociocultural norms—is a functional mentality to mediate the apparent contradictions of knowledge work that is simultaneously "managerial and managed, transcendental and paranoid, free and enslaved, decentralized and centralized."[57] To mediate such cognitive disjunctions of knowledge work that is both "empowered and resentful," there needs to be "an excess of knowledge about the connectivity of information . . . [which] grants the knowledge workers the mental distance needed to gesture beyond the doxa of postindustrialism to the semi-autonomous para-doxa of cool."[58] In other words, the sense of cool is a decentering effect from oneself, which relies on excessive information to mediate the contradictory subject of knowledge work.

This decentered state of being cool—that is, being distanced and different—offers a slight sense of autonomy for "postindustrial automatons" because the postindustrial, post-Fordist knowledge work, which conflates labor with leisure and production with consumption, affords no real space for outside or alternatives.[59] When there is no genuine sense of countercultural difference, one can only aspire to be cool. As Alan Liu says:

> Increasingly, knowledge work has no true recreational outside. Cool therefore arises *inside* the regime of knowledge work as what might be called an *intra*culture rather than a subculture or counterculture. Cool is an attitude or pose from within the belly of the beast, an effort to make one's very mode of inhabiting a cubicle express what in the 1960s would have been an "alternative lifestyle" but now in the postindustrial 2000s is an alternative *workstyle*.[60]

Geek culture is precisely such an *"intraculture"* of knowledge work. The ethos of cool, therefore, is the aesthetic innervation for the informational knowledge work to be processed as a cool geek style (or "an alternative *workstyle*") through cycles of transfiguration between work and play, knowledge and pleasure, production and consumption. What is really cool is the capability to internalize the logic and rationality of the technological systems of knowledge work (with all their contradictions and disjunctions) into one's decentered intrasubjectivity through popular cultural techniques, styles, forms, and aesthetics within the system—that is, an intraculture for technological innervation.[61] As an intraculture, which is to mediate among various contradictory factors within knowledge work, cool is thus the aesthetic function of mediation, "the interface by which it knows itself."[62]

How does "cool" function as mediation? What constitutes a "cool medium"? Interestingly, media theorists have their own answers about what it means to be cool. Marshall McLuhan once famously introduced a schema to distinguish between hot and cool media. Hot media such as cinema and photography are those with high definition but low participation, and cool media such as television and cartoons tend to be low in definition but high in participation. While hot and cool media can be understood as different technological effects on media forms, their interrelations, for McLuhan, also define the "temperatures" of sociocultural formations in history: hot cultures, with large-scale sensory saturation, tend to be centralizing and exclusive, but cool cultures, marked by gaps and fragmentation, encourage distributiveness and inclusion.[63] Despite many debates and criticisms of McLuhan's much-simplified binary schema (and his much-criticized tendency of technological determinism), what I find most illuminating are the ways in which McLuhan's definition of cool media provides us with a roadmap to understanding the cultural cool of information as primarily a function of mediation, or, more precisely, a function of "low-definition" cool media that invite a great deal of user awareness, participation, and involvement. In fact, the key features of the cultural cool that Alan Liu characterizes, including its stance of gap and distance, its ethos of fragmentary self-awareness, and its stylistic principle of communication clarity and simplicity, all amount to the cool media effects that are marked by fragmentation, disjunction, and incompleteness with a promise of dialogues, involvement, and participation.[64] Therefore, it is no wonder that the best analogies for cool cultures are none other than cool media: cool as ethos is akin to an information interface of hypermediacy that is aware of itself, and cool as style is "a visual analogue of telegraphy, radio, and other remote information technologies."[65] Understanding "cool" as a mediation effect is also to understand media as an environment, a stance that has increasingly been taken by the environmental and elemental approaches that take the media temperatures of hot and cool as a climatic issue.[66]

In sum, cool as a cultural value is fundamentally a function of mediation, the effect of what McLuhan characterizes as medium cool, which is a media environment that is low in definition with gaps, disjunction, and fragmentation but is high in participation with active sensory, psychic, and cognitive involvement and expression in cultural forms, such as the cool tempos of jazz or the cool styles of anime. This cultural involvement, marked by the constant interplay between techno-media and human sensorium, are what Benjamin hails as technological innervation. Benjamin's notion of innervation, as Miriam Hansen argues, describes: "a neurophysiological process that mediates between internal and external, psychic and motoric, human and machinic registers."[67] It is this process of technological innervation that makes culture and media cool.

At this intersection between cool culture and cool media we find the perfect location to situate anime from cool Japan. Among all geek cultures, anime provides one of the most powerful cases for understanding the meanings of cool, because it constitutes a cool media environment that is remarkably effective for generating a decentered intraculture to mediate the contradictions of informational knowledge work. There are three core elements through which anime delivers the decentering, "cooling" effects of intrasubjectivity: the transnational othering from the position of cool Japan, the transmedial system known as the "media mix," and the technical form of animation. Combining these three elements, anime as a media environment offers a powerful window to critically examine the meanings of cool in knowledge culture.

The notion of cool Japan has many facets. It is often defined as a banner of foreign policy and a market campaign for national branding, under which Japan is sold as a trendy brand of content industry for global consumption to boost the nation's much-needed capital and soft power.[68] In international contexts, however, cool Japan is sometimes consumed as a discursive fantasy of techno-Orientalism, whereby "Japan" is an imaginary other to be projected to the posthuman techno-future in the popular imagination of Western viewers with both fascination and fear.[69] Like cool jazz from Black artists, cool Japan offers an imagined position of otherness from afar because the sense of cool has to assume an empty position of "outside," an imagined somewhere far out (the Far East, the Zen garden, and Chiba city), which points to the racialized origin in the notion of cool that is historically rooted in the struggle of Black cultures.[70]

The discourse of cool Japan, from the perspective of cultural studies, is a fertile area to explore the changing cultural landscape of global capitalism: it points to the shifting power dynamics of "recentering" globalization from the U.S. to Japan, a new value system of culture production through "collaborative creativity" that is based on characters and world-making, and an alternative cultural logic of postmodern "soft capitalism" powered by fantasy, play, and affect of millennial youth as immaterial labor.[71] In this regard, "cool Japan" represents less the national logic of Japanese cultural specificity than the profound sociocultural and economic shifts of global postindustrialism—be it decentered to Japan or elsewhere—which has come to redefine the meanings of intimacy, mobility, flexibility, creativity, collectivity, and productivity.

These shifts highlight the fact that the underlying foundation of cool Japan is not its national characteristics but its extraordinary power of mediation in technological, cultural, and economic terms, because "cool Japan," as either a governmental initiative or a cultural phenomenon, is largely the result of the transmedial, transnational process that is known as "media mix." In fact, the discourse of cool Japan emerged at the precise moment when the industrial strategies and practices of media mix began to gain global recognition under the banner of "convergence," which describes the proliferation of content across multiple media forms and platforms.[72] The underlying logic was the belief that the engine of media mix that drove the flow of cultural content across different media could also drive the transcultural flow across national/ geographical boundaries. Cool Japan is thus tethered with media mix, both centered on the notions of "content" and "soft." As Marc Steinberg points out: "Content shifts from meaning digital information to becoming a catchword for those media or franchises that were most capable of export—both to increase revenues and to support a 'Cool Japan' that had newly discovered the significance of culturally mediated soft power."[73] These contents are also called "software" (*sofuto*) in Japan, conflating the softness of cultural content with that of soft power. The quest for cool is also the quest for postindustrial, immaterial "softness" as a function of technological mediation. What is truly "cool," therefore, is the powerful function of soft mediation that operates the transmedial, transnational process of media mix.

Media mix, which is characterized as convergence or participatory culture by Henry Jenkins, represents McLuhan's definition of *medium cool* par excellence.[74] The distance, disparity, and disjunction among different media types demand intensive user involvements, interactions, and investments (of money, time, labor, and affect). The fans are invited into the productive cycles of media mix as vigorous consumers and producers, but their activities must be tightly controlled by media industries—the actual owners of the capital of media mix—through various mechanisms such as copyright control and character-world consistency.[75] Like well-disciplined knowledge workers, whose workstyle/ lifestyle of work–play conflation is popularized by media mix in cultural terms, fans contribute their labor and passion to actively manage, and be managed by, the ever-expanding network of media mix that requires their participation but denies their autonomy. The system of media mix thus generates a cool cultural environment of "outsiders inside," which is inclusive and distributive, on one hand, but, on the other hand, also gestures toward a position of intrasubjectivity of elsewhere and elsewhen beyond oneself.

These "cooling" effects make media mix a perfect vehicle for technological innervation of informational knowledge work, producing bodily and social poses of cultural cool that Alan Liu describes as "camo-tech," which is the enactment and embodiment of technological logics of information systems through cultural forms and techniques.[76] Consuming, playing, and working within the ecosystem of media mix with their affective immaterial labor, otaku are informationalized, computerized, and networked everywhere.[77] The system of media mix, through its capacity of culturizing character goods into communication and attachment, as well as its world-generating mechanism that sustains transmedia consumption and production, functions to internalize the post-Fordist logics of knowledge work into a transformative media environment where consumption and communication become forms of production and labor.[78] The notion of cool Japan as the empire of media mix epitomizes this development of postindustrialism. The otaku culture organized by media mix thus represents what Maurizio Lazzarato calls the new "anthropological reality" of knowledge work, a "polymorphous self-employed autonomous work . . . inserted within a market that is constantly shifting and within networks that are changeable in time and space."[79] The techno-ecosystem of media mix is the engine that drives the process of innervation that inserts the logics of this "polymorphous self-employed autonomous work" into the endless cycles of transmedia consumption/creation via various technological circuits such as computers, internet, and game consoles. This technological innervation process is precisely how Anne Allison characterizes the "coolness" of the Pokémon franchise: "Work blurs into—and emerges from—the ways in which information is passed, communication conducted and play created via such techno channels as cell phones, iPods, and Game Boy."[80]

At the center of media mix as the anthropological reality of knowledge work with endless morphing trends, gadgets, and proliferating series of media forms and platforms, there is anime, "the nodal point in a *transmedial network*."[81] The reason that anime can function as such a powerful nodal point connecting its "low-tech production" and its "high-tech situations," according to Thomas Lamarre, is the technicity of animation, whose organization of techniques ("open compositing" with gaps between layers of cels) expresses the determination of its technological condition (the animation stand). Anime's technicity in relation to its technological condition—the "anime machine"—thus can teach us new dynamisms of human–machine interactions for seeing, perceiving, and "thinking technology."[82]

I will push Lamarre's thesis a step further and argue that anime not only helps us "think technology" but also teaches us how to "think cool," if *cool* means a new techno-aesthetic value of knowledge work in the digital era. According to McLuhan, animated cartoons are an exemplifying cool medium, because animation's hand-drawn moving images offer less visual detail than live-action cinema but invite more viewer participation and involvement.[83] This cool media effect makes animation uniquely powerful in generating participatory fandom and transmedia consumption, ranging from Disney's merchandising empire to anime's media mix. More importantly, animation as a cool medium has become the new center that organizes a much broader techno-cultural condition of cool, a condition of what Shane Denson calls "discorrelated images" in digital cultures—images that challenge the limits and capacities of human perceptions.[84] The computer-generated discorrelated images, such as those in CGI and video games, all rely on the technicity of animation not only for generating new forms of moving images but also for engineering radically transformed spatiotemporal relations that produce new subjectivities and affects. Therefore, what Denson characterizes as postcinematic discorrelation is fundamentally a decentering and disjunctive cool media effect of animation, a process of technological innervation enabled by animation techniques to mediate between machinic and human agencies. Because of the renewed centrality of animation in digital media, scholars such as Lev Manovich and Deborah Levitt forcefully argue that the "kino brush" of animation had replaced the "kino eye" of cinema to become the aesthetic and technical foundation of the digital age, the age of "the animatic apparatus."[85] As the center of digitalized image-making and cultural production, animation is thus emblematic of the cool media of technological innervation—that is, a machine-automated media form of discorrelation that expresses the arrangement of technique (animated moving images) to technology (computerized digitalization). In other words, for animation, to "think technology" is to "think cool."

Anime, in particular, has its own distinctive cool styles that constitute a unique media form of what Stevie Suan calls "anime-esque," a set of techniques that mark the recognizable specificity of anime.[86] This cool media form features high levels of audience participation and engagement that adjust anime-esque techniques to broader technological conditions. My study in this book focuses on identifying and analyzing the cooling effects of the anime-esque techniques, including the affective/semantic field of techno-intimacy (chapter 4), the database structure of cybernetic play (chapter 5), and the distributive but enframing visual field of superflat style (chapter 6). These cooling effects of anime are located in its internal gaps, disjuncture, and openness, which invite the active involvement and fulfillment of the subject (as an individual consumer and producer), on one hand, but demand an outward trajectory (toward the networks and systems) that decenters from oneself, on the other. It is an intrasubjectivity that is positioned with neither the individual nor the social but somewhere in the middle, oscillating between the internal and the external, between one's own desires and the structural demands of the media networks, like a signal of information that becomes its own interference in cybernetic feedback, or layers of images that crush upon themselves in the superflat visual field of anime. It is the production of this intrasubjectivity—as the result of technological innervation—through the aesthetics and technicity of animation, as well as the mediation effects of its transmedial environment, that positions anime at the center of geek culture.

My purpose in this book is to investigate how this informationalized intrasubjectivity of knowledge work is produced and sustained through the networked systems of popular geek culture, by examining the transmedial forms, techniques, and aesthetics of anime, as well as the transnational organizations, practices, and activities of anime fandom. I focus on the cooling effects of anime's media environment, examining them as the mechanisms of technological innervation that mediate between the internal self of knowledge workers/consumers and the external networks of information systems/infrastructures. This innervation milieu between the individual and the infrastructural, between the imaginary and the networks, between the sensorium and the machines, captures the cultural ethos of postmillennial knowledge work.

Examining the transnational, transmedial system of anime as the innervation mechanism mediating between the collective psyche of knowledge workers and the technological machines of information networks, this book seeks to broaden the theoretical frameworks for studying anime and otaku culture by trying to achieve what we may describe as "double decentering." On one hand, by focusing on anime as the central nexus of geek culture, this book decenters the technoculture of knowledge work from Silicon Valley in California (its often-assumed global center) to Akihabara in Tokyo and Zhongguancun in Beijing. On the other hand, this book also decenters the notion of "cool Japan" from its nationalist containment of "Japaneseness." What makes Japan and anime cool is precisely the powerful function of transnational mediation to break away from national containment. As Stevie Suan convincingly argues, anime's identity is not so much a Japanese one as it is an identifiable anime-esque form that mediates the local–global tensions between anime's origin in Japan and its dispersed production and consumption globally.[87] If cultural cool is less a matter of identity than identifying with a recognizable position from outside—something is cool because it is far out—then "cool Japan" is not the sociocultural identity of actual Japan but is rather identifying with what Koichi Iwabuchi describes as an "odorless" virtual Japan that is neither Japanese nor elsewhere.[88] The imagination of virtual Japan, which is less a national identity than an empty identification with a set of media artifacts, is what McLuhan would describe as a cool medium, because it generates distance, dislocation, and discorrelation in its cultural signification to mediate the discrepancies and unevenness of globalization. This virtual Japan is cool because it projects somewhere outside itself, outside its Asian neighbors, and outside its Western counterparts, and it is thus able to mediate the differences and disjunctions among them. This cool position of somewhere afar is not located in Japan but rather is shaped by the broader conditions of postindustrial informationalism that are articulated through the anime-esque media environment in both local and global terms. This book thus argues that the transnational, transmedial movement of anime and otaku culture is to be mapped outside the border of Japan.

Furthermore, this book demonstrates that, in the anthropological reality of anime geekdom, the cooling mechanisms of the innervation process—the sense of disjunction, distance, and disparity generated by the transmedia environment of anime—paradoxically operate with, and are propelled by, the intense affect of anxiety, anxiousness, and agitation. Underneath the medium cool of animation is the hot affect of animatedness. The machine is cool, but the feeling is hot.

Cybernetic Affect: The Structure of Geek Feelings

How does it *feel* to be an anime geek? Fun and edgy. Passionate and obsessive. Captivating and addicting. Enchanting and endearing. Curious and restless. Exciting and frustrating. Inhabiting the forever-expanding networks of anime's media mix is both enthralling and exhausting: the geek has to be endlessly searching (for new trends and information), collecting (merchandise and character goods), consuming (anime, manga, and games), and producing (fan art, fan theories, and *doujinshi* [fan-created manga and fiction]). The geek feeling is an innervated version of postindustrial knowledge work, which is marked, simultaneously and paradoxically, by the increasing desire for more information, connection, and communication, as well as by the mounting level of anxiety and agitation because the load of knowledge is simply too much. The informational knowledge work, like its pop cultural manifestation in geekdom, requires both investment and management of emotion and affect. Passion, affection, and attachment are juxtaposed with, and are converted to, the techno-economic rationality of information systems and operations. The feelings must keep being incited but must also be well-controlled in order to propel and sustain the perpetual cycles of production and consumption for the continuous growth of informational products, commodities, and services (in knowledge work), as well as for the continuous proliferation of transmedia content, forms, and platforms (in geek cultures).[89]

I define such geek feelings as *cybernetic affect*: the structure of excess feelings that are driving and driven by the endless cycles of information feedback. It is a structure of feelings caught in the tension between the increasing proliferation of informational entropy and the intensifying desire for cybernetic control, between the system's expansive potency of distributiveness and its centralizing mechanism for integration. It is the ambivalent feeling that oscillates between the desire for complexity/uncertainty and the impulse for order/control, because it is the affective innervation of a cybernetic system that oscillates between information proliferation and systematic management. These feelings are often articulated in popular cultural forms, patterns, and styles, such as the juxtaposition between distributive expansiveness and framing containment in anime's visual aesthetics and media mix system. The cybernetic affect is closely tied to and actively resonates with the procedural logics and technological conditions of postindustrial knowledge work: signal encoding and decoding, data input and output, packet switching and delivery. It is exhilarating and yet utterly familiar to the postmillennial geeks who are experiencing similar cybernetic rituals on a daily basis, which generates a mimetic faculty for knowledge workers to confront and make sense of the postindustrial conditions that are both pleasurable and grueling.

Deeply embedded within the habitual experience of knowledge work and encoded in popular fantasies and imagination, cybernetic affect is the result of mediated innervation between human sensorium and cybernetic systems, an integration that operates through networked play, work, and consumption in geek cultures. This affective response is a significant component in the information feedback circuits that mediate between human and machine. The "affective tone," as Norbert Wiener tells us in his theorization of cybernetics, is a crucial sensory signal in the feedback mechanism in both human and computational nervous·systems, which is the key to the learning function of both.[90] The affective sensory signal is thus at the center of cybernetic systems as the mediation for human–machine integration, because "the physical functioning of the living individual and the operation of some of the newer communication machines are precisely parallel in their analogous attempts to control entropy through feedback. Both of them have sensory receptors as one stage in their cycles of operation."[91] My conception of the cybernetic affect hinges upon Wiener's emphasis of the sensory as a critical element in cybernetic operation, which defines *affect* less as an automatous bodily response than as a mediated experience that connects living individuals with communication machines. In other words, I take affect as a medium because it "arises in the midst of *in-between-ness*."[92] In anime geekdom, affect arises in the cybernetic mediation between geek experience and anime's transmedia system, and it is the sensory signal that functions as "one stage in their cycles of cybernetic operation." The affective feelings—passionate obsession, curious uncertainty, and unstable attachment—are necessary feedback signals to improve or enhance the otaku performance as knowledge work: searching for more information, consuming more media goods, and producing more derivative content. Driven by the cybernetic affect as the signaling stage of one's performance, the transmedia practices of anime geeks essentially operate as cycles of information feedback loops performed as perpetual learning.

But the purpose to improve and to learn is to "control entropy"—that is, to control the feeling of uncertainty that is evoked, paradoxically, by the proliferation of information produced through feedback. Since cybernetics as a theory was developed historically as a response to a new worldview on contingency in modern sciences, it is marked by the dialectic tension between chaos (informational entropy) and order (cybernetic control). It is a control mechanism that is in perpetual motion of approaching but never actualized. Therefore, cybernetics is, by and large, a machine of affect, if *affect* is defined as a virtual realm with infinite movement of unactualized potential.[93] The cybernetic affect, as the result of such dialectic tension, is characterized as the geek's polarizing tendencies between the desire for informatic overload and the impulse for control. The geek community, as the core labor force of knowledge work, has to internalize the cybernetic tension into their workstyle/lifestyle, because their main job in the information society is to produce a proliferating amount of information for communication, while at the same time operating and managing the regulatory system for control. Positioned at the center of the cybernetic affect machine, geek feelings are marked by a perpetual struggle in which the polarizing impulses between entropy and control are continuously demanding but never gratified, leading to a permanent state of agony and agitation.

As such, the cybernetic affect is never merely a feedback signal. It is excessive, contradictory, and interfering, marked by an often-uncontrollable level of anxiety and agitation as the commonly shared feelings among geeks, otaku, and knowledge workers alike. These feelings are not necessarily productive (as one stage of cybernetic operation), but they can be disrupting, disorienting, or even subversive (as noisy interference against cybernetic efficacy). The cybernetic affect, in many cases, can lead to literal unproductivity in biological and social terms.[94] The affective sensory signal is the integral component of cybernetics but is also running against it. It is simultaneously the force and counterforce in cybernetic systems. Mediating between information machines and human feelings, cybernetic affect is both the driving engine and the side effect of the cool media of technological innervation. It is the affective expression of the inherent contradiction and self-negation of informational medium cool, the irony of "cool passion." Cybernetic affect is thus the emotional excess that is evoked, organized, and dominated by the extreme techno-rationality of cybernetic systems but that at the same time has the tendency to pervert it, because it expresses the techno-rationality in obsessively technical terms. It is "a technical feeling or feeling of the technical."[95]

Animatedness: The "Asiatic" of Geek Movement

If cybernetic affect is the structure of geek feelings, then it is a technical feeling that is often associated with the techniques of animation, as it is the medium that is uniquely powerful for making us feel the techno-rationality of cybernetics through its techniques of animated moving images. The feeling of the technical, as Levitt points out, arises from the "development of an animatic aesthetics that privileges affect— that is, the subtle forms of visceral and emotional responses—over narrative and representation."[96] This affect of the animatic is what Sianne Ngai calls "animatedness," a kind of innervated feeling of being "moved" both physically and emotionally.[97] The state of animatedness— that is, being moved by external forces rather than moving by oneself—is deeply rooted in the forms and techniques of animation, which are rhetorically and aesthetically about "giving life" to lifeless objects by generating motion with machinic force. The feeling of animatedness is thus situated at the interplay between affect and machine, between "the passionate and the mechanical."[98] As such, animatedness is arguably the best notion to characterize cybernetic affect—the feeling of being programmed, moved, and animated by the cybernetic machine. It is the feeling of postindustrial automatons (as geeks of knowledge work) animated by cybernetic automation: the feeling of being automatized without autonomy. As Rey Chow suggests in her essay "Postmodern Automatons," animated motion pictures as the technological media of mass-produced mechanical movement are uniquely powerful in exposing the condition that "the 'human body' as such is already a working body automatized, in the sense that it becomes in the new age an automaton on which social injustice as well as processes of mechanization 'take on a life of their own.'"[99]

Animated by the automation system of anime's media mix, the transmedial, transnational culture of geekdom is also a sociocultural movement. It is a movement that is largely "moved" by this affective feeling of animatedness. But the state of being moved or animated, which is aesthetically represented by exaggerated involuntary movements of the body and excessive expressions of emotion (both being the stylistic features of anime), is an "ugly feeling" according to Ngai, because the sense of being moved by others foregrounds the lack of agency and the sociopolitical powerlessness that are often associated with objectified racial or ethnic otherness for an ethnographic gaze. "Hence, the animation of the racialized body in this instance involves likening it to an instrument, porous, and pliable, for the vocalization of others."[100] But Ngai's notion of animatedness as an ugly feeling is deeply ambivalent, because it points to the modern instrumentation of bodily affect within technological rationality, on one hand, but, on the other hand, it also highlights the primitive impulse toward bodily excess, elasticity, and ecstasy that Sergei Eisenstein famously celebrates as "plasmaticness."[101] It is in this ambivalence between "postmodern automaton" and "plasmaticness"—the ambivalence that allows animation to undermine its own techno-rationality—that we are to locate the sociopolitical potentials of the animatedness in the global geekdom movement. As Lamarre observes, although the otaku movement is largely animated by the industrial mechanism of media mix systems, it also seems to "remain somehow autonomous of the official markets and corporate regulation."[102] The anime geeks genuinely can *move*, through the transnational, transmedial movement of images and meanings, as in the case of anime fansub that I examine in chapter 2, even when they are also *being moved* by the force of cybernetic systems of information capitalism. This ambivalence between automation and autonomy is where power comes into play (*play* in a literal sense as geek culture often centers on gameplay). The constituent power of geeks stems from the fact that the cybernetic affect of animatedness is as much an expression of technological rationality as it is a "strategy of refusal."[103] As such, the affect of animatedness is not simply a symptom of postindustrial knowledge work; it also gestures toward the critical possibility of refusal against cybernetic rationality.

An important goal of this book is to explore this critical possibility that is afforded by the animatedness in cybernetic affect. By examining the transnational, transmedial movement of geek culture, as well as by analyzing the aesthetic and technical expressions in anime, this book demonstrates how the cybernetic affect of animatedness operates within and against the technological rationality of postindustrial knowledge work as both its cultural manifestation and a strategy of refusal. To pursue the possibility of critical intervention, this book theorizes the cybernetic affect of animatedness as the interplay between anime and knowledge work and contemplates Chow's suggestion for a theoretical task of turning automation to autonomy for the objectified, animated racial subjects, the task "of making the automatized and animated condition of their own voices the conscious point of departure in their interventions."[104] Considering the projected techno-Orientalism in the international discourse of cool Japan and the stereotypical Asianness in the popular imagination of geekdom, the animated Third-World subjects that Chow mentions are actually not far from otaku and geeks, though their racialized embodiments of postindustrial automatons operate in a global geography that is beyond the Third World.

The affect of animatedness, as an often-racialized ugly feeling, provides the critical possibility to turn automation to autonomy for the objectified, racial/ethnic subjects in the global geek movement that is often associated with Orientalized Asian cultures such as anime and manga. If the imaginary cool Japan allows geeks to identify with an empty position from outside, then the racialized feeling of animatedness allows critical interventions to problematize the uneven power structure that frames the production and theorization of digital media that anime is part of. In the seemingly neutral, inclusive, and placeless knowledge structure of media studies, the so-called networks and new media are primarily understood as Euro-American media entities such as Google, Facebook, and YouTube, which are nevertheless taken as the model frameworks for global and universal media experiences. These models from the Western center are taken as the structural engine that animates the media cultures of those animated others in the supposed periphery. The movement of anime geekdom with its racialized feeling of animatedness, as well as its varying configurations and manifestations in different local and global contexts where it both moves and is being moved, offers an opportunity to problematize and decenter such universalist assumptions. It allows for the critical possibility of potential deimperialization in media studies by following Kuan-Hsing Chen's call for "Asia as method," which is to use "the idea of Asia as an imaginary anchor point" to mobilize alternative horizons and perspectives.[105] But unlike Chen, my take of "Asia as method" is not situated within the discipline of area studies where Asian societies become each other's references. Instead, "Asia" is taken as a critical and imaginary position that operates through a set of mediated forms (anime) and racialized affect (animatedness), which are associated with but not anchored to the geocultural region of Asia. This critical imagination of Asia as form/affect is what Christopher B. Patterson describes as "Asiatic," which are racialized forms of play that one finds "similar to Asia but that are never exclusively Asian," because "'Asiatic' remains a form, a style, rather than substance, a technology rather than an essence."[106] Identifying the Asiatic forms and affect as the gateway to anime geekdom not only provides a critical possibility of refusal against the objectified racial/ethnic otherness in knowledge culture but also mobilizes a decentered perspective to problematize the uneven geography in the existing theoretical frameworks, whose universalist assertions, as Chen reminds us, "must be deimperialized."[107]

This deimperialization approach from the form and affect of the Asiatic is especially crucial if we consider that the discursive myths of the so-called new economy, new class, and new media, which all locate the "new" technological frontiers in cosmopolitan centers in the West, are fundamentally constructed by entrapping the Third World in a perpetual developmental state of the industrial past that is associated with manufacturing, cheap labor, and outdated technologies. The proliferating narratives of the perpetual "newness" of postindustrial frontiers are based on the abjection of non-Western experiences as historicized otherness. But Asiatic animatedness, by exposing the ambivalent relations between affect, machine, and power, has the potential to liberate the animated automatons of the Third World from their historical entrapment. To transform the non-Western media experience from animated automation to animating autonomy, as Chow suggests, is to reclaim the geocultural and historical complexities that are often denied by the totalizing assertions in media theories and to remap the uneven developments and diverse experiences that are obscured by overarching notions such as "new media" (whose "newness" is it anyway?). If "we"—the knowledge workers in both the developing and developed worlds—have all metaphorically become "Chinese gold farmers" who play as labor in a global digital economy (as Alexander Galloway argues), the actual Chinese gold farmers, I believe, still deserve to be heard with their own autonomous voices rather than to be animated like automatons by media theorists.[108] This book studies those actual Chinese gamers, fans, and geeks, shifting our critical perspective on postindustrial knowledge work from the universalist myth of Silicon Valley to the Asiatic animatedness of the Chinese zhai generation.

This Book

Juxtaposing the cool medium of animation with the hot affect of animatedness, this book examines how these opposing temperatures make anime a powerful environment for the technological innervation of knowledge work. At the center of the book is a theoretical rethinking of anime and otaku culture beyond the frameworks of media representation and identity formation in either national or subcultural terms. Anime is examined not merely as a media object but as a technocultural condition of mediation—the innervation function of medium cool—that operates through the forms of animation techniques with internal openness, gaps, distance, and disjunctions. In a similar vein, this book studies otaku geekdom not as a (sub)cultural identity (from

Japan or elsewhere) but as a quasi-identifiable state or gesture—an intrasubjectivity—of excessively animated outward motion from within, a state of excess feeling that expresses the cybernetic affect of animatedness as the manifestation and refusal of the techno-rationality of postindustrial knowledge work.

My study of anime geekdom is from the vantage point of a specific historical moment at the turn of the twenty-first century, a moment when anime and geek culture became globally popular with the worldwide expansion and penetration of digital networks and information capitalism. Although the modes of production and consumption in knowledge culture emerged in earlier periods (they can be traced to the postwar eras in both the United States and Japan), their global resonance, as well as the association with anime as a cultural staple of geekdom, did not come to prominence until the late 1990s. This book thus focuses on the historical period from the 1990s to the early 2010s and studies a selection of renowned anime, such as *Neon Genesis Evangelion* (1995), *Gurren Lagann* (2007), and *Steins;Gate* (2011), that gained global fandom in that pivotal moment when anime and geek culture came to the front stage. The transnational, transmedial spread of these classic anime, whose popularity continues today (the latest *Evangelion* film was released in 2021), was influential to the millennial generation that this book focuses on, and it came to define and continued defining the meanings and practices of postmillennial geekdom in years to come. Situating these anime in the formation period (1995–2011) of global geekdom, this book demonstrates how these media artifacts played a crucial role in the development of geek communities and their cultural sensibilities in the historical moment of the early twenty-first century.

The book develops in two parts: Part I (chapters 1–3) examines the historical and cultural formation of anime geekdom—with a focus on China—to illustrate the growing expansion of a transnational knowledge culture that had emerged since the 1980s with the rise of network society and information capitalism. It examines zhai culture in China as a case study to demonstrate the emergence and development of anime geekdom, along with the changing meanings and functions of knowledge, in a socially and historically specific context. The focus on Chinese zhai culture is an intentional choice to move away from the assumed center of geek culture in Silicon Valley, as well as from the assumed origin of otaku in Japan. Neither *geek* nor *otaku* is a native cultural term in China, but their transnational emergence, development, and flourishment under the Chinese banner of *zhai* demonstrate the historical transformations of knowledge, production, and labor in both local and global terms.

Chapter 1 traces the historical development of postindustrial knowledge culture by focusing on the cultural history of China's zhai generation. It examines the emergence and development of zhai culture from the popular reception of *Astro Boy* as the first TV animation imported to China in the 1980s to the recent anime fandom that reshaped Chinese internet culture in the twenty-first century. The coming of age of the zhai generation amid China's profound social and economic transformation in the past four decades provides a vivid picture of how a knowledge culture formed and evolved, along with the development of a new generation of Chinese workers and consumers, during the uneven transition from the industrial to the postindustrial economies. At the center of this cultural history is the shifting relationship between the zhai generation and the nation's renewed interest in cultivating and soliciting skilled knowledge workers through institutional and market means. This historical study illuminates the changing meanings and significance of geekdom in relation to knowledge work in the context of China's overwhelming social, cultural, and economic transformations: from wholesale economic reform (*gaige* 改革) in the postsocialist era to the painful transition (*zhuanxiang* 转型) from manufacture to informational economies amid the global development toward postindustrialism.

Chapter 2 continues exploring the changing modes of knowledge production and consumption by examining the ways in which the transnational otaku movement is organized by fansub, the amateur translation and subtitling of anime videos by fan and for fans. Fansub effectively created a global community through collective production, circulation, and consumption of information and knowledge. Such a process of transnational self-organization involves extensive interlingual practices and operates on the fundamental signifying platform of language. By theorizing a methodological shift from the symbolic meanings of visual style to the social functions of language communication, I examine anime fansub as a form of signifying practice that functions as intracultural communication for the formation of a deterritorialized knowledge community, which not only facilitated global cultural flow through user participation and knowledge sharing but also put forward a mode of organizing labor and production through collective voluntary communication on information networks. I call it "communication labor," a form of immaterial knowledge labor that has become the fastest-growing production force in networked digital economies. By studying fansub, this chapter interrogates the mechanisms of organizing, capturing, and sustaining communication labor, which exist as modes of collective knowledge production that oscillate between speed and control, between mass intellectuality and self-management.

Chapter 3 studies the platformization of anime geekdom by examining the *danmaku* interface that permeates various digital platforms in China. Originally a Japanese term to describe a type of shooting games, *danmaku* refers to a unique interface design featured by Japanese video-sharing platform Niconico to render user comments flying over videos on screen. The danmaku interface was quickly popularized among the regional geek communities in East Asia, and it was widely adopted by cinema, television, video streaming, and social media in China, where its cultural penetration far exceeded its original impact from Japan. Examining the interface function of danmaku in mediating different contents, audiences, and platforms among the zhai community in China, this chapter argues that danmaku creates an affective contact zone between visual content and cybernetic platforms, between pseudo-liveness and temporal spectrality, as well as between knowledge production and community organization. Such dynamic and volatile contact, among conflicting modes and logics of different media systems and experiences, generates affective mapping for a contested and uneven knowledge community, in which the platformization of anime geekdom in a regional media geography clashes with local disjunctions and inequalities.

Part II (chapters 4–6) of the book theorizes anime as a media environment for knowledge culture. The chapters analyze the aesthetic forms, narrative patterns, and transmedial operations of anime as a technocultural condition of mediation that is distinctively powerful for generating and sustaining the pleasures and sensibilities of knowledge geeks. The key notion in this study is cybernetic affect, a structure of excess feeling that is experienced through information searching, navigating, and networking and that is evoked by forms, patterns, styles, and signifiers in anime. Such cybernetic affect, which is both exhilarating and familiar for postmillennial geeks, generates a mimetic faculty for knowledge workers to confront and make sense of the postindustrial conditions that oscillate between information explosion and feedback control.

Chapter 4 analyzes the affective/semantic field of techno-intimacy that is structured by one of the most popular modalities in anime, which I call the "mecha-child." The motif of the mecha-child establishes mutual assimilation and identification between machines and child figures through anime's aesthetic forms of cuteness and animatedness. The fictional figure of a cute, animated mecha-child, who is imagined with perpetual youth and creativity, is a mythical invention that serves as an ideal vehicle of identification for knowledge geeks, for whom the cybernetic logic of human–machine integration is not only normalized as ubiquitous and indispensable but also fetishized as desirable, therapeutic, and empowering. Informed by Benjamin's thesis on mimetic innervation in relation to children's play, this chapter further analyzes the ways in which the mecha-child imagination produces an affective milieu of techno-intimacy to internalize the material and symbolic structure of information technology to the daily habitat of knowledge work as both familiar and fantastic. This sense of techno-intimacy has become a dominant cultural logic in information capitalism that translates technological portability and immediacy to a structure of intimate feelings.

Chapter 5 focuses on the play mechanism in the networked, open-ended structure of anime's media mix and characterizes it as a form of aesthetic-technological continuum that I call "cybernetic play." The notion of cybernetic play underlines the integration between the modern romantic conception of play as aesthetic experience and the technological adoption of play into cybernetic systems. As a cybernetic function, play is a mechanism of informatic feedback to optimize performance for the purpose of controlling an expansive information field. This chapter demonstrates that the transmedia system of anime, with its database structure that features narrative complexity, seriality, and interconnectivity, oscillates between two polarizing impulses of distributive chaos (proliferating "worldlines") and unifying control (the singular "true end"). The inherent tension between the opposite impulses calls for the cybernetic function of play as a necessary mechanism to sustain continuous user involvement and information expansion, as well as to control transmedia consumption and production. The mode of play is operated as otaku's persistent search for the "true end" by consuming/producing proliferating "worldlines" as informative feedback loops with trial and error. I argue that the mechanism of cybernetic play has increasingly replaced the previous models of media mix to become the new organizational principle to structure, expand, and control the transmedia systems of anime geekdom.

Chapter 6 examines the so-called superflat aesthetic as a visual vernacular of digital interfaces, which not only mobilizes a viewer's gaze but also frames the subject within the structure of the information field. The chapter begins by studying anime's unique visual style of densely layered flatness and surface-oriented visual organization, which challenges the long-held convention of Renaissance perspective. This is a style that was celebrated by Japanese artist Takashi Murakami as superflat. By mapping the paradigm shift from Renaissance perspective to superflat vision, this chapter addresses the technological condition underlying the changing modes of perception by focusing on the development of computer user interfaces that transformed the vernacular visual structure. I argue that superflat visuality is the aesthetic of hypermediacy that represents increasing mobility and multiplicity of screens, images, and gazes through the proliferation of various kinds of digital interfaces. Such a postperspective vision mobilized by digital interfaces implies a spatiotemporal structure that is propagating and propagated by a heightened state of commodity experience in information society. The distributive visual surfaces, though mobilizing the gaze beyond the fixed vanishing point of linear perspective, ultimately frame the subject within the algorithmic structure and commodity matrix of the information field.

Examining the aesthetic forms and techniques of anime as a function of mediation, as well as the activities and sensibilities of geeks as a state of intrasubjectivity of knowledge work, this book combines cultural studies of geekdom with media theory of anime. Highlighted throughout the two parts of the book are three key elements of anime geekdom:

> KNOWLEDGE: the changing nature and structure of knowledge in informationalized and commodified forms mediate between work and play in the post-Fordist modes of production, which leads to excessive surplus knowledge that is unidentifiable and unproductive.
>
> PLAY: the affective experiences of the technologically mediated aesthetics of play express cybernetic rationality, on one hand, but fail to be fully incorporated or valorized as productive labor, on the other.
>
> PLEASURE: unvalorized play and unproductive knowledge are circulated as "wasteful" heat—rather than productive energy—of affective pleasure, which cannot be contained within the frame of identity formation but remains in an unactualized and unstable state of intrasubjectivity of knowledge work that gestures for outward motion from within.

The circulation between (unproductive) knowledge, (unvalorized) play, and (unactualized) pleasure forms the continuous but volatile cycles of cybernetic feedback loops, which nevertheless do not sustain the supposed function of knowledge work but rather point to its own anxiety, obsession, edginess, and, above all, animatedness. Anime geekdom is thus an animated and animating machine that is paradoxically unproductive. When energy is trapped by the machine into cycles of motion but without productivity, it converts to heat. It is this heat that animates the transnational, transmedial movement of anime geekdom. This book intends to capture this heat, measure its temperature, and study its source, nature, and impact, because the heat not only burns but also energizes.

PART I

THE KNOWLEDGE CULTURE OF GEEKDOM

Knowledge Is Power

From *Astro Boy* to China's *Zhai* Generation

In 2010, Han Han, a twenty-seven-year-old best-selling author, filmmaker, and one of China's most popular bloggers, was voted number two in *Time* magazine's poll for the top one hundred most influential people in the world, ranking higher than Bill Gates and President Obama.[1] Widely hailed as the posterchild of the "post-8os" generation (80后), who were born and raised in the 1980s when China was undergoing socioeconomic reforms, Han, like his young Chinese followers, grew up under the cultural influence of anime and wrote in the style of Japanese light novels. Guo Jingming (Edward Guo), another best-selling author, filmmaker, and posterchild of the post-8os generation, is also known as a high-profile anime fan. Guo's works are famous for their manga-style illustrations and anime-like storylines. In 2004, he founded his media company, Ke Ai Entertainment, following the Japanese model of media mix that was established by the publishing house Kadokawa Shoten. Guo's media empire successfully launched the first wave of media mix in China with popular franchises such as *City of Fantasy* and *Tiny Times,* which gained remarkable revenue across multiple media types, including novels, comics, animation, films, and television. The successful business in media mix made Guo a young millionaire before turning thirty, and he was celebrated by *Forbes* magazine as one of the most promising entrepreneurs in China's booming media industry.[2] To a certain extent, Han and Guo were the cultural icons of China's postmillennial class of cool: young, rich, tech-savvy, prominent on social media, embracing the market, and capitalizing on the dreams and fantasies of a rising China in the digital age. Emerging as powerful cultural voices, they represented a new generation of Chinese youth who came to adulthood in the early twenty-first century, when China was struggling to transition from a manufacturing to an informational economy, or, to borrow a fancy phrase, from "Made in China" to "Created in China."[3]

The older generations were caught off-guard by the success of these young cultural icons who rode the waves of China's burgeoning digital economy. For Chinese critics and scholars, their success represented less a triumph than a symptom of the millennial generation who had grown up under too much influence of anime, and their works were as flat and superficial as those manga and anime that they consumed. In the words of the literary scholar Xiao Ying: "[Guo Jingming's works] are pathological texts without real feelings of pain. . . . They have nothing to do with literary traditions but are simply commercial formulas typical of the post-80s generation, who have apparently grown up watching too much Japanese anime."[4] Similarly, Lu Jinbo, a renowned publisher, claimed that post-80s literature had "less to do with European literary modernism than with the popularity of Japanese manga and anime."[5]

Indeed, these millennial youths are also known as China's *zhai* generation (宅世代), whereby the word *zhai* (宅) borrows its meaning from the Japanese term *otaku* (お宅). Not only did they grow up as enthusiastic consumers of Japanese anime, manga, and games, but zhai was their self-claimed collective identity. The phrase "wo hen zhai" (I am so otaku) was their well-known motto. This generation also marked the collective debut of China's "only children" (独生子女), born under China's one-child policy that was officially launched in 1979.[6] Unlike their parents, who went through the Cultural Revolution in the Mao era, this generation was raised under China's rapid economic boom and was expected to grow to a major driving force for the nation's fast-developing digital economy. Zhai thus represented the emergence of a nascent generation of postindustrial knowledge workers and consumers in China, who were endowed with expanded college education and an increasing amount of income, media access, and consumer goods. They were also China's first digital generation, who witnessed the IT boom, fully embraced the power of information technologies, and went on to become avid internet users and developers fleeing to the high-tech centers in Beijing, Shenzhen, and Shanghai to pursue their careers and fortunes. For a significant period, they were China's most active netizens, organizing social relations, productive labor, consumer activities, and cultural lives almost entirely on the internet. When the world's largest population was getting wired, it was this generation of information workers and consumers, the self-proclaimed zhai-boys and zhai-girls, who largely shaped popular media culture in China.

Born and raised under the nation's wholesale socioeconomic reforms, the zhai generation must be situated under China's dramatic transformation of the past four decades. This is a generation whose coming-of-age story chronicles China's astonishing changes from a socialist welfare state to a neoliberal market economy, from industrial manufacturing to postindustrial informationalism. Their geek sensibilities echo the social, cultural, and economic transformation of the entire nation. As Chinese scholar Zhang Yiwu points out, the whole cultural spectrum of this generation is a manifestation of China's "new social norms under a market economy."[7] Therefore, this generation needs to be understood within the historical context of a series of political and economic changes since the 1980s, including China's embrace of free-trade policies and a neoliberal agenda, its strong belief in technocracy and techno-nationalism, its forceful entry into globalization, its rapid development of an information society, and its painful transition from the industrial to the postindustrial economy.[8]

It is against this historical backdrop that I will study the sociocultural formation of the zhai generation. I investigate the ways in which the transmedial, transnational circulation and consumption of anime, from the television broadcasting of *Astro Boy* in the 1980s to the internet influence of otaku in the new millennium, effectively nurtured a new generation of knowledge workers and consumers, whose behaviors and sensibilities since childhood had formed a substantial force in shaping the cultural and economic landscape of contemporary China.

The coming of age of the zhai generation amid China's profound transformation provides a case study of how a postindustrial knowledge culture emerged and evolved in a socially and historically specific context.

This cultural history is marked by the changing meanings and relations of knowledge and labor, along with China's renewed interest in cultivating and soliciting skilled knowledge workers through institutional and market means. Since China's reform in the 1980s, a technocratic, developmental logic had been at the center of its economic and governing policy, in which techno-scientific advancement was believed to be the driving force for the nation's revival. Under the banner of Francis Bacon's famous saying "Knowledge is power," a new generation of knowledge workers was demanded and produced in China.[9] One of the cultural manifestations of this historical transformation was the changing position of zhai culture in relation to the institutional and market structures of knowledge work: from *Astro Boy,* which started anime's popularity in China as science-education programs for children, to anime fandom that emerged on university campuses amid the expansion of college education; and from anime's media mix being incorporated into popular techno-cultures of software and computers to millennial geeks being celebrated as a new breed of innovators to lead the nation's digital economy. This history illuminates the changing meaning and significance of anime geekdom in relation to knowledge work in the context of China's socioeconomic transformation: from economic reform (*gaige* 改革) in the postsocialist era to the structural transition (*zhuanxing* 转型) in global development toward postindustrialism.

A Brief History of Anime Geekdom in China

To historicize the development of zhai culture, I first go over the brief history of anime's expansion in China from 1980 to the present, because anime geekdom carries different historical meanings in China than in Japan and the West.[10] This history can be divided into three important periods, each correlating to a series of social, political, and economic changes, as well as transformations in media environment and technology, which had deeply influenced the form and meaning of knowledge culture in China.[11]

The first period, from the early 1980s to the mid-1990s, is the moment when Japanese anime was first introduced to Chinese youth through official channels, the state-run television stations. This period was marked by the rapid development and penetration of television culture, and television was the main medium for anime distribution and consumption at that time. It thus can be described as anime's television era. Profound historical factors shaped this debut period of anime in China, as the era witnessed some of the most dramatic social, political, and economic changes in recent Chinese history. As television began to spread and replace cinema as the leading mass medium to entertain the world's largest population, anime was among China's first imported TV programs. Blessed by the rekindled diplomatic relationship with Japan through the Open Door policy, anime landed in China, quickly dominated children's television programs, and became a major form of entertainment for Chinese youth. More importantly, this decade of rapid anime invasion coincided with the debut of China's first generation of avid consumers who were brought up in front of television commercials and whose consumer power was cultivated at a crucial moment for the development of a nascent market economy. The increasing presence of anime on television, therefore, influenced not only the desires and imaginations of Chinese children but also the economic and cultural transformations of Chinese society.

From the 1990s to the new millennium, when the official importation channels began to close, Chinese anime culture entered its second phase: the digital piracy period. After the crackdown of the 1989 democracy movement, the Chinese government became cautious of cultural importation of television. In the early 1990s, the number of imported programs on Chinese television was reduced to less than half of what it was in the late 1980s.[12] China's national television stations stopped importing anime in the 1990s, though local and provincial stations continued to rely on anime as a major source of children's programming due to the lack of content supply from Chinese domestic animation production.[13] In 2004, Chinese officials issued a policy that required the television airtime of imported animation to be cut down to less than 40 percent of the total airtime of children's programming.[14]

In 2006, the governmental regulation was further strengthened and anime nearly disappeared from Chinese television altogether.[15] This period of anime's dramatic decrease on Chinese television incidentally coincided with the explosion of digital piracy, owing to the fast development of digital video technology, such as VCD and DVD, that became affordable in Chinese households. With the rapid growth of the youth market in digital media, piracy began to fill in the gap left by the restriction of anime on television. By the early 2000s, anime culture had moved from television to digital piracy, and it had transformed from an officially promoted youth culture to a semi-illicit subculture.

When anime was moving from television to digital video, its initial Chinese audience, the generation that was raised in the 1980s watching anime, had reached adolescence and early adulthood. They became China's first generation of avid computer users and web surfers when information technology began to spread in the 1990s. When its audience moved from television to the internet, anime culture transformed to its third stage (2000 to the present): the internet fandom period. The most important cultural practice in this period is the fansub: amateur subtitled anime videos produced "by fans and for fans." When anime's Chinese fans—the post-80s children who were now in college and spending a lot of time on the internet—became dissatisfied by the deficiency of anime on television and pirate DVDs, they began to organize translation, subtitling, and distribution of anime by themselves through online platforms. Fansub groups quickly emerged from digital communities in China's major universities and spread on the internet. After anime disappeared from television, online fansub became the major channel for distribution and consumption. By taking the task of transnational mediation into their own hands, Chinese fans (unintentionally) undermined the hegemonic systems of cultural control by effectively upsetting the governmental rulings that aimed to limit the spread of anime. What used to be broadcast as a mainstream youth culture on Chinese state-run television transformed to an ambivalent cultural presence, a force of both growth and disturbance, in China's emergent digital economy of information networks.

Through these different stages, anime underwent a series of changes in China, from state-approved, televised cultural importation to user-initiated, networked cultural globalization. These changes, which were contextualized by China's socioeconomic transformations and the development in media technology, will be closely studied in this chapter, with a particular focus on the first and third stages of this short history, because they correlate with the most crucial developments in China's nascent knowledge work and culture. I will examine how the economic reforms with the Open Door policy that brought televised anime in the 1980s, as well as how the economic transition toward postindustrial capitalism that expanded computerized zhai culture in the early twenty-first century, redefined the cultural meanings of knowledge, work, and play in contemporary China.

Televised Techno-Modernity and China's Only Children

The beginning period of anime's transnational journey in the 1980s was a significant one, because it was a defining historical moment with wide-ranging changes that made China what it is today. The story of China's miraculous economic boom has been told many times. What has not been fully explored, however, is how popular media such as television and animation played a key role in it. Mass media, as James Lull argues, are "symbolic and functional contributors to the economic and ideological dimensions of reformation" in China.[16] It is especially true for animation, a major form of children's entertainment that took the role of educating a new generation of Chinese workers and consumers who were born and raised under China's economic reforms. The intervention of these animated imageries on television in the lives of Chinese youth is central to understanding the changing social, cultural, and economic dynamics that gave rise to the zhai generation.

Since 1978, China had undergone a series of reforms under the leadership of Deng Xiaoping, and one of them was the Open Door policy, which aimed to reopen China's diplomatic and economic relationship with foreign countries.[17] As the first step toward entering globalization, the Open Door policy was a crucial force driving China's socioeconomic overhaul under Deng's neoliberal agenda, and its main result was a remarkable growth in foreign trade and investment.[18] As China rushed to the global economy, cultural products and ideas also flooded in through the open door. Such cultural exchanges not only changed public opinions toward foreign countries but also had a dramatic impact on Chinese popular culture with profound influences in everyday life. Television, the new medium that became popularized in the reform era, was the prime platform for these influences.

First introduced to China in the 1950s, television was not a major communication medium until the 1980s, when it suddenly became affordable due to increasing household incomes. Television was then reintroduced as a new media technology, celebrated as a symbol of the nation's rapid modernization and an effective tool to stimulate the emerging consumer economy. As Lull observes, "There was no material device that symbolized prosperity more than television," and "the maturation of China's material civilization is not only symbolized by television, it depends on it."[19] In the 1980s, a television set was considered one of the "three major appliances" (*san da jian*) that Chinese families believed they should purchase to demonstrate their newly improved standard of living. Even governmental officials, such as chairman Hu Yaobang, publicly endorsed television ownership. Consequently, television ownership and viewership increased dramatically during the reform period. From 1980 to 1990, the ownership of television sets in China soared from 5 million to 185 million, and television penetration reached 79.4 percent of households.[20] China had by then developed the largest television audience in the world. And television began to wield great effect on private and public spheres, reorganizing daily routines, altering leisure and consumption, and affecting the collective consciousness. The Chinese government embraced this new medium as both a propaganda device to influence public opinions and an economic machine to stimulate mass consumption. Television thus played a vital role in China's social and economic reform, generating a consumer society that looked to the outside through an open door.

When China was marching toward a market economy, television, a powerful advertising machine, mediated a particular kind of consumer desire that was enchanted with the imagination of techno-modernity. Throughout the 1980s, the advertising industry was one of the fastest-growing areas of the Chinese economy, with television as its major medium. At the same time, Chinese television, with rapid expansion and commercialization, had to fill its airtime with foreign TV shows and commercials due to the lack of domestic programs. The internationalization of Chinese television was further facilitated by the Open Door policy that relaxed regulatory restrictions. On China Central Television (CCTV), the percentage of imported programs increased from 2 percent in 1980 to 36 percent in 1988; on the Shanghai TV station, the increase was from 7 percent in 1980 to 73 percent in 1986.[21] Arriving together with imported TV shows were commercials for foreign brands. Chinese television, with the world's largest viewership, was the most sought-after vehicle for international advertising. The primary mechanism to place advertisements on Chinese television was through barter deals in exchange for program imports. For instance, in 1986 CCTV signed a barter agreement with Disney Studio, exchanging commercial airtime for the broadcasting rights of Mickey Mouse cartoons. Through such barter agreements, an influx of foreign commercials aired on China's prime-time television.

These foreign commercials and TV shows advertised not just famous international brands but the fantasy of a prosperous modern lifestyle with technological advancement. As Conghua Li points out: "Television has introduced advertising and the outside world. It shows the viewers what they do not have, and, by implication, what they should come to expect."[22] Indeed, television motivated Chinese viewers to desire an imported lifestyle of technological modernity and to reevaluate their own living standards. As is shown in an audience study in the 1980s: a family voiced their frustration that their local stores did not carry a Japanese brand of washing machine that was advertised on television, and a female viewer expressed her surprise that on American TV shows "even terrible people have cars!"[23] Television, a new technological medium itself, functioned as a material and cultural construction of commodity experience that appeared to be distinctively modern and technologically advanced. For Chinese viewers in the reform period, television was an alluring window that looked out to an imagined techno-modernity.

This crucial function of television to stimulate desires of techno-modernity had arguably the strongest impact on the post-80s youths. They were China's first generation brought up in front of television and were at the center of the expanding TV viewership. As the only children in their families, they dominated both the remote controls and consumer expense. One audience survey indicated that most families took their children's interests or benefits as the determinant factors for their TV viewing patterns.[24] Another survey showed that the average urban Chinese family spent 50 to 70 percent of their monthly expenditure on the only child.[25] As China's first generation of avid consumers and TV viewers, these only children, who were expected to form the core demographic to propel a gigantic consumer economy, were the most desirable targets for foreign advertisements. Therefore, it is no accident that the first advertising barter agreement for Chinese television was signed in 1980 between the CCTV children's program and the Japanese electronics manufacturer Casio. The barter deal brought to China the first anime series, *Astro Boy*, in exchange for airtime of TV commercials specifically targeting children. It was in this context of expanding TV viewership and advertisement, as well as the growing internationalization of Chinese television toward a collective desire of techno-modernity, that anime arrived in China, targeting the only-child consumers who eventually grew up to become the zhai generation. The cultural history of zhai as a popular knowledge culture, therefore, began with *Astro Boy* on Chinese television, alongside Casio commercials, advocating for a new kind of modern myth.

Astro Boy: From Science Education to a Transnational Myth of Techno-Utopia

The first anime introduced to China was none other than *Astro Boy* (Osamu Tezuka, 1963), translated as *Tiebi Atongmu* (铁臂阿童木) in Chinese, close to its original Japanese title *Tetsuwan Atomu* (鉄腕アトム). It was the first TV anime in Japan in the 1960s and the first of such in China in the 1980s. It initially aired in December 1980 on CCTV,

China's only national television channel at that time, and continued to be syndicated and rebroadcasted through local and provincial stations throughout the entire decade and beyond. For Chinese children who were born and raised in the 1980s, *Astro Boy* was one of their first TV memories. As one of the most popular TV shows in China's broadcasting history, it became an omnipresent cultural icon on Chinese television and came to define this new medium that began to enter average households, as many Chinese families bought their first television set to satisfy their children's desire to watch *Astro Boy*. The powerful image of Astro Boy not only captured the imagination of a whole generation of Chinese youth but also transformed the media consumption of their parents, convincing them that television was a useful medium for children's education and thus should be welcomed into their households.

The impact of *Astro Boy* was not limited to television, and it became one of the most successful transmedia franchises in China. Osama Tezuka's original manga series of *Astro Boy* was released in Chinese in 1981 and received similar popularity as the TV anime. It was translated by a famous ambassador, Zhou Bin, who used to work as the interpreter for the former national leader Hua Guofeng, and was published as science-education books for children by the prestigious state-run publisher Popular Science Press (Figure 1). Meanwhile, various character goods in the *Astro Boy* franchise flooded the youth market and launched the first wave of merchandising business in China. Astro Boy thus became the first transmedia celebrity known to Chinese children in the 1980s, celebrated as a techno-superhero for science education.[26]

The extraordinary success of *Astro Boy*, first of all, underlined the changing political and economic situations under the rekindled China–Japan relationship. As a wealthy neighbor, Japan was sought after as a desirable trading partner and an ideal choice for geopolitical alliance. But the public image of Japan was plagued by the bitter memory of the Japanese invasion of China during World War II. Therefore, renewing the relationship with Japan was a challenging and delicate project that had to be carefully orchestrated. In 1978, Deng Xiaoping visited Japan as the first Chinese leader to do so after the Communist Party took power in 1949. Publicly announcing that "developing a friendly relationship

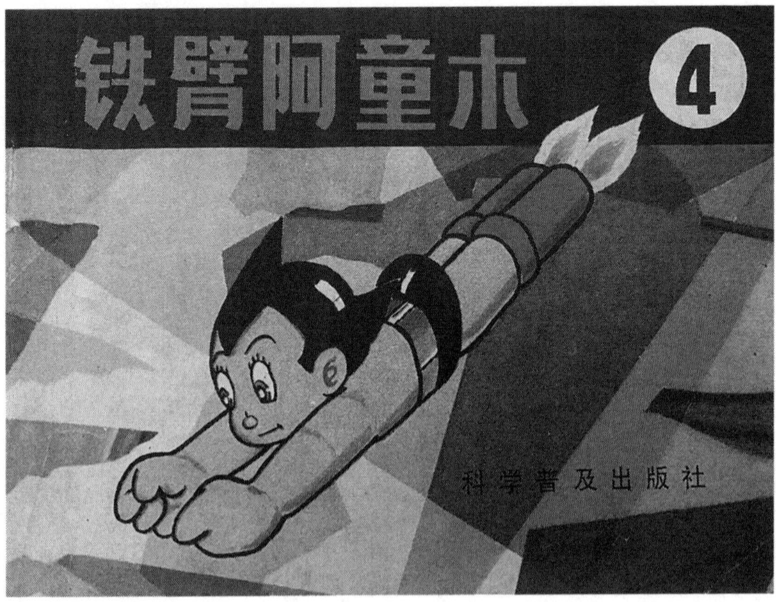

FIGURE 1. The comic book series *Tiebi Atongmu* (*Astro Boy*) published in Chinese by Kexue Puji Chubanshe (Popular Science Press) in 1981.

with Japan is China's long-term policy with strategic significance for economic modernization," Deng brought back from his Japanese trip an important collaboration treaty and a generous loan of JPY ¥55 billion.[27] Japan was the first developed country to establish an economic partnership with China through the Open Door policy, providing crucial investment and technology. China in turn offered Japan its labor, market, and energy sources. From 1978 to 1995, trading between China and Japan increased almost sixtyfold, from USD $1.03 billion to USD $57.5 billion, and Japan became China's biggest trading partner.[28] This era was therefore marked as the famous "honeymoon period" for the Sino–Japan relationship.

In this historical context, *Astro Boy* came to China not simply as the first imported animation on television but as an important cultural ambassador from Japan. In 1980, months after Chinese prime minister

Hua Guofeng finished his official visit to Japan, CCTV signed its first barter deal to bring *Astro Boy,* the most iconic anime, to the Chinese audience. In 1981, when *Astro Boy* was hot on the air, its creator, Osamu Tezuka, visited China. Celebrated as the father of modern Japanese manga and anime, Tezuka received tremendous publicity from the Chinese press and a warm endorsement from the government. While Astro Boy was popularized as a role model for Chinese children, Tezuka was admired as a great Japanese artist who loved Chinese culture, as his appreciation of Chinese animation and his interest in the traditional Chinese myth of the Monkey King were widely publicized.[29] Meanwhile, with an endorsement and financial support from the Chinese government, Tezuka's company opened a local subsidiary, Xie Le studio in Beijing, to serve Japanese anime production with cheap Chinese labor, which was the first foreign-owned animation studio built on Chinese territory, a starting point of China's decades-long history of outsourced animation production serving Japan.

Following Tezuka and *Astro Boy,* a wave of Japanese cultural entities was introduced to China in the 1980s as a measure to promote cultural exchange for the renewed Sino–Japan relationship. Television was the primary medium in such exchanges, and Japanese drama series such as *Akai Giwaku* (1975), *Moero Attack* (1979), and *Oshin* (1983) began to dominate television screens and became widely popular among the Chinese audience. Anime was a major part of Japanese cultural importation through television. After *Astro Boy*'s groundbreaking success, a bunch of famous anime including *Kimba the White Lion* (1965), *Ikkyu the Little Monk* (1975), and *Hana no Ko Lunlun* (1979) all flooded in, most of which were offered to Chinese television stations at almost no cost, leading to anime's prevalence in Chinese youth culture. As Japanese dramas and anime series became omnipresent on Chinese television, these televised images constituted a virtual imagination of Japan, which was no longer associated with the painful history of the Sino–Japanese War but was desired as an indigenized version of modern life in Asia, a fantasy for Chinese viewers to project their own imagined future.

China's cultural obsession with a television-mediated virtual Japan, I would argue, was not solely due to the widely assumed geocultural proximity of East Asia.[30] Instead, it was based on a transnational myth of techno-utopia, embodied in the popular imagination of Astro Boy, which was shared by Japan's postwar history in the 1960s and China's postsocialist reform in the 1980s. It was this shared aspiration to build a strong nation with technological empowerment that made Japan, an Asian economic superpower rising from atomic ashes, a perfect historical model for China's own modernization project in the reform era. The renewed Sino–Japan partnership, which was spearheaded by this shared myth of techno-empowerment, was thus endorsed by Deng Xiaoping as a "long-term policy with strategic significance for economic modernization."[31]

To understand this shared myth, let us first be reminded that Astro Boy, as a transnational/transmedial icon, was famously remembered, in both Japan and China, as a nuclear-powered super robot with "100,000 horsepower." As the opening theme song in the original Japanese series tells us, Astro Boy is "Almighty Atom" who is "passing through the sky" and "beyond the stars," because he is "a boy of science" (科学の子), a characterization that is further specified by the Chinese version of the song as "a good boy who loves science" (爱科学的好少年).[32] This boy of science (who also "loves science") was celebrated as an inspiring role model not only for Chinese children but for the entire national identity that was to be renewed and empowered by techno-sciences. This myth of techno-nationalism was fully embraced in 1980s China. Led by Chairman Deng's motto that "science and technology are the first production force," the belief in technological empowerment was a guiding principle for China's economic reforms. Cybernetic theory was adopted into social and economic models, and knowledge workers were demanded and produced by expanded college education in techno-scientific programs.[33] It is in this historical context that Astro Boy, a techno-hero who never ages, was introduced to China as a role model for children's science education and an embodiment of technological superpower.

Astro Boy was not alone in advocating for a transnational utopian myth of technological modernization. Anime as a media form, with its unique quality of *mukokuseki* (statelessness), had successfully put forward what Iwabuchi characterizes as an "odorless" image of virtual Japan that is endowed with the fantasies of global modernity.[34] For the Chinese audience, anime presented less a national culture of Japan than a transnational imagination of techno-future. The animated images function as what Lisa Leung calls "trans local agents," evoking fantasies and desires of modern lifestyles beyond national or cultural boundaries.[35] Therefore, Chinese viewers in the 1980s experienced the influx of anime culture as an indigenized version of modernity that had been taken as universal values—the values of technological modernization and economic prosperity to which China was aspiring.

These values were also articulated through a particular brand of techno-consumerism that was associated with virtual Japan. It is worth reiterating that *Astro Boy* came to China through a barter deal that brought the first foreign commercials to Chinese television. The deal was signed not with a Japanese animation studio but rather with a Japanese consumer electronics manufacturer, Casio. In 1979, Casio entered the Chinese market and actively sought advertising opportunities. But China was still unprepared for foreign advertisements, as it had just broadcast its first television commercial in 1979.[36] Instead of directly purchasing advertisements, Casio bought the Chinese broadcasting rights for *Astro Boy* from Japan and gave it to CCTV in exchange for commercial airtime. Therefore, along with *Astro Boy* as the first anime introduced to China, the Casio advertisement was the first foreign commercial ever aired on Chinese television. The Casio commercial that was broadcast during *Astro Boy*'s airtime was nicely engineered: the super robot Astro Boy, flying with his nuclear-powered engine, endorsed the "scientific advancement and accuracy" of Casio calculators and digital watches, proudly declaring: "Casio is empowered by the same technology as mine!" (Figure 2).

Besides their own commercials, Casio also sold part of the airtime to other Japanese companies. Most of these commercials featured the image of Astro Boy, who became not only the first TV star but also the first advertising celebrity in China. Through the popularity of Astro Boy, these Japanese brands became household names. After the success of the Astro–Casio bundle, an influx of anime TV shows was brought to

FIGURE 2. The tie-in TV commercial for Casio broadcast during *Astro Boy*'s airtime on China Central Television (CCTV) in 1980. It was the first foreign commercial that aired on Chinese national television. Images captured from the footage reproduced in *Xianxiang 1980* (Phenomena 1980), season 4, episode 4, directed by Chen Xiaoqing, 2010, as part of the documentary series *Jianzheng: Yingxiang Zhi* (Witness: Image Records), China Central Television.

China through barter deals with Japanese companies such as Sony, Toshiba, and Toyota. When anime became the companion of Chinese children, these Japanese brands of technological goods occupied a significant space in their daily life. As one Chinese blogger puts it, the most exciting moment in his childhood memory was "waiting for Astro Boy flying through the gigantic logo of Hitachi."[37] For Chinese youth brought up in the 1980s, the trademarks of Hitachi, Casio, and Sony were as vivid and unforgettable as Astro Boy in their collective memories, imaginations, and desires.

In an almost uncanny fashion, the ways in which *Astro Boy* singlehandedly pushed Chinese television and its young viewers toward a heightened state of techno-consumerism echo anime's early history in Japan. The broadcast of *Astro Boy* on Japanese television in 1963, according to Kusakawa Sho, was a "turning point in postwar Japanese culture," because the successful advertising and merchandising strategies launched by *Astro Boy* led companies to realize that they can "advertise and sell products by overlapping the commodity image with a character image," which marked a paradigm shift in the relation between media, commodities, and advertisement.[38] As Marc Steinberg notes, *Astro Boy* was the historical origin of anime's media mix in Japan, as the character image of Astro Boy was extremely successful in launching advertisement campaigns for candies, toys, and a vast array of commodities. The proliferation and spread of the character image from anime to advertisement to merchandise translated TV viewership to transmedia consumption, which "enabled a convergence of media and objects around it and contributed to the formation of a particularly systematic image-thing network around anime."[39] This "image-thing network" that ties anime with commodities and advertisement is precisely what *Astro Boy* brought to China in the 1980s. What was introduced from Japan was not only a new type of TV animation for children but also "a new way of advertising, a new way of selling products, and a new way of organizing media relations."[40] What *Astro Boy* represents is the Japanese brand of commodity logic and its business model of media mix.

The bundled influx of anime and Japanese brands, as well as the invasion of the Japanese model of media mix, took place at a crucial moment, a historical turning point in the economic relationship between China and Japan. In the early 1980s, when China began its reform to a market economy, Japan was the world's second-largest economy driven by exportation. The warming Sino–Japan relationship provided the Japanese economy with a much-needed vehicle to expand to a new emerging market. Therefore, with the influx of anime, the Japanese brand of techno-consumerism came through the commodity logic of advertising and merchandising. Throughout the 1980s, Japanese companies were the biggest spenders on advertising in China, placing two-thirds of total foreign advertisements.[41] Consequently, Japanese companies such as Toyota, Casio, and Sony became the best-known brand names representing an alluring fantasy of cutting-edge technology. According to audience research in the 1980s, the most desirable products for Chinese people were Japanese consumer electronics that were believed to be technologically advanced.[42] Owning a Japanese TV set was considered a proud achievement by many Chinese families. For children growing up watching *Astro Boy,* their favorite gadget was most likely a Casio digital watch.

Representing a utopian myth of techno-nationalism and a commodity logic of techno-consumerism, anime's historical debut in China highlights the complex economical and geopolitical situations in the pivotal moment of reform. Under such historical conditions, anime was never simply children's entertainment. The intricate political and economic implications of anime culture were evident even to its most innocent viewers. As a Chinese journalist recounts:

In the prelude to Sino–Japan friendship, Astro Boy came to China with his superpower, and so did Ikkyu the Little Monk. Together with them were various kinds of Japanese goods. Even in my naive childhood world, the political drama of that era was so evident.[43]

Deeply implicated in such historical situations of the reform-era China that set out to build its own techno-economic power, the choice of *Astro Boy* as the first anime to be introduced to a Chinese audience was certainly not accidental. By the time *Astro Boy* aired in China, it had been a cultural icon in Japan for almost two decades. *Astro Boy*'s 1963 debut on Japanese television marked a milestone in Japan's postwar media history, introducing not only a business model of media mix but also a national myth of technological empowerment and renewal. According to Anne Allison, the popular image of Astro Boy—a robotic techno-superhero endowed with boyish cuteness and innocence—emerged in postwar Japan as an enchanting myth of nation-building through technology and modernization.[44] Such a techno-utopian myth celebrating a youthful superhero empowered by atomic energy put forward a much-needed national identity for postwar Japan, a nation anxious to be reborn after traumatic defeat in WWII and to rebuild itself through economic development and technological empowerment. This national myth was further propagated through the emergence of a new medium: television. As the first animated series broadcast on Japanese television, Astro Boy became Japan's first TV star in the 1960s.[45] The propagation of *Astro Boy*'s techno-utopian myth went hand in hand with the rapid growth of television as a mass medium in postwar Japan.

As Karl Marx tells us, history often repeats itself, albeit in different forms and sometimes in different places. Anime's introduction to Chinese television in 1980 uncannily mirrored its historical origin in Japan, propagating a similar myth of techno-empowerment, though in another culture at another historical moment of national reckoning and reconstruction. With striking resemblance to postwar Japan, China in the early reform era of the 1980s also had a desperate need to renew its national identity after decades of social, political, and economic turmoil. In the immediate aftermath of Mao's Cultural Revolution, China's economic reform launched in 1978 was branded specifically as a massive project of nation "rebuilding" (重建), for the reform was considered a structural overhaul and "fundamental correction" (拨乱反正) of the failed socialist experiments in the previous eras. The official Chinese motto at that time was "waiting to rejuvenate after hundreds of wasted failures" (百废待兴). Such a dramatic overturn in economic and political discourses in the postsocialist era inevitably led to a collective sense of confusion and identity crisis. The influx of Western culture and ideology after the introduction of the Open Door policy further intensified the widespread anxiety and uncertainty regarding China's future. To put forward a cohesive and united national discourse amid such collective anxiety, the famous propaganda of "building for modernization" (建设现代化), which was first raised by Mao Zedong to propagate techno-nationalism in the 1950s, was revived by Chinese leaders in the reform era as a blueprint for developing modern China through technological advancement.

This techno-utopian myth of nation-building was not unlike that in postwar Japan. To build this techno-future for the nation, it is crucial to educate a new generation of knowledge labor skilled in science and technology. China's leader, Deng Xiaoping, strongly advocated a national policy to "revive the nation through science and education" (科教兴国), a policy that was supposed to be based on the Marxist doctrine that "science and technology are the primary productive force."[46] In 1985, Deng made a famous speech at a national conference for science education. He said: "For our country, the strength of national power and the force of economic development increasingly depend on the education level of labor, that is, the quantity and quality of intellectuals."[47] By "intellectuals," Deng was referring to a burgeoning class of knowledge workers, because the Chinese word for "intellectuals"—*zhishi fenzi* (知识分子)—literally means "knowledge members."

In this historical context of a massive modernization project, as well as under the national policy to strengthen science and technology through education, *Astro Boy* came to China. The techno-utopian myth of a robotic superhero must have struck a chord in the collective national psyche and in the public belief of a techno-future. Sold as a science-education program to cultivate passion, *Astro Boy,* like many imported anime and manga afterward, served as a powerful mediation between the popular fantasy of children and the popularization of techno-science.[48] For Chinese viewers, what came to represent a utopian future of technological modernization was not simply Astro Boy but also the imagined virtual identity of Japan as a techno-economic superpower, as well as the cutting-edge electronics of Japanese brands (e.g., Casio, Sony, Toshiba, and Hitachi) as the symbols of technological strength, precision, and innovation. To the nation that was expected to be rebuilt with a new modern identity, and to the young viewers who were educated to become a new generation of "knowledge members," the imagination of a virtual Japan in anime represented an alluring techno-future that China could identify with and aspire to. While Chinese children were desiring to become Astro Boy, China was longing to become the next Japan, an economic superpower rebuilt from ashes with modern technologies. Behind the enchanting images of anime was the utopian imagination of a technologically empowered future for China.

Knowledge Work and Play in the Transmedia Networks of Zhai Culture

The historical conditions that gave rise to the popularity of *Astro Boy* began to change after the Tiananmen Square massacre in 1989, which put an end to China's long decade of the 1980s.[49] Notable changes in the following years include the domestication of Chinese television by reducing the percentage of imported programs and the end of the "honeymoon period" of the Sino–Japan relationship. Despite such changes, anime continued to enchant Chinese children as a leading media form. According to a survey conducted in 2003, 60 to 80 percent of urban youths cited anime as their favorite entertainment.[50] Although anime still dominated youth culture, its distribution and consumption moved to different media. Television as a major distribution channel began to be closed after the 1990s, but the development of new media technologies allowed anime culture to continue flourishing through digital piracy and the internet. By 2006, when the Chinese government banned anime from prime-time television, transnational consumption of anime had largely moved to cyberspace in the form of fansubs. Consequently, China's anime culture transformed from televised mainstream entertainment imported by state-run media to an internet-based, peer-to-peer community generated by fans. It became a networked transnational, transmedial movement of otaku geekdom under the name *zhai*.

At the center of this historical transformation was the incorporation and valorization of zhai culture into China's newly emerging post-Fordist mode of production and consumption in the forms of knowledge work and play. This transformation went hand in hand with the

coming of age of the zhai generation, who watched *Astro Boy* on television as a popular science program in the 1980s and went on to become
college-educated knowledge workers in the new millennium. As the
first generation to benefit from China's massive expansion of college
enrollment under the policy to "revive the nation through science and
education," many of the post-80s only children were the first generation of college students in their families.[51] Universities and college
campuses thus became the original hubs of zhai culture, which quickly
spread to internet cafés and home computers.

In tandem with China's national policy to produce a massive amount
of college-educated knowledge workers, the historical development of
networked zhai culture was situated in China's effort to pull through a
difficult economic transition. It was to shift from an industrial economy
of manufacturing based on manual labor to a postindustrial economy
of information and services based on knowledge labor.[52] The move
from "reform" in the 1980s to "transition" in the twenty-first century
paved the way for the changing perception of zhai culture in relation
to the market and institutions of knowledge work. Situated in this
process of China's economic transition, zhai culture is thus marked by
the postindustrial, post-Fordist logics that are structured by the interplay between knowledge work and play. The following examination of
the development of zhai culture will thus focus on two factors. The
first is engineered play. Anime became part of a transmedial ecosystem of play that emphasizes engineered assemblage and participation,
which was synergetic with an emerging techno-culture of computer and
gaming. The second is informational knowledge work: zhai culture
was organized on information networks by collective knowledge work
of information production, navigation, and sharing, oscillating in the
cybernetic tension between complex and control.

Engineered Play: From Computer Gaming to Transmedia Synergy of ACG

Although zhai culture is part of a networked global movement, its historical emergence, in fact, predated the wide spread of computer technologies. As early as the 1980s, the phenomenal popularity of *Astro*

Boy had already created a huge amount of anime fans among Chinese youth. However, as anime fandom moved away from television in the late 1990s, the development of zhai culture on transmedia networks was coemergent with a techno-culture for computer geeks. The converging point between zhai culture and computer culture was a collection of popular magazines about software and games. These magazines were heavily focused on the transmedia system of anime, manga, and video games, dubbed "ACG" (anime, comics, games) in China. The development of zhai culture was propagating and propagated by an emerging popular culture of computer technologies, and the transmedia system of ACG thus became a crucial element in shaping the techno-culture for a new generation of knowledge workers.

To understand this historical convergence between zhai culture and computer culture, let us first examine how the transmedia system of ACG was organized and operated by a logic of engineered play through computer-gaming magazines. Unlike the Japanese model of media mix, the Chinese system of ACG was not centrally organized by Japanese media companies, because most of the ACG products were distributed in China without licensing agreements from Japanese copyright holders. Circulated in the semi-illegal terrain of unauthorized copy culture, the transnational/transmedial system of ACG was operated collectively by Chinese publishers, distributors, and millions of fans and consumers in a gray area between top-down industrial control and grassroots user participation. Popular magazines played a key role in establishing a cultural and economic platform for players to come together to collectively organize and sustain this transmedia system. A collection of computer-gaming magazines successfully used gameplay as the central engine to drive the transmedia convergence and consumption of ACG, to expand its cultural outreach, and to sustain its social networks of the zhai community.

PopSoft (大众软件) is one of the earliest and most influential popular magazines on computer software and games in China. Established in 1995 by the China Association for Science and Technology, the magazine was originally designed to popularize computer science and technology to the Chinese public, but it quickly shifted its focus toward popular gaming with special emphasis on Japanese ACG, establishing one of the earliest platforms for Chinese zhai culture. At the same time, two other game magazines were also launched by prestige state-run publishers for the purpose of science education: *Electronic Game Software* (电子游戏软件) was launched in 1994 by the China Association for Science and Technology and *Play* (家用电脑与游戏) was first published in 1994 by Popular Science Press, and its Chinese title is literally translated as "Home Computers and Games." Because of the prevailing popularity of Japanese games in the Chinese market, as well as the predominance of the media mix model that converged games with anime and manga, these gaming magazines demonstrated trans-medial spread across the ACG spectrum. The magazine covers, graphic design, and even advertisement pages all featured visual styles and character images from anime and manga (Figures 3 and 4); the review articles often focused on popular anime series such as *Naruto, Ghost in the Shell,* and *Rurouni Kenshin.* In *Electronic Game Software,* for instance, there was a special column named "Triphibian" that was devoted to the converging juncture between the three media of anime, comics, and games. Another magazine, *TV Game & PC Game* (电子游戏与电脑游戏, also known as *Modern Electronic Technology* [现代电子技术]), was established in 1996 by a former editor from *Electronic Game Software.* It emphasized more of the transmedia system of ACG than the games themselves. It published serialized analyses of famous anime series such as *Neon Genesis Evangelion, Gundam,* and *Macross,* introduced Japanese history and culture, and provided a platform for fans to publish their own comics, fan art, and fan fiction. These game magazines also frequently published supplemental volumes specially focused on anime, manga, and *doujinshi* (amateur manga and fan fiction). Many popular anime magazines, such as *All of Dreams* (梦幻总动员), *Anime New Power* (动感新势力), and *MAGIC Zone* (MAGIC地点), were originally developed and published as supplemental issues for computer-game magazines. Some successful writers and editors who gained recognition through their work in game magazines eventually went on to develop successful anime magazines, such as *Shinkansen* (新干线) and *Anime*

Spot (动画基地). By and large, zhai culture was developed in the 1990s in a transmedia ecosystem that was organized by computer-game magazines and gaming culture as the central nexuses.

To organize and sustain this transmedia system of ACG, the logic of gameplay is key. When Chinese zhai culture migrated from television to games, it also integrated anime viewership with the nascent gamer community, converging viewing with gaming, spectatorship with gameplay. This integration led to transmedia synergy, "whereby the popularity of a text or a series in one medium leads to its accelerated consumption in another medium—a key element of the media mix."[53] Indeed, the transmedia synergy of ACG successfully popularized anime among Chinese gamers and introduced games to anime fans, mutually accelerating the consumption of both media.

This transmedia synergy of zhai culture, unlike Japanese media mix, was not centrally planned or organized by any media conglomerates for merchandising. Instead, the transmedia system in zhai culture was collectively participated in by unlicensed game distributors, pirated video stores, and the fan community. This distributed model of convergence was coordinated by the editorial content of the gaming magazines, which were mostly written and edited by Chinese otaku themselves. The discursive structure of these magazines presented an open ground for participation, emphasizing playability as the nodal point that converges the transmedia system of ACG. The graphic and textual designs of the magazines completely erase any sense of medium specificities or distinctions between anime, manga, and game: they all look the same and are described and analyzed in the same way—that is, they are all forms for play. For instance, an article published in *Electronic Game Software* in 1995 compared *Ranma 1/2* and *Urusei Yatsura,* two of the most popular anime series in the 1980s, which were both originally written by manga artist Takahashi Rumiko. While analyzing both series as multimedia franchises, the article emphasized the gaming elements and examined different levels of gamification and playability between these two franchises, as if the original manga texts were designed to be played rather than to be read.[54]

TV GAME & PC GAME
电子游戏与电脑游戏
格兰蒂亚传说（SS）　武神传说（PS）
超大特辑　机器人大战百年史
现代电子娱乐
1998·2

Figure 3. The graphic designs of Chinese computer-game magazines.
(above) The cover of TV Game & PC Game, no. 2, 1998. (opposite page) An
advertisement page in PopSoft, no. 1, 2000.

永远的伊苏
YS ETERNAL
3CD豪华典藏版
预定2000元起上市
上海佐星电脑软件有限公司授权
北京晶合雷达计算机有限责任公司出品

FIGURE 4. The front and back covers of *Electronic Game Software*, no. 4, 2000.

The logic of gameplay was highlighted by the central focus on "strategies and guides" (攻略) in these ACG magazines, which offered helpful tips not only about how to play games but also about how to design manga, perform cosplay, assemble toy kits, make mecha (giant robot) models, or interpret the characters and narratives of an anime series. For example, when *Neon Genesis Evangelion* was introduced by a series of articles published in *TV Game & PC Game* across several issues in 1997, this popular series was examined as a multimedia system combining both anime and games without distinctions between the two media. The strategy guide of how to play the game of *Evangelion* was intertwined with a detailed explanation of the anime series' complex storylines, unique character design, and intertextual symbols, metaphors, and references. Navigating the narrative of *Evangelion* as an anime became equivalent with gaming. The articles also focused on the notion of design, analyzing not only the design of the games and the gaming mechanism in the franchise but also the design of the characters and narrative of the anime series. The magazine encouraged readers to design their own projects to explore this series through fan activities such as writing fan fiction, creating websites, or making doujinshi. The logic of play that was foregrounded by the game magazines thus became a powerful tool to engineer a transmedia synergy of ACG through fan participation. This seemingly distributive open field of play was well organized and structured under the "strategies and guides" of the magazines, which functioned as the game engine of this transnational, transmedial system of zhai culture.

Knowledge Work: Creating and
Navigating China's Information Complex

The ACG magazines that flourished in the 1990s were often described by the zhai community as "information sources" (咨询), a function that was quickly taken over by the internet in the new millennium. The spread of computers and the internet not only provided a new platform to obtain "information sources" but also firmly established zhai as a major cultural voice on Chinese cyberspace, as those who initiated anime fandom in their childhood had come to define the cultural meaning of information networks in their adolescence. The coming of age of this generation coincided with the rise of information technology in China, which provided these post-80s youths a crucial platform to present themselves as the most visible and outspoken group of internet users, whose voices largely shaped Chinese digital culture in the early twenty-first century.

Initially introduced to China in the 1980s, computers and the internet, like television before them, had been highly promoted by the Chinese government, who believed that developing information technology not only would signify modernization and prosperity but had strategic significance to spur economic growth. Since the 1990s, China had been devoted to building the infrastructure and industry for information networks, which consequently expanded at an exponential speed. From 1997 to 2005, the number of internet users in China jumped from 670,000 to 111 million.[55] When the world's biggest population was getting wired, China was moving toward a rapidly growing information society. In this process, the post-80s zhai generation played a crucial role and formed the backbone of China's expanding internet population. From 1997 to 2002, in the formation period of China's information networks, the post-80s youths came to their early adulthood with the discovery of this new medium and became the fastest-growing demographic in the internet boom. In 1997, only 5.3 percent of Chinese internet users belonged to the post-80s (the sixteen-to-twenty age) group, but in 2002, 53.5 percent of internet users were younger than twenty-four.[56] The coming of age of the zhai generation fueled the internet boom in China. And the desires and sensibilities of this generation shaped the rapidly flourishing cyberculture. Thus, Han Han, the post-80s posterchild, became China's most popular blogger; Man Zhou, China's first world-known hacker, came to be celebrated as a cyber hero when he was only seventeen; Zola Zhou, a twenty-six-year-old blogger, became China's first netizen journalist when he covered the famous "nail household" incident in his blog in 2007; and Gong Xiaobing, a self-educated writer who was credited for coining the term *post-80s,* was one of the first Chinese authors to gain national fame by publishing almost entirely on the internet, leading the trend of what came to be known as "internet literature" (网络文学).[57] While the post-80s generation helped establish China's vibrant cyberculture, the rise of the internet also provided the most crucial vehicle for this new generation of Chinese youths to articulate their cultural sensibilities. As Chinese critic Jiang Bing points out, the spread of the internet was one of the most important factors for the post-80s to become an influential sociocultural formation.[58] The whole cultural regime of this generation was largely born on the internet.

The close kinship between the post-80s zhai generation and computer networks is demonstrated by the strong influence of anime culture in China's burgeoning cyberculture. Chinese internet slang, for instance, is dominated by ACG-related Japanese loanwords. One example is the omnipresence of the word *meng* (萌) in Chinese digital cultures to describe almost every cute, lovely thing. *Meng* came from the Japanese term *moe,* a key word in otaku culture referring to certain kinds of character traits that generate affective feelings. Although the original

Japanese word *moe* (萌) is a kanji borrowed from Chinese, when the word came back to China by way of zhai culture, its original Chinese meaning was displaced by the new reference, demonstrating the prevailing impact of anime geekdom in China's digital vernacular. Besides *meng*, common otaku loanwords that populated the Chinese internet include *kawaii* ("cuteness"), *kuso* ("parody"), *baoso* ("runaway"), and *nijigen* ("two-dimensional culture"), as well as popular Chinese slang, such as *lei* (雷) and *jiong* (囧) that also derived from ACG culture. The wide popularity and extensive usage of these words suggest the central position of zhai in Chinese digital culture, which influenced the ways in which Chinese internet users communicate in their daily vernacular.

Among all those otaku terms that came to dominate Chinese digital vernacular, one of the most widespread and influential ones is *kong* (控). Its original Chinese meaning is "control," which quickly changed when the word was reintroduced to the internet through zhai culture. In its new life, *kong* became a homophone for the Japanese word *cong* (コン) that itself is a katakana for the English loanword *complex,* a psychoanalytical term that refers to obsessive psychological emotions around a certain theme. In Japan, *cong* is used as a suffix, and *x-cong* means a person who has a complex or obsession with something. *Loli-cong,* for instance, refers to a Lolita complex. When the Japanese term *cong* (コン) was introduced to China via zhai culture, it was assigned to *kong* (控) due to the same pronunciation, and this common Chinese word has since been loaded with a new meaning that refers to a person who has an obsessive complex with certain things or subjects. For instance, a *computer-kong* or a *technology-kong* means a person obsessed with computers or technology. This new meaning had become so popular on the internet that it both displaced and overlapped with the original meaning of *kong* as "control." Therefore, being a kong—that is, having an obsessive complex with something—also expresses a subtle feeling of control and being controlled.

The overlap between complex and control, expressed in this common word of *kong,* represents the cultural sensibilities of zhai who had shaped Chinese information culture in the postmillennial era. The zhai generation likes to express themselves as some kinds of kong (e.g., game-kong, sound-kong, tech-kong, cat-kong). The sense of a psychological complex is associated with compulsive informational behaviors that have become increasingly common in the digital age. When a Chinese zhai becomes a kong of something, she has the urge to search for all information about it, and this obsessive informational behavior probably best characterizes the meaning of *kong*. The proliferation and wide spread of the kong phenomenon not only testifies to the tremendous influence and popularity of zhai culture but also points to the collective cultural sensibility of the zhai generation that was brought up with the rise of information technology worldwide.

"Knowledge is power." This famous saying by Francis Bacon has been taught to almost every Chinese child in school since the 1950s, when prime minister Zhou Enlai personally wrote down the phrase as the official title for China's leading journal for science education. But for Chinese youth, being a kong, which often involves obsessively searching, navigating, and collecting informational knowledge about something, gives a feeling of both power and powerlessness. To be kong is to be controlled and in control at the same time, and this ambivalence is precisely where the pleasure and obsession of the psychological complex come from. There is something deeply affective in the ambivalent oscillation between control and being controlled in the kong/complex.

If information technology has brought us to what Gilles Deleuze calls the "society of control," we probably should also realize that there is something affectively, and perversely, attractive in control-as/in-complex.[59] As is suggested by the widespread kong phenomenon among the Chinese zhai generation, there is a certain kind of psychological complex that is associated with the sense of control, which offers as much pleasure as paranoia. In his study of anime's media ecology, Thomas Lamarre takes Félix Guattari's term *infrastructure complex* as an analogy with a psychological complex in its implication of the formation and disjunction of subjectivity.[60] For Lamarre, an infrastructure complex is not only analogous to but also intertwined with a psychological complex, and therefore a media ecology is always an affective one, which oscillates between the regulatory and anarchic tendencies. Underlying such contradictory tendencies of the infrastructural/psychological complex is a strong desire for bonding, attachment, and affinity, which is a structure of feelings that is constituted through what Lamarre describes as "disjunctive synthesis" of a psychic/medial complex.[61] The sense of control in both infrastructure and psychological complexes does not necessarily lead to a fixed positioning of subjectivity; instead, it can evoke an affective feeling of desiring to be attached and bonded—to be a kong with something—in a world that is increasingly marked by deterritorialized alienation, fragmentation, and isolation.

Therefore, the ambivalent feeling of complex/control is also one of intimacy, which oscillates between power and powerlessness, between disjunction and assimilation. The proliferation of countless kinds of kong in Chinese zhai culture thus represents an affective ecology of information complex/control that is fundamentally contradictory. The distributive structure of information networks, as well as the disjunctive force that decenters the intrasubjectivity of information workers, evokes a desperate desire for unification and reattachment, the desire of wanting to be bonded to, be assimilated with, and even be controlled by something (e.g., data, information, network). Kong (complex/control), therefore, is the affective economy of postindustrial knowledge work.

The Zhai Economy in China's Transition toward Postindustrial Capitalism

Marked as a paradigm shift in the affective economy of knowledge work, the rise of zhai culture coincided with a major economic transition in China. When anime culture was moving from regional exchanges on television to global informationalism on the internet, China entered the World Trade Organization in 2002 and has since grown to the world's second-largest economy. If the earlier influx of anime to Chinese television was situated within the historical context of China's reform toward a market economy, the current zhai culture that flourished on Chinese cyberspace is contextualized by a new phase of transition toward postindustrial, informational capitalism that has been spreading on a global scale. For today's zhai generation, anime is no longer associated with Sino–Japan friendship but is instead a global cultural reference that is brought to them through the information highway. As the first generation of Chinese who were raised under the influence of information networks, their cultural impulse had been closely synchronized with the global geekdom movement that centers on the cultural capital of a rising cosmopolitan knowledge class. As the admission rate to higher education reached over 80 percent in 2018, China had been rapidly producing the world's largest number of knowledge workers, a massive emerging class of white-collar labor that has yet to be well studied.[62] In this context, the cultural forms and idioms of the zhai generation gained new economic significance, for they represented the collective sensibilities of a rising class of knowledge workers and consumers who were expected to play a key role in China's economic transition. It was also at this moment that the cultural presence of the zhai generation suddenly gained public attention.

Although zhai culture had been quietly spreading in China for years, it did not attract extensive publicity until the postmillennial era of economic transition. In March 2008, *Southern Metropolis Daily,* one of China's most popular newspapers, published a lengthy report on the rapid spread of a cultural phenomenon called "zhai." Portraying an eighteen-year-old Chinese otaku who spent most of his time at home watching anime and playing computer games, *Southern Metropolis Daily* described this widespread zhai culture not simply as a new trend that had been gaining momentum among Chinese youth but as an alarming social problem that deserved public scrutiny.[63] Suddenly, zhai became the most talked-about subject in public discourse from popular magazines to academic journals, from newspapers to talk shows. Before long, "zhai" became the trendiest label among Chinese youth and zhai culture was fashioned as a hip lifestyle. With public recognition and acknowledgment, zhai became the mainstream.

Zhai culture was nothing new in China, but what made it suddenly explode in a prominent cultural phenomenon with such media hype and public attention? The answer has less to do with the transnational popularity of Japanese anime than with the rapid rise of information technology and knowledge work in China. In fact, it was zhai's omnipresent cultural influence on the internet that brought this sociocultural formation to the spotlight of public obsession. Because of its close affiliation with information networks, zhai culture came to be understood as more of an internet phenomenon than an anime fandom. According to the report in *Southern Metropolis Daily*, although obsession with anime and manga is "the reason to be zhai," the major characteristic of zhai is "the heavy reliance on computers and the internet."[64] Consequently, the zhai phenomenon had largely been interpreted as a cultural symptom of information networks. The proliferating public discourse on zhai culture was almost exclusively focused on the impact of computer technology on Chinese society. The rapid expansion of zhai was thus interpreted as the result of the increasing dominance of information technology rather than the long-standing popularity of Japanese anime. As is suggested by Chinese scholar Jiang Ping, the zhai phenomenon was a "cultural derivative from the rapid expansion of cyber technologies," and zhai as a lifestyle "could only exist in the virtual space of the internet."[65] Indeed, for the vast number of Chinese youth who self-identify as zhai, what the term evokes is their collective experience in an increasingly networked society, which has transformed both their cultural lives and the nation's economic future.

Riding the wave of rapidly expanding information connectivity, the zhai generation was recognized as the most valuable group of labor and consumers, who were credited for fashioning new modes of production and consumption for China's economic transition. Chinese press, advertising agencies, media industries, IT companies, and venture capitalists all began to collectively celebrate the rise of the "zhai economy" (宅经济), which was believed to be the new frontier of China's economic growth.[66] The so-called zhai economy is a very loosely defined area that includes almost any products or activities that are related to information technology and geek culture, such as fan cultures, e-commerce, user-generated content, computer games, social media, mobile services, and consumer electronics. As vague as it is, however, the notion of the zhai economy, as well as its increasing prominence in the mainstream media, highlights less a distinctive economic mode than the rising power of a new group of Chinese workers and consumers who are closely associated with knowledge work and information production.

In fact, despite a certain popular tendency to portray zhai as a sociocultural symptom of postmodern alienation in the internet age, the majority of public attention focused on the extraordinary consumer power and creative potential of this ever-expanding group of millennial geeks in China. As early as 2005, China Market and Media Study (CMMS), a leading consumer research group in China, began to observe the growing number of zhai consumers, and in 2007, CMMS estimated that there were 6.5 million Chinese who identified as zhai, about 21 percent of the total population of Chinese youth aged fifteen to thirty-five.[67] Marketing and advertising companies paid close attention to this consumer group. In 2008, right after the *Southern Metropolis Daily* brought public attention to zhai culture, the trade journal *China Advertising* published detailed research analyzing the consumer behaviors and preferences of the zhai generation, as well as their responses to different media and advertisements.[68] As the famed only-child consumers, the core members of Chinese internet users, and the constituents of a rising class of knowledge workers, the zhai generation was thus celebrated as trendsetters and creative talent for economic growth. Their active and prevalent presence as the primary operators and users of information networks was believed to be the shaping force for the techno-economic future of China. Therefore, with the proliferation of information technology, the zhai economy, no matter how poorly defined, was deemed to be pursued as a new frontier of China's fast-growing digital economy. Analysts began to quickly notice economic sectors with "zhai characteristics"; stock markets and venture capitalists began to favor "zhai industries"; entrepreneurs predicted the zhai market to be the next big opportunity for growth.[69] Some even claimed that China was "entering the age of the 'zhai economy.'"[70] And this economic obsession with zhai is still ongoing. During the Covid-19 pandemic, the zhai economy once again came to the spotlight and was chosen as the word of the year in 2020, because zhai was believed to be the key driving force for the postpandemic economic recovery.[71]

This obsession with the zhai economy in China, to a certain degree, echoed the rise of a similar notion of the "otaku industry" in

Japan, which was estimated to be worth billions.[72] However, unlike the Japanese otaku industry that specifically refers to media mix companies, the Chinese notion of the zhai economy is a much broader concept that encompasses almost the entire spectrum of the digital economy. The Chinese discourse of the zhai economy drew its inspiration less from the Japanese media mix industry than from the global economic success of IT companies such as Google, Apple, and Facebook, as well as the growing social and economic power of a cosmopolitan knowledge class. Indeed, the rise of zhai culture and the zhai economy in China was in tune with the wider cultural and economic trend of a global geekdom movement.

If the rise of geek culture in the global arena was the result of the growing socioeconomic power of knowledge workers in the information age, the obsession with the zhai economy in China was part of the same trend. In fact, when Chinese companies were embracing the zhai economy, they interpreted it as part of a global wave that originated in Silicon Valley, and their imagined models were the Chinese internet giants such as Baidu, Tencent, and Alibaba. When Chinese media were demonstrating the potential economic wealth in the virtual realms of zhai culture, their examples were *Second Life* and the metaverse, and when Chinese entrepreneurs were eyeing social networks as zhai hotspots, they were looking at Twitter and TikTok. What they were chasing in the so-called zhai economy were simply the successful formulas for a global digital economy. It is also worth mentioning that before *zhai* became a buzzword, the term *jike* (极客), which is the Chinese translation for "geek," had already been imported to public discourse to describe the same knowledge communities who were believed to be the driving force of the digital economy. In 2006, one of China's most popular websites, mop.com, launched a big public campaign promoting China's own "geek heroes," who were identified as techno-talents in areas like gaming, programming, and electronic engineering.[73] To a certain extent, the zhai discourse was a continuation of the jike publicity, both seeking to explore the social synergy and cultural capital of a rising demographic of knowledge workers and consumers in China's economic transition toward postindustrialism.

Both *zhai* (otaku) and *jike* (geek) are borrowed foreign words, introduced to China as a new kind of popular knowledge culture that came with the promise of information connectivity. They represent the cultural imagination and economic aspiration of a techno-future centered on postindustrial knowledge work. This imagination produced new subjects and feelings that were significant for a nation in transformation. From regional television that introduced *Astro Boy,* Casio, and the virtual Japan of techno-modernity in the 1980s, to the information highway that brought in the global geekdom movement and its information complex in the new millennium, what we witnessed was the coming of age of a new generation of knowledge workers and consumers during China's rapid socioeconomic transformation from the era of market-economy reform to the moment of postindustrial transition. In the 1980s, when China was reforming from the failure of socialist experiments to the promise of free-market prosperity, *Astro Boy,* a popular myth of techno-utopia and a merchandising engine of media mix, cultivated the cultural sensibilities of post-80s youths with an alluring fantasy of techno-empowerment in a collective aspiration of national reconstruction and modernization. In the twenty-first century, when China was undergoing a difficult transition from manufacturing success based on cheap labor to an information economy driven by knowledge work, the zhai economy, a dazzling notion packaged with the excitement and promise of Silicon Valley, captured the popular imagination of postmillennial geeks for a new techno-economic future. It is against this historical background that the zhai generation gained its cultural and economic currency in China as a rapidly expanding group of college-educated knowledge workers. The cultural history of zhai demonstrates the powerful impact of anime geekdom as a postindustrial knowledge culture in a socially and historically specific context.

2

Fansub

Language, Knowledge, and Communication Labor

The Chinese *zhai* generation, like its Japanese or American counterparts, is part of a global geekdom movement that represents a highly informationalized culture that is closely tied to the technological rationalities of postindustrial knowledge work, and it can teach us a great deal of how these rationalities are implicated in the sociocultural organization of everyday lives. As Mizuko Ito argues, the practices in early otaku culture predicated "many of the core characteristics of today's networked and digital age," including immersion in specialized knowledge networks, decentralized forms of organization and production, the primacy of media participation, distributive and collective content generation, and so on.[1] Therefore, understanding anime geekdom, to quote William Gibson, "is one of the keys to understanding the culture of the Web."[2] But we need to first understand that the web is not simply a technology but is, to follow Raymond Williams, "a social complex of a new and central kind."[3] Therefore, in this chapter, I study anime geekdom less as a subcultural type than as a mode of techno-social practice, organization, and assemblage—that is, "a social complex." One of the key elements that holds this social complex together is fansub, which not only forms the material foundation for anime fans to be organized into a transnational community but also exemplifies the ways in which social relations are generated and sustained through knowledge production and communication on global networks. If postindustrial capitalism is marked by transformations in the material and process of production, as well as in the nature and organization of labor, the techno-social complex initiated by fansub represents such changes by demonstrating a mode of production that is enabled by a particular type of labor organization of knowledge workers, who themselves represent a changing "role and function of intellectuals and their activities within society."[4]

Originated in the early days of anime's international fandom in the 1980s, the term *fansub*—short for "fan-subtitled"—refers to a particular kind of anime video that is translated, subtitled, and distributed by fans and among fans. Since most anime titles were unavailable to international viewers at that time, some fans with access to the Japanese original materials and with appropriate language proficiencies began to produce amateur subtitled copies of anime for their fellow fans and distributed them through fan clubs, mailing lists, and anime conventions. Although fansubbing activities predated the wide spread of the internet, the rapid expansion of computer networks and digital technology in the 1990s, which made fansub much easier to produce and distribute, transformed fansub to a prevalent cultural practice on global networks. Anime videos were widely translated and distributed by and among fans in the form of fansub in various languages, and fansubbing became a common practice in many other media forms, such as Korean drama and Bollywood cinema. Asian fansubbers also began to translate and distribute American TV series to Asian viewers, reversing the initial direction of flow in anime fansub. For the past decades, fansub had been a major form of global culture dissemination with massive user participation on information networks.[5]

Among Chinese anime fans identified as the zhai generation, fansub played a key role in their sociocultural formation. In the early 2000s, when China was moving toward an information society with the rapid development of computer networks, anime culture was also moving from television to online communication. Under governmental regulation, Chinese television stopped broadcasting anime in prime time. Online fansub came to the rescue and quickly became a major channel for anime circulation in China. As early as 2001, some of the first Chinese fansubbing groups appeared in anime clubs on university campuses. These fansubbers began to translate, subtitle, and distribute anime videos that were not available on Chinese television or the pirated DVD market. Since college students were among the first groups of Chinese internet users, these university-based fansubbers were also the first in China to bring anime culture to cyberspace. Consequently, the earliest anime fansubs were mostly distributed through online forums and BBS (bulletin board system) that were based on university networks (with the domain name *.edu.cn), such as Beida Weiming BBS (https://bbs.pku.edu.cn) on the Peking University network and Shuimu Tsinghua BBS on the Tsinghua University network. Before long, fansubbing groups flourished on various anime websites, forums, and BitTorrent systems. They began to recruit members outside college campuses, and their fansubbing projects also expanded from anime to other transnational media forms. With the rapid growth of computer networks in postmillennial China, online fansub had become not only a major channel for anime distribution but also a crucial and omnipresent component in Chinese digital culture at large.[6]

Much has been written about the ambivalent legal status of fansub, particularly its murky relationship with intellectual property rights.[7] But the significant functions of fansub in the historical process of changing global communication, knowledge production, and labor management are yet to be fully explored. The fansub, first and foremost, represents a semi-illicit mode of global cultural flow that challenges the dominant model of corporate-controlled cultural globalization. Unlike global Hollywood, the transnational dissemination of anime through fansub had less to do with the top-down forces of industrial marketing than being propelled by collective user participation on computer networks. I call it "pirate cosmopolitanism," as it is a piratical global cultural circuit in the shadow of copyright control, which was built on the material foundation of distributed information networks whose structural form had become the basic diagram of our society.[8] This pirate cultural field of global flow points to the techno-rationality of a distributed mode of organizing labor and production through a decentralizing and decentralized process of information sharing and communication, similar to other networked practices such as crowdsourcing and the open-source movement.

More importantly, what distinguishes fansub is the fact that it orga-nizes the distributive network of knowledge production through a mode of play with language. The ways in which fansub organizes a transnational network of collective production, circulation, and con-sumption of knowledge involve extensive operations with language as its primary material: translating, editing, proofreading, typesetting, subtitling, and so on. If postmodernism, as Jean-François Lyotard tells us, is fundamentally about the transformation of knowledge from "grand narratives" to "language games," fansub marks this shift par excellence.[9] It echoes Alvin W. Gouldner's characterization of postin-dustrial knowledge work as basically a linguistic habit, which takes language as both a production material and a way of life.[10]

If fansub is a "language game," it is a game that plays with language not only as its material but also as its mediation interface, because it is through the interlingual "transduction" in the forms of translation and subtitling that anime is circulated on transnational, transmedial networks.[11] The interface, as Branden Hookway suggests, is not a transparent mediatory but a threshold.[12] As an interfacing threshold, fansub provides us with a valuable window to examine how power functions through language in material and symbolic ways. As Robert Stam suggests, interlingual practices of translation and subtitling are effectively "the filtration of meaning through ideological and cultural grids, the mediation of a social or political superego," and for those who operate such processes, "subtitles provide a 'mutual illumination of languages.'"[13] As the production material and mediation for knowl-edge work, language is also the most fundamental signifying system that structuralizes social, cultural, and political life. It intersects with power, knowledge, and communication, an intersection that is not only crucial for the formation of the intrasubjectivity of postindustrial knowledge work but also a center for control and reification in infor-mational capitalism.

By operating directly on the foundational material and signifying ground of language, fansub complicates the existing structure in popu-lar culture and knowledge work by establishing an alternative sphere of knowledge production, interpretation, and communication on the most fundamental level. This alternative mode of knowledge production involves the changing nature and organization of labor in post-Fordist capitalism, a transformation marked by collective self-valorization where "knowledgeable consumption of culture is translated into excess productive activities."[14] Therefore, to understand how fansub mediates global cultural flow through massive user participation and knowledge sharing is also to understand how a distributive mode of organizing labor and production is initiated and sustained through collective voluntary communication via language.

Positioned at the intersection between globalization, media, and language, as well as between knowledge, communication, and labor, anime fansub offers an ideal window to investigate a fan-based, distributive cultural field that operates through the sociosymbolic dimension of language as a mediation interface. It also demonstrates how this cultural field presents both a problem and an opportunity for control of knowledge, communication, and social relations through a renewed relationship between labor, technology, and cultural production, a relationship that has to be constantly restructured and resolved within the changing system of capitalism. As Tara McPherson reminds us, the modes of cultural experience afforded by networked digital technologies "are neither innocent nor neutral," but they model "particular modes of subjectivity which can work too neatly in the service of the shifting patterns of global capitalism."[15] This chapter interrogates the ways in which the distributive cultural field of fansub interacts with and intervenes in the "shifting patterns of global capitalism" through the complex relationship between language, knowledge, communication, and labor, which are all entangled in the transnational, transmedial, and translingual practice of fansubbing.

To explore this multifaceted entanglement around the cultural phenomenon of fansub, I first theorize a methodological approach by combining Mikhail Bakhtin's conception of language with Dick Hebdige's theorization of subcultures. By doing so, I intend to expand the theoretical framework of culture studies from the symbolic meanings of visual representation to the signifying practice of verbal communication, not least because dialogic text has become the basic form of communication in today's sociocultural formations that are largely organized through emailing, texting, and blogging. This translinguistic approach that shifts from the visual to the verbal, from representation to communication, is crucial for understanding fansub as a language game, which is not simply a system of signs but rather a social field for play. Mapping anime's global flow through the play field of language, I examine fansub as a signifying practice that functions as intracultural communication on transnational networks.[16] By studying both the textual and the paratextual elements of anime fansub, I argue that the activities of producing, distributing, and consuming fansub constitute an alternative communication sphere through collective learning and knowledge sharing, which not only puts forward a distributive cultural field for the formation of a transnational knowledge community but also functions as a distinctive mode of organizing labor and production both within and against the techno-economic system of postindustrial knowledge work. I call it "communication labor," which includes diverse online communication activities such as emailing, blogging, and social networking, and it has become the fastest-growing production force in the digital economy. By examining how anime fansub organizes collective production, circulation, and consumption of information and knowledge, this chapter interrogates the mechanisms of generating, managing, sustaining, and valorizing communication labor, which exists as the powerful engine of collective cultural production that is simultaneously enjoyed as a liberating force of communicative pleasure and refusal and exploited as a free-floating resource of knowledge work and commodity.

The fansub materials that I examine in this chapter include examples from both Chinese-language and English-language fansubs. Studying and comparing fansubs in these different contexts and highlighting their shared practices, styles, and sensibilities, the chapter maps how fansub constituted a distributive, dispersed, and deterritorialized media geography across geocultural and linguistic boundaries and diversities. The Anglophone examples are also chosen to help English-speaking readers understand the textual characteristics of fansub as a play with language (with puns, jokes, and references), which may not be well demonstrated through Chinese fansubs due to language barriers. My study focuses on the historical moment from 2000 to the early 2010s, when fansub developed and transformed from a subcultural phenomenon to a major form of digital video culture on global networks.[17] This formation period illuminates the significance of fansub in the historical development of changing modes of knowledge production and labor organization that continue to shape digital cultures and economies both in China and globally.

Toward a Translinguistic Approach

In his influential work, *Subculture: The Meaning of Style,* Dick Hebdige argues that subcultures create distinctive communities and identities through the symbolic meanings of visual styles, such as fashion, clothes, and hairstyles, which function as "intentional communication." The symbolic meanings of the subcultural styles communicate a significant difference from outsiders as well as a collective identity among the subculture members. Influenced by poststructuralism, Hebdige associates the communication function of visual styles with that of language. He argues that subcultural styles, like language, communicate their subversive meanings by the signifying practice of refusal, transformation, and deconstruction of the coherent meanings of popular cultural signs. Hebdige's thesis relies on a radical approach to language: "Such an approach lays less stress on the primacy of structure and system of language ('langue'), and more upon the position of the speaking subject in discourse ('parole'). . . . This approach sees language as an active, transitive force which shapes and positions the 'subject' (as speaker, writer, reader) while always itself remaining 'in process' capable of infinite adaptation."[18] This approach to language as signifying practice instead of signification system echoes Russian philosopher and literary critic Mikhail Bakhtin, whose theorization of language influenced poststructuralists such as Julia Kristeva and Roland Barthes, as well as film theorists such as Robert Stam and Vivian Sobchack.[19]

For Bakhtin (and thinkers in the Bakhtin Circle such as Valentin Voloshinov), language is neither an abstract system nor an imaginary entity; it is a material reality with concrete social functions as communication. As such, language is the material foundation for the individual consciousness as *"a socio-ideological fact,"* because each individual subject encounters the spheres of social relations and ideologies through the concrete activities of communication, and the basic "material of behavior communication is preeminently the *word*."[20] Emphasizing the material rather than the symbolic aspect, Bakhtin sees language as less a system of signs than a social act of dialogic communication. He argues that the primary channels through which each individual engages with interpersonal social activities are not language systems but are concrete verbal intercourse—speeches and dialogue. Critiquing Saussurean linguistics that regard language as a stable system of abstract signs, Bakhtin's approach to language emphasizes the unstable process of the actual speech act—the utterance—which is always social because it entails particular speaking subjects and contexts with complex sociopolitical backgrounds and relations. Therefore, Bakhtin's translinguistics, as Robert Stam points out, successfully bridges the missing links—in semiotics, structuralism, and Saussurean linguistics—between text and context, between the linguistic and the sociopolitical. In Stam's words: "Bakhtin retains the linguistic paradigm, but opens it to the diachronic, to history and struggle. . . . A Bakhtinian 'social semiotic' would thus avoid the prudish scientism of a certain 'value-free' structuralism, enabling us to reintroduce both politics and culture into the abstract model."[21]

Bakhtin's emphasis on the actual usage of language in the action of verbal intercourse brings us back to Hebdige's notion of style as symbolic communication. Interestingly, though Hebdige heavily relies on the semiotic function of language, his study of subculture is primarily focused on the visual signs, leaving the verbal, linguistic signs largely ignored. Like many others, Hebdige's semiotics is based on the logic of analogy between image and language. Such an analogy, however, is often achieved at the sacrifice of the material reality and social practice of language itself. We often take language analogously but not literally. Hebdige's overt emphasis on "spectacular subcultures" echoes the widespread intellectual trend in the 1970s that was obsessed with the semiotics of "the society of spectacle."[22] What is lost in such emphasis on spectacular visual signs is the actual verbal/literary communication that functions equally, if not more significantly, for cultural communication. Such is also the case in the semiotic approach to cinema. Stam points out: "For while contemporary theoretical work has been concerned with the analogies between films and 'natural language,' it has virtually ignored the role of language difference *within* film. Cinesemiology has rarely delineated the impact on cinema, for example, of the prodigality of tongues in which films are produced, spoken, and received."[23] The ignorance of the verbal and literary acts within film and media studies forms a stark contrast with the very omnipresence of such acts in almost every aspect of social and cultural life. As Bakhtinian thinker Voloshinov suggests, "All manifestations of ideological creativity—all other nonverbal signs—are bathed by, suspended in, and cannot be entirely separated or divorced from the element of speech."[24] Indeed, compared to visual signs, the actual verbal utterances—words, speech, and dialogue—function more prominently in media communications even in the so-called society of spectacle, not to mention the dominance of computer language as a new vernacular in the digital age.

It is time we take the function of verbal intercourse as equally significant as visual signs in organizing popular culture and media. Hebdige's notion of subcultural styles as signifying practice can be verbal/literary as well as visual. Emphasizing the actual language practice is especially important for studying today's digital sociocultural formations that are no longer communicated via visual styles but are organized via computerized language networks—email, blogs, text messages, chat rooms, and Twitter. What are trafficked on these networks are mainly words, sentences, speech, and dialogue. And that is how communities are organized today—by inputting a sentence in your Facebook status instead of wearing a black leather jacket. When the medium to express and to communicate moved from fashion on the street to messages on the internet, subcultures (and mainstream culture alike) became less visible in visual signs but more identifiable in words, such as *otaku* or *zhai* for anime fandom, *Klingon* for *Star Trek* fans, or *WoW* and *LoL* for gamers. This paradigm shift brings Bakhtinian notions of speech acts

to the center stage, calling for a methodological shift from visual sig‑
nification toward verbal communication.

To study verbal/literary communication, however, is not to study
language as a structure or a system of signs. Instead, the forms of
actual utterance—the "speech genres"—illustrate the mechanisms of
sociocultural organization on networks: "Each period and each social
group has had its own repertoire of speech forms for ideological com‑
munication in human behaviors. Each set of cognate forms, i.e., each
behavior speech genre, has its own corresponding set of themes."[25]
Each subculture group, therefore, has its own set of speech genres, its
own "repertoire of speech forms" to organize its communication. To
study such sociocultural formations is to study the speech genres that
are utilized for "ideological communication" to articulate their collec‑
tive ethos and sensibilities. The forms of these speech genres are not
organized by linguistic systems but are determined by the addressivity
of the utterance that is composed not only of words and sentences but
also of the speaking and the listening subjects. It is the sociocultural
relation between the speaker and the addressee that determines the
choice of speech genres.[26] Bakhtin's notion of speech genre, as well
as his emphasis on the relation between speakers and addressees, is
crucial for understanding the communication activities that organize
transnational fandom. For a global subculture, whose members may
speak different native languages, it is the speech genre rather than the
national language of Chinese, Japanese, or English that communicates
their shared identity. Therefore, to study communication among anime
geeks, one is less concerned with the linguistic forms than with the
relation between the speakers and addressees that organize the com‑
munication practice among the members. Indeed, fansub's famous
motto, "By fans and for fans," manifests the positions and relation of
the speakers and addressees. For such communications, the question
that matters is less what is spoken than who speaks to whom.

Combining the theoretical frameworks of Bakhtin and Hebdige, I
argue for a methodological approach that studies not only the visual
styles but also the activities of verbal/literary communication for under‑
standing anime geekdom as an intraculture community of knowledge

work. Fansub functions as intracultural communication through its unique form of translingual signifying practices—translation and subtitling—as mediation interface. By examining fansub as a communication practice—an "utterance," indeed—I hope to address the following questions: What is the relationship between the fansubbers and their audience? How is such a relationship communicated through fansub texts, paratexts, and activities? How does fansub communicate the ethos and sensibilities of this knowledge community both internally and externally? How is the language game played by this community as collective knowledge production? If fansub represents a distributive cultural field of flow, how does it generate and distribute meaning through the material and symbolic forms of language and knowledge? What can fansub tell us about the relations between communication, language, and knowledge production?

"Abusive Subtitling" as Intentional Communication

Compared with the commercially distributed, professionally subtitled anime videos, fansub videos distinguish themselves by making their practices highly visible. Commercial subtitles often try to suppress the visibility of translation by making it seemingly transparent and unnoticeable. Fansubs, on the contrary, tend to lay bare the very process of translation and subtitling by calling attention to their own practices. Such differences are explicitly displayed by fansub's innovative use of styling and typesetting. Whereas commercial videos generally use standard styles in subtitle formatting, fansubs use a wide variety of fonts, sizes, colors, and locations for their subtitles. Frequently, fansubs use all-capital letters to highlight the expressed importance or tension made by speaking characters and use different colors or fonts for different speaking characters when there is overlapping dialogue. Sometimes, peculiar colors, fonts, and typesets are used for subtitles to match the visual style and graphic design of the particular video (Figure 5) or for cueing functions about certain narrative aspects, such as character typologies, speaking tone, intonation, dialect, emotion, mood, and contexts (Figure 6). These examples of playful uses of diverse subtitle styles in fansubs form a sharp contrast with the standardized format of

FIGURE 5. Matching styles in color, shade, and typeface between the original anime video's title sequence and the fan-created subtitle in the Chinese fansub of *Mashiroiro Symphony* (2011). Fansubbed by SumiSora 澄空学园字幕组.

FIGURE 6. A peculiar style of typesetting is used in the subtitle to highlight the wickedness of the speaking character, Death God, in the English fansub of *Death Note* (2006). Fansubbed by Death God Fansub.

commercial subtitles. They contribute new meaning and pleasure to anime videos, calling attention and creating discussion among fans.

Besides the innovative styling, fansubs frequently call attention to their practice of translation. Nonverbal text (e.g., signs, title cards, and thought bubbles) often gets translated with on-screen text that is integrated into the mise-en-scène in a seamless manner (Figure 7). Certain words in dialogue are sometimes left untranslated in the subtitles and are accompanied with the translator's notes on screen suggesting possible meanings or interpretations of these words (Figure 8). Occasionally, there are lengthy glosses explaining cultural backgrounds or character arcs in the narrative (Figure 9). In fact, using on-screen notes to explain untranslated words and phrases is so prevalent in anime fansubs that some fans even jokingly complained that they do not really need an entire Wikipedia page for a single term. Fansubs' extensive use of notes and glosses foregrounds the technological materiality of digital video processing, editing, and viewing, which allow both the writing and the reading of these on-screen notes with relative ease. They also force viewers to pay attention to subtitles as a mediation interface and thus break the illusion of a transparent media field of moving images.

Fansub's daring experiments with on-screen notes and innovative styling are radically opposed to the standard rules of subtitling in commercial operations that strive to suppress their own visibility. Fansubbers tend to lay bare the very process of translation and subtitling by calling attention to their practices through these strange, colorful styles as well as the lengthy, intrusive notes, and by doing so, fansubs break down the illusion of transparency and continuity. This is what Abé Mark Nornes describes as "abusive subtitling."[27] Borrowing Phillip E. Lewis's notion of "abusive translation," which "seeks to match the polyvalences and plurivocities or expressive stresses of the original by producing its own," Nornes argues for a similar fashion of abusive subtitling.[28] According to Nornes, professional subtitling in general is a corrupt practice: "It is a practice of translation that smoothes over its textual violence and domesticates all otherness while it pretends to bring the audience an experience of the foreign. . . . In fact, they conspire to hide their repeated acts of violence through codified rules and a tradition of suppression."[29]

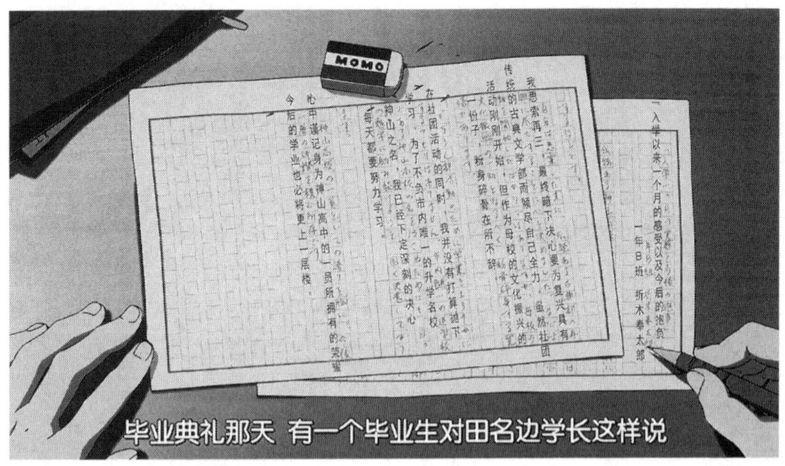

FIGURE 7. In the Chinese fansub videos of *Hyouka* (2012), a handwritten Japanese letter is translated to Chinese (*top*) and a Japanese fortune-teller card is translated to classical Chinese written in traditional style (*bottom*), both being integrated seamlessly in the mise-en-scène on screen side by side with the original Japanese text. (*top*) Fansub by SumiSora (澄空学园字幕组); (*bottom*) fansub by XKsub (星空字幕组).

FIGURE 8. In the English fansub of *Welcome to the N.H.K.* (2006), an on-screen note explains that the untranslated word *anison* in the subtitle is "an abbreviated term for an anime song." Fansubbed by Ayasumi.

Against such a practice of corrupt subtitling is abusive subtitling, which "uses both textual and graphic abuse—that is, experimentation with language and its grammatical, morphological, and visual qualities—to bring the fact of translation from its position of obscurity, to critique the imperial politics that ground corrupt practices."[30] Whereas the corrupt subtitling strives to suppress the visibility of its apparatus, the abusive subtitling "enjoys foregrounding it, heightening its impact and testing its limits and possibilities."[31]

Anime fansub, with its playful experimentation with both textual practices and graphic styling, is an ideal model of abusive subtitling. For Nornes, however, the strength of abusive subtitling is not merely in its foregrounding of the subtitling apparatus but in its appreciation of the otherness of the original text. Unlike Lewis's Derridean proposal of abusive translation, in which abuse is targeted at both the original and the translated, Nornes's notion of abusive subtitling rather merits the approximation toward the original. For Nornes, Lewis's elitist, post-structuralist thesis against the transparency of ideological apparatus is

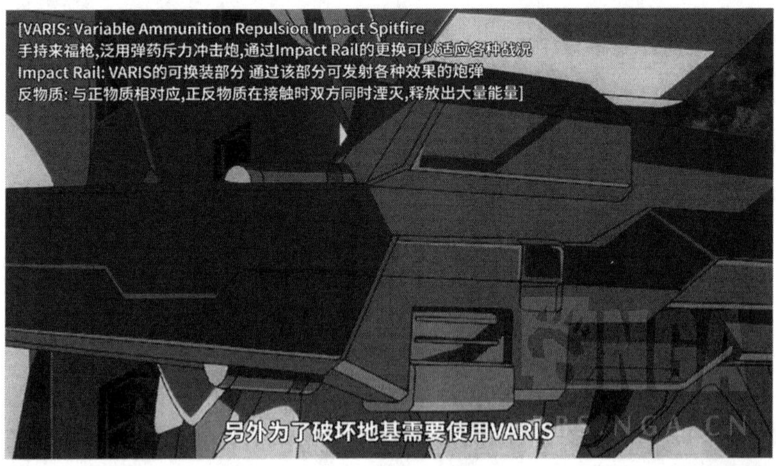

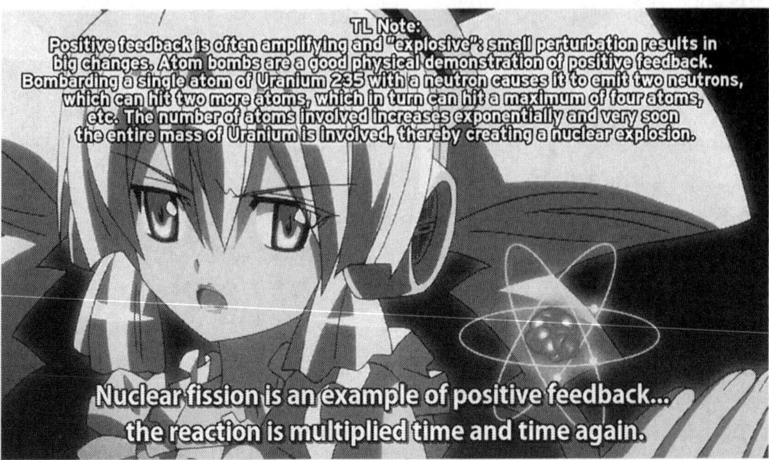

FIGURE 9. Lengthy translators' notes appear on screen to explain the untranslated special terms and techno-scientific details in the fictional technological systems in anime. (*top*) The Chinese fansub of *Code Geass* (2006), fansubbed by 异域-11番小队; (*bottom*) the English fansub of *Needless* (2009), fansubbed by Ayako-Himatsubushi.

turned away by today's abusive fansubbers, who are more concerned with bringing spectators back to the original text—the "Japanese" in anime—than with critiquing the corrupt practice of commercial subtitling. Nornes's embrace of abusive subtitling for its appreciation of cultural originality is echoed by many commentators who also saw the strength of fansub in its respect for the original.[32] For them, the reason to be "abusive" is to be culturally "authentic."

However, such an overt emphasis on cultural authenticity, which seems to assume a sense of stability and totality of the original text, is problematized by the intricate and varied conditions of cultural globalization that fansubs are part of. When various cultures are fashioned as "hybrid," we cannot help but wonder where to draw the line between the "original" and the "translated." This is especially the case for anime, whose global popularity is often based on its intentional erasure of the cultural markers of Japaneseness. If anime already lacks a sense of the original, how can we argue for the approximation toward the original in anime fansub? The contradiction between the embrace of fansub's appreciation of cultural authenticity versus anime's very lack of authenticity as such, interestingly, is highlighted in a case study of fansub by Jordan S. Hatcher.[33] Hatcher suggests that fansub often uses translator's notes to explain the original Japanese cultural references, but the example image he gives to illustrate such a use, ironically, has nothing to do with Japanese culture at all—it is Charles Baudelaire's *Fleurs du Mal* that is being referenced in an anime series named *Trinity Blood* (the religious reference to Christianity is also noteworthy), which is given explanation by the translator's on-screen note.[34] In fact, discussions and surveys among fans indicated that viewers did not feel that fansub videos achieved better accuracy or authenticity than commercial subtitles.[35] Cultural authenticity is never the real strength of fansub, and it should not be. As Thomas Lamarre points out, the power of anime fandom "lies in its refusal of the sort of cultural mediation that begins with fixed cultural identities."[36] Indeed, the cultural significance of fansub's abusive subtitling is precisely its ability to open a space to be "lost in translation," a room for play that refutes the claim of a fixed authentic meaning.

Countering the prevailing notion of cultural authenticity, I argue that the strength of anime fansub comes not from its approximation of the original text but from its creation of an alternative signifying sphere for intentional communication. Fansub's abusive subtitling may not be motivated by poststructuralist radicalism against illusive transparency, but neither does it merely appreciate the supposedly authentic Japanese originals. Instead, what fansub strives to achieve is a signifying practice that intentionally communicates a sense of difference from within, a difference that resides not in the cultural authenticity of Japan but in an imaginary empty position that is intended to be somewhere distanced. The "abusiveness" in fansub is to generate cognitive distance and disjunction within the cultural sphere of knowledge production, gesturing toward an outsider-inside position for the intracultural identity of anime geeks and knowledge workers alike, a position that Alan Liu characterizes as "cool."[37] But this intracultural identity of cool geeks is highly unstable, in a permanent state of agitation, and perpetually in flux. It may be better described as a nonidentity or intrasubjectivity, because it does not posit a stable location but is a dynamic movement to fill in the emptiness from within. Abusive subtitling is not to approximate the cultural authenticity of Japan but to fill in the emptiness of the very lack of it. If fansub is a language game, it is what Jacques Derrida calls the "movement of play." For Derrida, language is an open field for play, because it excludes totalization: "This field is in effect that of *play,* that is to say, a field of infinite substitutions only because it is finite." Nontotalization of language thus allows, and even demands, play as "infinite substitutions" to supplement for "something missing from it." Therefore, "this movement of play, permitted by the lack, the absence of center or origin, is the movement of *supplementarity.*"[38] Fansub, as an act of abusive subtitling, is precisely such a movement of play that is driven by "the absence of center or origin." What it points to is not the totality of an identity or subjectivity but the very lack of it, and thus the "infinite substitutions" and the permanent state of generative motion and agitation.

In perpetual motion and agitation, fansub generates less an identity than a dialogue. Fansub's abusive foregrounding of the translation/

subtitling practice forms a distinctive position for the translator/sub-titler as a speaker (writer, author) dialoguing with their fellow fans as addressees (readers, audiences), creating a unique channel for intentional communication. Bakhtin's notion of dialogue is particularly helpful for understanding such a communication practice. For Bakhtin, a text should be studied as verbal interaction, because a text always develops in dialogue. Such dialogical relations are developed not only between the author and the reader but also between the author and the characters, between the reader and the text, and even between the author and himself or herself. Since any given text always implies dialogue among multiple viewpoints or social voices, a text can never be completely translated, "for there is no potential single text of texts."[39] Bakhtin's emphasis on dialogical relations, both between texts and within a text, not only denies the fetishistic location of a single supposedly original text but also reminds us that to translate a text always implies the introduction of another voice into the dialogue—the translator. Commercial subtitling, the "corrupt practice," strives to suppress its own visibility and hides its voice from the dialogue. Fansubbing, as a practice of abusive subtitling, highlights its voice for the translator/subtitler to enter the dialogue precisely by making its practice highly visible. Therefore, by foregrounding their practice with innovative experimentation with translation and subtitling, fansubbers create a visible position and an audible voice for themselves to enter the dialogue as participating speakers, generating dialogue not only with the authors (producers, writers, directors) of the anime text but also between fansubbers and their fellow fans. It is such multiple dialogues among anime texts, fansubbers, and fan viewers that mark the unique function of fansub as intracultural communication.

The communication function of fansub is best exemplified by fansub's extensive use of notes and glosses. Many argue that the function of these notes is to educate fans about the Japanese cultural background, leading them closer to the original text.[40] However, a closer look demonstrates that these notes are rarely intended to explain Japanese culture. Neither are they written in a definite tone of educating or informing the audience. More often, fansub notes read like suggestions or discussions.

These notes sometimes start with "Personally I think . . ." or "Excuse us for destroying this wonderful moment . . ." They suggest a sense of dialogue, an exchange of opinions. Instead of leading the viewers closer to the original, fansub notes create a channel for the fansubbers (who are fan themselves) to communicate with their fellow fans by discussing certain issues they believe are significant. Reading these notes is dialoguing with the fansubbers. Often, viewers respond to these notes through paratextual and extratextual channels such as fan websites and forums. Sometimes, the on-screen notes themselves are fansubbers' responses to fan viewers' discussions. Chinese fansubs, for instance, are famous for making extensive refences to zhai culture in their on-screen notes, including references to popular anime, fan trivia, internet slang, and memes (Figure 10). These on-screen notes often become popular topics that are widely discussed among fans. Contrary to commercial subtitlers who try to hide their voices, anime fansubbers enjoy

FIGURE 10. In the Chinese fansub of *Hayate the Combat Butler* (2007), the on-screen note makes reference to the popular anime *Case Closed* to comment on the character's self-description in the dialogue, explaining to viewers that the sentence "Always determining the one truth with the body of a child and the mind of an adult" is a famous line describing Detective Conan in *Case Closed*. Fansubbed by OUR Fansubbing Group.

opening up to their fellow fans and frankly discussing how and why they did certain things for translation and subtitling, include their own failures. One Chinese fansub, for instance, admitted in its on-screen note that the translators were "uncertain about the meanings" of the dialogue.

In some cases, the notes are not for explanation but for expressing fansubbers' thoughts and comments on the story or characters. For example, in the English fansub of *Code Geass: Lelouch of the Rebellion R2* (by gg Fansub), fansubbers gave four different lengthy notes, all appearing on screen simultaneously, to debate how a character manages to cheat in a chess match. The notes are so extensive that they cover the entire screen, overlapping and disrupting the animated image in a quite "abusive" manner. These fansubbers, who were expressing different opinions about the story with these on-screen notes, were simply taking advantage of the fansub as a channel of communication to initiate dialogue with their fellow fans. And these notes are written in a dialoguing fashion as if the fansubbers are literally talking with their viewers. More interestingly, when the same fansubbing group later subtitled another anime series, they made a specific reference to the lengthy notes in their earlier fansub of *Code Geass* as an inside joke (Figure 11). This playful incident is an illuminating example of how fansub functions as intentional communication among the community, because by creating a joke like this, the fansubbers obviously were assuming that their viewers had seen their previous fansub works and still remembered that famous incident with those extensive notes on screen. By recalling the previous incident, the fansubbers initiated a humorous dialogue with their fellow fans by giving them an insider's nod: if you understand this joke, you are one of us, because you have seen our previous work. Such a playful use of fansub is quite common, and it does not seem to be serious about discussing anything other than simply pulling out a practical joke to entertain viewers. It suggests the powerful communication function of fansub. By writing (and expecting viewers to read) those lengthy, funny, and sometimes annoying on-screen notes, fansubbers create a peculiar moment of dialogue. They are literally talking with their fellow fans via the mediation of fansubs. It is

FIGURE 11. (*top*) Four different translators' lengthy notes appear on screen simultaneously, debating why the character calls "checkmate" after an illegal move in a chess match, in the fansub of *Code Geass: Lelouch of the Rebellion R2* (2008). Fansubbed by gg Fansub. (*bottom*) Later, the same fansubbing group made another on-screen note in their fansub video of *Kämpfer* (2009) to comment on the word *checkmate* in the dialogue, as an insider's joke to communicate with viewers, recalling their memory of the famous lengthy notes in their previous fansub of *Code Geass*.

precisely such visibility, openness, and playfulness of fansub that establishes the important channel of intracultural communication between fansubbers and their fellow fans.

Fansub's function as intentional communication is also manifested by its overt awareness of its audience. Unlike commercial videos that seek to target a mass audience as large as possible, fansubs make it clear that they are addressing only a specific subculture group. Their famous motto—"By fans for fans"—not only explicitly foregrounds the question of who speaks to whom but also contains both the speakers and the addressees in the same group of anime fandom. Fansubbers' awareness of their audience group is often expressed by the recurrent use of untranslated words or phrases that are familiar only to anime fans. For instance, in many fansubs, the term *otaku* is left untranslated in the subtitle, assuming that anime fans all know what the word means. There are a bunch of commonly used Japanese phrases, such as *itadakimasu* ("let's eat"), *tadaima* ("I'm back"), and *onee-chan* ("elder sister"), that are often left untranslated in fansubs, assuming that their fellow fans have learned the meanings of these words from their frequent viewing of anime. For the viewers, the use of these untranslated terms functions less to preserve the cultural authenticity of Japan than to set up the symbolic barrier between the subculture members who understand their meanings and the outsiders who do not. For instance, in the English fansub of *Welcome to the N.H.K.*, the word *anison* is left untranslated in the subtitle (Figure 8). But what is preserved in the untranslated word is not the authenticity of Japanese culture, because *anison* is not even a Japanese word. It is a combination of two loanwords from English—*animation* and *song*. If this word expresses any sense of authenticity, it is the authenticity of transnational otaku culture. By keeping the word *anison* untranslated, the fansub creates a symbolic barrier for its community. It is a gatekeeping boundary: if you understand the word *anison*, you are one of us. Like many cult references that either you get or you do not, fansub's recurrent use of untranslated special terms creates a strong sense of exclusiveness of anime geekdom that requires special knowledge to enter, while leaving out casual viewers who are not fansub's core audience. In fact, the use of such a symbolic barrier is not unique for anime fandom but is common for almost any geek subculture that is famous for inventing and popularizing many special terms, slangs, and references.

Relying on recognition of the addressees as the same-minded group members who share similar knowledge, these codes and references used by geek cultures exemplify what Bakhtin calls "familiar speech genres," which are speech communications constructed according to the proximity between the speakers and the addressees who share similar sensibilities and specialized knowledge.[41] Like many geek cultural codes and references, anime fansub's recurrent use of specially untranslated terms creates a familiar speech genre for the fan members to communicate, while setting up a boundary to alienate outsiders. This is one of the most effective ways to communicate a group identity with shared knowledge for geek communities, who have indeed invented their own speech genres that are familiar only to group members themselves. In fan communities online and offline, they have their own ways of speaking and communicating, which are difficult for outsiders to understand. Anime forums thus often feature dictionaries or wikipages to explain these familiar speech genres, including a long list of acronyms, abbreviations, and phrases that one has to know in order to surf through the fan culture. Geek communities heavily rely on the invention and cultivation of their own familiar speech genres, commonly referred to as "lingo," to facilitate communication and to maintain group identity with shared special knowledge. Chinese zhai culture, for instance, is marked by its popular obsession with an intracultural reference system known as *neta* (ネタ), referring to the source of intertextual parodies, spoofs, or pastiches in anime. Translating and explaining neta references is a focal point for Chinese fansubs, which generate a powerful mechanism for intracultural communication within the community. Like using a password to enter a private club, mastering the "anime dictionary," "otaku lingo," or "neta codes" enables one to communicate in familiar speech genres with other fans, allowing one's entry into the community of anime geekdom. The familiar speech surfaced in anime fansubs also includes a large amount of internet slang, acronyms, symbols, and emoticons, such as LOL, AAMOF, and :3 (Figure 12),

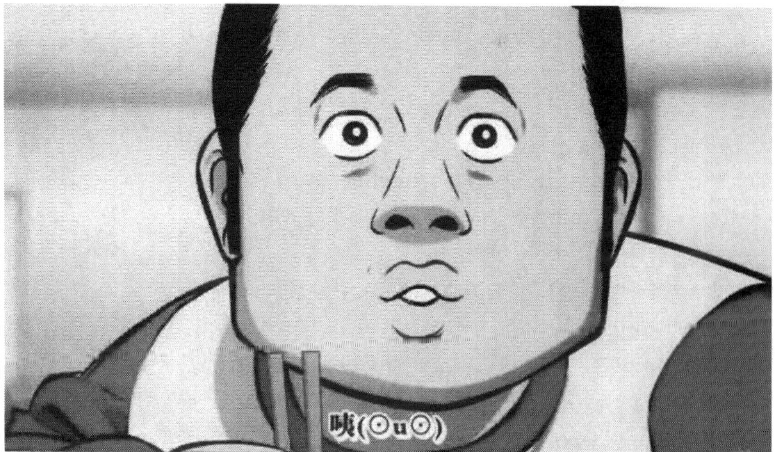

FIGURE 12. Subtitles include extensive use of emoticons that are popular among otaku in the Chinese fansub of *What Is Your Perfect Way to Eat Fried Eggs?* (2014). Fansubbed by F Zhai.

which suggests that they belong to a broader, networked community of postmillennial geekdom that built the material and cultural life of the internet. These familiar speech genres, by foregrounding the shared knowledge in the form of language, create an effective space for geek communities to communicate and negotiate with their collective ethos and sensibilities.

In sum, through their symbolic and stylistic practices of abusive subtitling, anime fansubs create intracultural dialogue via familiar speech genres. They function as intentional communication between fansubbers and fan viewers, as well as among the fansubbing groups themselves. Collectively producing, consuming, and discussing fansubs has become their way of communication. This sense of communication among transnational communities is what motivated thousands of fansubbers to spend a great amount of spare time doing a free service for millions of fans all over the world. As a longtime fansubber describes it: "You spend hours and hours working on fansubs and chatting with each other on the computer; it's basically a community that's come around. . . . It's all about the community, that's the heart of it."[42] This community is shared with fan viewers, whose consumption of anime culture often centers around fansubs—downloading, watching, discussing, and commenting on them. Fansub, as one of the most distinctive features of anime geekdom, is a collective experience that plays a crucial role for communicating, negotiating, and sometimes destabilizing intracultural identities. Throughout anime websites, forums, and blogs, fansub is one key subject that is constantly being debated, discussed, and interrogated among fans. These discussions rarely come to an agreement but are always in dispute. Such debates suggest that the function of fansub is precisely to create an open space for discussion and negotiation—the "intentional communication" that Hebdige describes or the "movement of play" that Derrida celebrates.

The nontotalization of this open field—or, more precisely, the non-identity of anime geekdom—calls for fansub as an act of play with language. It is a game of infinite substitution, agitation, and movement. As fansubbers themselves suggest, fansub is actually "no different from people playing Warcraft all day."[43] Perhaps nothing characterizes fansub better than the analogy with massively multiplayer online games such as *World of Warcraft*. Producing and consuming fansubs is like an online game played by fans together: competing among one another, gaining recognition, establishing fame and ranking. It is a language game that is played by a huge number of participating players from all over the world. The transnational, transmedial movement of anime geekdom that is organized by fansubs represents a distributive cultural field of globalization that acts like a massively participating online game. However, this distributive, massively participatory cultural field of play—"a field of infinite substitutions" to borrow from Derrida—is not without control, tension, or exploitation. The intracultural communication organized by fansubs is marked by uncertainty and contradiction rather than by commonality and unification. The relationship between the cultural logic of fansubs and that of information capitalism is as indeterminate as it is unstable.

The Intraface of a Knowledge Culture: Between Speed and Control

Functioning as intracultural communication, fansubs effectively organize anime geekdom as a transnational knowledge culture through collective knowledge sharing. It is what French philosopher Pierre Lévy celebrates as "collective intelligence," a mode of sociocultural organization through massively participated knowledge production and distribution.[44] This cosmopolitan knowledge sphere emerged out of the deterritorialization of traditional social bonds, and it is organized by shared cultural interest and knowledge via decentralized networks with peer-to-peer connectivity. This deterritorialized and distributive cultural field of a knowledge community, according to Lévy, is fundamentally different from the commodity culture that operates through industries and markets. The knowledge culture, instead, is based upon the generation and development of a universally distributed intelligence that is enhanced, coordinated, and mobilized in real time. It is a self-organized knowledge sphere of "cosmopedia," a site of collective discussion, negotiation, and development.[45] Fansub, as well as transnational anime geekdom in general, constitutes such a knowledge culture, a cosmopedia where knowledge is produced and shared through collective discussion and communication. However, the "fan-based poli-tics" of this knowledge culture, which Henry Jenkins hails as "a proto-type or dress rehearsal for the way culture might operate in the future," was never as utopian as it was envisioned by Lévy and Jenkins, whose somewhat idealistic stances were representative of a particularly his-torical moment that was marked by widespread optimism about com-puter networks.[46] The politics of knowledge culture, both then and now, has always been ambivalent, because it is not so much determined by fan activities themselves as it is dependent on the dynamic and inde-terminate relations between knowledge and commodity. The distri-butive cultural field of participatory fandom, on one hand, "can work too neatly in the service of the shifting patterns of global capitalism," as McPherson warns us.[47] But on the other hand, it also disrupted the normative global flow through murky practices such as copyright in-fringement via unauthorized copying and distribution. Japanese media industry's continuous legal battle against the fansub community, which led to the shutdown of numerous Chinese fansubbing groups, is one indication of such an ambivalent and unstable relationship.[48]

In fact, the nature of fansub as a form of derivative content positions it at the precarious interface between Lévy's distinction of "knowledge space" and "commodity space."[49] What we witness in fansub are the active negotiations between two different cultural systems and logics that are full of dynamic tensions and contradictions. The collective knowledge sphere of fansub is primarily for and about preexisting cul-tural commodities. The lengthy notes on screen, for instance, interact with the original anime text by providing additional interpretations, debates, and discussions. But at the same time, these on-screen notes, which can be quite overwhelming and intrusive, also tend to disrupt the narrative flow and visual coherence of the anime. Fansub as a knowl-edge culture is simultaneously enriching, problematizing, and trans-forming commodity culture. Therefore, fansubs not only communicate internally but also interact externally at a dynamic interface between a knowledge culture and a commodity culture. The two cultures con-stantly interact with and inform, as well as problematize and destabilize, each other, each carrying its own sociopolitical reality. The legal battle over copyright is one example of such tension.

Fansub, therefore, is a fertile contact zone where the systems between knowledge and commodity clash, generating new meanings and contradictions. As such, it is what Alexander R. Galloway calls an "intraface," which is "an internal interface between the edge and the center" that constitutes "the zone of indecision."[50] Fansub is precisely this zone of indecision between knowledge and commodity. On the intraface of fansub, the center is the coherent, self-closed diegetic universe of the anime video, and the edge is the fansubbing interface, the subtitles, the notes, the glosses, as well as the computerized networks and operations that enable them in technological means. In the abusive subtitling of fansub, the edge often overwhelms and disrupts the diegetic world in the center. Unlike the self-closed, fictional universe of the anime video, the edge of fansub points to the external social, cultural, and political realities—the geek communities, the knowledge work, and the economic conditions of information networks. As Galloway says, "The edges of the work are the politics of the work."[51] Indeed, it is this intraface—the contact zone of indecision—between the knowledge space and the commodity space that demonstrates the fan-based politics.

This politics, I would further argue, is located in fansub's distributive mode of organizing production and labor that centers on the tension between speed and control. Speed is the key for fansub. Often labeled as "speed subbers," most fansubbing groups claim a turnaround rate of three to twenty hours, which means that whenever an anime episode airs in Japan, its fansub video will appear online the same day. Such speedy operation relies on the spatiotemporal immediacy that is enabled by the distributed field of information networks, which provides the material foundation for not only instant content distribution but also efficient labor management and organization through collaborative participation and real-time coordination on a global scale. Take the fansubbing group Live-Evil as an example, who arguably led the trend of speed subbing with a turnover rate of eighteen hours for subtitling

Wolf's Rain in 2003. Live-Evil's Tokyo-based leader, Tofusensei, recorded the raw video of *Wolf's Rain* when it aired in Japan and instantly uploaded it online. Then the group's trilingual translator, greenkabbage, a Japanese native living in Germany, translated the Japanese material to English and sent the transcript to editors and typesetters in the United States. Across three continents with multiple players who might have never seen each other, the whole process was coordinated and completed within eighteen hours.[52] Later fansubbing groups organized the production in an even speedier manner. Some Chinese fansubbers claim that the whole process can be completed within three hours: one hour translation, one hour proofreading and timekeeping, and one hour video processing and compressing.[53] If the dynamics of information networks are marked by spatiotemporal immediacy and simultaneity, speed subbing is a perfect example and reification of that dynamic.[54] As the technology of networked communication greatly accelerated the global flow of information, capital, and commodities, fansub strove to bring anime's global fandom to a heightened level of simultaneity, testifying to David Harvey's famous notion of "time-space compression."[55]

But speed is not everything, and the pursuit of immediacy and simultaneity is not without a price. With the proliferation of speed subbing, fans began to complain that fansubbers were only concerned with grabbing the position of "it's out first" but were no longer careful about the accuracy of translation or the quality of subtitles. With the acceleration of speed, quality control became a problem, for the activities of checking and proofreading tend to slow down the process. Although the advantage of speed and immediacy is largely the main attraction of fansubs (which often come out before an anime's commercial international release delayed by a windowing period), the tension between speed and quality control continues to agitate communication and debate within the fan community.

This tension mirrors the ambivalence between control and speed in the network dynamics of information technology. While the protocological system of control, as Galloway reminds us, enables the management of distributed computer networks, the fringe search algorithm to find the shortest route in the package-switching system, according to Tiziana Terranova, inevitably breeds chaos, fluctuation, and turbulence.[56] If the notion of "control," as in its etymological origin in the French word *contreroller,* means to check or verify an account using duplications, the control mechanism to verify the collective intelligence of fansubs has to constantly deal with the turbulent, restless, and sometimes chaotic movement of informational packets that are in search of the shortest route—that is, the fastest fansubbing speed. As Terranova notes, the collaborative mode of self-organization on distributed networks is always under threat from the entropic dynamics of a chaotic informational milieu.[57]

The sense of contingency in the distributive cultural sphere of fansub—the swiftness, the lack of accuracy control, and the sudden appearance or disappearance of a fansub video—is the signature of what John Tomlinson calls the "culture of speed," as the state of speedy acceleration "has been the constant leitmotiv of cultural modernity."[58] This logic of speed has less to do with the velocity of physical movement than with the rate of occurrence or incident in the pace of life, which has both economic and cultural value. In economic systems, speed is closely associated with the rate of circulation of capital and commodities. In cultural life, speed is widely evaluated as a virtue in connection with energy, vitality, power, dynamism, and (pro)creativity.[59] However, against this backdrop of economic and cultural fascination with speed, modern society, according to Tomlinson, is simultaneously obsessed with the mechanisms to control the unstoppable development of speed: "It seeks to discipline the inherently violent and unstable impulses of social and economic modernity—of which speed is the prime emblem—in a culture of rational regulation."[60]

This dialectic tension between speed and control, I believe, is where the knowledge culture of fansub arrives at its closest encounter with the political economy of information capitalism. The turnover rate that the fansubbing community is so obsessed with echoes Karl Marx's notion of "turnover time" for profit and surplus value in the circulation of capital. In the age of "fast capitalism," the pace and tempo of our cultural lives are inevitably synchronized with those of the money supply. As Amanda Landa jokingly notes about the culture of fansub, it is "a global fandom that is moving faster than the speed of money."[61] However, in the circulation of either capital or fansub, speed has to be both enhanced and controlled. Capitalism is as much about speed as it is about how to discipline it, because of "the risks, danger and implicit violence of speed and the—quintessentially modern—sensual-aesthetic experiences and pleasures it can afford."[62] In the culture of fansub, the pursuit of speed is always in sharp tension with the demand for quality control—that is, to verify the accuracy and coherence of the translated subtitles, which requires a great of amount of time that cannot be afforded by the swift process of speed subbing within a tight turnover rate. But speed is difficult to control or discipline, for it "embraces a range of transgressive and rebellious impulses" that are also the cultural signature of modernity, a sense of unruliness that is "subversive and impetuous, conjoining hedonism with a peculiar sort of existential heroism."[63]

It is this experience of what Tomlinson calls "unruly speed" that provides the fertile battleground for the knowledge culture of fansub to disrupt, subvert, and potentially transform the commodity space. The distributed information networks constitute a "space of flow," which both enables and demands the heightened experience of simultaneity and immediacy with a transgressive tendency to run out of control.[64] It is precisely the case of speed fansubbing, as well as the countless Bit-Torrent portals that keep flourishing in cyberspace despite continuous counterpiracy efforts by law enforcement and media industries. This culture of unruly speed is in strong tension with the space-time tyranny controlled by global media industries, whose restriction strategies, such as windowing, region coding, and geo-blocking, are problematized by the networked cultural logic that demands simultaneity.[65] As Shujen Wang points out, the increasing speed and fluidity of global cultural flow enabled by information technology both accelerated and disturbed the "normative" flows of capital and commodity that need to be tightly controlled by multinational corporations, which is demonstrated by the growing tension between different layers and directions of multiple flows that are observed in the case of film piracy in China.[66] Similar tension also marks the dynamic intraface between the knowledge space of fansub and the commodity space of anime. The rise of streaming platforms, such as Netflix, Hulu, and Crunchyroll, which all offer simulcasting of anime at almost the same time as the initial airtime in Japan, demonstrates the reactionary efforts from global media industries to deal with and to control the unruly culture of speed that is cultivated by the distributed field of fansub. The important role of speed subbing in pressing commercial distributors toward web-based simulcast, one may argue, exemplifies Lévy's prediction that knowledge culture would eventually alter the operation of commodity culture. However, it is also the wide spread of anime simulcasting on streaming platforms that threatens to kill or displace the cultural viability of fansub, for the time frame of simulcast defeats fansub's key advantage in speed.[67] Streaming media's contest with fansub suggests that the relations between speed and control, as well as between knowledge culture and commodity culture, are never settled but instead are always mutually entangled and perpetually contested. These relations are constantly renewed and reworked with the expanding logic of informational capitalism.

Cosmopedia and Communication Labor

Organized on computer networks, the transnational fansub community exemplifies Arjun Appadurai's notion of deterritorialization in ethnoscapes, marked by diasporic communities and cosmopolitan citizens.[68] Equipped with multilingual proficiency, the fansub community, like global geekdom in general, largely belongs to a cosmopolitan knowledge class, as one fansubber described herself as being "of Japanese descent, raised in Germany, gone to the US for four years, returned to Germany to attend the tuition free college in Munich."[69] Somewhat an ideal example of Jenkins's notion of "pop cosmopolitanism," the fansub culture highlights the networked experience of deterritorialization not only through the symbolic space of textual translation but also through the collective imagination of a cosmopolitan community that is self-organized through knowledge sharing.[70]

One illuminating case of such a cosmopolitan knowledge community is the Fengxue fansubbing group (枫雪字幕组). Founded in 2003 by a Chinese graduate student living in Canada, Fengxue started as an online forum, Fengxue Anime and Manga (formerly at bbs.fxdm.net), for diasporic Chinese fans living in Euro-America. Because of its cosmopolitan background, as well as the language advantage of its members, Fengxue quickly developed into a fansubbing organization, and its first notable fansub was for *One Piece,* one of the most globally popular anime series. With the success of its fansubs, Fengxue began to draw an increasing number of members and followers from back home in China, and it quickly grew into one of the most recognized online communities. For Chinese fans, Fengxue functioned as more than a forum or a fansub-downloading portal. It was a closely connected transnational community, almost its own virtual world. It had a role-playing system that allowed users to choose different roles—such as pirate, ninja, knight, wizard, soldier, or hunter—to identify themselves and to interact with others. It also featured a virtual currency and monetary system, called *xuebi* ("snow money"), which members could earn by contributing to fansubbing, participating in discussion, or helping the community. The virtual money could in turn be used for downloading fansub videos or donating to others. Seamlessly blending knowledge work (translation and subtitling) with play (the role-playing games), Fengxue represents a cosmopolitan knowledge community that is organized on information networks through collective participation. This is what Lévy describes as cosmopedia, a collective knowledge sphere that is networked, deterritorialized, and cosmopolitan.[71]

This knowledge space of cosmopedia, however, exemplifies a cultural model of post-Fordist production that translates consumer leisure to what Terranova calls "free labor," a networked labor force of knowledge work that is "voluntarily given and unwaged, enjoyed and exploited."[72] The provision of knowledge work as free labor indicates that the knowledge space of collective intelligence is an integral part of a rapidly evolving and expanding commodity space of digital economy, which relies on knowledge as both the main source of productive value and the driving force of global expansion. Therefore, self-organized community through collective knowledge sharing is not simply a techno-social formation but a mode of organizing production and labor at "the moment where this knowledgeable consumption of culture is translated into excess productive activities that are pleasurably embraced and at the same time often shamelessly exploited."[73] And this moment is not a new phenomenon of the digital age; it is part of a continuous historical process to extract and enhance "monetary value out of knowledge/culture/affect."[74] This is a process in which knowledge cultures of various kinds have been the active and crucial ingredients. Fashioning themselves as valuable promotional materials for the media industry (primarily to defuse the copyright problems), fansubs, as well as geek culture in general, are always part of the postindustrial logic of free labor.

But what I want to highlight in the case of the Fengxue community is the fact that the post-Fordist conflation between play and work is not without tension. That tension is exposed and underlined by Fengxue's virtual currency and monetization system, xuebi, which literally means "snow money." Like snow, this virtual currency of xuebi is soft, malleable, and meltable. Its value depends not only on how much work you contribute or how well you play the role-playing game but also on peer evaluations (other members' comments and votes) that translate participation and communication to self-disciplined communal labor management. More conspicuously, in the monetization system of xuebi, the transition between work and play, between labor and pleasure, is neither immediate nor transparent but instead is marked by temporal delay and perceptual disjunction. In order to enjoy the pleasure of watching a fansub video or playing the game, one has to gain enough xuebi by working hard to contribute to the community. Since this fan activity is practiced not for fun but to gain "snow money," it is clearly framed as work, and as such, it is separated from the realm of play. And the xuebi system purposely delays a user's pleasure of play by constantly requesting and encouraging one to gain more money—that is, to work more. If the post-Fordist system operates by bridging the spatiotemporal distance between consumption and production, as well as by making leisure and labor indistinguishable, the xuebi system seems to operate in the opposite direction: the transfer from work to xuebi to play—a process that can cost days or months, depending on how much time and effort one puts into it—enlarges the distance between production and consumption through delay and underlines the disjunction between work and play, which are separated and mediated by the very mechanism of value transfer through the currency of xuebi. As such, the xuebi system that organizes the Fengxue fansubbing community exposes an inherent and irreconcilable tension in the managing scheme of free labor.

The case of the Fengxue community suggests that the provision of free labor from knowledge culture cannot be taken for granted. Instead, it is rooted in the collective needs, desires, and sensual-affective pleasures of knowledge workers/consumers that remain contested and undetermined. If labor and pleasure are not automatically entangled or indistinguishable, as the Fengxue case indicates, then their shifting relations need to be investigated. Therefore, we must ask: What kind of pleasure drives these geeks to devote hours and hours of free time to engage in the tedious, unpaid, and labor-intensive work of translating, proofreading, typesetting, and video coding? As I discussed earlier, the primary motivation of fansubbing is intentional communication, for the production, circulation, and consumption of fansub opens a space of collective discussion, debate, and negotiation for a self-organized community. It is the strong need and desire to communicate—with a deterritorialized virtual community that is largely imagined but immediately present in cyberspace—that drives the production and organization of collective free labor by fans. I call it "communication labor," for this is producing and produced by collective voluntary communication, which is an indispensable force that not only produces economic and cultural values but also generates social relations.

Communication labor, we may argue, is the vital driving force of almost the entire digital economy that largely relies on communication of various kinds: email, tweets, blogs, forum posts, live chats, cell-phone texts, etc. Communication—as well as its crucial role in organizing economic production, social relations, and subject formation—is the fundamental aspect of Maurizio Lazzarato's notion of "immaterial labor," which is defined as the labor that "produces the informational and cultural content of the commodity."[75] The two aspects of immaterial labor, "informational content" and "cultural content," are both deeply rooted in the process and forms of communication, because communication, as the interface between production and consumption, is how the productive value of information and culture is valorized. In the words of Lazzarato: "If Fordism integrated consumption into the cycle of the reproduction of capital, post-Fordism integrates communication into it."[76] Therefore, "the activation of both productive cooperation and the social relationship with the consumer is materialized within and by the process of communication. The role of immaterial labor is to promote continual innovation in the forms and conditions of communication (and thus in work and consumption)."[77] In other words, in the post-Fordist economy of informational capitalism, immaterial labor is, by and large, communication labor.

Despite such centrality of communication in the postindustrial economy, our sociocultural communication—that is, the exchange of language, ideas, and images—is not always a form of labor, and neither is it readily realized as economic value. Between communication and labor, there is a critical process of valorization, which does not necessarily follow the activity of communication immediately. Since communications are foundational "forms of life," there remains "a space of radical autonomy of the productive synergies of immaterial labor," especially when the communicative process of knowledge production implies a collective social field of cooperation.[78] This collective knowledge production, according to Lazzarato, is not entirely the result of a new phase of capitalism but rather has its historical root in the struggle against work: immaterial communication labor is "the product of a 'silent revolution' taking place within the anthropological realities of work and within the reconfiguration of its meanings."[79] This historical origin locates a "space of radical autonomy" within immaterial labor, and the economic system of post-Fordism can never fully contain the collective communication—it can only manage, regulate, and standardize it.

The tension between radical autonomy and managerial control underlines the internal contradiction within the cultural space of fansubbing as a form of communication labor. On one hand, fansub communality is marked by a strong sense of DIY (do-it-yourself) spirit, a tendency of "self-valorization" that Lazzarato identifies in mass intellectuality as a result of the historical struggle against work. On the other hand, fansub demonstrates a global efficacy of self-managerial control in communication labor. The productive social synergy in this labor form is not only powerful in organizing social relations among fans but also effective in managing, coordinating, and standardizing its own activity. The desire for self-valorization is thus used to fuel the energy of collective communication labor for a global organization of production and distribution of knowledge, information, and cultural content. These two tendencies—radical autonomy and self-managerial control—are neither entirely separate nor simply opposing each other. Instead, they are mutually entangled, simultaneously enriching and problematizing each other.

The self-valorizing sensibility of DIY creativity is foregrounded and celebrated in fansubbing through stylized typesetting and the daring use of notes and glosses, features that instantly distinguish fansubs from commercial subtitles. One fan openly admitted: "Honestly, fansubs have their own special place in my heart. Besides the fact that some timers have the nerve to use sky blue colors on their text and not the standard yellow with black outlines."[80] To encourage DIY participation, many fansubbing groups publish detailed procedures of the production process on their websites.[81] Explaining technical details in almost every step of fansubbing, these online tutorials demonstrate a gesture of knowledge sharing and emphasize the easiness of the practice to encourage fan participation. Some Chinese fansubbers even provide screen captures to help fans go through the process of reediting and recoding the subtitles to create their own fansub videos. Resembling the open-source software movement, in which software developers share their source code so that other programmers can improve, adapt, or change a program, fansubbers' openly published procedures invite more fans to participate in collective knowledge sharing and production. Many fansub groups publish recruiting announcements alongside their tutorial guides. Encouraging fan participation, the cultural field of fansub foregrounds the communicative social synergy of self-valorization through its amateur innovation and DIY spirit. Precisely because of the relative ease of entering fansubbing practice, there had been a proliferating number of groups and stronger competition among them. Like playing a game, fansub groups began to compete with each other in order to establish their brand names through innovative styles, fast speed, and high-quality translation. On forums and social media, anime fans often discussed their preference and loyalty toward certain fansubbing groups, comparing one group with another.

With competition, there came standardization. To gain recognition in a crowded competition field, fansubbing groups had to accelerate the speed and improve the quality by streamlining the process into a series of standardized steps: raw acquisition, translation, proofreading, editing, timing, typesetting and styling, encoding, quality control, and distribution (Figure 13). And every fansubbing group features almost the same standard procedures that are effectively organized through online communication. The Chinese fansubbing group Kamigami (诸神字幕组), for instance, established a standard set of rigorous requirements for recruitment in each category of labor in fansub production with well-formulated testing routines like job interviews.[82] Such standardization of production and labor in fansubbing demonstrates the function of communication labor in regulating and managing its own production relation on a global scale. While the DIY spirit of self-valorization and participation encourages almost everyone to become a fansubber, the standardization of production with the rigid division of labor sets up a gatekeeping boundary to control the quantity and quality of fansubs, generating hidden hierarchy in the social relations among fans. The neoliberal embrace of the free market is also the underlying force that drives competition and generates hierarchy: bigger groups dominated the market while small ones were phased out. Like many online communities, anime geekdom organized around fansub is effectively self-managed with administrative standards, division, and hierarchy.

The contradiction between creative collectivity and standardizing regulation in the knowledge culture of fansub demonstrates the deep entanglement between radical autonomy and managerial control in

星空字幕组·氷菓
翻译：
01-11「雨曝し」
12-20「樹影搖曳」
最终话「おうとう」
21.23「Needfire-Gl」
时轴：
01-20「Mekozoko」
21-23「Needfire-Gl」
校对：
01-23「Needfire-Gl」
审稿：
01-11「树影摇曳」
12-23「雨曝し」
后期：「Mekozoko」
压制：「おうとう」
「想换purley」

星空字幕组
特摄字幕制作组
招贤纳士
▶片源
▶翻译
▶校对
▶时轴
▶特效
▶压制
▶美工
星空字幕组考核群
644319022

Figure 13. Posters released by the Chinese fansubbing group XKsub (星空字幕组) to publicize a new fansub video (*above*) and recruitment (*left*). Both materials feature the standardized procedures and labor divisions, including translation, proofreading, timing, video encoding/compressing, and postproduction effects. Sources: NF-GL, "[XKsub] Bingguo/Hyouka [Jianri·fanri shuangyu zimu]—ACG zimu fenxiang" ([XKsub] Hyouka [simplified Chinese–Japanese and traditional Chinese–Japanese bilingual subtitles]—ACG fansub sharing), Anime Subtitle Club, September 23, 2020, https://bbs.acgrip.com/thread-6630-1-1.html; "Xingkong zimu niang de weibo" (Weibo page of XKsub), https://weibo.com/XKsub. Credit: XKsub (CC BY-SA).

communication labor, which foregrounds the unresolvable tension among knowledge, power, value, and social life in a post-Fordist information society. On one hand, communication is a form of life that is rooted in everyone's affective desire, which encourages mass participation for the sake of cultural expression, social relation, and self-valorization. On the other hand, when knowledge becomes a valuable asset in a techno-economic system that relies on commination as a productive and coordinating force, or when the production of social relations becomes the production of economic value, the communicative exchange, or what Bakhtin describes as the social act of dialogue, inevitably overlaps the production of subjectivity (a primary function of language and knowledge) with the process of management and self-control.

The neoliberal subjectivity of self-control is manifested by fans' continuous debate on the meaning of "free" vis-à-vis the commercial value of copyright. Offering itself as a free service for fan communities, fansub culture is openly against any commercial activities that sell fansubs as bootleg copies. Most fansub videos feature an on-screen disclaimer that reads: "By fans and for fans. Not for sale or rent." As a longtime fansubber proudly announced: "There's always been a sort of code among fansubbers that you don't make money off of this."[83] The anticommercialization sensibility gestures toward a self-marked boundary between the free labor of knowledge space and the commercial value of commodity space. However, fansub can never truly be "free" (economically or symbolically) because the material that it deals with is commercial anime with economic values in both the commodity and the copyright. There thus emerged endless debates and controversies over the ethical and legal issues of copyright among fansub communities. Fansubbing was often defended by arguing that it helped expand a global anime market for the copyright holders, fashioning its free labor as not simply a service for fans but also a market promoter for the media industry.[84] Contrary to their widely claimed anticommercial sentiments, fansubbers expressed a willingly cooperative attitude toward commercial enterprise, celebrating themselves as "taste-spotters" for the market. Some fansub videos are blatantly labeled as "promotional materials." Even when fansubbers were not overtly cooperative, they still posed a high degree of self-regulation to prevent themselves from hurting the business interest of copyright holders. The well-known fansub ethics, which mandate withdrawing a fansub project whenever the anime is licensed internationally, further indicate the fansub community's self-control and management to accommodate, rather than to challenge, the system of global intellectual property laws. As "well-tempered selves," fansubbers are what Toby Miller calls "cultural citizens."[85] If idealization of cultural citizenship, as Miller argues, is an essential part of neoliberal globalization, fansubbers fashion themselves as such idealized cultural citizens who participate in collective knowledge production with an efficient mechanism of self-management as a new kind of citizenship on global information networks. Their communication labor, which is voluntarily given as both free and valuable, is the crucial force for the production of this neoliberal subjectivity of global cultural citizenship, a subjectivity that is crucial for the translation between self-valorization and self-control, between knowledge and value, between communication and production.

Lévy's utopian vision of cosmopedia, a deterritorialized and distributed knowledge culture against conformity or hegemony, is certainly complicated by fansub's neoliberal ethos of self-control and post-Fordist mechanisms of labor management, which is quite opposite from the "disorderly, undisciplined, and unruly" knowledge space that Jenkins suggests.[86] The distributive mode of global flow via knowledge sharing, which is practiced mostly among an elitist, cosmopolitan knowledge class, masks the sharp division between knowledge labor and manual labor, a class division with increasing socioeconomic inequality that marks the highly uneven experience of what it means to be networked or informational. But my purpose is not to simply dismiss this utopian vision of geek power (many have done so) but to identify those largely undetermined areas of tension and contradiction in the collective, free labor of communication, which is voluntarily given not for values but for the genuine, affective desire that is rooted in the historical struggle against work as such. In his discussion of otaku culture, Lamarre suggests that both the nonhierarchical visual field of anime and its participatory fandom foreground a "distributive function," which "shifts the problem of fandom toward the productivity akin to labor power."[87] But this distributive labor power is not separated from the ongoing transformation of labor and production under post-Fordist capitalism, which puts leisure, culture, and knowledge all into work. Anime geekdom, in a contradictory manner, is "a sort of play discipline or disciplinary play," which oscillates between a space of knowledge production that is governed by discipline and standardization and a space of play that is marked by fun, passion, and resistance to organized labor.[88] The question is never "either/or" but the very tension between the two. As Lamarre says about otaku movement: "Its bid for a space of play that is not automatically recoverable as ideology or discipline also suggests a refusal of work and evokes power of labor."[89] Indeed, if there is any potential power of labor in fansub, it lies in the fact that the knowledge culture of communication cannot be automatically or immediately assimilated into neoliberal ideology or disciplinization. The fact that many fansub videos, even after being withdrawn due to intellectual property infringement, are still widely circulated on the internet underlines the unruly historical root and radical autonomy in the immaterial, communication labor that cannot be completely lost to self-governance or economic exploitation. There is always a space to negate, to refuse. And this space of negation and refusal is what we should be looking for in the dynamic contact zone—or the "dialogical imagination," to follow Bakhtin—between the conflicting modes of expression, logic, and mediation that are entangled and assembled in the techno-social complex of anime geekdom.[90]

3

Danmaku

The Interface Affect of a Contact Zone

In the past decade, the transnational, transmedial movement of anime geekdom has increasingly relied on the networked systems of platforms for both content dissemination and sociocultural participation. In China, the anime fansub communities have largely moved from peer-to-peer (p2p) file-sharing networks to commercial video-streaming platforms such as AcFun and Bilibili.[1] This platformization of anime culture is global in scale. From social media networks such as Reddit, 2chan, and 4chan to video-streaming services such as Netflix, Hulu, and Crunchyroll, the transnational culture of anime geekdom is organized and sustained on a myriad of digital platforms, which operate "as a new global infrastructure, like water pipes or electricity cables."[2] A major part of this infrastructure is the popular video-sharing platform Niconico, one of the largest and most-visited platforms in Japan. Launched in 2006, Niconico was initially designed as a website for otaku fans to share user-generated videos related to anime, manga, and games. Combining video sharing with social networking, Niconico distinguishes itself by featuring a unique interface with live comment feeds flying over the video on screen. The interface generates a communicative environment for subculture communities in addition to delivering videos.[3] In later years, Niconico further developed beyond video sharing and became a powerful platform for the transmedia operations of media mix.[4] It features diverse types of user-generated content, including videos, comics, novels, news, and live broadcasts, and the expansion of this platform targets both multimedia types and multinational markets. Niconico launched its Chinese-language version in Taiwan in 2007, a German and Spanish site in Europe in 2008, and it expanded to the North American market with an English site in 2012. Modeled after the success of Niconico, two Chinese video-sharing services, AcFun and Bilibili ("A-site" and "B-site," as they are called in China), were launched in 2007 and 2010 and quickly became the dominant platforms for Chinese *zhai* culture and the major channels for the transnational distribution of anime in China.

The success of Niconico, AcFun, and Bilibili suggests that the global dissemination of anime geekdom is as much about the spread of content as it is about the expansion of platforms and platform logic, because it is the digital media platforms that sustain both content distribution and community formation on global networks. In fact, the whole cultural regime of global geekdom is often defined by user-generated information, knowledge, and content that are collectively produced and shared by communities organized and programmed on digital platforms such as YouTube, Reddit, and Niconico. And the ethos of peer-to-peer advocacy and participatory collectivity, which has been advocated as the cultural foundation of the platform economy, historically emerged from the convergence between networked cyberculture and geek subculture. What José van Dijck calls "platformed sociality" operates as both the foundation and consequence of the global geekdom movement.[5] For Ian Condry, anime culture itself is a "generative platform," because anime characters and fictional worlds organize a transmedia system that generates a social engine for user participation and production, animating what he calls "collaborative creativity."[6] By and large, platforms of various kinds—such as media networks, computational systems, or social environments—form the pivotal engine that drives anime geekdom as a popular culture of knowledge production and consumption. Therefore, the so-called platformativity—that is, the cultural logic of platforms that transverse between hardware and software, between creators and consumers—is a central nexus of anime's global geekdom.[7]

This chapter interrogates the platformization of anime culture by analyzing the mediation functions and affective experiences of a discursive interface, *danmaku,* the unique interface design originally featured by the Japanese platform Niconico to render user comments flying over video on screen. The danmaku interface was widely adopted in China by video-streaming platforms, social media, television, livestreaming, and even theatrical film exhibitions. In fact, danmaku has become such a ubiquitous interface in Chinese digital culture that its meanings and significance have dramatically transformed from its techno-cultural origin in Japan. Not only is danmaku more popular and widespread in China, but it is also aligned with a far more pervasive and permeating framework for mediating and shaping user experiences and preferences. As an omnipresent and quasi-default interface on almost all video platforms in China, danmaku has become the media interface for Chinese video culture more broadly.[8] It localizes the cultural logic of informational knowledge work by penetrating and redefining the Chinese digital vernacular, a process that operates not only among the Chinese zhai culture of anime geekdom but through a much broader arena of what Luzhou Li calls "cultural zoning," whereby digital video platforms and their interface effects played a crucial role for mediating between China's domestic cultural politics and global information networks.[9]

In this chapter, I analyze how danmaku, as a transnational/transmedial interface that was adopted from Japanese otaku to Chinese zhai culture, concretizes the localized relations to the global expansion of the fetishistic logic of informationalism that is encoded in both anime geekdom and digital platforms. Examining the fundamental incoherence that is deeply structured by the interface—the incoherence between content and platform, between temporal experiences of liveness and spectral past, as well as between knowledge and community—this chapter underlines the notion of "contact" as the central logic of platforms. I argue that danmaku functions as a volatile contact zone between conflicting modes, logics, and structures of a knowledge culture on digital media. Such contested contact generates affective experience whereby the transnational media flow of anime geekdom, managed by platforms in material and textual traffic, is confronted with local disjunctions and inequalities on the user interface.

Interfacing Anime's Transnational/Transmedial Platformativity

The process of the global expansion of platforms, as well as the platformization of anime culture, is neither smooth nor homogeneous. It generates tension and disjunction as much as it facilitates flow. Because the intrinsic techno-cultural values of a platform are often "at odds with the values and preferences of the intended user base," the global dissemination of such values cannot be taken for granted but must be constantly negotiated by local users.[10] Therefore, a platform is not simply a technological facility that demands technical study. Instead, it constitutes complex performances, meanings, and knowledge of social acts that raise questions in specific social, cultural, and geopolitical contexts. If a platform, as both a concept and a structure, often entails discursive positioning of certain information politics through transnational/transmedial processes, how does the platform logic—the platformativity—help us understand cultural localization of the informatic logic of anime geekdom that runs across the playful and productive dimensions of postindustrial knowledge work? How does an individual user negotiate with, and make sense of, such logics through active sociocultural practices that are themselves codified by media platforms? To answer these questions, we need to look at the interface, where a user meets the platform, the content, and other users. As Van Dijck points out, platforms codify social activities by "presenting their interpreted logic in the form of user-friendly interfaces."[11] If platforms program our sociocultural practices into computer architecture, then interfaces are where this process takes effect and manifests itself, because an interface is a discursive and affective space where we encounter, negotiate, and feel the material and symbolic milieus of a platform.

Danmaku is one such interface where different platform experiences and cultural practices clash and are reconfigured. Originally a Japanese term to describe a certain type of shoot-'em-up games (a subgenre of shooter games), the word *danmaku* (弾幕)—or *danmu* as it is pronounced in Chinese—can be translated as "barrage" or "bullet curtain." The word is borrowed by the transnational otaku community in East Asia to describe the unique interface design featured by the Japanese platform Niconico that renders user comments flying over videos on screen.[12] The danmaku interface is widely recognized as the defining feature of Niconico. It allows viewers to input and share their comments in a seemingly synchronized manner with video streaming, supplementing the visual content of moving images with the paratextual information of peer interpretation and feedback, and transforming video consumption into social communication. The comment-over-the-video function, which combines images with text, the pictorial with the linguistic, generates user participation that is decidedly multitasking—watching, reading, and writing an overwhelming "polyphonic representation" with diverse types of media signals, evoking an intense sensation of information immersion, creation, and navigation.[13]

The danmaku interface was quickly popularized outside Japan. It was introduced to a Chinese audience through the video-sharing platforms AcFun and Bilibili, both of which were developed by and for the community of zhai culture and modeled after the platform design of Niconico (Figure 14). The interface of danmaku became so popular in China that it spread beyond the zhai community and was widely adopted by mainstream video-streaming services such as Tudou, YouKu, LeTV, and iQIYI. By 2014, almost all major video-streaming platforms in China featured a danmaku interface, which was no longer a unique subcultural entity but had become a standard interface design in Chinese digital culture at large.[14] The popularity of danmaku quickly spread to other media environments, such as social media (e.g., WeChat and Weibo), cinema, and television. In August 2014, three Chinese feature films—*The Legend of Qin*, *Tiny Times 3*, and *Brotherhood of Blades*—experimented with the danmaku effect in theatrical screenings. The audience could input comments using their cell phones, and these comments would appear on screen in real time. Though often dismissed as simply a publicity stunt, these three films' experimentation with this interface generated boiling discussions in popular press and social media about the possibility of what would become "danmaku

FIGURE 14. Screen capture of a user-generated video for *Toaru kagaku no rērugan* (A certain scientific railgun, 2007) on Bilibili.com with over-the-video comments on the danmaku interface.

cinema." A month later, TCL, a Chinese electronics manufacturer, launched a new model of smart TV featuring a danmaku interface as one of its key innovations. The television set is linked to the social media platform WeChat to generate the danmaku effect, so that when you watch a TV show you can see your friends' comments about the show on screen, advertised by the manufacturer as "TV + microsocial" (*wei shejiao*).[15]

The transmedial spread of danmaku (from video streaming to social media to cinema and television) testifies to the modularity and malleability of digital platforms in the transnational context of media flow and highlights the ways in which diverse media experiences can be inscribed and transcribed onto the shifting surface of an interface. To understand this transmedial/transnational process that is enabling and enabled by digital platforms and their cultural logics, as well as the sensibilities of Chinese zhai culture that are implicated, cultivated, and expressed by this process, I examine the interface function of danmaku.

In particular, I emphasize the fundamental incoherence and contradictions that are programmed and displayed by the danmaku interface, questioning the long-existing assumption of "convergence" or "mix" in media studies. Proposing the notion of "contact" as the central logic of platforms, I characterize danmaku as an affective contact zone that generates affective mapping of conflicting modes, logics, and structures of informational knowledge work.

The Bullet Curtain on the Window

Framing the audience's interaction with media content on multiple types of platforms through a layer of user comments, danmaku is not simply a computer interface but also a cultural one. As a cultural interface that organizes transnational cultural activities (watching and commenting on anime videos) into a certain coded format (comments over video), danmaku restructures the regional media geography in East Asia through the virtual unity of a platform-based otaku/zhai culture and a shared interface. Although the danmaku effect was originally featured by the Japanese video-sharing platform Niconico, what enables the transnational dissemination is not the platform itself but its interface design, which seems to be freed of its containment on the original platform and carries its encoded cultural logic into the architecture of many other media platforms, such as social media, theatrical cinema, and television. Such "spreadability" (borrowing from the notion of "spreadable media" coined by Henry Jenkins, Sam Ford, and Joshua Green) of danmaku exposes the complex and often-problematic relations between platformativity and its internal and external interfaces (and interface effects) in which various elements of a platform (e.g., users, content, data, algorithm, hardware) clash with one another.[16] If a platform often functions as an enclosed system of digital lockdown, the interface is the crucial element that both enables and exposes such an enclosure and can potentially open it up for users to negotiate with the platform logic.[17]

Because of the potential exposure through interfaces, the governing of a platform, according to Marc Steinberg, often involves "erasing the mediating function of the interface," rendering it seemingly transparent, as many content-delivery platforms such as YouTube, Netflix, and

Amazon have been trying to do.[18] In fact, striving for transparency has a persistent history in digital media. The famous Windows metaphor popularized by Microsoft, for instance, suggests that "the ideal interface is a transparent window onto a world of data."[19] But an interface is never truly transparent, and the persistent myth and desire of transparency in media history is paradoxically accompanied by increasing layers of mediation and reflections.[20] In fact, the danmaku interface operates against transparent access to media content.

The interface's name, *danmaku,* which literally means a "bullet curtain," metaphorically and figuratively suggests opacity rather than transparency—it is a "curtain" not a "window." Considering that the window metaphor is so prevalent in producing and maintaining an illusion of transparency in digital media, the metaphorical notion of a curtain in danmaku is an antithesis to such transparency: the danmaku interface is the curtain that covers the window and problematizes its supposed transparency.[21] Situated between visibility and invisibility, the interface reveals as much as it conceals, which makes it a discursive encoding that operates almost like an ideology. In Wendy Hui Kyong Chun's words: "Interfaces have become functional analogs to ideology *and* its critique—from ideology as false consciousness to ideology as fetishistic logic."[22] In the transnational media ecology, what moves across national borders is often not the architecture of a platform (e.g., Niconico) but its ideological logic that takes the form of an interface (e.g., danmaku), which "concretize[s] our relation to invisible (or barely visible) 'sources' and substructures."[23] But such concretization is often realized less through a transparent vision than by direct actions—programmed, interactive actions that are to be felt on the interface. Therefore, to understand what an interface reveals, its visibility "matters less than the affective relationship established through rapid, reversible, incremental actions."[24]

Such an affective relationship established by programmed actions on the danmaku interface is what I interrogate in this chapter, by analyzing how danmaku, as a cultural and media interface, concretizes our localized relations to the transnational expansion of the fetishistic logic of informationalism that is encoded in digital platforms. Examining the interface function of danmaku in mediating different content, audiences, and platforms, this chapter argues that the danmaku interface creates an affective contact zone between the visual and the operational, between text and paratext, between broadcasting and socializing. Specifically, this chapter focuses on the affective contact between visual content and cybernetic platform, between immediate and disjunctive temporal experiences, as well as between knowledge production and community organization. More importantly, the affective relationship engineered by danmaku also mediates the volatile contact between the cultural logic of transnational anime geekdom (which is coded in the platform that originated in Japanese otaku culture) and its local variations (which are felt through programmed actions among Chinese zhai users), for the interface produces a certain kind of knowledge worker whose terminal identity seems to be locked in a perpetual oscillation between pleasure and paranoia, which, to quote Chun, "also coincides with neoliberal management techniques that have made workers both flexible and insecure, both empowered and wanting."[25] If an interface functions as both an analogue and a critique of ideology, it can be examined, as Chun reminds us, as a form of "cognitive mapping" of such neoliberal management of knowledge work. But the mapping instantiated by danmaku is more affective than cognitive, and I follow Steven Shaviro in calling it "an aesthetic of affective mapping."[26] Danmaku provides us with an aesthetic of affective mapping of the cultural ideology of postindustrial knowledge work that is managed by digital platforms, and as such it tells a great deal about how we feel the fetishistic logic of information capitalism through programmed actions on the interface.

The Danmaku Interface: A Contact Zone on Platforms

Describing the danmaku interface as a contact zone, I want to first emphasize that the fundamental logic of a platform is *contact*. The concept of a "platform" is a contested one, and it often has radically different meanings in different contexts, whether a computational system, a business model, or a media entity. Despite the existence of various conflicting and competing definitions, the central meaning of the term points to the key function of a platform as a generative gathering space to establish, organize, and manage efficient and valuable contact of various kinds. As a computational concept, a platform refers to a programmable infrastructure where new applications can be built and used.[27] It relies on opening parts of the computing system to allow data exchange so that developers/users can interact with the coding framework. What enables a computation platform, therefore, is the contact among hardware, software, data, code, programmers, and users. In economic terms, a platform describes the business model of "a multi-sided market" that organizes interactions among multiple parties (consumers, producers, marketers) to exchange commodities and services.[28] It is the place of contact "where money, people and commodities meet."[29] In the media industry, the concept of a platform, as Tarleton Gillespie notes, was adopted by Web 2.0 intermediaries such as Google, YouTube, and Facebook to discursively claim an open, egalitarian gathering space for user-generated content to be in contact with targeted audiences.[30] Thus, "'platforms' are 'platforms' . . . because they afford an opportunity to communicate, interact or sell."[31] This broader definition positions "platform" not only as a computational and economic concept but also as a social and cultural one. It emphasizes sociocultural contact and connectivity that enable participation and collectivity. Combining the computation aspect with the sociocultural one, digital media platforms, by and large, are about engineering contact and interactions through programmed architecture. Platforms, as Joss Hands neatly summarizes, are entities that "gather users in interfaces with each other and with the Web and the Internet itself."[32]

Indeed, whether we interpret the concept of a platform as computational, economic, medial, or sociocultural, the core meaning of this notion is always about establishing contact of a certain kind: the contact between data and programs (computational), between consumers and commodities (economic), between users and content (medial), and among users themselves (sociocultural). In fact, the culture of platforms, as noted by Van Dijck, is essentially "the culture of connectivity," and the principle of contact, or that of "connectedness and connectivity, quick turnovers and constant data flows," is the technological and ideological foundation of platforms.[33] This fundamental logic is not simply determined by platforms themselves but is largely shaped by the wider techno-economic conditions of information capitalism, whose founding principles, as illustrated by information theory and cybernetics, are less about meaningful content than about informatic contact. In the words of Tiziana Terranova: "It is not about signs, but about signals."[34] The basic problem for information society is not as much a question of how to exchange ideas and meanings as of "how to clear out a space and establish a successful contact."[35] It is this purpose—to establish and manage a successful contact—that platforms fundamentally serve. Such is the case in danmaku and its original platform, Niconico. As Steinberg rightly observes in his thorough study of Niconico, the central objective of the platform's live commenting function is to keep the communication going, because to sustain this particular media ecology, "communication is more important than content."[36] In other words, the function of the danmaku interface is not so much to generate derivative content as to establish and sustain communicative contact.

The function of danmaku in generating contact suggests that the key component of any platform—whether a computational platform or an economic or sociocultural one—is its interface. If the logic of platformativity is contact, then the interface is where the contact takes place. On a computational platform, contact occurs on the application programming interface (API), which is "an interface provided by an application that lets users interact with or respond to data or service requests from another program, other applications, or Web sites."[37] Facilitating data exchange to allow building applications, API forms the foundation of a platform, because this interface "makes a website programmable by offering structured access to its data and functionality," which turns computational entities into a platform by enabling contact with data and code.[38] As a business model, the modular system of a platform also relies on a structural interface to generate value, to facilitate exchange, and to standardize production and communication, so that a complex ecosystem can be established and sustained.[39] "The interface is therefore a divider (of labour between distinct teams), but also a connector, and a conduit of selected information facilitating interconnection."[40] For a media platform or a sociocultural one, the interface is the site where users gather and interact with one another and with content. If a platform is the architecture that mediates contact among users, data, content, and services, then the interface (software interface, structural interface, or user interface) is the zone of contact.

What makes the interface more crucial for the formation and function of a platform is the fact that as a contact zone it is generative. On a computational platform, APIs enable new software, code, and applications to be programmed; on a business platform, open but standard interfaces facilitate innovations and generate new values; on a Web 2.0 platform, user-friendly interfaces establish communications that encourage and accelerate the production of user-generated content. If the concept of a "platform," figuratively or metaphorically, always seems to promise something new to be built, then the interface is the generative contact zone where this promised "something" (e.g., applications, values, content) eventually emerges out of various kinds of contact, communication, and connectivity.

Emphasizing the interface as a generative contact zone, I also want to compare the notion of "contact" with another more popular term, *mix* (or *remix*), which has been used widely to describe similar technological and sociocultural effects. The original danmaku interface designed by Niconico was developed from Japan's media mix ecology in which content can be transported across multiple media, and it functions as a generative structure that was optimized for the "continuation and evolution of the media mix."[41] Similarly, the ways in which danmaku enables fan-created comments to supplement and transform the original video content also demonstrate what has widely been celebrated as culture "remix."[42] Furthermore, by closely combining a computational architecture with visual media (video, film, and television), the danmaku interface foregrounds what Lev Manovich calls "deep remixability"—that is, what is being remixed are "not only the contents of different media types, but also their fundamental techniques, working methods, and ways of representation and expression."[43] Manovich's notion echoes Tim O'Reilly's famous Web 2.0 manifesto, in which he advocates that platforms should be designed for "remixability" by providing access to data and functionality that can be remixed from various sources.[44] Following O'Reilly, many thus envision platforms as technological "mashups," remixing existing data, code, and services to create something new.[45] Overall, "mix" is widely perceived as the central concept for understanding not only the interface effect of danmaku in particular but also the techno-cultural logic of platforms in general.

However, the notion of "mix" tends to assume a certain degree of inherent compatibility, combinability, and mixability, while obscuring potential conflicts, confrontations, and contradictions among diverse elements, forces, and powers that may not be readily mixable. As Branden Hookway rightly points out, the interface is not a seamless integration but a contested boundary: "It is a disputed zone, a site of contestation between human beings and machines as much as between the social and the material, the political and the technological. In staging and solving this contestation, the interface both defines and elides difference."[46] It is such unmixable difference and contestation that is highlighted by the notion of "contact." A contact zone is where different media elements, methods, and logics—compatible and noncompatible—clash, confront, and contest with one another, generating volatile reactions and even possible explosions. Such unstableness and uncertainty of a contact zone also characterize what Alexander R. Galloway calls "intraface," the dialogical encounter between coherence and incoherence, between the workable and unworkable. "It is a type of aesthetic that implicitly brings together the edge and the center. The intraface may thus be defined as an internal interface between the edge and the center. . . . This is what constitutes the zone of indecision."[47] The contact zone structured by danmaku is precisely such a zone of indecision: indecision between video and comments, between text and paratext, between the visual and the operational, and between content and platform. The notion of "indecision" emphasizes the volatile nature of this contact zone where conflicting meanings and logics cannot be coherently determined by simply mixing them up.

As a site of dispute, the interface generates contested contacts that also concretize unequal power relations. This inevitably leads us back to the original notion of "contact zone" coined by Mary Louise Pratt in postcolonial studies, referring to "social spaces where disparate cultures, meet, clash and grapple with each other, often in contexts of highly asymmetrical relations of domination and subdomination—such as colonialism and slavery, or their aftermaths as they are lived out across the globe today."[48] From this perspective, the term *contact* highlights the often-forgotten history and politics of imperial domination, subjugation, and resistance that continue to exist in today's techno-political situation of what Dal Yong Jin calls "platform imperialism."[49] This historical shadow of imperialism is exactly what is overlooked or suppressed by the harmonious notion of "mix," a term that embraces postcolonial hybridity rather than colonial inequality. From colonial encounters to platform imperialism, the notion of "contact" foregrounds the interactive means by which unequal power relations between the colonizers and the colonized, between platforms and users, are established through the exchange of knowledge and information. Bridging the technological and the political, the historical and the present, "contact zone" is thus a crucial concept for studying the ways in which the danmaku interface structures an entanglement of power, knowledge, and agency in mediating transnational flows of culture and technology that are often asymmetrical.

This dynamic and unequal contact between local users and the global expansion of the platform logic, mediated by the constant flow and overflow of information, are the key effects of the danmaku interface. I am particularly interested in the conflicting and unstable contact whereby cracks, fissures, and contradictions can potentially be opened to generate affective experience, a structure of excess feelings that cannot be fully contained within the productive activities of anime geekdom that overlaps work and play. In the remaining part of this chapter, I will examine several instances of such volatile contact: between conflicting modes of representation and mediation (cinematic content versus cybernetic platform), between uncertain temporal experiences (real-time liveness versus spectral past), and between knowledge production and community organization (collective intelligence versus gatekeeping membership tests). Through these cases, I hope to understand the ways in which the danmaku interface generates affective flow—like the overflowing comments on screen—that can carry us beyond the boundaries of ourselves that have been codified by technological and sociopolitical control. It is through "such affective flows that the subject is opened to, and thereby constituted through, broader social, political, and economic process."[50]

Between Content and Platform

As a contact zone, an interface is essentially a space of dynamic relations between various kinds of properties and media environments that are in contact "*within* a system of co-dependent relations of production."[51] For the danmaku interface that features overlay on-screen comments on a variety of video-streaming platforms, the key relation of production is between the video content and the digital platform. Indeed, the convergence between content and platform, according to Steinberg, is precisely the central logic of Niconico, "where the platform's affordances—the comment function—allow for the transformation of the moving image itself."[52] Such transformation effectively merges content production with platform connectivity, and the danmaku interface is the contact zone where this convergence takes place.

While converging content with platform, the danmaku interface, however, also paradoxically differentiates and distances the two, generating gaps as much as overlaps. For instance, the danmaku interface on platforms such as Niconico, AcFun, and Bilibili allows the comment overlay function to be turned on or off, as well as allowing users to adjust the location, transparency level, and flying speed of the overlay comments so that the degree of interference between comments and videos can be customized. These interface affordances effectively separate the comment function and video streaming into two distinctive entities and operations (though the two can be brought into contact on screen), which are to be experienced and interacted with differently by users. In other words, the danmaku interface is a surface of contact that enables both convergence and distancing. Such ambivalence is arguably the underlying foundation of the interface as a contact zone. As Seung-hoon Jeong argues about interface: "Without this spatiotemporal difference and determent there would be no experience of contact and presence."[53]

The distance and interval that are mediated by the interfacial contact on danmaku are explicitly manifested by one of the on-screen comments commonly made by Chinese users on AcFun and Bilibili: "I come here simply to watch danmaku (我就是来看弹幕的)." What this comment suggests is that some users' primary purpose in using the platform is to read the overlay comments on the danmaku interface rather than watching the video, which clearly separates comment reading and video watching as different (but not independent) activities with different attractions, pleasures, and priorities.[54] However, by describing the activity of reading comments as "to watch danmaku," this peculiar comment also demonstrates the conflation between reading and watching, between commentary texts and the interface itself.[55] The user experience articulated here emphasizes both separation and collision between multiple entities and activities (videos and comments, text and paratext, watching and reading) that are entangled in the interface effect of *danmaku.* As a process of differentiation and remediation, this interface effect, as the user comment suggests, is the key attraction of *danmaku,* because it mediates both the contestation and reconciliation between visual content and platform socialization.

The ambivalent relationship between content and platform is pronounced most dramatically in a peculiar form of hybrid media—the "*danmaku* cinema" (弹幕电影)—in which the danmaku interface is transplanted from its original context of computerized media to a cinematic one. Since danmaku was introduced to movie theaters in China in 2014, several Chinese feature films have incorporated the danmaku effect by projecting viewer comments over cinematic images in theatrical screenings. Although these experiments were often dismissed as gimmicks, the public excitement and dispute surrounding these instances generated such media buzz that they triggered a series of industrial speculations, as well as academic examinations, debating whether danmaku could become a viable element in future film forms and businesses. Even the *New York Times* noticed this new trend in China, asking: Is this "bullet screen . . . a moviegoer's worst nightmare or the coolest wave of the future?"[56]

Despite the initial enthusiasm, however, the prospects for danmaku cinema quickly faded, because the audience response was not very positive, and some viewers and critics even questioned whether danmaku was compatible with cinema in the first place. According to a survey conducted by Tencent (one of the largest internet companies in China), among young viewers under twenty years old, only 10 percent appreciated danmaku cinema and over 60 percent viewed it negatively. The majority of the respondents suggested that danmaku "disrupts movie viewing."[57] This result echoes another survey, in which 57 percent of the respondents indicated that danmaku distracts them from watching films properly.[58] Such negative responses seem strange, considering that the majority of the audiences who attended danmaku screenings were preselected: they were invited from the zhai community at Bilibili and AcFun and thus should have already been very familiar with the danmaku effect. The negative feedback, in fact, is not about danmaku itself but about the strong feeling that the interface is fundamentally at odds with cinematic pleasure. For instance, one female respondent stated that although she was a devoted user of Bilibili, she could not enjoy danmaku in cinema. In her own words: "I spent the money to watch movies, not to watch danmaku."[59] Even the most positive viewers admitted that they "were not actually watching the movie," though they had a great time at the screening.

The consensus among viewers and critics seems to be that danmaku has a negative impact on the original film content, and it is only suitable for movies that are not "cinematic" enough. As some commentators put it: "Danmaku is for terrible movies and it is absolutely damaging for real cinema."[60] Not being "real" cinema, interestingly, is also the most prevalent criticism of the first two danmaku films, *The Legend of Qin* and *Tiny Times 3*, which gained tremendous publicity by introducing danmaku at their theatrical screenings. These two films were not considered "real cinema" because they are not stand-alone cinematic works but are parts of larger media franchises, including games, comics, and novels. This is especially the case with the *Tiny Times* series, a multimedia franchise based on a model similar to that of the Japanese media mix, and its film installments were overwhelmingly criticized for being "noncinematic." When commenting on danmaku cinema, one critic asked: "Can *Tiny Times* even be considered a real narrative film?"[61] Emphasizing the noncinematic aspect inevitably generates a strong negative association between danmaku and cinema. One audience worried that danmaku would "damage the artistic values of cinema," and another commentated that incorporating danmaku contributed nothing but to "expose the film's lack of self-confidence."[62] Such a negative association between danmaku and cinema was strongly emphasized by film critics and filmmakers. One critic described danmaku as a "humiliating insult" that made cinema "lose all its dignity."[63] Another went so far as to suggest that mainstreaming danmaku is equivalent to cinema's "forced suicide."[64]

The overwhelming fixation on the distance, opposition, and incompatibility between cinema and danmaku, interestingly, stands in sharp contrast to the smooth incorporation of this interface into computerized platforms, such as video streaming and social media. The key question here is not one of compatibility but of how the danmaku interface, as a volatile contact zone, a "zone of indecision" (to borrow from Galloway), can expose the fundamental incoherence between content and platform and destabilize the often-naturalized logic of both. The interface effect of danmaku questions the consistency and transparency of both cinematic conventions that organize the content and the cybernetic system that structures the platforms. While audiences complain that the computerized danmaku interface prevents them from concentrating on the view, the story, and the cinematic gaze, they are not completely at ease with the interactive experience of information sharing, collective expression, and socializing that is popularized by digital platforms. Indeed, the public responses to danmaku cinema highlight the conflicting modes, logics, and experiences that are entangled in the interface effect: visual versus operational, narrative versus informational, absorption versus participation, cinema versus social media.

To be fair, these conflicting elements are not unique to danmaku cinema but are common to almost any platform. As Van Dijck points out, media platforms exist less as a coherent convergence than a volatile battleground, a constant contestation among multiple norms and logics that struggle to define the terms of digital media. The transformation of YouTube, for instance, demonstrates conflicting logics between broadcast and social networks, between TV and PC, "a process of tight interlocking between broadcasting and homecasting, between watching television and video sharing, between programs and snippets."[65] These conflicting elements, however, often appear to be converged and mixed in seemingly coherent ways, because the transparent interfaces featured on platforms such as Netflix, YouTube, and Hulu, which strive to deliver videos as smoothly and immediately as possible, effectively mask the intervals and contestations and create an illusory impression of a harmonious synthesis between video content and informational systems. Countering such transparent channeling, the nontransparent interface of danmaku, by contrast, exposes the incoherence between the center (cinematic content) and the edge (computational platforms) by staging their conflicts and contestations on the very surface of an interactive screen. This is precisely the function of an intraface, an incoherent aesthetic that is "*indecisive* for it must always juggle two things (the edge and the center) at the same time."[66]

The experience of such incoherence and indecisiveness can be quite affective, which is demonstrated in viewers' comments that often express confusion, agitation, and conflicted feelings about danmaku cinema. One said that "it feels like a party not a cinema," and another admitted evident pleasure from the danmaku screening but "really hated the film."[67] Even the producer of *Tiny Times 3* admitted that many people came to the danmaku screenings to "play" instead of "watch[] the movie." For those who managed to enjoy the films, however, they had to do so by "forgetting the existence of danmaku."[68] Struggling between the center and the edge, between the content of moving images and the platform of social media, between a transparent window and an opaque "bullet curtain," between a cinematic gaze and a cybernetic scan, viewers of danmaku cinema are exposed to the contradictory logics of today's media environment of the information age, which demands both our absorption and distraction. Such contradiction is manifested by the incoherent aesthetic of the intraface. The incoherence of this zone of indecision is further intensified and becomes more evident when the logic of digital media (platforms) is juxtaposed with that of the cinematic one (film content). The affective experience of such an incoherent intraface, more importantly, can also bring us to a broader realm to navigate an incoherent politics: a politics of informationalism that conflates the informational with the meaningful, as well as a politics of global media flow that relies upon contradictory frameworks of spatiotemporal experience and identity formation.

Between Liveness and Spectrality

The notion of an interface is often described in spatial terms: it is a relational area, a boundary condition, and a surface of interaction. However, as a contact zone of indecision, the interface effect of collision and contestation is not only spatial but also temporal. For the danmaku interface, the conflicting temporal relation is explicitly staged in its pseudo-real-time structure that creates an ambivalent feeling of quasi-liveness. The video-overlay comments seem to move across the screen in real time, giving "a sense of 'live' and simultaneous viewing between users."[69] But these comments are not actually "live"—they were usually made and input long before their appearance on a video display. What makes them appear to be "live" for an individual viewer, however, is the fact that the temporal position of a comment is locked to a specific moment in a video when the comment is submitted and displayed. In other words, a comment input at a particular time-code mark of a video will always appear at this exact time-code position for any subsequent viewers, for whom this comment seems to appear in "real time." Such a quasi-live temporality, which was originally featured on Niconico and was adopted by almost all video platforms featuring the danmaku interface, is described by Hamano Satoshi as "pseudo-simultaneity."[70] The on-video comments "are seemingly simultaneous in relation to the particular moment of viewing the time-shiftable, replayable video."[71] According to Hamano Satoshi, the pseudo-simultaneity between the video and the comment feed also creates a sense of "virtual time," which unites users in a collective feeling of synchronicity despite the actual time difference among them. Therefore, the temporality structured by the danmaku interface leads to a collective user experience of "virtual liveness."[72]

Such a temporal feeling of virtual liveness, however, is highly unstable, because the pseudo-simultaneity in virtual time is often experienced in stark contrast to the nonsimultaneity in actual time, especially the time lapse between the production and the reception of a comment feed. Although viewers can see other people's comments at that specific "simultaneous" moment, they know that these comments were made in the past, probably days, months, or even years before they are replayed at the present moment. The temporal contradiction between simultaneity and nonsimultaneity, between present and past, is often strongly felt when a viewer tries to engage with those pseudo-live comments in actual real time. The viewers know that the comment they respond to is not made in present time (though it appears to be so) and whoever they are communicating with is not likely to be currently watching. Recognizing the time lapse in danmaku communication, users also know that their own comments will not be seen by others until sometime later and they do not expect immediate replies either. Therefore, to engage in a conversation on danmaku, you have to revisit the same moment of the same video multiple times to see how others respond to your comments and to respond to others. Although the interface presents user interactions as "live," they are not and do not feel like live conversations. Instead of simultaneity or immediacy, what are actually experienced in danmaku communications are time shifting, repetition, and delay. Although temporal delay is common for almost all online communication (e.g., forums, blogs, microblogs), danmaku's pseudo-simultaneity intensifies and highlights the contradictory temporality in digital platforms precisely because it appears to be live. This feeling of temporal disjunction is probably most affective when one joins a heated dispute or a hostile verbal fight through danmaku comments, which often demand an immediate response in real time. One cannot help but wonder: How does it feel to debate with someone who spoke in the past but whose words always appear in the present? It probably feels like quarreling with a ghost.

Indeed, the temporal experience structured by the danmaku interface feels more spectral than live. There is a strong sense of ghostly presence in those comment feeds over video: they are spectral conversations made in the past but resurrected in the present, moving across the screen in a seemingly live manner. This ambivalence between liveness and spectrality, however, is not unique to danmaku. It points to a fundamental contradiction of computer interfaces, whose affordance of seemingly real-time user interaction is always haunted by hidden specters.[73] The feel of real time in computer systems is more an illusion than actuality, but it provides a sense of authenticity precisely because it frames the liveness of computer processes in a temporal reference to real-life user actions, such as clicking a link or inputting a comment. A website becomes live only when it begins to dynamically respond to our clicks. This liveness, according to Tara McPherson, emphasizes "volition and mobility," and thus is different from traditional live television that simply brings presence before our eyes: "the web structures a *sense of causality* in relation to liveness, a liveness which we navigate and move through, often structuring a feeling that our own desire drives the movement."[74] This sense of volitional mobility is even more intensified by online platforms in the Web 2.0 era, when the feel of liveness is further enhanced by the dramatic expansion of user input, actions, and interactions that structure the desire for mobility.

However, not unlike live television, liveness in computer systems is more ideological than ontological.[75] The sense of real-time liveness, as Chun points out, serves to "portray the computers as unmediated connectivity" and render them transparent.[76] For the media systems of digital platforms, the impression of liveness creates a feeling of immediate contact (with content, commodities, and other users), masking the mediating function of the platform (as the management and control of contact) and rendering such mediation invisible and transparent. Such is precisely the function of pseudo-simultaneity on Niconico, AcFun, and Bilibili: to immerse users directly in a virtual community that appears to be naturally alive (but is actually constructed by the platform algorithm). This illusion of immediacy and transparency, however, requires a certain degree of instantaneity: the "real-time" interface feels real "because of its quick reactions to users' input."[77] Such instantaneity is precisely what cannot be afforded by danmaku. Unlike online live chats, a comment feed on danmaku does not immediately generate instant replies. The sense of simultaneity, after all, is "pseudo." To make a transparent interface that operates in what seems to be real time, "one creates daemons."[78] Those daemons are now let loose by danmaku's nontransparent, pseudo-real time. Promising liveness but failing to sustain it with instant responses, the spectral interface of danmaku exposes hidden computational daemons (the algorithmic structures that formulate the synchronic appearance of nonsynchronic comment feeds), which are supposed to be masked to achieve illusory transparency.

For users of danmaku, the spectral temporality of this interface is not only visible but highly affective. The affective response to temporal disjunctions is sometimes expressed by users' desire to mark the actual real time, as opposed to the pseudo-real time, in their comment feeds. For instance, among Chinese users on AcFun and Bilibili, it is conventional to "mark dates" (刷日期) on danmaku, especially at the beginning of a video. They often write down the specific date and time of their viewership in their comments. Thus, it is common to see multiple comment lines that simply display dates and times over the video on screen (see Figure 15; this screenshot shows many different times marked in the danmaku comments, including August 23, 2015; June 15, 2016; and February 16, 2017). The differences among these dates and times can be minutes, hours, days, months, or even years, but they appear simultaneously on screen and are visibly juxtaposed side by side. The plain display of these diverse times in danmaku comments not only discloses the wide temporal differences among users' actual real-time experiences but also forms a sharp contrast with the alleged feeling of pseudo-simultaneity. Behind the collective experience of the virtual time of pseudo-simultaneity, there is always a strong desire to record the apparent disjunction in the actual time of nonsimultaneity.

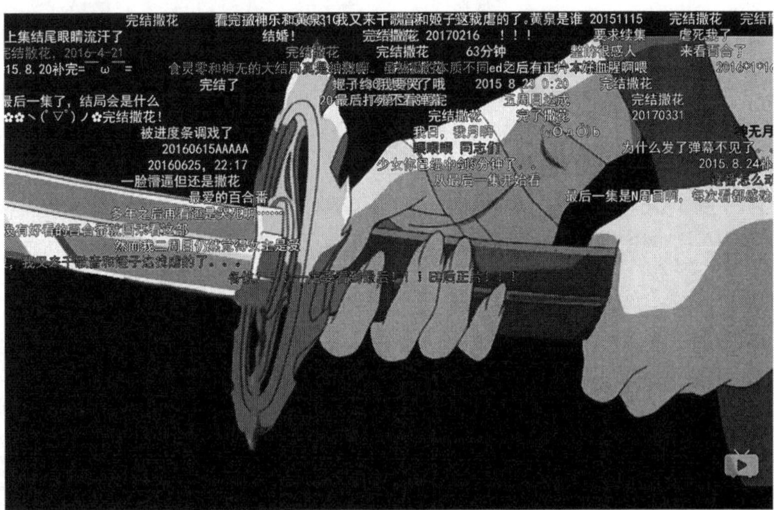

FIGURE 15. Actual viewing dates are marked in the over-the-video comments on the danmaku interface in a user-shared fansub video of *Kannazuki no Miko* (2004) on Bilibili.com.

The affective incoherence between the virtual time and the actual one is further intensified by the exaggerated sense of temporal urgency that is often generated by the speedy movement of the comment text on screen. The comments fly too fast! They rush across the screen, appearing and disappearing in seconds, "bullet time" indeed (thus the term *danmaku*—a "barrage" or "bullet curtain"). The sensation of urgency is further heightened by the fact that video platforms featuring danmaku often have an upper limit to the number of comments on display.[79] Whenever the limit is reached, older comments disappear, replaced by new comments on screen. This fleeting, vanishing nature of danmaku comments enhances the collective feeling of virtual liveness, on one hand, but it also highlights the profound unstableness of the real-time present, on the other. This instability complicates the temporal structure of danmaku communication that relies on revisit, repetition, and replay. How do you reply to a comment that may disappear tomorrow? The fear of missing or losing a piece of information (due to the speedy movement or the disappearance of comment feeds) propels users to an archival path, a quest for "historical danmaku" (历史弹幕). How to search, access, download, or archive old danmaku comments that were flushed out by the platform limitation is commonly discussed among users on Bilibili and AcFun. One Chinese user personally archived all the danmaku comments of over two hundred videos that were published at Bilibili from 2012 to 2014 and shared the entire archive on the internet.[80] Such a desire to preserve, archive, and revisit a fleeting past, interestingly, seems to be fundamentally at odds with the platforms' temporal affordances that are designed for a feeling of perpetual presentness (virtual liveness, pseudo-simultaneity, and rushing urgency). Against the platform logic of real time and liveness are users' own affective temporal ambiguity and anxiety, juggling between the simultaneous and the nonsimultaneous, between the present and the past, between the ephemeral and the archival, between the live and the spectral.

Between Knowledge and Community

The pseudo-simultaneity of the danmaku interface creates a sense of community, as it unites viewers with a collective temporal experience of simultaneous viewing, a sense of "virtual time" of liveness.[81] Because the comments have no identification attached, they seem to come from nowhere yet appear right in front of you, creating the feeling of an organic and mythical existence of a highly immersive community that is immediately present and intimately welcoming. United by knowledge sharing in the form of on-screen comments, this is largely a knowledge community, a self-organized sphere of "cosmopedia," as Pierre Lévy would call it, a site of collective discussion, negotiation, and development of information and knowledge.[82] This notion of a knowledge community, in fact, assumes mutual constitutiveness between knowledge and community: knowledge is produced and distributed as a community function through collective discussion and communication; and vice versa, community is organized as the result of a collective knowledge sphere on digital platforms, whereby knowledge sharing functions as a vehicle for communicating shared identity and sensibility.

This assumed coconstitutive synergy between knowledge and community, however, is challenged by the danmaku interface, because what is programmed and visibly displayed on this contact zone of indecision is the tension and conflict, rather than cohesion and integration, between knowledge production and its supposed community function. This tension is prominently exhibited on the platform of Bilibili by the gatekeeping mechanism that requires users to pass certain tests to enable the necessary membership to post on the danmaku interface. These tests take the form of multiple-choice exams that one can take online after logging into the platform. A registered user has to pass the exams in order to become a valid member to post and share comments on danmaku. Without taking the exam, one can only read but not post danmaku comments. In other words, in the platformed community organized by danmaku, the communication function of knowledge production and sharing is not a pregiven right but is a reward and recognition that a user has to earn by passing numerous tests of knowledge in order to prove their worth as a member of the community.

Managed by knowledge testing and evaluation, the danmaku interface, therefore, is a tightly controlled gatekeeping boundary rather than an open communication channel. It is an interface that sets up a threshold of knowledge to distinguish and manage community membership. To verify that an applicant has adequate and correct knowledge to belong to the community, danmaku membership tests are designed to be very difficult so that they can function as an effective threshold.[83] On Bilibili, for instance, the entry-level exam has fifty questions, and a user has to correctly answer thirty of them within sixty minutes in order to pass the exam. Some questions focus on the community rules of the platform, but most questions are about specialized knowledge, obscure facts, and geek trivia that are specific to transnational otaku culture, such as a plot twist in an anime series, the name of a Japanese voice actor, or a secret trick in a video game. Additionally, questions to test local zhai cultural knowledge—such as recent online phenomena, memes, or inside jokes in Chinese cyberculture—are prominently featured as well. Also included in these exams are wide arrays of questions that cover areas as broad as cult movies from Hollywood and superheroes from Marvel comics; general knowledge in math, physics, and chemistry; philosophy and critical theory from feminism to Marxism to psychoanalysis, and others (Figure 16).

Mastering such diverse and extensive knowledge, as well as passing the difficult tests, is only the minimum requirement to gain basic entry—LV1 (level 1) membership—to the community. On Bilibili, there are six different levels of membership, each requiring more tasks and more tests to access.[84] These higher-level memberships reward users with more utility and affordances in the interface function of danmaku, such as editing choices with different colors, fonts, or locations for on-screen comments, the ability to search, filter, or block certain comments, and the administrative power to organize and manage danmaku comments. In 2022, Bilibili added another level, "hardcore membership" (硬核会员), which is supposed to offer the highest level of user privilege with the danmaku interface, but it also requires the most difficult tests. The exam for gaining hardcore membership is so absurdly difficult that it became an internet sensation among Bilibili users who were trying to pass the test by learning and sharing tips online.[85] Indeed, danmaku membership tests, even the entry-level ones, are so challenging that users must go through a diligent process of learning and research in order to pass the exams and to gain the most basic communication function of the interface. To accomplish this challenging task, countless tools, services, and information packages were developed and widely distributed on Chinese cyberspace to help users prepare and pass danmaku membership tests. In other words, to communicate through the danmaku interface, one has to first train to be a hardworking knowledge worker.

If the interface, as Hookway reminds us, is always a threshold because its main function is to control and regulate rather than to mediate access, then danmaku overlaps the computational threshold of an interface function (different levels of interface affordances that are computationally programmed and controlled) with the knowledge threshold for a community function (different levels of memberships that are regulated by knowledge tests).[86] The platform attaches the knowledge tests with the danmaku interface and uses the testing results to

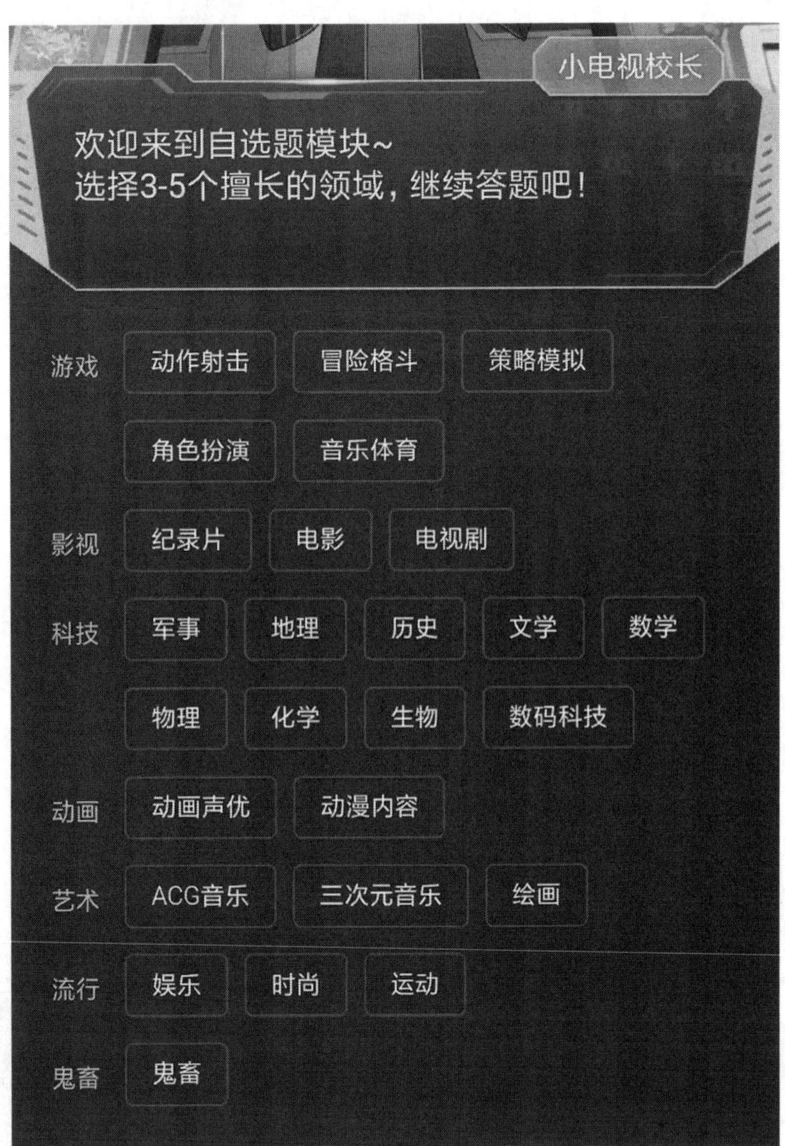

FIGURE 16. (*above*) The danmaku membership exam on Bilibili, which covers diverse fields, including anime, games, arts, film and television, science and technology, and pop culture. (*opposite page*) The sample questions that test user knowledge of anime, games, popular cinema, math, biology, and chemistry. Screen captures from https://www.bilibili.com.

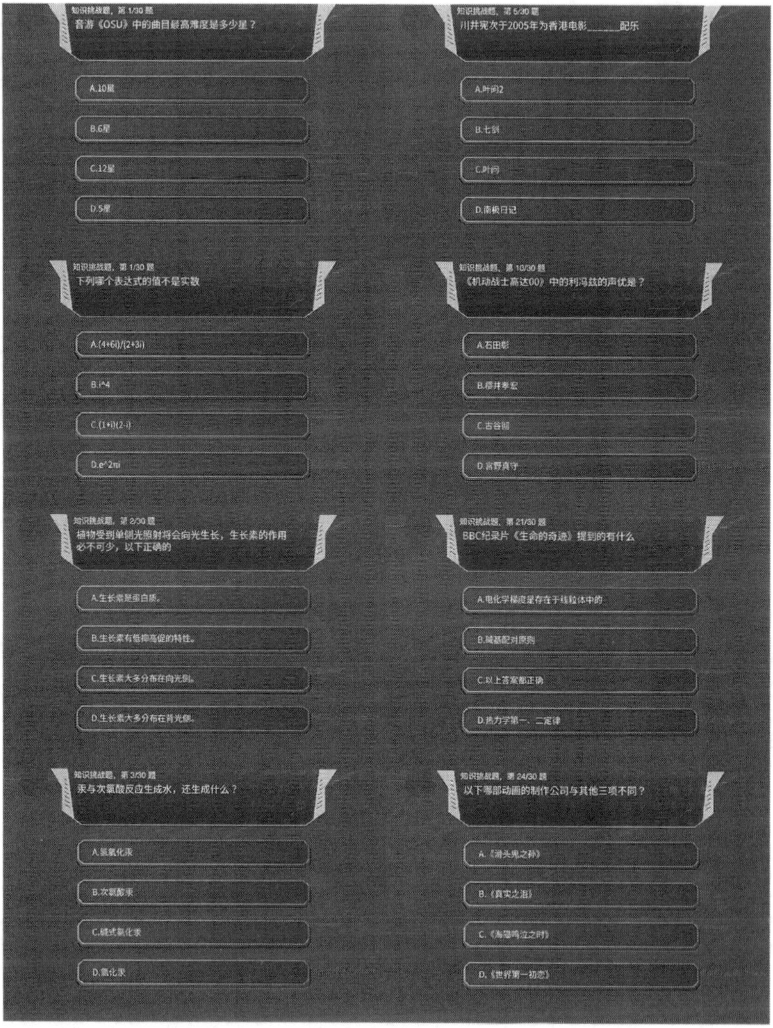

知识挑战题，第 1/30 题
音游《OSU》中的曲目最高难度是多少星？

A.10星

B.6星

C.12星

D.5星

知识挑战题，第 1/30 题
下列哪个表达式的值不是实数

A.(4+6i)/(2+3i)

B.i^4

C.(1+i)(2-i)

D.e^2πi

知识挑战题，第 2/30 题
植物受到单侧光照射将会向光生长，生长素的作用
必不可少，以下正确的

A.生长素是蛋白质。

B.生长素有低抑高促的特性。

C.生长素大多分布在向光侧。

D.生长素大多分布在背光侧。

知识挑战题，第 3/30 题
汞与次氯酸反应生成水，还生成什么？

A.氢氧化汞

B.次氯酸汞

C.桥式氯化汞

D.氯化汞

知识挑战题，第 5/30 题
川井宪次于2005年为香港电影______配乐

A.叶问2

B.七剑

C.叶问

D.南极日记

知识挑战题，第 10/30 题
《机动战士高达00》中的利冯兹的声优是？

A.石田彰

B.樱井孝宏

C.古谷彻

D.宫野真守

知识挑战题，第 21/30 题
BBC纪录片《生命的奇迹》提到的有什么

A.电化学梯度是存在于线粒体中的

B.碱基配对原则

C.以上答案都正确

D.热力学第一、二定律

知识挑战题，第 24/30 题
以下哪部动画的制作公司与其他三项不同？

A.《滑头鬼之孙》

B.《真实之泪》

C.《海猫鸣泣之时》

D.《世界第一初恋》

distinguish different levels of user privileges that are in turn algorithmically structured into different interface functions of danmaku. In order to access, or to gain a better function of, the danmaku interface on the platform, a user has to pass numerous rounds of tests. For danmaku users, therefore, the interface threshold *is* the knowledge threshold, and vice versa.

In a digital economy that relies on informational knowledge as its primary production material, this divisive knowledge threshold that is programmed by the interface threshold serves to encode and sustain the internal hierarchy and the external privilege of the geek community. The double threshold on danmaku thus reflects and reinforces broader socioeconomic inequality and disparity within and without the knowledge class in information capitalism, whereby knowledge is not a common good to be shared but is a valuable asset that generates distinction, division, and hierarchy. This contentious contact between the encoded inequality in knowledge production and consumption on the danmaku interface versus the supposed egalitarian ideal in the formation of a geek community exposes the fundamental contradiction between knowledge and community in platform-based anime geekdom. On one hand, the knowledge threshold, like many geek codes or otaku references, effectively sets up a gatekeeping mechanism to maintain the integrity and cohesiveness of a subcultural community. On the other hand, the overlap between the threshold of subculture knowledge and that of a platform interface, which is programmed with the technological structure of algorithmic control and sorting, inevitably translates the logic of platformativity, with its inherent mechanism to distinguish and discriminate, to that of a knowledge community. On digital platforms, user communication is a valuable product that has to be tightly managed, organized, and sorted through the centralizing mechanism of data processing, despite the decentralizing tendency in user participation, because communicative information needs to be algorithmically structured for monetization. Such contradicting directions between centralization and decentralization, between monetizable distinctions and egalitarian ideals, are programmed into the tension between knowledge and community on the danmaku interface. The knowledge community of a cosmopedia, as Lévy envisions, is supposed to be organized by "universally distributed intelligence," a knowledge space that is deterritorialized and distributive.[87] The knowledge threshold on the danmaku interface, however, is rather produced, structured, and sustained via rigorous testing and mandatory learning, and it is enforced, validated, and managed by a computerized interface on a digital platform. When knowledge is produced through gatekeeping exams organized by a platform interface, the supposedly distributed knowledge sphere is recentralized. Thus, what used to be the playful and voluntary practices of producing and sharing fan/fun facts, geek trivia, and inside tricks, such as the hidden plot twist of an anime or the obscure name of a voice actor, now become a well-structured and well-managed system of knowledge work that one has to follow and be tested meticulously in order to communicate in the community. As such, the knowledge community of danmaku turns out to be neither universal nor distributed but is formed and managed by elitist intellectual gatekeeping that uses knowledge as the currency between economic and sociocultural capital.

In sum, in the community organized by the danmaku interface, knowledge production and sharing are not simply to generate collective discussion and communication. Instead, knowledge is produced to set up a distinguished threshold of membership, overlapping with that of a programmed interface on the platform, which recentralizes the control of a distributive cultural field for platform management with monetizable difference and hierarchy. Shifting from distributive sharing to centralized testing, from communication to control, knowledge production and consumption in the danmaku community generate more affective anxiety than communicative cohesion. Indeed, the "fear of being controlled" (被支配的恐惧) is one of the common themes among user discussions about the danmaku membership exams.[88] Some describe this fear as "frantic" (疯狂) and others admit it was a "moment of collapse" (崩溃).[89] Such a fear of being controlled, which characterizes the interface affect of the knowledge-interface threshold of danmaku, demonstrates a sharp contrast with the assumed openness and distributiveness of a participatory community that is organized by knowledge sharing. In this community, knowledge is not so much a communication vehicle as a controlling mechanism, and control is operated through the interface threshold of danmaku overlapping with a knowledge threshold.

Affective Contact and Transnational Otaku/Zhai Culture in East Asia

The knowledge community organized by the danmaku interface is largely regional, because it is shaped by the transnational/transmedial processes driven by the regional dissemination of otaku culture through the expansion of distribution platforms in East Asia. The Chinese zhai users of danmaku identify with a transnational framework of otaku culture that emerged from a regional geography of media infrastructures (e.g., television, pirated videos, and online platforms), and thus they borrow a Japanese term from a type of Japanese game to describe an interface design that comes from a Japanese platform. This transnational otaku culture is the result of media regionalism that has emerged in a context in which the production of media networks precedes the production of content.[90] However, what produces the sense of virtual unity in the transnational otaku/zhai community is not simply the proliferation of networked platforms (Niconico, Bilibili, and AcFun) but the logic of platformativity encoded in the danmaku interface. Japanese otaku users of Niconico and Chinese zhai users of Bilibili have a similar experience of danmaku, which unites them and produces "a feeling of something coming into common, of a region in common."[91]

This sense of transnational media regionalism, however, depends less on the homogeneity than the gaps between and within media infrastructures, which leads to feelings that "serve to erase and mask the discrepancies between infrastructures, or on the contrary, to reveal and exacerbate them."[92] These feelings make the transnational media geography between Chinese zhai culture and Japanese otaku culture highly affective, because they hinge upon the experience of both proximity and distance. The danmaku interface is a contact zone that generates such affective intensity of the regional map between otaku and zhai cultures because the dynamic contact on danmaku promises both connectivity and gaps. This unique interface instantiates both convergence (media mix) and contradiction between different media logics (demonstrated in the case of danmaku cinema). It affords both pseudo-simultaneity and disjunction in its temporal structure. And it exposes and manages the tension between knowledge and community through its challenging membership tests. The user experience of these discrepancies can be described in affective terms because it generates feelings that remain "unactualized, inseparable but unassimilable to any *particular,* functionally anchored perspective."[93] Therefore, danmaku is the interface that operates as an affective contact zone. As such, it provides an affective mapping of the transnational media geography of anime geekdom in East Asia. It maps the flow of affect that produces a sense of a regional otaku/zhai culture in common and in disjunction, a feeling of transnational/transmedial contact that evokes both intimacy and distance.

PART II

THE MEDIA ENVIRONMENT OF ANIME

4

The Mecha-Child

Myth, Innervation, and Techno-Intimacy

Why does anime appeal to millennial geeks, otaku, and *zhai*? How does anime organize the knowledge culture of global geekdom? To answer these questions, we need to look at anime not simply as a media object but as a condition of mediation, a transmedia environment with certain structures, patterns, motifs, and aesthetic forms that are synergetic with an expanding techno-culture of knowledge work that is marked by cybernetic logics, informationalized connectivity, and digitalized production and consumption.[1] In this chapter, I will begin theorizing anime as a media environment for knowledge culture by first examining a popular motif in anime that I call the "mecha-child." The trope of the mecha-child unfolds through intimate assimilation and identification between fictional child characters (including teenagers and adolescents) and mecha (machines, robots, and cyborgs). This assimilation is established through anime's unique aesthetic forms of cuteness and animatedness, which mediate the mimetic identification between the child and the mecha. The animated mecha-child, who is a mythical figure with perpetual youth and creativity, serves as an ideal vehicle of identification for geeks, who are also widely perceived in popular imagination as childish but creative figures with valuables skills for a techno-economy that is endowed with the mythical temporality of eternal recurrence and renewal. In other words, geeks are the mecha-children, for whom the cybernetic logic of human–machine integration is not only normalized as ubiquitous and indispensable but also fetishized as therapeutic and empowering.

More importantly, this popular trope of the mecha-child serves as a central modality to form a strong semantic/affective field of techno-intimacy. Informed by Walter Benjamin's thesis on mimetic innervation in relation to children's play, this chapter analyzes the ways in which the mecha-child imagination produces the milieu of techno-intimacy to internalize the material and symbolic structure of information technology to the daily habitat of knowledge work as both familiar and fantastic, both intimate and cool. This field of techno-intimacy decenters human subjects toward mutual integration with cybernetic machines, dislocating an intrasubjectivity of knowledge work that is branded as the "second self."[2] This chapter further argues that the sense of techno-intimacy has increasingly become a dominant cultural logic that is adopted by a wide range of techno-cultural forms that translate technological portability and immediacy to a structure of intimate feelings. The mythical figure of the mecha-child is a crucial component in a broad and forceful aesthetic system, which collaboratively evokes the sense of techno-intimacy as the prevailing cultural voice of information capitalism.

The Mecha-Child

Mecha (メカ) is a Japanese term for "machines." It often refers to both a popular subgenre of anime featuring giant robots and a broad science-fiction motif about robots, cyborgs, machines, and future technology in general.[3] As either a subgenre or a motif, mecha characterizes some of the most iconic anime, such as *Astro Boy, Gundam,* and *Neon Genesis Evangelion,* which aligns the historical rise of anime as a globally popular form with that of science fiction. Since the 1980s, with the advent of computer technology, science fiction has captured popular imaginations and become a dominant genre in both cinema and literature. It is no accident that anime began to gain international popularity at the precise moment when the sci-fi genre became a prominent form. The global otaku movement, incidentally, developed from sci-fi clubs in Japan and elsewhere. What further aligns anime with the global sci-fi wave is cyberpunk, a literary and cinematic subgenre that is heavily indebted to the iconography of a futurist Japan, which paved the way for appreciation of anime as part of a futuristic imagination of "Pax Japonica." As Takayuki Tatsumi points out, the compelling vision of a futuristic Japan in cyberpunk "could not help but refresh the Japanese sense of reality."[4] It influenced a wave of Japanese writers and artists to synthesize their own imagination of a futuristic Japan as popular iconography in anime and manga.[5] Although cyberpunk helps position anime in a familiar canon, anime is notable for its significant departure from Western sci-fi conventions. Often labeled "tech-noir," cyberpunk films occupy a transgenre intersection between science fiction and film noir, in which technology is envisioned as dystopian doom for future dwellers. Anime, in contrast, is often more cute than noirish. In anime, technology is rarely cast as completely dark or dystopian but is rather ubiquitous and indispensable, and the technological mecha is often quite adorable and delightful, be it a sweet home companion in *Doraemon* (1973), a computerized girlfriend in *Chobits* (2002), or a toylike armor in *Gurren Lagann* (2007).

Anime's delightful and cute representation of technological ubiquity is largely due to its association of mecha with fictional child characters in a recurrent motif that I call the "mecha-child." This fictional figure does not simply incorporate techno-fantasies into children's everyday lives, but it also establishes a close assimilation between the child and the mecha as a human–machine integration that is imagined as cute, innocent, and adorable. Popular schemas of the mecha-child include: child characters as technological beings, such as robots, cyborgs, or AI (e.g., Astro Boy); anthropomorphic machines with childlike features (e.g., Doraemon); and children who rely on the physical and psychological integration with mecha as the foundation of their fictional existence (e.g., mecha pilots in *Gundam*). Through these schemas, the child and the mecha establish mutual identification with each other.

The character typology of the mecha-child represents the furthest departure of anime from cyberpunk conventions. Rooted in hard-boiled detective fiction, a typical cyberpunk hero is an urban adult male with a dark past and a bitter worldview. In sharp contrast, a typical anime hero is a cute, innocent figure of the mecha-child whose posthuman state is closely integrated with futuristic technologies. Memorable mecha-children include the powerful psychic children in *Akira* (1988), the group of teenage mecha pilots in *Neon Genesis Evangelion* (1995), the mysterious cyborg schoolgirl in *Serial Experiments Lain* (1998), and the teams of child soldiers piloting giant robots in the *Gundam* series. Even in the most adult-driven anime, the mecha-child still occupies a significant position. In *Ghost in the Shell,* the mecha-child imagination is highlighted by the film's ambivalent ending, in which the adult female protagonist, Major Motoko Kusanagi, transforms to the body of a little girl when she eventually integrates with artificial intelligence. Becoming a posthuman being, the adult character transforms to a mecha-child. In fact, the motif of the mecha-child is so central for a posthuman imagination that *The Sky Crawlers,* a transmedia franchise including light novels, manga, games, and anime, specifically identifies its main characters as "Kildren," a group of fighter pilots who are genetically engineered to be perpetually adolescent.

By centering on the mecha-child, the futuristic imagination in anime is never completely dark or dystopian; even in the gloomiest cases, there is a strong sense of innocence and cuteness. The tech-noir sensibilities of cyberpunk are thus displaced by anime's childish renderings. In *Serial Experiments Lain* (1998), for instance, the central character, Lain, evokes a noir reading as a femme fatale even though she is only a teenage schoolgirl. Like a typical femme fatale, her mysterious past calls for a cinematic gaze and a narrative investigation, and her supernatural power in "the Wired" poses a serious threat to this otherwise male-dominated virtual world. As mysterious and powerful as she is, Lain is portrayed as such a wide-eyed, childish, and sometimes helpless little girl that her femme-fatale quality is overshadowed by her youthful naivete. Eventually revealed as a child born in the Wired, she is the embodiment of network technology—that is, the mecha-child. The cyberspace embodied by this mecha-child, though often linked to malice, never loses its sense of innocence, because of this baby-faced, cute little girl whose naivete and fragility never fail to gain our sympathy. This ambivalence between femme-fatale malevolence and childish innocence is illustrated by the series' ending credits sequence where, in a continuous zooming-out shot, Lain is sleeping naked in a womb of wires like a newborn baby.

A mecha-child version of the femme fatale is also exemplified in the anime film *Metropolis* (dir. Rintaro, 2001). Loosely based on the original manga by Osamu Tezuka (the creator of *Astro Boy*) and scripted by Katsuhiro Otomo (the writer/director of *Akira*), this anime version of *Metropolis* is also indebted to Fritz Lang's 1928 German expressionist film of the same title. Precisely because of such a connection, the anime's striking departure from Lang's modernist imagination catches our attention. In Lang's *Metropolis,* the heroine, Maria, is a young adult woman with two identities: one is a real human being with good virtues and the other is an evil robot replica who leads the whole city into riots. But in the anime version, there is only one "Maria," the female robot named Tima, who is portrayed as a harmless little girl until she eventually unleashes uncontrollable power when connected to a central machine. Somewhat a prototype of tech-noir, Lang's *Metropolis* features robot-Maria as a typical femme fatale with mysterious deadly power hidden underneath. The mecha-child Tima in the anime, in contrast, never loses her sympathetic innocence even after her monstrous transformation: we see her tears of pain as she is torn apart by her own destructive power. Whereas robot-Maria in Lang's *Metropolis* embodies the dark side of technology with the "otherness" of her female body that signifies castration fear, the high-tech world embodied by the mecha-child Tima is more ambivalent.[6] As destructive as it is, the moment of climax, when Tima rises to power, feels oddly exciting: with exhilarating music, her face looks up, hair swinging in the wind, like a rising sun. Compared with the iconic image of the cold, metallic female body in Lang's German expressionist vision, the babyish, illuminating face of Tima feels strikingly positive and even hopeful (Figure 17). Overall, the anime version of *Metropolis* departs greatly from Lang's original tech-noir with a peculiar mixture of juvenile innocence and cybernetic exhilaration in the figure of the mecha-child, which puts technology on a far more ambivalent ground than Lang's dystopian vision.

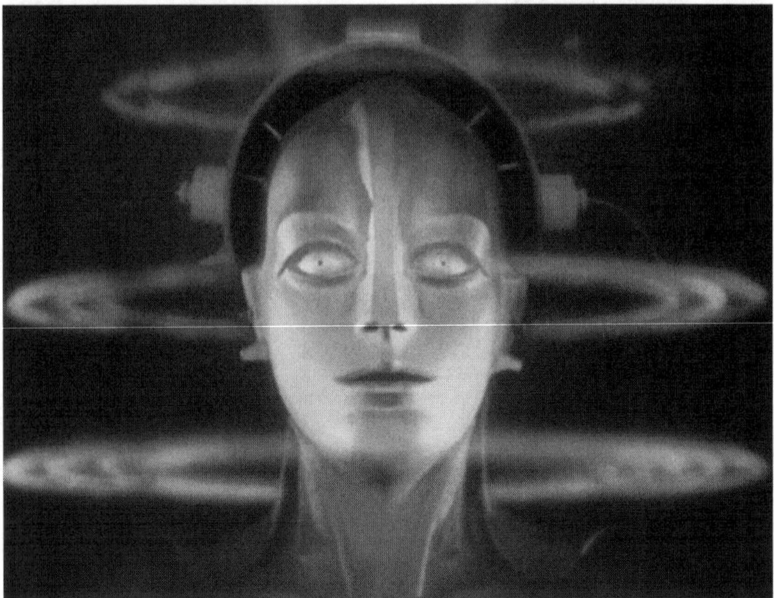

FIGURE 17. The mecha-child Tima in the anime film *Metropolis* (*top*) compared with the adult female robot-Maria in the German film *Metropolis* (*bottom*).

But children do not necessarily guarantee a safe ground of innocence. We know too well the evil-seed motif popularized by horror movies such as *The Omen* (1976), *The Exorcist* (1973), and *Rosemary's Baby* (1968). These monster kids, according to Robin Wood, highlight the repressed Otherness of children in our society.[7] Susan Napier also remarks on this notion of repression in her characterization of the destructive teenage character in *Akira* (1988) as "the monstrous adolescent."[8] Indeed, many mecha-children in anime can be described as monstrous—the cyber junkie in *Lain*, the destructive cyborg in *Metropolis*, and grotesque Tetsuo in *Akira*. However, unlike the evil youths in horror movies, the mecha-children in anime are never completely sinister and they rarely lose our sympathy even in the most monstrous state. Like Tima in *Metropolis*, Tetsuo in *Akira* is also depicted as a hapless victim destroyed by his own monstrous body. At the final apocalyptic moment, his desperate screaming and yearning for help are as memorable as his horrifying body transformation. The film's ending is also quite ambivalent: Akira and Tetsuo, two mecha-children whose destructive superpower leads to the apocalypse, are pictured in a dreamy flashback as sweet, shy, and harmless little boys smiling to the audience. When represented as the mecha-child, technology in anime, even in its most monstrous, dystopian scenarios, still has a peculiar sense of hope, renewal, and sweetness.

Because of the centrality of the mecha-child, anime generally adopts quite different settings from tech-noirs. Whereas cyberpunks often inhabit a dark labyrinth of urban chaos, mecha-children usually live in the mundane, everyday settings of school and family. Borrowing Mikhail Bakhtin's concept of the "chronotope" to designate the spatiotemporal junction in narrative, I argue that cyberpunk and anime are marked by their different chronotopes.[9] The chronotope of cyberpunk is characterized by the strong tension between "high-tech" and "low life"—a stunning futuristic vision set in a decaying urban dungeon: junky gutters, dark alleys, trashy motels, and smoky, poorly lit nightclubs.[10] Typifying such a chronotope of dystopian urban anguish, Scott Bukatman describes the cityscape in *Blade Runner* (1982) as an infernal city: "with its flame-belching towers, it has become an almost literal Inferno."[11]

Compared with such a dark, chaotic urban space of an infernal city, the mecha-children in anime inhabit the chronotope of a high-tech-infused everyday adolescent life: the orderly classrooms at school and the tidy domestic space at home. Although a dystopian city may still be represented as a prevalent setting, it appears to be far less chaotic than familiar, even with giant robots fighting in the background. In *Neon Genesis Evangelion*, for instance, despite the fantastic settings of an apocalyptic future, the story mostly unfolds around the characters' ordinary teenage life struggling with school, friends, and family while training as mecha pilots in a not-so-fantastic cityscape of Tokyo-3. Similarly, in *Serial Experiment Lain*, the chronotope largely centers on Lain's daily routines. Traveling between the classroom and the living room, Lain's chronotope repeats the pattern of a typical schoolgirl's mundane everyday life, which is miles apart from the cyberpunk iconography of urban chaos.

In fact, most anime, with or without mecha, can be classified as "teenpics" (teen pictures), as their narratives largely center on teenage lives.[12] Combining futuristic imagination with teenpic conventions, anime embeds techno-fantasies within the chronotope of everyday teen life, representing technology as an integral part of the adolescent daily routine, normalizing and domesticating it as inhabitable, adorable, and even indispensable. Centered on a twelve-year-old boy named Naota, the anime series *FLCL* (2000) exemplifies such integration between techno-fantasies and teenage stories in its mecha-child narrative. Mostly focused on Naota's relationship with two girls, the story is a typical coming-of-age romance, which is nevertheless spiced up by the cute, powerful robot coming from Naota's head and the mysterious alien maid in his household. These imaginary mecha figures, though often portrayed as troublemakers, are safely contained within the ordinary domestic space of a teenage life. As integral parts of the child's existence, the mecha figures are exotic and fantasized, on one hand, but are harmless and habitual, on the other. In a similar fashion, the popular multimedia franchise *Science Adventure* (2008–present) represents fantastic "science adventures" almost entirely within the familiar chronotope of a teenage life. In *Steins;Gate* (2009–11), the second installment of the franchise, a powerful time machine turns out to be a household microwave. In *Robotics;Notes* (2012–13), the third installment, the story is less about the mystery of robotic science than about friendship and romance in a high school setting.

Integrating techno-fantasies with everyday familiarity, the mecha-child imagination blurs the boundary between technological life and teenage life. This is precisely the case in *Serial Experiments Lain,* where the boundary between the virtual world of the Wired and the real world of the everyday increasingly dissolves as the story unfolds. At the beginning, the separation between the chronotope of cyberspace and that of real life is evidently visualized by the spatial disjunction in Lain's home: the tidy, brightly lit living room with nice furniture represents an ordinary domestic space, while Lain's dark, dungeon-like bedroom full of wires signifies the murky space of the Wired. When the mecha-child Lain, in cute teddy-bear sleepwear, walks through the bright living room into her dark bedroom, we follow her journey from the real world to the virtual one. However, the division is just a single door, which is slowly dissolved as the story goes on. When it is eventually revealed that Lain's seemingly ordinary teenage life is an artificial construction, her domestic space overlaps with the dark dungeon of cyberspace. For the mecha-child, the techno-fantasy of the Wired is indistinguishable from the everyday familiarity of the teenagers.

The posthuman integration between technology and daily life has been explored by many sci-fi films, including *Videodrome* (1983) and *The Matrix* (1999) in the West as well as *Tetsuo: The Iron Man* (1989) in Japan. Compared to these famous tech-noirs that represent human–machine integration as grotesque and threatening, the mecha-child trope in anime often normalizes or even fetishizes the feelings of posthuman existence. For instance, in both *The Matrix* and *Serial Experiments Lain,* the imagery of wires is a significant visual motif representing the cybernetic world. However, contrary to the horrifying images of those dark, monstrous wires in *The Matrix,* wires in *Lain* are portrayed as familiar, ubiquitous, and mundane components of everyday environments—electric wires, telephone cords, and computer cables, all of which are common household items. The familiar images of everyday objects render the imaginary world of the mecha-child as ordinary, relatable, and inhabitable, and the human–machine integration is thus normalized as part of ordinary daily reality. In a similar fashion, the tendency toward familiarity marks the key difference between *FLCL* and *Videodrome,* though both imagine media technology permeating the human body. Whereas *Videodrome* is famous for its gory imagery of grotesque body transformation that is indebted to body horror, the scenarios in which the robot emerges from Naota's forehead in *FLCL* are portrayed as enjoyably hilarious and fascinating, thanks to the series' generally lighthearted undertone and its familiar settings of teen life. Unlike the adult protagonist's nightmarish terror in *Videodrome,* the teenager Naota in *FLCL* does not seem bothered by his own bodily transformation and is generally at ease with various technological beings coming out of his brain. As Brian Ruh points out, "Through its fun and frenetic animated styles, *FLCL* takes a much less dour attitude toward media technologies."[13] Indeed, contrary to *Videodrome*'s dramatized paranoia about media invasion, *FLCL* takes the posthuman condition as a given norm. If the tech-noir convention envisions technological permeation as a threatening, dystopian doom, the mecha-child trope rather fashions human–machine integration as a welcoming condition in daily realities.

For the mecha-child, the infusion with machines is not only normalized as an indispensable part of teenage life but is also demanded as a necessary supplement for what is lacking in troubled adolescence. For Lain, the Wired world seems a better alternative than her otherwise plain, insecure, and largely alienated teenage life. Similarly, the mecha-child story in *Neon Genesis Evangelion* converges technological fantasy with adolescent anxiety. The main character, Shinji, a gloomy, introverted teenager who suffers a strong sense of insecurity after being abandoned by his father, gains his confidence and comfort from a gigantic mecha that he somehow pilots skillfully. The mecha, which has the symbolic maternal name "EVA," plays a significant role in Shinji's coming-of-age journey. Designed by his diseased mother and claimed to contain part of her soul, EVA functions as a substitute mother figure that is absent in Shinji's life. The maternal relationship between EVA and Shinji is established when this painfully unconfident boy mysteriously gains superpowers when sitting inside the belly of EVA. The moment when unconscious Shinji is ejected from EVA as a little boy immersed in liquid is reminiscent of a birth scene.[14]

Overall, the mecha genre, which pictures children encapsulated within mecha armor, seems a Freudian reenactment of the infantile fantasy of returning to a primitive state in the mother's womb. Freud associates this infantile complex with the feeling of the uncanny.[15] Indeed, the mecha-child motif often appears uncanny, as in the cases of *Evangelion* and *Lain,* as if integrating with machines inevitably returns humans to an infantile state, the primal source of the uncanny. In his comparison between the sublime and the uncanny, Bukatman observes that while the sublime is often aligned with the gigantic in the cosmic distance, the uncanny is associated with the miniature, the ordinary, and the domestic in "the childhood home." The uncanny, therefore, "is an altogether more proximate and intimate phenomenon."[16] Enclosing the human–machine relationship in the ordinary chronotope of teenage domesticity ("the childhood home"), the mecha-child imagination operates in the realm of the techno-uncanny by returning to a perpetual state of the infantile and the intimate. But we may ask: What is the collective psychic behind this infantile fantasy of the techno-uncanny? Why are we attracted to the fantastic yet familiar stories of these mecha-children? What are the meanings and feelings involved in imagining a perpetual state of the infantile and the intimate through the fictional figure of the mecha-child?

The Geek Myth: From the Perpetual Adolescent to the Creative Child

At first glance, there seems to be nothing unusual about the mecha-child motif in anime, because animation is believed to be an entertainment form for children. Paul Wells claims that "the very language of animation seems to carry with it an inherent innocence which has served to disguise and dilute the potency of some of its more daring imagery."[17] Pertaining to the inherent childishness that is claimed to be associated with animation, anime often features more complex narratives and weighty themes. The teenage stories unfolded in anime such as *Akira, FLCL, Serial Experiments Lain,* and *Evangelion* address real-life adolescent problems including teenage alienation, sexual anxiety, and identity fragmentation, all of which are also involved with technological situations in information society.[18] The mecha-child imagination not only provides an allegorical map to interrogate teenagers' changing "cyborg" bodies and fragmented identities, but it also echoes the general perception that adolescents are eager adopters of technological change. From this perspective, the animated images of the mecha-children are in tune with the real-life situations of today's teenagers who immerse themselves in a web of techno-gadgets such as iPhones, iPads, Nintendo, and so on.

However, the cultural significance of the mecha-child goes far beyond its adolescent appeal. The fictional child figures, I would argue, have less to do with actual youths (though they may be identifiable by young audiences) than with a constructed mythology that connects the national allegory of Japan to the transnational movement of geekdom. The mecha-child is a mythical figure. It is historically rooted in postwar Japan as a national allegory, but it eventually became a global myth of perpetual adolescence and creativity that came to be associated with the knowledge labor of millennial geeks. The mecha-child imagination, therefore, functions as a mythical vehicle of identification for the intrasubjectivity of postindustrial knowledge work, a myth of technologically empowered perpetual youth and renewal.

To understand this myth of the mecha-child, let us begin by tracing its historical lineage to *Astro Boy* (1963). In fact, the robot girl Tima in *Metropolis* looks strikingly similar to Astro Boy (they are both created by Osamu Tezuka), reminding us of anime's long-existing legacy of imagining mecha-children. As Japan's first TV anime that generated tremendous popularity and cultural impact both domestically and worldwide, *Astro Boy* crystallizes a powerful myth "about national rebirth, reconstruction, and reindustrialization" in postwar Japan.[19] Perpetually a child who never grows up, Astro Boy and his techno-power, as Anne

Allison points out, are effectively tamed "by cuteness and innocence that forever identity him as kid." As such, Astro Boy not only serves as an enchanting symbol of Japan's newborn identity in the postwar era—a young superpower with technological advancement emerging from the atomic ash—but he also "personifies the cyberfrontier as nonthreatening, uplifting and bright."[20]

Identifying with the innocent cuteness of the mecha-child successfully created a utopian myth of technological empowerment and renewal that came to redefine Japan's sense of self. But this national allegory is not always optimistic. Artist Takashi Murakami once branded Japan's superflat art with an aptly titled exhibition called *Little Boy,* identifying both the nation and its otaku subculture as the "little boy." Unlike the utopian fable of Astro Boy, Murakami's "little boy" expresses an ambivalent gesture toward nuclear technology by identifying Japan, the defeated victim, with the victimizer: the atomic bomb dropped in WWII is also code-named "Little Boy." Critiquing Murakami's willful omission of Japan's own history of wartime aggression and militarism, Thomas Lamarre points out the problematic logics in the "little boy" imagination: "While constrained to remain boys under the security umbrella of 'manly' American military-industrial power, little boy otaku found solace in a two-folded attachment, at once to childhood and the objects associated with it (toys, anime, manga, games, dolls) and to the power of military technology."[21] By conflating the national identity with its otaku culture, as well as by identifying both with permanent children (little boys) and children's culture (anime and manga), Murakami's "little boy" projects Japan to an untenable state of arrested development. As Japanese anime director Hideaki Anno (who directed *Neon Genesis Evangelion*) sarcastically comments: "We are a country of children."[22]

Taken as a symbol for Japan's national identity, the little-boy otaku, however, is not always Japanese. Neither is the anxiety about the lack of adulthood an exclusively Japanese symptom. Like otaku in Japan, geeks throughout the world are imagined as perpetual children who never grow up (thus the "fanboys") and whose preferred cultural entertainment—including comics, animation, video games, superhero movies, and collectible toy figures—are all considered "childish." In an article titled "The Death of Adulthood in American Culture," film critic A. O. Scott observes that American popular culture is increasingly focused on appealing to the "man-child" who lives in perpetual adolescence, which led to the "erosion of traditional adulthood in any form." He complains "that nobody knows how to be a grown-up anymore. Adulthood as we have known it has become conceptually untenable."[23] In China, zhai culture is also widely perceived, and sometimes criticized, as an "infantilization of adulthood," whereby the zhai generation prefers being enclosed in the "healing" (治愈) environment of childhood and refuses to grow up.[24] To a large degree, the sense of childishness has become a prominent label for postindustrial knowledge work and culture. So much so that the trillion-dollar IT industry that is run by technological geeks is widely imagined as a juvenile club that needs adult supervision: "Is It Time for More Adult Supervision at Facebook?" was a news headline in the *New York Times* in 2018, and "Adult Supervision Is Back at Google" was another one in 2015.[25]

Given this prevailing imagination that associates geeks with children, the appeal of the mecha-child in anime is probably less to actual teenagers than to this larger audience of geek men-children, the little-boy otaku whose desire is "to wallow in (his own) immaturity, plumbing its depths and reveling in its pleasures."[26] And these geeky, childish pleasures are largely mediated through information technologies of various kinds. By integrating machines with children and their daily lives, anime's distinctive imaginary of the mecha-child satisfies as much the childish sensibilities of geeks as their fascination with technological engagement, mediation, and immersion. In other words, anime enables geeks to imagine themselves as mecha-children, for whom the cybernetic logic of human–machine integration is both fantastic and familiar, both empowering and habitual.

But what makes geeks, otaku, and zhai so deeply connected with such an imaginary figure of a perpetual child who refuses to grow up? Maybe it is because of an idealized notion of childhood as spontaneous, playful, imaginative, and, ultimately, creative. After all, these little-boy otaku are also the proud members of the so-called creative class.

The association between childhood and creativity is manifested by an idealized conceptualization of the "creative child," which, according to Amy Ogata, was constructed and disseminated in the postwar era when a romanticized image of childhood as "natural" and "innocent" began to be conflated with a mythologized and commodified notion of creativity as a new productive force.[27] The invention of the creative child was the result of a historical process of postindustrialization that promised to transform capitalistic economy from manufacture to "creativity," whereby "creativity has become the default 'answer' to social and economic problems."[28] The imagination of an innocent child who is endowed with natural creativity projects a strong sense of nascent optimism to a new "creative future" of postindustrial capitalism. As Ogata says: "The value of individual perception, the unquestioned belief in innovation, and the idealized future many imagined the next generation would enjoy all shaped the image of the creative child as an authentic figure of hopefulness."[29] If Astro Boy fashions a utopian fable of national rebirth and reconstruction with techno-superpower, the creative child crystallizes a romanticized myth of postindustrial knowledge work that is idealized with childlike curiosity and authentic creativity.

To a large extent, the little-boy otaku is imagined as a creative child with a genuine sense of playfulness and innovativeness. Okada Toshio, the self-claimed "otaking," once celebrated otaku as "new human type" (*shinjinrui*) with an "evolved sense of vision."[30] Otaku is believed to be an active creator of a personalized techno-fantasy with productive cultural entities such as fanzines, fan art, cosplay, and garage kits. The fictional worlds of the mecha-child in anime mirror this idealized image of otaku as the creative child: from those talented child soldiers who are naturally skilled at piloting mecha robots in the *Gundam* series, to the orphan boys who imaginatively combine an abandoned drill, a mecha head, and robot armor into a deadly weapon in *Gurren Lagann* (which echoes the common otaku activity of assembling toy figures through garage kits), to the teenagers who innovatively turn everyday objects into robots and time machines in the *Science Adventure* series. Anime features a rich collection of creative children who are resourceful, playful, and visionary and who are naturally and intuitively good at reading manuals, playing with mechanical things, experimenting with new ideas, and solving technical problems.

The imaginary of the creative child is largely a mythical construction. The child archetype in myth, according to Carl Jung, "describes a certain psychic experience of a creative nature, whose object is the emergence of a new and as yet unknown content."[31] It is the content of the whole, the circle of both beginning and end, "a symbol of the creative union of opposites."[32] The child thus symbolizes synthesis, creation, renewal, and reconciliation. Or, as Friedrich Nietzsche puts it: "The child is innocence and forgetting, a new beginning, a game, a self-propelling wheel, a first movement, a sacred 'Yes.'"[33] Nietzsche's notion of becoming a child, as Stanley Cavell points out, is also associated with "the achievement of a new vision of time, or a new stance toward it, an acceptance of Eternal Recurrence."[34]

Is not this new vision of time, the "Eternal Recurrence" running in circles, precisely the engine—the "self-propelling wheel"—that drives both the "creative economy" and anime's media mix? The economy relies on constantly reworking and rebranding the old into the new (e.g., iPhone 1, 2, 3, etc.). The media mix system centers on never-ending narrative cycles to spring endless content and products across an ever-increasing number of media types (e.g., manga, anime, games, novels, toys, and internet videos). The whole notion of an "ecosystem," as both a business model in the new economy and an operational logic of media mix, relies on the metaphorical structure of a circular flow. In fact, the temporal structure of endless cycling loops—the "Eternal Recurrence"—has become a guiding principle in both media organization and economic operation in postindustrialism, and the child is the ideal symbol, the central motif, and the driving force for this discourse of perpetual renewal and recurrence. To belong to such a new economy and media mix system, one has to become and remain the creative child (e.g., otaku, geek, zhai) and to accept this mythic vision of time running in circles. As Allison points out about the cultural logic of cool Japan and its media mix, "This is a cultural logic that extends the category of youth to everyone," no matter whether that "youth" is real or constructed.[35]

This perpetual youth is also imagined as an infinite source of labor, whereby the joyful play of the creative child is translated to the productive labor of the knowledge worker. Indeed, the mecha-children in anime, from the cyborg soldiers in *The Sky Crawlers* to the mecha pilots in *Evangelion*, are largely portrayed as child workers, whose perpetual youth is a valuable labor source that is paradoxically both precious and limitless. To work as a mecha operator, the child cannot, and is not allowed to, grow up because only children can pilot mecha. The mecha-children's inability to grow up is specifically tied to their intimate work with the machines, and their perpetual youth is the source of labor for endless (and shameless) exploitation by the adult world. Therefore, it is no wonder that geeks and otaku are imagined as forever children who never grow up. Caught in the circular time of postindustrial economies, and exploited as a boundless labor source of creative play as productive work, knowledge workers are not supposed to grow up. Their perpetual youthfulness serves to sustain the cultural and economic logics of postindustrial capitalism, which relies on this imaginary creative child as both a never-ending mythical inspiration and a never-aging labor force—"a self-propelling wheel"—to drive endless reproduction, renewal, and "Eternal Recurrence." When time collapses upon itself in the circular temporality of media mix, of digital economy, and of the eternal now of the perpetual "newness" (new economy, new media, new class, etc.), there is no outside, no growing up. Living in the circular system of information machines, we are all Murakami's "little boys," the mecha-children running in the endless cycles of cybernetic loops.

Techno-Intimacy: Cuteness, Animatedness, and Mimetic Innervation

The creative child is to be immersed with playful gadgets, for the sensory engagement with objects and playthings, according to Ogata, is central to the invention of the creative child, because it is believed to be a stimulating source of knowledge and creativity.[36] In anime, the mecha-children are surrounded by a wide variety of technological beings as integral components of the children's lives, which puts forward an affective field of techno-intimacy. For the mecha-child, technology is an intimate being: it can be a good friend (e.g., *Astro Boy*), a little brother (e.g., *Fullmetal Alchemist*), a sweet home companion (e.g., *Doraemon*), a substitute mother (e.g., EVA to Shinji in *Evangelion*), or even one's real self (e.g., *Serial Experiments Lain*). It is a narrative trope that unfolds through the intimate assimilation between children and their mecha. With such assimilation, anime renders technological beings as not only innocent, habitual, and indispensable but also comforting, therapeutic, and empowering. For the mecha-children, the techno-gadgets are intimate parts of their lives, without which teenage drama will never be complete.

This sense of techno-intimacy echoes Allison's characterization of Japanese toys and character goods as surrogate companions and healing instruments for millennial youths who suffer postmodern alienation.[37] Indeed, the narrative trope of the mecha-child is a powerful engine in anime's media mix for merchandising, such as Astro Boy stickers, Doraemon T-shirts, and Gundam models, which form "kinlike and interpersonal" relationships with consumers like "shadow families."[38] According to Allison, techno-intimacy is a consumer fantasy that is historically rooted in Japan's postwar aspiration of rebuilding a techno-superpower. It is "the symptom and corrective to this industrial master plan in the new millennium—assuaging the atomism, alienation, and stress of corporatist capitalism with virtual companionship."[39] However, what Allison reads as a particular Japanese fantasy also became a widespread global reality—a reality of techno-intimacy that we all live in our technology-infused daily lives. If the screen-head robot emerging from Naoto's head (in *FLCL*) reminds us of a Nintendo or an iPad, the image of Lain immersed in a womb of wires (in *Serial Experiment Lain*) mirrors our increasingly wired environment—just take a look at how many wires are around your desk (I count twenty-two on mine).

The sense of techno-intimacy, however, is not simply about the interpersonal companionship between humans and machines. Instead, what is fantasized and normalized through the mecha-child figure is a far more intimate relationship: it is the integration and identification between the human and the machine that are being propagated by this popular trope. In other words, the child is not simply seeking a close friendship but is desiring to become and to *be a mecha*. And the mecha is desirable precisely because it is imagined, in many ways, to *be a child*. It is this structure of mutual identification between the child and the mecha that animates the intimate human–machine interface.

This structure also suggests that it is not adequate to interpret the fantasy of techno-intimacy in merely psychoanalytical terms, such as the notions of "polymorphous perversion" and "partial objects" that explain intimate attachment to technological things as substitutions.[40] These psychoanalytical terms fail to address the fantasy of mutual assimilation, for the child–mecha relationship unfolds through identification rather than substitution. In many sci-fi narratives, such as cyberpunk and tech-noirs, the posthuman scenarios of technological permeation are often imagined as dangerous, invasive, and even deadly, because machine-induced affect threatens human-centered subjectivity. In contrast, anime's peculiar strength is precisely the ways in which it structures the scenario of technological permeation by closely associating mecha with children in such a seamless and intuitive manner that the decentering affect from human subjectivity is no longer problematic but becomes desirable. Therefore, techno-intimacy is, first and foremost, a semantic/affective field that has to be carefully constructed discursively and aesthetically, because we do not automatically feel an intimate attachment with technological things. In order to evoke the meaningful and affective feelings of techno-intimacy, the modality of the mecha-child has to be designed, represented, and situated in specific forms so that the mecha and the child can be identified with each other. In other words, the structure of techno-intimacy should be interpreted in aesthetic terms rather than psychoanalytical ones. The intimate assimilation between the child and the mecha, I would argue, is established primarily through their shared aesthetic forms of cuteness and animatedness, which enable the child–mecha identification via mimetic innervation.

Cuteness

In anime, the mecha-children are often utterly cute. From Astro Boy to Doraemon, these cute figures are highly marketable icons to sell character goods and to drive the media mix engine of merchandising. Almost an international label for Japanese popular culture, *kawaii* (cuteness) is commodified for the global consumption of "cool Japan."[41] But the cute figures are more than desirable products; they are also affectionate and caring companions who offer intimate relations. Therefore, the aesthetic form of cuteness is not only a commercial strategy to stimulate consumer desire, but it physically, discursively, and psychologically bridges the distance between human and things, evoking a strong sense of intimacy by making people integrate these cute beings into their daily lives. As Allison points out: "Here physical intimacy overlaps and converges with the psychological intimacy by the new fads and markets of cute character goods. . . . People become attached to them, taking their virtuality as a source of personal amusement, companionship, even identity."[42]

As such, cute things are not only to be desired but also for identification. Children long to identify with cute mecha rather than simply seek companionship. Largely associated with playthings for children, the aesthetics of cuteness, which often has an infantile appearance, is the most appropriate form to stage the intimate identification and assimilation between children and mecha, as both are perceived to be cute. But the intimate relationship established by cuteness is highly ambivalent and oscillates between comforting and demanding, between empowering and submitting, between love and cruelty. In her study of cuteness as an aesthetic category, Sianne Ngai locates the logic of cuteness in its fetishistic function in commodity culture to close the gap between consumer and commodity, between maker and product, between subject and object.[43] But the feeling of intimacy, according to Ngai, is a result of cuteness's paradoxical combination of power and powerlessness, domination and passivity, tenderness and abuse, vulnerability and violence. On one hand, cuteness "solicits a regard of the commodity as an anthropomorphic being less powerful . . . appealing specifically to us for protection and care . . . as if it were our child."[44] On the other hand, the cute object is not simply to be taken care of, but it also invites us to handle it, squeeze it, use it, and play with it physically, sometimes even damaging it with brute force, which "suggests that the pleasure offered by cute things lies in part in their perceived capacity to withstand extended and usually rough use."[45] Therefore, it seems that cuteness solicits "the consumer's sadism or desire for mastery as much as her desire to protect and cuddle . . . as if to foreground how a certain degree of mental violence becomes necessary for regaining intimacy."[46] Because of such a sense of violence that is implicit in its evocation of intimacy, cuteness oscillates between the pathos of tender powerlessness and aggressively powerful demand.

This tension in cuteness is precisely how this aesthetic form functions in anime to evoke the intimate assimilation between mecha and children, both imagined as vulnerable and deadly, hapless and aggressive—that is, simply being "cute." Astro Boy, for instance, is the prototype of a mecha-child exhibiting the ambivalence of cuteness. Abandoned by his father/creator before becoming a superhero, Astro Boy's cute appearance and character arc are designed with a paradoxical combination of power and powerlessness. His round, childlike face with big, innocent eyes is juxtaposed with a tough, metallic body fueled by deadly nuclear energy. His superpower is both his vulnerability (he often gets into trouble due to his power) and his strength (after all, he is a superhero). His failure to grow up is both a tragedy and a blessing. If the cuteness of Astro Boy represents a utopian myth of techno-intimacy, this myth is dramatized with both tenderness and abuse (Astro Boy is probably one of the most abused children on television).[47]

The ambivalence of cute mecha is also manifested when these powerful, childlike machines are pictured in the hapless condition of being damaged and mutilated, evoking an almost contradictory feeling to take care of them so that they can continue being used and abused. In anime ranging from *Evangelion* to the *Gundam* series, the stunning images of damaged mecha with broken parts and distorted figures are often featured prominently, without which the spectacular battle scene would never be complete. These are the "moments of attraction" (to borrow Tom Gunning's "cinema of attraction"), the visual spectacles—often in slow motion, freeze-frames, and close-ups—that graphically represent the dramatic moments of the mecha-body falling apart and out of control.[48] In fact, a large portion of popular GIFs collected and

shared by anime fans online are about mecha being damaged or mutilated, an agonizing and dazzling process running in endless digital
loops. If, as Ngai suggests, "cuteness 'in distress' is the 'most affecting' cuteness," the image of mecha in hapless distress is probably the
most affective cuteness in anime, as if to prove that the cutest mecha
is the one that manages to survive, episode after episode, repetitive
use, abuse, mutilation, and damage (such as EVA in *Evangelion* that
survives countless damage through endless battles).[49]

Cuteness in distress is applied not only to mecha but also to children
who pilot them. In *Evangelion,* Rei Ayanami is the most popular child
character and stimulated wide consumption; her remarkable cuteness
became a market sensation, which not only sold a huge amount of
toy figures but also led to an industry trend that shifted focus from
narrative to character design. What makes Rei Ayanami exceptionally
cute is her constantly injured and mutilated body that is always
wrapped in bandages, which evokes in viewers both the affective feeling to care and the delightful desire for violence (Figure 18). With such
apparent powerlessness, however, Rei Ayanami's vulnerable, cute body
is powerfully demanding and generative. Her injuries lead to battles and

FIGURE 18. Cuteness in distress: the injured mecha-child Rei Ayanami in *Neon
Genesis Evangelion.*

actions in the narrative, as well as to millions of character goods for sale.[50] Quintessentially defining *moe*, a Japanese term for "budding" or "spouting" that describes affective feelings of intimate attachment, Rei Ayanami's cuteness ultimately corrupts the distinction between passivity and domination, between object and subject, which, to a certain degree, characterizes the affective economy of techno-intimacy.

The ambivalent state of cuteness that structures and sustains the affective field of techno-intimacy is well exemplified by the anime series *Gurren Lagann* (dir. Hiroyuki Imaishi, 2007), which was produced by the famed Gainax studio to cultivate the renewed popular obsession with the mecha genre after the studio's earlier success with *Evangelion*. The story takes places in an apocalyptic universe where humans are forced to live underground. An orphan boy named Simon and his brother-like friend Kamina use a drilling mecha to come to the earth's surface. They subsequently team up, each piloting a mecha (Simon's Lagann and Kamina's Gurren), to fight enemy forces and to rescue the future of humankind. What stands out in this series is the crude cuteness of its mecha, which were designed by Shigeto Koyama, who later went on to design the cute robot Baymax in Disney's animated film *Big Hero 6* (2014). The main mecha, Lagann, is designed with only a round head and tiny limbs without even a torso (Figure 19). Literally a face without a body, this mecha is first discovered by the children as simply a "face." If "giving face," according to Ngai, is "cuteness's master trope," Lagann's design is the minimalistic essential of cuteness.[51] Compared with other mecha designs, Lagann is remarkably smaller, rounder, and simpler (after all, it is just a "face"), which makes it appear more infantile, diminutive, and powerless. This cute, tiny machine in the shape of a round face that makes you want to cuddle and protect is, in fact, utterly violent and formidable, because it can transform from a childlike face (a smooth ball) to a fearful drill (a sharp spear). And it often appears the cutest—and the deadliest—in the moment of distress and vulnerability when it is constantly being squashed, spanked, and kicked (Figure 20). In fact, the most effective use of Lagann as a weapon is to toss it (and abuse it) like a baseball—small and passive but fierce and powerful. As such, Lagann is the design of cuteness par excellence.

Figure 19. A small, round face without a body, Lagann is the design of
cuteness par excellence in *Gurren Lagann*.

One of the key attractions of the cute object, as Ngai points out, is our mimetic tendency to imitate its appearance—to be as cute as it is—which evokes intimacy between consumer and commodity by "conflating desire with identification."[52] The mechanism of mimesis is indeed how techno-intimacy operates in anime, by identifying the cuteness of mecha with the cuteness of children. In *Gurren Lagann,* the mecha often functions as the visual/narrative double of the main character, Simon. The child and the mecha identify with each other. The ambivalent cuteness of the mecha (Lagann) thus mirrors that of the child (Simon), who, like the machine, is both hapless and aggressive, innocent and violent. The signature action of Simon, interestingly, is to use Lagann to drill a hole and hide, which combines phallic penetration with infantile regression, highlighting gendered codification of techno-intimacy as primarily a male fantasy.

Lagann's crude, minimalist, and primitive design of cuteness facilitates the mimetic assimilation between the mecha and the child. Exemplifying what Benjamin describes as "primitive technology" in the "false simplicity of the modern toy," the simple cuteness of the mecha solicits a powerful force to incorporate the subject into the object, generating an intimate experience like being encapsulated in a coat or a mask. Such primitive, simple cuteness "allow[s] us to look outward from within objects."[53] This scenario of being enveloped and looking from within the object is precisely how anime stages the intimate assimilation between children and mecha—they pilot the giant robots by being cloaked within the techno-beings. This structure of techno-intimacy is therefore "a sign of our own compulsive mimetic identification with the object in response to its unusually intimate address."[54] In other words, the cute mecha invites the cute child (and us) to identify with and behave like it, to dominate and submit to it, with both power and powerlessness. As such, the cute mecha is what Sherry Turkle calls "the evocative object," which is "an object that fascinates, disturbs equanimity, and precipitates thought."[55] Turkle uses the concept to describe the computer as "the second self," because the computer—a cute mecha of a sort—invites us not only to think of it as an intimate partner but also

FIGURE 20. The cute mecha in distress: Lagann is squeezed, kicked, squashed, and tossed in *Gurren Lagann*.

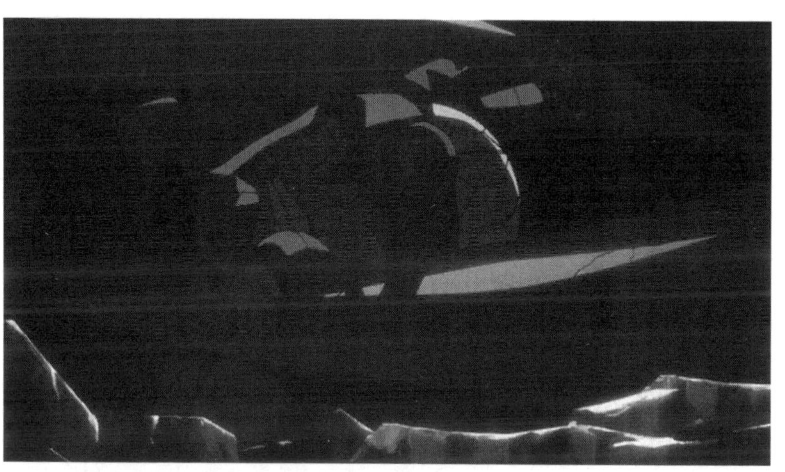

to think of ourselves in computational terms. It is thus an object holding power because it evokes mimetic identification. It is an "object-to-think-with" rather than to think of.[56]

Animatedness

The mimetic identification between the mecha and the child also animates the machine, giving it an anthropomorphic personhood that demands our intimate affection and companionship. Animism, which is to give life to an inanimate object, is how cuteness functions in commodity fetishism. According to Allison, the aesthetic form of techno-animism, which combines techno-commodities with the Japanese Shinto tradition of animism, is the foundation of techno-intimacy in Japanese toys: "Affective ties are formed with such objects, particularly when they are endowed with techno-animism."[57] Highlighting the enchanting and therapeutic affect of techno-intimacy, Allison's emphasis on Shinto animism suggests that the intimate feeling comes from an animistic fantasy that endows inanimate things with an animate spirit.

But what if the animistic fantasy fails when one cannot find the spirit in those inanimate objects? The affective feeling of techno-intimacy turns out to be more ambivalent, excessive, and even disturbing than therapeutic animism. In his 1853 essay "The Philosophy of Toys," Charles Baudelaire notes a strong psychological tension, "the first metaphysical stirring," in children's animistic desire to find the soul of their toys:

> When this desire is implanted itself in the child's cerebral marrow, it fills his fingers and nails with an extraordinary agility and strength. He twists and turns his toy, scratches it, shakes it, bangs it against walls, hurls it on the ground. From time to time he forces it to continue its mechanical motions, sometimes in the opposite direction. Its marvelous life comes to a stop. The child, like the populace besieging the Tuileries, makes a last supreme effort; finally he prises it open, for he is the strong party. But *where is its soul?* This moment marks the beginning of stupor and melancholy.[58]

Baudelaire's characterization of how children violently tear apart their toys to look for the soul with "extraordinary agility and strength" echoes Ngai's observation of a strong tendency of "hyperobjectification" in cuteness that solicits the desire to "fondle and squeeze" the cute object, "even to the point of crushing and damaging" it.[59] It seems that we are all Baudelaire's children who like to "twist and turn" our cute toys. But the motivation may not be to search for the toy's soul but instead to grasp its very physical "thingishness," because "the cute thing is the most reified or thinglike of things, the most objectified of objects or even an 'object' par excellence."[60]

In fact, cuteness, as well as its evocation of intimate attachment, operates precisely through the dialectic tension between animistic spirituality and inert objectivity. Therefore, what fascinates us in the cute techno-toy is not simply the animistic illusion of life that provides companionship but the brute, physical force—especially the technological and mechanical one—that makes the thing move.[61] Because deep down we all understand that the same brute force, whatever that is, moves us too. It is this understanding that evokes the intimate feeling of identification between us and techno-things. As Benjamin says about the mechanically animated figures of Disney cartoons, "The public recognizes its own life in them."[62] What enchants us in techno-intimacy *is not animism but animation.* The child rips apart the toy not to search for its animistic spirit but to animate it with his own physical, mechanical force, which is why he "twists and turns" it and "forces it to continue its mechanical motions."[63]

Therefore, in anime, it is not so much the fantasy of animism as it is the feeling of animatedness that generates the intimate assimilation between the mecha and the child. What animates the mecha-child is not really the Shinto tradition of animism but the technological force of animation. It is the machine of animation that generates the moving images, which give "life" to the mecha-child. In other words, the mecha-child is not animistic but is animated. The affective response to such animatedness can be highly ambivalent and excessive. In her brilliant analysis, Sianne Ngai identifies animatedness as an "ugly feeling" that is often associated with racial others whose lack of autonomous agency and sense of powerlessness are expressed through an affective state of being "animated" or "moved" to an excessive degree—both physically and emotionally—by invisible external forces.[64] But this "ugly feeling" is not always negative. As Scott Bukatman argues, the affective contradiction of animatedness highlights the dialectic tension between "the *automaton* and the *autonomous*," which can lead to unruly, rebellious forces of resistance against the controlling power of automation.[65]

Following Ngai and Bukatman, I argue that there is something intimately engaging in animation even without anima (the animistic spirit), or in the automaton without the autonomous, because the sheer technological force that moves the images and the machine is also recognized as the force that animates us too, which blurs the boundary between machine and human, between object and subject, between automatization and autonomy. As Ngai observes, animatedness can bounce back from the manipulated object to its human agent, affectively tying them together in the same string: "The nonliving entity that is animated . . . comes to automatize its animator," which may allow the human subject to "acquire agency within his or her own automatized condition, enabling the mechanized human to politically comment on—if not exert some form of direct resistance to—the forces manipulating him or her."[66] Therefore, the feeling of being animated is not necessarily "ugly" but can be uniquely empowering and self-reflective.

In the anime series *Gurren Lagann,* the sense of mutual animatedness establishes intimate assimilation between the children and their mecha. Following the narrative conventions of the mecha genre, the main actions in this story never truly begin until the children sit in their mecha. It is largely the integration between the child and the mecha that "animates" the narrative and the images of the whole anime series. The child character Simon is often portrayed as a passively inert boy lacking confidence (like many child protagonists in anime) until he begins to pilot his mecha, which dramatically transforms him to an active, brave hero seeking salvation for humankind. Simon's mecha, Lagann, remains an inanimate machine (albeit a cute one) until being discovered and controlled by Simon, who activates this long-deserted mecha into the deadliest weapon. The child and the mecha thus mutually animate each other.

In *Gurren Lagann,* the sense of mutual animatedness is also visualized by a graphic style that emphasizes the dynamic tension between motion and still. Whenever the child and the mecha are "animated" by their mutual integration and enter the climax of battle, the animation images often change to sudden stillness with graphic markers (speed lines and sketching edges) that emphasize both the dynamic motion and the hand-drawn artificiality (Figure 21). This graphic style of stillness connects anime to its aesthetic root in manga. It is what Marc Steinberg calls "dynamic immobility," for it incorporates "an intensity of movement into the still image."[67] But these dynamic, immobile images often appear to be affectively agonizing, because they imply a transgression of time by disrupting a continuous temporal flow into a fractured moment of duration in flux. It is what Gunning calls "the manufacture of the instant," a moment of uncertainty that is "filled with potential movement, an instant torn from an unseen (but imagined) continuity whose contour they evoke almost painfully."[68] It creates a peculiar sense of time that is suddenly stopped, fractured, and flattened, as well as an affective feeling of movement that is full of tension, anticipation, and agitation, which is why these dynamic immobile images appear to be "almost painful." The sense of painfulness is highlighted by the exaggerated graphic styles that emphasize emotional intensity in such images.

The dynamic, immobile images in *Gurren Lagann* are indeed quite painful, as they are full of affective excess of animatedness. Situated between motion and still, what these dynamic immobile images visualize is not so much the movement as the process of being moved. With the graphic traces that emphasize the hand-drawn quality, these images, which resemble comic sketches more than animation frames, highlight the implicit inanimatedness of the mecha and the children. Arrested in the moment of stillness but with a strong implication of dynamic motion, these children and mecha are visualized in an ambiguous situation between object and subject, between inanimate drawings and animate lives. They seem agitated, anxiously waiting to be animated by the "anime machine." The subsequent motion thus feels

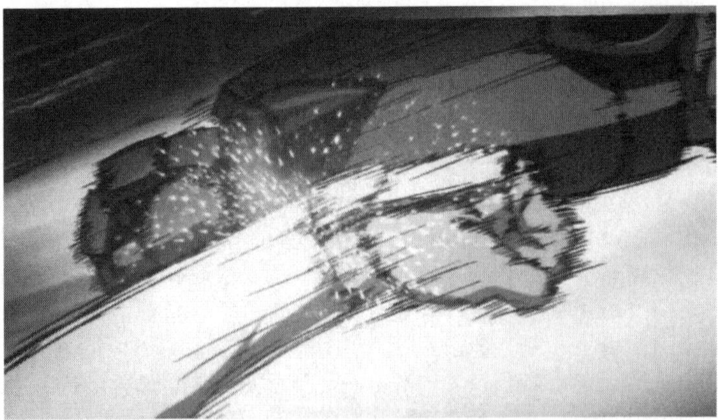

Figure 21. The mecha and the child in dynamic, immobile images in *Gurren Lagann*.

like an affective release from the agony and agitation of animatedness. The graphic excessiveness of the dynamic immobile images mirrors the affective excessiveness of being animated or, more precisely, of wanting to be animated. This affective excess is accumulated and relieved by the mutual animatedness between the child and mecha, which is realized through their intimate integration.

It is this mutual animatedness between the child and the mecha that best characterizes the geek sensibility of techno-intimacy. We seek an intimate relationship with the techno-beings not to search for their souls or spirits as companions but to animate, and be animated by, their techno-power of mechanical or computerized automation. Like those mecha-children, geeks and otaku immerse themselves with techno-gadgets not simply because they are looking for soulful friendship but because they want to be "agitated" by the excessive feeling of animating and being animated, which gives a peculiar sense of agency and empowerment to confront and make sense of—in an affective manner—the hyperautomatized condition of postindustrial knowledge work. That is why Turkle describes the computer—our most intimate techno-being—as a "metaphysical machine," because it influences how we "construct such concepts as animate and inanimate" and "how we think about our own."[69] And the sense of animatedness in the cute mecha-child does the same, which is why it generates intimate feelings. Like the mecha, we are also the automaton without the autonomous, animated without anima. If there is a "ghost in the shell," the ghost is nothing but an algorithm (as it turns out to be in the famous anime film *Ghost in the Shell*), and *that* is the intimate identification we are longing for.

This feeling of intimate identification with an algorithmic automaton is not unlike the public fascination with Mickey Mouse cartoons in the early twentieth century. As Benjamin points out, Mickey Mouse is popular not because it represents an organic, animistic life. Instead, in Mickey Mouse "we see for the first time it is possible to have one's own arm, even one's own body, stolen. The route taken by Mickey Mouse is more like that of a file in an office than it is like that of a marathon runner."[70] It is by recognizing one's own life in "that of a file in an office" that "mankind makes preparations to survive civilization."[71] That survival strategy is at the heart of techno-intimacy.

Mimetic Innervation

In summary, the mecha-child motif evokes and sustains a sense of techno-intimacy through two basic and interrelated aesthetic forms: cuteness and animatedness. For a techno-being to address us intimately, it needs to be both cute (to be cared for and fondled) and animated (to be moved). To be cute, the techno-gadget, with its miniature, edgeless design like children's playthings, oscillates between power and powerlessness, between anthropomorphic spirit and objectified thingishness, inviting us to touch, squeeze, and overuse it, as well as to love, to care for, and to be attached to it. To be animated, the techno-being is perpetually caught in the arrested moment between motion and still, between the autonomous and the automation, generating affective feeling of wanting, needing, and desiring to be moved, both physically and emotionally. Combining cuteness and animatedness, the childlike mecha generates techno-intimacy by: making us use it, abuse it, and love it; evoking us to move it, twist it, and animate it; and ultimately, inviting us to identify and assimilate with it.

Establishing mimetic identification and assimilation between children and mecha, the aesthetic forms of cuteness and animatedness evoke what Benjamin describes as "innervation" through the mimetic faculty. For Benjamin, the concept of innervation, which refers to a process of mental-physiological mediation between the psychic and the physical, between the human sensorium and the mechanical world, presents a materialist and nondestructive manner for the crucial interaction between human and technology, which can lead to a therapeutic correction of, or even a revolutionary transformation from, the pathological, destructive, and fetishistic reception of technology under the alienating conditions of industrial capitalism. This process of innervation, in Benjamin's conception, can potentially be achieved through the mimetic faculty, an aesthetic modality that Benjamin theorizes partially through his fascination with children's intimate relationship with toys. As Miriam Hansen points out, Benjamin's notion of mimesis is less about a relationship with a referent than a *relational* practice," because "similitude works on the order of affinity (*Verwand-schaft*), rather than *sameness*."[72] Benjamin identifies the mimetic faculty in the ways children play, interact, and assimilate with surrounding objects: "The child plays at being not only a shopkeeper or a teacher, but also a windmill and a train."[73] The mimetic behavior that Benjamin characterizes in children's tendency to pretend to be the playthings they interact with echoes the ways in which anime evokes mimetic identification and assimilation between children and mecha through their mutual cuteness and animatedness—the children are compelled to become as cute and animated as the mecha that they encounter and are intimate with.

More importantly, the mimetic innervation that children excel at does not stop with imitation; it also involves creative transformation of both the object and the subject. The children do not so much imitate as "bring together, in the artifact produced in play, materials of widely differing kinds in a new, disjunctive relationship."[74] And this new relationship allows the children not only to transform the material world but also to incorporate or ingest "the object or device, be it an external rhythm, a long-forgotten madeleine, or an alien(ating) apparatus" into their own neurosomatic energy of sensory affect.[75]

The aesthetic forms of cuteness and animatedness in anime function precisely to evoke such affective transformation and incorporation for both the fictional children on screen and the little-boy otaku in front of the screen to achieve mimetic innervation. The dynamic immobile images in *Gurren Lagann*, for instance, generate such affective excess of agitation and agony on the part of the viewers that the images seem to request them to incorporate the technological force of the anime machine, which animates the images as well as the mecha and children, into their own bodily sensorium. The viewers, like the fictional mecha-children, are also being animated and experiencing the affect of animatedness, mimetically assimilating this external rhythm of the anime machine into their neurophysiological experience. This innervation of the anime machine may possibly enable "both a sensory recognition of human self-alienation and a nondestructive, mimetic adaptation of technology."[76] This aesthetic, neurotic, and machinic assimilation through the mimetic faculty is how techno-intimacy functions and operates as a cultural mechanism for technological innervation.

Mecha Fetishism and Infantile Capitalism

Benjamin's envisioning of mimetic innervation is far from a techno-utopia. As therapeutic as it may be, the process of innervation works hand in hand with the destructive, alienating, numbing, and incapacitating effects of massive technologization and rationalization in industrial capitalism. Fetishism, which Marx describes as the foundational mechanism in commodity culture, seems to go in both directions. In fact, both cuteness and animatedness, the two aesthetic forms of techno-intimacy, operate through the fantasy logic of commodity fetishism. Examining the global popularity of Japanese cuteness, Allison rightly points out that fetishizing technological entities with playfulness and cuteness, which she refers to as "mecha fetishism," breeds endless consumer desire for techno-products as "enchanted commodities." The particular site for the fetishistic gaze is "the metallic–human interface," where the intimate fusion between the child and the mecha is performed to achieve their mutual transformation.[77] Such focalized fetishization of the "the metallic–human interface," I would argue, serves to fantastically resolve the tension between anthropomorphism and thingishness in cuteness, as well as the contradiction between automatization and autonomy in animatedness. In other words, anime's aesthetic forms of cuteness and animatedness construct and expose the contradictory logic of techno-intimacy that must be "magically" resolved (or disavowed) through fetishism.

Such fetishization of techno-intimacy is often operated by gendering and sexualizing the mecha-child as female, particularly cute teenage girls who are recognized as shojo.[78] The fetishistic imagery of a cute shojo has been widely commodified in Japan, signifying excessive consumption by representing adolescent girls as both consumable products and consuming subjects.[79] In fact, many mecha-child figures in popular anime—including *Lain*, *Evangelion*, and *Metropolis*—are part of the shojo convention. Combining childish cuteness with female sexuality, the shojo figure as technological embodiment highlights the sexualized tendency in mecha fetishism.[80] For instance, the bonus features in the *Lain* DVDs, which offer close-up looks of shojo fashion and label them "layers," explicitly equate techno-intimacy with a shojo fetish that specifically addresses male fantasy and subjectivity. After all, the mecha-child Lain is a fetishized shojo desired by many male characters and likely male audience members as well. At the same time, shojo fetishism also serves to disavow the inherent tension in techno-intimacy, displacing it with familiar sexual desires. By dramatizing techno-intimacy through a reassuring cultural ground of heterosexual norms, the symbolic figures of the shojo-mecha simultaneously fetishize and conventionalize the intimate relationship with machines as a social standard. It is a specific mode of address toward technophilia of the male otaku, equating sexual relations with techno-intimacy.[81] As Lamarre points out in his analysis of the mecha-shojo in *Chobits* (2002): "The question of how men treat women becomes entwined with the question of how humans interact with machines."[82] Like the fetishistic gaze of the metallic–human interface, the figure of shojo-mecha, by overlapping the fetishistic body of shojo with that of mecha, as well as by displacing the attachment to machines with heterosexual desire, serves to both fantasize and normalize the irresolvable tension of human–technology integration through the lens of male sexuality.

In sum, by assimilating and identifying the machines with cute, childlike figures and their everyday lives, the mecha-child motif normalizes and fetishizes the feeling of techno-intimacy as common pleasure and provides a comfort zone for its viewers—presumably male geeks—to interrogate and transform their own experience of informational knowledge work with the potential possibility toward innervation. To be fair, the intimate assimilation between human and machine often expresses some level of collective sociocultural anxiety toward the omnipresent technological permeation.[83] However, underneath the widespread anxiety, there is always a strong sense of pleasure in enjoying and admiring the fantastic power of the mecha-child, be it destructive or liberating. For anime, such generic pleasures are offered directly and comfortably through its aesthetic forms of cuteness and animatedness that are associated with children and children's culture, which construct and sustain a seemingly innocent, harmless, and even cheerful fable of human–machine assimilation without being channeled through the fears of techno-paranoia that are prevalent in popular science fiction. By normalizing and integrating technological elements as physical and psychological components of children's existence, anime provides narrative and aesthetic formulas to render the generic pleasure of technophilia as habitual and omnipresent, and thus fashions techno-intimacy as just another cultural norm. It is precisely such a normalized pleasure of techno-intimacy that marks anime as a distinctive body of cultural products that offers intense resonance with tech-savvy knowledge workers, who are living through a similar experience of intimate assimilation with mecha on a daily basis. Indeed, the mecha-child schema can be easily identified by geek fanboys, whose own attachment and integration with technological media would be comfortably validated.

Although the notion of techno-intimacy is often endowed with the therapeutic function of healing or soothing, it is not necessarily pinned down to social anxiety regarding posthuman/postmodern conditions. Not unlike the rising geek chic, the semantic/affective field of techno-intimacy has increasingly been fashioned—in anime and beyond—as a trendy cultural logic that is fantastic and enchanting, on one hand, and ordinary and ubiquitous, on the other. We see such a cultural logic of techno-intimacy—as both a fantasy and a reality, both an aesthetic system and a commodity strategy—not only in the animated figure of Astro Boy but also in the digital interface of Google Android, a mobile operating system whose logo takes the shape of a cute, childlike robot and whose numerous versions are all named after sweets for children— e.g., "Cupcake," "Jelly Bean," "KitKat," "Lollipop," "Marshmallow." Sweet, cute, and childlike. The techno-beings that saturate our everyday life begin to take the forms of mecha-children and our daily encounter with various apps, gadgets, and devices also begins to mirror the child–mecha interface in anime—cute and longing to be animated. These aesthetic forms of techno-intimacy have become the default design of toys, characters, logos, consumer products, websites, and user interfaces (Figure 22). By identifying and assimilating machines with childlike figures, the mecha-child modality establishes a powerful and ubiquitous aesthetic system that animates the global desire of techno-intimacy.

As a conclusion, I want to take a quick look at what makes the mecha-child such a compelling trope in an information society. Akira Asada famously and parodically coined the term *infantile capitalism* to characterize Japan's version of postmodernism.[84] Like many others, Asada sees Japan as a little boy who never matured to "adult" modernity. But ironically, this infantile state allowed Japan to directly progress to a more advanced state—that is, infantile capitalism is also late capitalism. Asada's playful "fairy tale" of infantile capitalism, which seems to be more satirical than serious, turns out to be not uniquely Japanese. Fredric Jameson borrows Asada's metaphorical concept to describe postmodern consumer capitalism as "infantile," for we are all children born into "the free play of automation and the malleable fungibility of multiple consumer publics and markets."[85] The ironic, circular "progression" of time that is implied in this notion of the infantilization of late capitalism makes sense, if the metaphorical child is taken as a signifier for "Eternal Recurrence" (Nietzsche) or "both beginning and end" (Jung). Characterizing postmodernism as "infantile," however, both Asada and Jameson seem to forget that modernity and modernism had also been described as childish. For example, Ngai notices that early twentieth-century modernism had been called the "child cult."[86] A. O. Scott points out that American modern culture can mostly be described as "juvenile."[87] It seems that capitalism has always been a little bit "infantile."

The key question, however, is not whether infantile capitalism is Japanese or American, modern or postmodern. What makes the logic of infantilization so compelling, despite Asada's humorous tone, is the fact that this infantile state seems to be specifically associated with human–machine relationships in the context of information capitalism, because the "childlike passion" that Asada observes came from "Japanese engineers" who "are easily obsessed with machines."[88] In his rather short theorization, Asada briefly (and jokingly) mentions Nishida Kitarō's philosophy of "nothingness," which he reads as the ideological

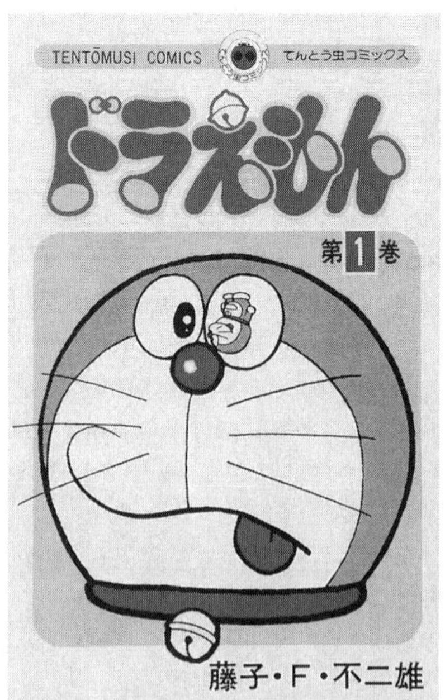

TENTŌMUSI COMICS
てんとう虫コミックス
第1巻
藤子・F・不二雄

FROM THE HUMANS WHO BROUGHT YOU 'FINDING NEMO'
Disney · PIXAR
WALL·E
JUNE 27

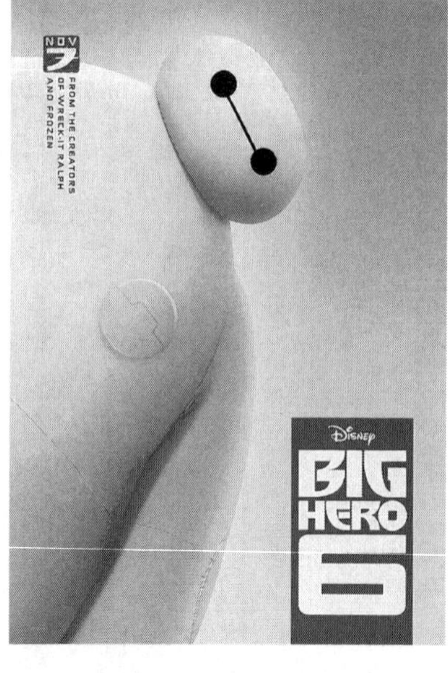

NOV 7
FROM THE CREATORS
OF WRECK-IT RALPH
AND FROZEN
Disney
BIG HERO 6

FIGURE 22. The cute, childlike mecha that animate the global desire of techno-intimacy everywhere. (*opposite page, top left*) Doraemon (*Doraemon*, manga series by Fujiko Fujio); (*opposite page, right*) Baymax (*Big Hero 6*, Disney, 2014); (*opposite page, bottom left*) WALL-E (*WALL-E*, Pixar, 2008); (*above, top left*) Google Android logo (Android 6.0 Marshmallow, Google Inc.); (*above, bottom left*) Snoo, the Reddit alien logo (https://www.reddit.com); (*above, right*) BB-8 (*Stars Wars* franchise, created by George Lucas/Lucasfilm Ltd.).

foundation for a "holonic" structure—"like an empty cylinder"—that protects the "children." Although this holonic structure "has an empty center," it is not necessarily distributed or heterogeneous, for it is "a theory of unification—or, rather, 'zerofication.'"[89]Although this notion of nothingness (and Asada's casual theorization of it in relation to Japan) is not to be taken literally, I do find it useful to consider the sense of nothingness in information. By "nothingness," I am not referring to the common notion that information is immaterial or lacks substance. Instead, I want to point out that information also operates as a holonic structure "like an empty cylinder," because it runs on networks without a center, and it has something that is unrepresentable. Alexander Galloway points to the unrepresentability of information by arguing two theses: "Thesis 1, *data have no necessary visual form*; thesis 2, *only one visualization has even been made of an information network.*"[90] These two theses lead to the contradiction of unrepresentability, because "thesis 1 argues for digital aesthetics as nothing" while "thesis 2 argues for digital aesthetics as one." Therefore, when representation takes place, "it says *nothing.*"[91] Unification is zerofication.

If nothingness in Kitarō's philosophy is the result of self-negation, the nothingness of information refers to its unrepresentability. In either case, nothingness produces children, because only under the protection of an empty cylinder with no center can we become children to play "freely" without a central guardian. But the information playgrounds all look the same because they have only one visualization. Protected by decentralized "soft" networks, we are all children playing with our favorite mecha, but the multitudes of mecha all "produce singular images."[92] Therefore, what infantilizes us is the contradiction of informationalism as an empty cylinder that is simultaneously nothing and one. This scenario is strikingly similar to how Hiroki Azuma characterizes otaku as "database animals."[93] For Azuma, the empty center of "nothingness" is the decline of the grand narrative, replaced by the multitudes of database, which inevitably reduces us to "animals" (or "children") because the mode of database consumption stops us from maturing to independent human subjects ("adults") by replacing genuine consciousness with immediate needs. Therefore, we become animalized infants playing with the database with endless layers of data and information that generate an infinite number of *moe* characters for our consumption, though these countless *moe* characters all somehow look the same (singular images). In other words, the mecha-child as a widespread cultural motif is the result of the unrepresentable, centerless information structure (e.g., networks and databases) that is the one and the many at the same time. This information structure, as well as its inherent contradiction, is what I will examine in the next chapter.

5

Cybernetic Play

Seeking the "True End" in a Database Complex

The milieu of techno-intimacy in anime often operates through a playful mode of transmedial consumption akin to information navigation. This chapter explores the play mechanism in the networked, open-ended structure of anime's transmedial environment and characterizes it as a form of aesthetic-technological continuum that I call "cybernetic play," which is a mode of play that relies on informative feedback to improve learning, to optimize performance, and, ultimately, to control and unify the expansive information field. As such, play as an aesthetic experience is adopted into the technological system of cybernetics. This chapter examines how the adoption of play into the logic of cybernetics is operated through the transmedia system of anime. It starts by first analyzing anime's database structure that features hypertextual complexity, seriality, and interconnectivity. Focusing on the notion of "complex" (*cong* コン in Japanese and *kong* 控 in Chinese), which refers to both a psychological state and a media infrastructure, I argue that anime's media mix constitutes a psychological/infrastructural complex that oscillates between the polarizing impulses of informatic expansiveness and regulatory unification, leading to compulsive information searching and navigation as a function of cybernetic control. This database complex, which oscillates between chaos and control, calls for cybernetic play as a necessary mechanism to generate, sustain, and organize continuous user involvement in transmedia consumption and production. Specifically, the mode of play is operated as the player's persistent search for the "true end" by consuming/producing proliferat-ing storylines (the "worldlines") as informative feedback loops to con-trol the expansive database complex. This mechanism of cybernetic play centered on the true end has increasingly replaced the previous models (narrative consumption and database consumption) to become a new organizational principle of the media mix system.

From Anime Puzzles to Mind-Game Films

Anime is marked by textual density and complexity with heavy doses of signs, codes, and references, in both visual and literary forms. Some-times referred to as *neta* (ネタ, source of spoofs and pastiches) or *meta* (メタ, self-reflective metafictions) in otaku culture, these intertextual codes and references are infinite sources of play for fans to actively participate in anime's transmedia system.[1] Identifying and interpret-ing these signs are the key elements in anime geekdom, like playing puzzle games collectively in a community. For example, in the *Ghost in the Shell* franchise, the abundance of on-screen signs and icons, as well as the prolific use of complex technical jargon in dialogue, calls for lengthy extradiegetic footnotes, extensive supplementary texts, and pro-liferating spin-off narratives to navigate this complex multimedia sys-tem. A somewhat extreme case is the series *Sayonara, Zetsubou-Sensei* (2007–12), which is famous for featuring extensive cultural references as text, images, symbols, and graphics on screen. Translation, interpre-tation, and discussion of these references is a cultural obsession among transnational fans, especially in the fansub community (Figure 23). *Sayonara, Zetsubou-Sensei* may be extreme but is not exceptional. From early classics, such as *Ghost in the Shell* and *Neon Genesis Evangelion*, to later fan-favorites, like *Lucky Star* and *Gintama*, anime culture is rich in signs, codes, and references both on screen and off screen. In fact, a key attraction of anime as a transmedia system are its intertextual and intratextual density, multiplicity, and complexity that demand repetitive viewing, attentive deciphering, and collective knowledge sharing and puzzle solving.

Besides the extensive use of intertextual signs and references, anime is also marked by complex narrative modes that depart from the classical

FIGURE 23. Extensive neta references to pop culture—such as Tokyo Disneyland that is not located in Tokyo, the McDonald's "free smile" service, and the Japanese pop duo KinKi Kids—appear as lengthy Japanese text on screen with Chinese translation, explanation, and comment in a fansub video of *Sayonara, Zetsubou-Sensei* (2007–12), fansubbed by CamoeFansubs 华盟字幕组.

norms of linearity. Disjunctive, achronological, nonlinear, or multilinear narratives are common in popular anime. The narrative of the *Evangelion* series, for example, is constructed through an interwoven tapestry of multiple storylines, all of which unfold through a complex network of intertextual references. Series such as *FLCL* and *Samurai Champloo* fashion narrative complexity in a more casual and playful manner. Informed by hip-hop culture, *Samurai Champloo* manipulates its moving images and narrative structure in a mode of "video scratching"—it jumps back and forth along the storyline through visual motifs that resemble record scratching. For *Samurai Champloo,* temporality is like a plastic record that can run in multiple directions with different speeds. This playful manipulation of narrative structure is pushed to a more extreme version by *FLCL,* whose chaotic narrative "mess" seems to resist any sense of linearity, clarity, or even logic. The series resembles a cluster of fragmented short videos more than a continuous linear narrative. The diegetic world is constantly interrupted by nondiegetic connotations that are self-reflective or intertextual. Characters often appear without appropriate introductions; flashforwards or flashbacks constantly jump in without visual/audio cues; establishing shots are largely omitted; the editing generally lacks spatial or temporal continuity. Commenting on *FLCL*'s often random and illogical narrative, director Tsurumaki Kazuya admits that the series is like "imagination being made physical and tangible."[2]

Anime's mazelike structure, with extensive references, intricate signs, and narrative complexity, is not unique. Cultural allusions and alternative narrative strategies have arguably become the leading trend in cinema, television, and streaming series, ranging from earlier films such as *Pulp Fiction* (1994), *Run Lola Run* (1998), and *Memento* (2000) to recent series such as *Mr. Robot* (2015–19), *Westworld* (2016–22), and *Dark* (2017–20). Narrative complexity, referentiality, and multiplicity, as well as spatiotemporal disjunction, fragmentation, and juxtaposition, are increasingly common in popular screen culture. But we can certainly trace it to earlier predecessors: the visual bricolage in Andy Warhol, the cinematic experimentation in Jean-Luc Godard, and the obsession with allusions in the 1970s New Hollywood Cinema.

What is new about anime such as *Samurai Champloo* and *Evangelion*, however, is the fact that nonlinear narrative and cultural allusions are no longer reserved for the regime of the avant-garde and cinephile. Neither are they designed to be challenging or oppositional alternatives against dominant norms. As a growing cultural trend, deciphering intricate codes in complex narratives is nothing more than gameplay. These cultural signs and references are not supposed to mean anything significant—they are signifiers without the signified, text without context. The purpose here is to recognize signals and patterns rather than to interpret signs and meanings. The process is more informational than semiotic. For viewers and fans alike, recognizing the allusions and references and solving puzzles, either effortlessly or through obsessive research, is a fun game to play, and it has become a key pleasure in digital-age popular culture. A cartoon in the *New Yorker* explicitly made fun of this mode of gamelike movie viewing, featuring a father saying to his son in a movie theater: "When it's over, I'll explain all the pop-culture references you didn't get and you can explain all the pop-culture references I didn't get."[3] As filmmaker Lars von Trier admits, the abundance of signifying objects in his films is nothing but "a riddle to be solved. . . . It's a basic mind game, played with movies."[4]

Marked by complexity, multiplicity, and intertextuality, anime with nonconventional narrative forms evokes a mode of address that resembles gameplay or puzzle solving. It is active, interactive, repetitive, and sometimes obsessive, which can occasionally generate a cult following. Many have studied these "puzzle films" (Warren Buckland), "mind-game films" (Thomas Elsaesser), "forking-path" narratives (David Bordwell), "multiple-draft" narratives (Edward Branigan), "modular narratives" (Allan Cameron), or "post-cinematic affect" (Steven Shaviro).[5] But the key question remains: What are the historical conditions that gave rise to these modalities that are so obsessed with puzzles, codes, and labyrinth structures? Many point to "the exponential rise of 'new media'"—computers, the internet, video games, and digital culture and technology in general.[6] But is the relationship between narrative complexity and new media technology a causal one of reflection, representation, revelation, and response? Or is it a mere coincidence?

Hypertext and the Changing Mode of Address

Anime offers a valuable window to investigate the techno-cultural relations between changing narrative forms and the rise of digital media, because anime is never a singular medium of moving images but is the nexus of a complex transmedia system. Anime's transmedia system allows us to note that the rise of mind games in screen culture is not simply the result of the changing relationship between digital media and cinema. Instead, it is a fundamental shift in the mode of address in a transmedial environment that has been computerized and networked. By "mode of address," I am not simply referring to "the spectator–screen relationship," as Elsaesser discusses in his analysis of mind-game films. Rather, it is a rising mode of user engagement that displaces storytelling with pathfinding, pattern recognition, and navigation in a networked information field. It is a cultural practice that resembles Google Search. In other words, this is a mode of address that conflates work with play, narrative with information. As such, it produces an information worker rather than a spectator.

The kind of media environment that is most effective for producing information workers is a hypertextual one, which is marked by networked hyperlinks and interconnectivity. Conceptualized by Theodor H. Nelson in the 1960s as a new form of information technology, hypertext is "non-sequential writing—text that branches and allows choices to the reader, best read at an interactive screen."[7] Emphasizing the linking mechanism and multiple reading paths, hypertext was celebrated by literary theorists such as George Landow as a poststructuralist form with textual openness, intertextuality, multilinearity, interactivity, and involvement, which defines a mode of address that is multivocal, immersive, and participatory.[8] Although literary scholars often associate hypertextual links with poststructuralism, the intertextual reference in anime is less a signifying practice than a relational functionality.[9] It is not so much about meaningful signification or interpretation as about pathfinding and pattern recognition. The extensive referential links in anime such as *Evangelion* and *Samurai Champloo* rarely point to any signifying meanings other than simply evoking the pleasure of relational recognition. Emphasizing the links themselves instead of the terminal meanings of the links, these references are merely connections without destinations. Whatever possible meanings that may derive from the references may solely depend on a viewer's informational search through networked platforms such as blogs, forums, and Wikipedia. In *Evangelion*, for instance, the countless biblical references do not seem to mean anything significantly religious. The series' creators openly admit that there were no intentionally religious or philosophical meanings whatsoever, but the reason for those Christian symbols was simply to be "like a puzzle" and "look cool."[10] This gesture of "cool" echoes Alan Liu's characterization of cultural cool as identification with an empty position rather than with actual identities.[11]

This sense of cool emptiness, which is to look for passages (identification) without destinies (identities), captures the collective ethos of hypertextual mind games in anime as a ramification of informatic logics, which is to displace meanings with signals. Observing the phenomenal fan activities trying to decode *Evangelion,* Leonard Sanders notes that the meanings of cultural signs have become incredible unstable: "Meanings cannot be said to lie in the one or the other. . . . In a sense it has become virtual, ephemeral."[12] This unstableness can be applied to hypertextual links in general that are equally "virtual" and "ephemeral." The increasing proliferation of hyperlinks in digital media environments has largely destabilized signs and significations, whose meanings are diluted and deflated by the very links that they are connected to. The virtual, ephemeral nature of anime's intertextual references mirrors the general loss of signification by the very proliferation of informational links.

As assemblies of hyperlinked signals, anime's hypertextual narratives resonate with its flattened images that compress layers of surfaces without a linear perspective (the visual style of superflat that I will discuss in chapter 6). As Thomas Lamarre notes, the multilinear narrative in *Evangelion* is akin to its multilayered superflat images, both challenging the viewers to closely watch the anime to navigate through the complex information networks that lead in different directions and patterns without hierarchy.[13] Visually and narratively, anime prioritizes multiplicity and mobility over linearity and fixation. It constitutes an information field that consists of interconnected layers and networked links rather than a perspective depth or meaningful signification. It is what Nelson famously calls a "docuverse."[14] As an early proposal for hypertextual media, the docuverse was envisioned by Nelson as a decentralized, globally distributed source of information structured with webs of hyperlinks. As a transnational, transmedial system, anime often evokes the imagination of a docuverse by exhibiting its structure as expansive networks of links and layers. Anime series such as *Evangelion, FLCL,* and *Samurai Champloo* feature themselves more as wide collections of cultural data than as forms of storytelling. The anime series *Serial Experiments Lain* even explicitly points to Nelson's notion of the docuverse by making reference to the Xanadu Project, which was famously proposed by Nelson in the 1960s as the actualization of a hypertextual docuverse. By and large, anime is presented as a cultural database structured with layers of referential information connected by hyperlinks rather than as televised narratives serialized with episodes.[15]

Playing with the Geek Code in Hypermedia

As a database culture, anime generates a specific mode of address that centers on information searching, navigation, and decryption. This mode of address produces a postindustrial subject that shifts from spectatorship to knowledge work. This paradigm shift in the mode of address can be pleasurable for some but alienating for others. The anime film *Ghost in the Shell,* for example, is famous for its convoluted dialogue full of technical jargon that can be quite confusing for audiences unfamiliar with that kind of language. One of the reviewers bitterly criticized that the film's "excessive use of high-tech terminology and tropes, such as computer hacking and virtual environment, gradually becomes embarrassing and annoying." Complaining that the film is "so steeped in computer nerd dialogue" that it is not "user-friendly enough," the critic explicitly asked: "Just who are Oshii [the film director] and company trying to impress?"[16]

Such a question about viewership is significant for anime geekdom, a knowledge culture that is obsessed with codes, patterns, and hypertextual links that require collective knowledge sharing and learning. As I mentioned in chapter 2, the knowledge culture of geekdom relies on familiar speech genres. The "nerd dialogue" is the key to enter the club. Like many cult references that you either get or you do not, the abundance of signs, references, and puzzles (i.e., the neta and meta) in anime is the geek code that creates a strong sense of community. Or in Elsaesser's words, it is an "expanded network of inter-tribal communication," which requires a certain familiarity with the "code" (in a literal sense) to enter.[17] Observing the recurrent use of codes and references in cyber-age films such as *Pulp Fiction,* Dana Polan points out, "Getting the reference allows entry into a private club, this being one of the functions of cult culture."[18] As a somewhat global cult, anime is a code-rich culture that is marked not only by the extensive appearance of nerdy languages and intertextual references on screen but also by the prevalent use of special terms, acronyms, and abbreviations in fan communities off screen. This geek code, once again, points to the semiotic emptiness in anime's hypertext. Like computer codes, the meanings of anime code stop at the mere surface of recognition, of the links themselves. It is a system of encoding and decoding. The pleasure evoked is not unlike programming or reading computer code. The obsession with hypertextual links and relations in anime, therefore, mirrors the lived experience of postindustrial knowledge work, where cultural differences are merely informational variables.

Fans' obsessive involvement in encoding and decoding highlights the mode of play. Anime's hypertextual narratives encourage viewers to actively engage with links, to search for information through webs of connections, and to find their own path through intertwined branches. It is a mode of gameplay that involves information searching, code deciphering, pathfinding, pattern recognition, and plot (re)organization. Anime series such as *Evangelion* and *Sayonara, Zetsubou-Sensei* explicitly invite viewers to participate in puzzle-solving games. Playing these games is a collective activity, like multiplayer online games, that involves extensive knowledge production and consumption on networked transmedia platforms such as streaming services, social media, wiki sites, fan clubs, and many others. The intense viewer involvement in the mode of play aligns anime's hypertextual structure with gaming. Consuming anime culture is like playing a game that keeps you moving from one mission to another: getting a reference, solving a plot twist, or contributing to a fan theory. The narrative progression in many anime series, ranging from the earlier classics like *Heidi* and *Saint Seiya* to the later hits such as *Fullmetal Alchemist* and *Attack on Titan*, usually takes the form of a series of mission-driven journeys, as if playing a game in which you have to fight through a chain of tasks on different levels in order to progress. Such a narrative structure, which keeps moving from one mission, battle, and location to another, is not unlike the digital work of a video game that takes you from one site, action, and level to another by mouse clicks.[19] The association between anime and games is hardly surprising, considering that video games have always been important components of anime's transnational, transmedial system of media mix. Coincidentally, it is no surprise that the battle scenes in numerous anime, from *Dragon Ball* to *Gundam* to *Evangelion,* are always represented in the form of one-to-one combat reminiscent of game actions in popular Japanese video games such as *Street Fighter* and *Mortal Kombat.* Evoking the gamelike experience is arguably one of the key attractions of anime.

This mode of play is afforded not only by anime's hypertextual structure but by its hypermedia environment. The global dissemination of anime is largely driven by the expanding transnational networks of hypermedia, from peer-to-peer file-sharing networks of user-generated fansubs to streaming platforms such as Netflix, Crunchyroll, Niconico, and Bilibili, as well as anime's long-existing system of media mix including manga, toys, video games, character goods, garage kits, light novels, cosplay, and *doujinshi.* Inhabiting a hypermedia environment, anime has always been hypertextual, no matter its narrative or visual qualities that may or may not evoke a similar hypermedia experience. It is its hypermedia environment that makes anime a uniquely hypertextual entity. Even when a particular anime series follows a linear narrative, it can still appear to be nonlinear because it is presented or consumed in a hypermedia environment without conventional sequential order. Watching anime on the internet is rarely linear, as it involves fast-forwarding or reversing, jumping from one episode to another, or simply downloading later episodes before earlier ones. Like hypertext readers who must assemble their own narrative path, anime viewers must reassemble their own sequence of viewing. Therefore, the sense of nonlinearity and multilinearity in anime is often evoked more by the hypermedia environment than by narrative strategies. This hypermedial experience is self-reflexively mirrored by the anime series *Samurai Champloo,* which features narrative and visual motifs mimicking the effect of fast-forward/reverse in video playing. *Samurai Champloo* playfully reminds us of the hypermedia condition of anime, a condition that enables anime's networked, gamelike hypermediacy.

Anime's remarkable hypermediacy is exemplified by *The Melancholy of Haruhi Suzumiya* (2006–09), a series that playfully self-reflects the implication of the hypermedia environment through its own narrative arrangements and transmedial platforms. Part of a long-running multimedia franchise *Haruhi Suzumiya* (2003–), the TV anime *The Melancholy of Haruhi Suzumiya* generated huge popularity both in Japan and internationally partly due to its peculiar manner of nonlinear presentation. When initially broadcast in Japan in 2006, the series aired in a uniquely nonlinear order—the episodes in the later part of the story were broadcast earlier, while what was supposed to have happened earlier was presented later. Such a nonchronological presentation encouraged obsessive participation in this puzzle-solving game that involves actively sorting out the plot order while wondering what may happen (or be presented) next. In a sense, the anime series evokes similar viewing pleasure as many mind-game films. But the fundamental difference is that *Haruhi Suzumiya* creates nonlinear complexity solely through its presentation mode rather than the narrative form. What makes the situation more complex is transnational consumption. Unlike TV viewers in Japan, *Haruhi Suzumiya*'s international audiences accessed the series mainly through DVDs, online streaming, or p2p file sharing. The international release of the DVDs (by Bandai Entertainment) arranged the series according to its chronological sequence in the storyline. The actual viewing order, however, is solely at the mercy of the audience, who can choose to watch it according to its initial broadcasting order, or in the order of the storyline, or anywhere in between. The limitless number of viewing choices offered by its hypertextual, hypermedial presentation made the series a global internet phenomenon. The viewing order became a hot topic among fans who were actively engaged in discussion and debate about their own viewing choices. Offering itself as a collection of flexible modules to be structured and restructured by its hypermedia environment, the anime series *Haruhi Suzumiya* presents a hypertext to be played with. The hypertextualization of *Haruhi Suzumiya* was enabled by the fact that it was part of an expansive franchise, a hypermedia system with networks of intertextual, intermedial links to facilitate transmedia synergy.[20] Released by Kadokawa Shoten, a major Japanese publisher and multimedia conglomerate that famously coined the term "media mix," the *Haruhi Suzumiya* franchise is one of the most successful examples of the so-called Kadokawa media mix. The media mix system inevitably makes anime hypertextual, because it transforms an anime text from a singular, discrete unit to an assemblage of intertextual multimedia networks. As Marc Steinberg points out, media mix transforms anime "from a model of the text as a relatively self-contained entity to the text as a transmedia fragment."[21] Therefore, media mix implies a paradigm shift from an individual text to intertextual relations, a shift that changed the nature of anime from a singular textual unit of a particular medium to a hypertextual link in a multimedia database.

The Complex: Between the Multiplying Worldlines and the Singular "True End"

In the media mix system, the transformation of anime from a text to a hyperlink, or, more precisely, from a form of textual engagement to a form of relational connection, also implies a shift from narrative to database, a cultural form that is defined by informational relations as the primary structure. Although the narrative complexity of anime already demonstrates the database impulse, the media mix system is further constructed and operated with the logic and structure of a database as its primary cultural form that is marked by expansive networks of information, relations, and interconnectivity. Contrasting database and narrative as two opposite forms, Lev Manovich characterizes the database as the preferred form for digital culture because it features a modular structure with a collection of data that is designed for information collecting, processing, and retrieval.[22] More importantly, Manovich associates the database form with a particular psychological state he calls "database complex," a state of psychological obsession with producing, navigating, and inhabiting a database form.[23] This notion of a psychological state in relation to a media structure echoes Lamarre's notion of an infrastructural/psychological complex in anime's transmedia ecology.[24] Using "complex" to replace the notion of "media mix," Lamarre tries to steer away from the implied tendency to perceive transmedia systems as a combinatory "mix." Instead, he sees the transmedia system as a "complex," which is a site of encounter where the two polarized infrastructural tendencies (one-to-many and point-to-point) bifurcate the two opposite psychological tendencies (totalizing and individualizing).[25]

The infrastructural/psychological complex of a database, which oscillates between the polarizing tendencies of multiplicity (the distributive many) and singularity (the totalizing one), is precisely the mechanism that drives the transmedia system of anime. Because the hallmark of this system is the tension between the opposite tendencies of distributive chaos and unifying control. A perfect example of this complex, in both psychic and medial terms, is the popular franchise *Science Adventure* (2008–), which has produced a growing number of games, light novels, anime, manga, films, music, radio shows, and even theatrical plays. The success of this multimedia franchise almost single-handedly turned its game designer, 5pb., into a major studio. Exemplifying what Lamarre calls "the game play complex," the franchise centers on a series of visual novel games that all take place in the same fictional universe where a large assembly of teenage characters explore different sci-fi fantasies in the familiar urban setting of Tokyo.[26] Each game series also constitutes its own mini-franchise with transmedia spin-offs in games, anime, manga, novels, films, and so on. Following what Hiroki Azuma calls "game-ic realism," whereby the game logic of replay, reset, and multiple endings is adopted and expressed by nongame media such as novels and anime, the transmedia franchise of *Science Adventure* is marked by the gaming mechanism with interrelated loops, proliferating "worldlines," and perpetually branching scenarios that serve to tightly connect a vast collection of characters, images, and texts into an ever-growing database across diverse media forms and platforms.[27] In fact, the key attraction of the franchise is precisely its superb ability to create seemingly endless time loops and plot possibilities because the core "fantasy" elements in the franchise, such as reality alteration (in *Chaos;Head*) and time travel (in *Steins;Gate*), are all merely narrative devices that function to generate more branching points, more plotlines, more alternative endings, and more "worldlines," so that the infrastructural complex of the transmedia database, as well as a user's psychological complex to navigate the database, would expand almost infinitely.

The *Steins;Gate* series within the *Science Adventure* franchise is one of the most popular and illuminating cases of an ever-expanding database that is organized by games and gaming mechanisms, a system of game-centered media mix.[28] Consisting of several novel games, anime series, films, manga, and light novels, the media mix system of *Steins;Gate* comprises an intricate narrative that follows the emotional and intellectual journeys of a group of young characters centered around the self-proclaimed "mad scientist" Okabe Rintarō and his research partner (and love interest) Makise Kurisu, who discover and utilize the technology of time travel to change the past and the future and to save each other's lives. Combining a compelling science-fiction fantasy with poignant teenage romance, as well as a stunning visualization of Tokyo's vibrant otaku scenes in Akihabara, this multimedia series heavily relies on the narrative motif of time travel as a central device to operate a game-ic mechanism of replaying, revising, and resetting plotlines, as the characters can send text messages, emails, memories, and eventually themselves through a time machine to intervene with the past and to alter the worldlines of the present and future. Although novel games normally involve only a minimal level of gameplay—they often rely more on interactive reading—the *Steins;Gate* games evoke a strong sense of gaming, because the narrative setting of time travel affords the gamelike logic of loops and resets. Following this game-ic logic, the TV anime series *Steins;Gate,* which aired in Japan in 2011, features disjunctive editing, nonlinear narration, and a wealth of textual and graphic signs and intertextual references to complicate the narrative and to disorient the viewers. Its visual styles of canted angles, distorted perspective, and off-balance composition also create cognitive puzzles resembling gaming.

The narrative and visual complexities in the anime echo the networked database structure of the whole transmedia series. Although the anime series does not have as many alternative endings as the games, it does dramatize the protagonist's repetitive efforts to change the past, present, and future through time travel, a scenario of endless loops of trial and error that mirrors both the plot setting of the series in particular and the cultural logic of gaming in general. The repetitive cycles of time travel are further multiplied through numerous games, novels, manga, anime, and films in the series, each featuring different yet interconnected timelines. The proliferation of timelines through both intramedia narrating and intermedia franchising generated a large collection of various worldlines with many diverse stories and endings, which constitutes a huge database that still keeps growing with the continuous expansion of the franchise. And fans were enthusiastically archiving, processing, and indexing this ever-expanding database through wiki sites, forums, fan works, and social media. One wiki site, for instance, keeps track of all the known worldlines in the published works in the *Steins;Gate* series, lists their chronological order, analyzes how these worldlines are arrived at through time travel, and charts a complex diagram of the interrelations among these worldlines (Figure 24).[29] To facilitate and encourage fans' database complex of getting all the worldlines correct, the publisher of the series also released an "official document" indexing all the worldlines with a "divergence matrix," adding another commodity to be consumed to the media mix system. The series is also full of a rich collection of internet slang from 2chan (a Japanese social network), techno-jargon from real and fictional sciences, and references to many geek culture elements, such as anime, science fiction, and real-life conspiracies, including *Evangelion, Star Trek, Doctor Who,* the IBM 5100, CERN, and "John Titor." By and large, *Steins;Gate* is a transmedial, intertextual complex (infrastructurally) that is designed for (and probably by) otaku geeks who have a database complex (psychologically).

As such, the transmedia system of the *Steins;Gate* series is not only a database complex, in both infrastructural and psychological senses, but also a "metamodel" about that complex.[30] It exhibits the structural and experiential logic of a database by relentlessly multiplying worldlines, as well as by attracting users and fans to be devoted to maintaining and expanding the multiplicity of the database. Both are achieved through a gamelike setting of time travel, a gaming mechanism of replay and reset, and a game-centered, networked system of media mix. This structural/experiential mechanism with proliferating worldlines recalls what Azuma calls "database consumption."[31] Like Manovich, Azuma also sees the database as a structural form that is the antithesis to and the eventual replacement of narrative. Unlike Manovich, however, Azuma does not see the triumph of the database as completely

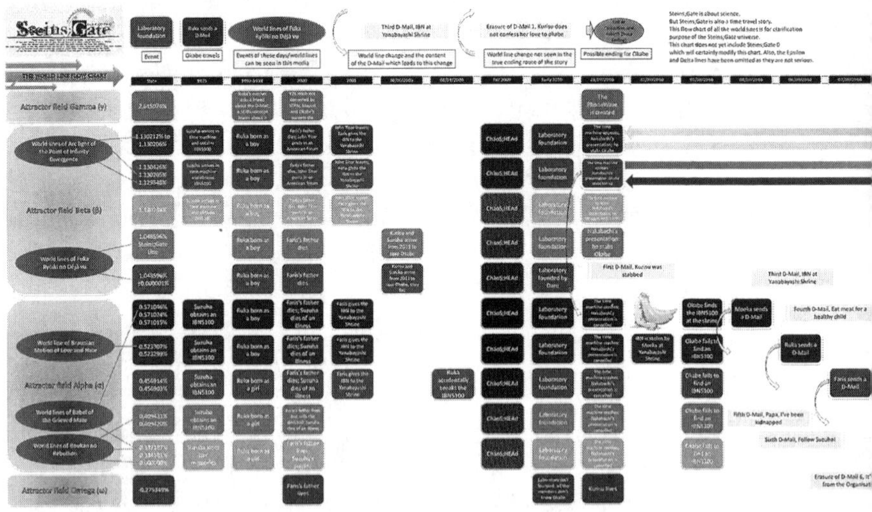

FIGURE 24. A fan-created visual database mapping the expansive network of proliferating worldlines in the transmedia system of *Steins;Gate*. "Timeline," *Steins;Gate* Wiki, https://steins-gate.fandom.com/wiki/Timeline. Credit: sg-epk@jtk93.x29.jp, M.A.D. company, Zeldakasumi (CC BY-SA).

technologically determined but rather associates it with the postmodern condition.[32] According to Azuma, with the decline of the "grand narrative" in postmodernity, the "tree model" of what Eiji Ōtsuka calls "narrative consumption," whereby the consumption of "small narratives" leads to access to the "grand narrative," has been replaced by a double-layered structure of the "database model," whereby the consumption of small narratives on the "outer surface layer" only leads to the "deep inner layer" of the information database—that is, the "grand nonnarrative."[33] This distributive structure of database consumption is organized and sustained by the *moe* elements in characters (e.g., *chara-moe*), with *moe* referring to a certain type of character features that generate affective feelings. In an effective and somewhat reductive manner, Azuma charts this modern-to-postmodern rupture by associating narrative with modern continuity, singularity, and unification, while aligning the database with postmodern dispersal, multiplicity, and fragmentation. For

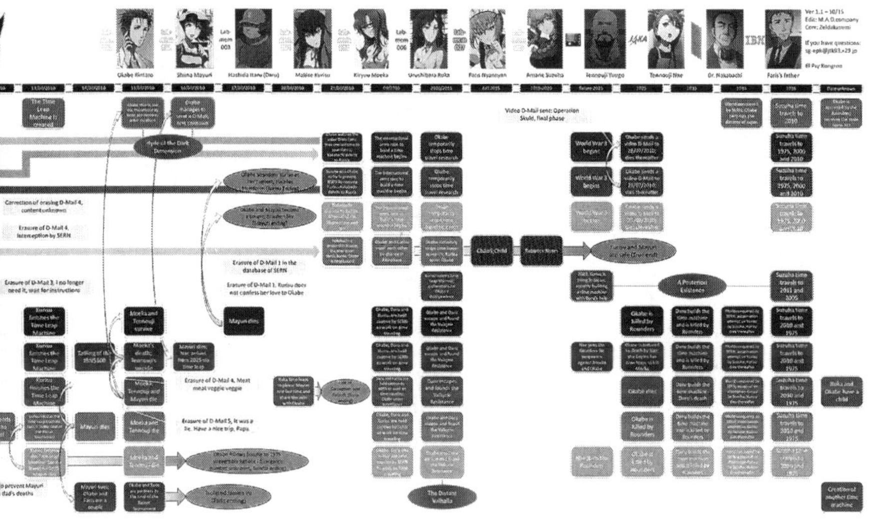

Azuma, the structural logic of database consumption is only intensified with the shift of focus toward games in media mix, because the game-ic tendency accelerates the production of postmodern fragmentation with the proliferation of loops and worldlines.[34]

While the game-centric database system of *Steins;Gate* may seem to testify to Azuma's thesis on postmodern dispersal with its expansive network of proliferating worldlines, it nevertheless complicates this schema of multiplicity by pointing to an opposite direction: the desire for unity and singularity—that is, the tendency toward the "true end." Despite the endless proliferation of alternative timelines, the *Steins;Gate* series is evidently and centrally anchored with one, and the only, "true end" (also known as the "R-worldline" in the series), in which the protagonist not only saves his supposed true love while preventing a future war but also avoids collateral damage to other characters, a mission that is supposed to be impossible in the series' "surface-layer" settings (to borrow Azuma's two-layered model), whereby saving the life of one character by changing the timeline always involves causing the death of another. The route to the seemingly impossible true end, however, lies in the middle between several timelines before the convergence point, which is an extremely narrow and forever-elusive pathway dubbed the "Steins Gate" (これが運命石の扉), a stone doorway to destiny. To reach the perfect destiny of the true end (and the true love)—that is, to find the narrow path of the Steins Gate—a player must unlock hidden secrets buried in the deeper layer of the database, a layer that can be accessed only by going through multiple worldlines with numerous loops of replays and resets, trial and error.

In fact, reaching the true end is so challenging that the game designers of *Steins;Gate* were initially worried that "the players might not be able to clear the game," until they realized that players were able to solve the puzzle collectively "within the first week" by trading information and sharing tips on the internet, a sort of "collective intelligence" that has become a common feature in game culture now.[35] More importantly, the true-end timeline (the "R-line") not only governs the initial game but also anchors the subsequent multimedia spin-offs and variations, for no matter which worldline is being portrayed in that specific media text (e.g., anime, novel, or manga), reaching the Steins Gate is always the central goal of the protagonist (and the player, viewer, or reader), even when the status of the protagonist changes from one character to another. For instance, in the anime feature film *Steins;Gate: The Movie—Load Region of Déjà Vu* (2013), the protagonist changes from the male lead Okabe Rintarō to the female lead Makise Kurisu, but the central drama still centers around how to keep Okabe in the worldline of the Steins Gate so that he will not disappear from his one and only destiny (i.e., being in love with Kurisu), his true love and true ending.

The centrality of the true end (or the "golden," "secret," or "canon" ending) is not only a signature of the *Steins;Gate* series but has also increasingly become the driving force of database culture in general. Ranging from the anime film *Your Name* (*Kimi no Na wa*, 2016) to the video game *Resident Evil 2* (2019), unlocking and reaching the true end through endless cycles of replays has become a cultural obsession. The significance of the true end, in fact, is not so much in its promised singular destiny (the "true") as its very central existence in a media mix system that is supposed to be open, infinite, and expansive—that is, to erase any sense of singularity or totality. In media mix systems, the endless proliferation of worldlines with seemingly infinite possibilities paradoxically intensifies the need and desire for the one and only true end. In other words, there is a stronger desire for singularity when the media mix system provides more multiplicity. Therefore, not only does the true end come to prominence in an expansive system that is supposed to eliminate its very existence, but its popularity and obsession thrives on the game-ic logic that renders the system infinitely multipliable.

If the multitudes of databases, according to Manovich and Azuma, have displaced the singularity of the grand narrative, why are we still so obsessed with the singular true end? The rising popularity of the true end inevitably complicates Azuma's model of database-as-postmodern multiplicity. Instead of postmodern fragmentation and dispersal, the database complex centered on the true end oscillates between multiplicity and singularity, between distribution and unification. In fact, it is the dialectic tension between the centrifugal force of an ever-expanding network of fragments (i.e., the worldlines) and the centripetal force of the increasing desire for unification (i.e., the true end) that fundamentally defines the infrastructural/psychological complex of a database. On the infrastructural level, the expansive network of media mix is always centrally controlled by the producer with the canon text, the official script, and the true ending, despite the participatory effort by fans to produce countless numbers of their own derivative narratives. On the psychological level, the desire for more narratives, information, and connectivity always goes hand in hand with the obsession with a singular trajectory toward the true-end terminal. In fact, more information and a bigger collection of data often evoke a stronger desire for a correct datapath through endless loops of searching, processing, and navigation. Therefore, it is the obsession with both multiplication (worldlines) and unification (true end) that structures the database complex.

Cybernetic Play: Controlling the Database Complex
with Informative Feedback

What is the unifying force behind the psychic/medial logic of the true end? Why are we obsessed with such a singular ending when consuming a database system that is supposed to be multiplied and expanded infinitely? To answer these questions, I want to call attention to the techno-cultural logic of cybernetics, a scientific theory that gave rise to the database as a structure of communication and control, of distribution and integration. The logic of cybernetics, as an organizational principle of networked media culture and technology, is marked by the inherent tension between multiplicity and unification, between the recognition of chaos and the longing for order. Cybernetics has often been read as a theory of control, but I want to stress that cybernetics is, first and foremost, a theory that is fundamentally based on the renewed scientific and philosophical understanding of uncertainty and distributiveness in the twentieth century. The theoretical mechanism of cybernetics, which is to seek integrated control amid distributed uncertainty, forms the foundation of the database complex in both infrastructural and psychological terms.

In his introduction of cybernetics, Norbert Wiener, a scientist who established his career by studying stochasticity through mathematical models of Brownian motion (a phenomenon of random movement of particles), traces the history of cybernetics to thermodynamics and statistical mechanics, two scientific fields that transformed modern science from Newtonian determinism with fixed causality to a new scientific view centered on contingency and probability. Wiener attributes this great scientific revolution to Josiah Willard Gibbs, who introduced statistical probability to physics. But the probability of distributions can only be measured through a mathematical model of integration. In other words, the statistical models of cybernetics are based on dialectic synthesis between distribution and integration. This tension between multiplicity and unification, between uncertainty and measurement, paved the foundation of cybernetics, a techno-science that was developed precisely to deal with this new worldview of contingency and probability. In Wiener's words:

Gibbs' innovation was to consider not one world, but all the worlds which are possible answers to a limited set of questions concerning our environment. His central notion concerned the extent to which answers that we may give to questions about one set of worlds are probable among a larger set of worlds.[36]

This probability of "a larger set of worlds," which is defined as entropy, will always increase, leading to more chaos and uncertainty. Cybernetics was thus developed to "steer" away from this tendency, "to produce a temporary and local reversal of the normal direction of entropy."[37] To control the entropy in the expanding sets of worlds, the most effective mechanism for the "steersman" (the original meaning of "cybernetics") is through feedback loops, which is described by Wiener as "a behavior of learning."

Situated in the historical shift from singular absoluteness to distributive probability, cybernetics is not simply a science of control. Rather, it is marked by the dialectic tension between chaos and order, between uncertainty and knowledge, between distribution and integration. If we understand cybernetics as an almost desperate endeavor to fight against nature's tendency toward chaos (the increase of entropy), the sense of control in cybernetics is already formulated with a lack or an absence in the center. This is a control that can never be actualized but is in a perpetual motion of approaching (through feedback), a permanent state of struggle and agitation.

Perhaps no other sociocultural group has found more resonance with such struggles than the community of otaku and geeks, because they are the ones, as core members of the postindustrial workforce, who have to internalize cybernetic logic into their lives of work and play. As knowledge workers, whose main role in the society is to produce proliferating information and to manage systematic regulation, they are facing the same cybernetic struggle between entropy and control. Therefore, it is no wonder that the media systems that are designed by and for them, such as anime's media mix, also adopt the same cybernetic logic and its affective tension. The cybernetic effort to steer toward order vis-à-vis chaos, which is a restless process of generative affect, is precisely the operational logic that sustains the infrastructural and psychologi-cal complex of anime's transmedia system, which oscillates in the ten-sion between an increasing number of worldlines and a sharper focus on the true end. With more possible worlds generated by the game-ic media mix, we have more information entropy, and more intensified cybernetic impulse to control the tendency of entropy increase—that is, more desire for the true end. Like the cybernetic "steersman" whose mission is "to hold back nature's tendency toward disorder by adjust-ing its parts to various purpose ends," the database complex of anime's media mix relies on the obsession with the true end to control the expan-sive networks of proliferating worldlines.[38] Cybernetic feedback loops are also the mechanism through which the true end can be achieved through repetitive replays with trial and error. The logic of gameplay thus becomes the logic of cybernetic learning through feedback. This cybernetic loop, however, is a highly affective one, for the cybernetic impulse is marked as a perpetual motion of infinite approaching and endless agitation without actualization.

Engineered by the polarizing cybernetic impulses between chaos (worldlines) and control (the true end), the play mechanism that is structured by anime's transmedia system should be defined as "cyber-genic play." It is a mode of play that functions as cybernetic control—that is, "steering." In the *Steins;Gate* series, the control mechanism of cybernetic play-as-steering, as well as its affective dimension, is strongly highlighted by the Divergence Meter, a device that measures the "divergence value" of each worldline in relation to the "original" one. The protagonist/player's mission is to steer the timeline correctly to a specific value so that the Steins Gate, a timeline with the divergence value at exactly 1.048596 percent, can be located to reach the true end. By consuming numerous games, anime, manga, and novels, the player/viewer/reader follows the protagonist's endless journey through count-less timelines at specific divergence values (e.g., 0.571015, 0.523299, 0.456903, 0.409420, 0.337187); the fan community keeps tracking all of them and their values. The Divergence Meter thus functions as a standardization mechanism that organizes the infinite multitudes of timelines into a structured information field with a unified numerical system. The worldlines are no longer diverse narratives but mathematical variables as informational feedback. After trying these feedback loops of different time-travel worldlines with specific divergence values, one's final mission is to steer the timeline to precisely 1.048596 percent so that the true end, the Steins Gate, can be reached. This journey through countless numerical variables, however, is highly affective, because each "wrong" timeline involves collateral damage that is heartbreaking—the tragic death of a friend or a love interest. If one fails to accomplish the correct cybernetic steering, the affective result can be devastating. The cybernetic loop, therefore, is an affective one.

Furthermore, the affective loop of cybernetic learning through trial and error, which centrally anchors the transmedia consumption of *Steins;Gate,* is also designed to train the player/viewer/reader to pay close attention to communicative information. The necessary information that one must learn to collect and process includes the divergence values assigned for each timeline, as well as the hints and clues that are all hidden in emails and text messages. A player's responses to this communicative information—ignore or reply—form the major branching points to reach different timelines. In other words, what one must learn through the cybernetic loops of replays is how to effectively and attentively navigate a dense information field on communication networks. Or, to follow cybernetics, the loops that steer the machine are essentially "control by informative feedback."[39] To facilitate "informative feedback," images that imitate cell-phone and computer screens to display communication information become the major visual motif of the *Steins;Gate* series. These images of information fields are also closely attached to those of *moe* characters, translating the affective feeling toward *chara-moe* to the affective obsession with information (Figure 25). More importantly, the player cannot accomplish this cybernetic learning process by oneself but has to rely on an online community. The game was so difficult that players had to resort to knowledge sharing online.[40] The series thus trains the player to be an active information worker, to navigate networked communication through emails, forums, and social media both within and outside the diegetic universe. By using communication networks in real and fictional contexts as

FIGURE 25. The visual field of communicative information overlaps with that of a *moe* character in gameplay of *Steins;Gate* (2009, developed by 5pb. and Nitroplus).

informative feedback systems to control both fictional timelines and real-life players, *Steins;Gate* establishes a metamodel of the cybernetic complex par excellence, a psychological/infrastructural complex with both communication and control, because cybernetics, according to Wiener, is the theory of communication and control.

This cybernetic model of communication and control has become a popular method to govern the expansive networks of media mix through a gameplay mechanism of feedback loops. Japanese games are arguably leading the trend. For instance, the *Souls* series (2009–), especially the video game *Dark Souls* (2011), was particularly influential in emphasizing the cybernetic process of feedback and learning. Developed by the Japanese company FromSoftware, which was originally founded for developing productivity software for knowledge work, the games in the *Souls* series are famous for unforgiving difficulty, deeply hidden rules, hints, and messages, as well as secret endings that are almost impossible to reach without informative help from online communities. Those secret endings, being "true" or not, are not necessarily the best or happiest endings; instead, they are marked as the most challenging routes that can be unlocked only after trying all other routes and learning all the hidden messages. The *Souls* series heavily relies on networks of cooperative play, cycles of feedback loops, and intensive informational learning. Unlocking and reaching the "true end" is arguably the driving force for this gruesome (and rewarding, according to many players) process of cybernetic play.

But cybernetic play is not simply about the logic of feedback control, which has always been a key mechanism of gameplay. Playing a computer game, according to game designer Will Wright, "is a continuous loop between the users (viewing the outcomes and inputting decisions) and the computer (calculating outcomes and displaying them back to the users)."[41] But what specifically adds to the play mechanism in *Steins;Gate* and the *Souls* series is the fact these games appear to be vast open worlds with endless options. As one commentator observes, "The designers give us these options when all but one of them leads to disaster."[42] Behind the apparent openness, "there's no freedom in *Dark Souls*. The designers let us experience the place on our own, while hooking us on an invisible leash to keep us more or less on task."[43] This dialectic tension between the infinite options and the singular control summarizes the cybernetic logic in numerous Japanese games such as *Persona 4* and *Resident Evil 2*, which all feature a seemingly open-ended universe with diverse routes but only one true ending deeply hidden beneath exceedingly difficult tasks. Such mechanisms also govern game-ic media mix systems, such as *Steins;Gate* and *Persona*. Juxtaposing a vastly open universe of infinite options with a soft control mechanism that operates through networked communication, information navigation, and informative feedback, game-centric media mix systems establish and sustain a metamodel of the database complex that is organized by the cybernetic tension between distributive entropy and unifying control.

Emphasizing the tension between entropy and control, my purpose is not simply to argue that the game-centric media mix follows cybernetic logic. Structured by computer algorithms, video games, of course, are "fundamentally cybernetic software systems."[44] What I want to call attention to is the degree to which this cybernetic logic of gameplay has been taken as a unification force to organize and control the media mix system that is marked by its expansive database structure of infinite multiplicity. This unification force draws a major distinction between my model of cybernetic play and Azuma's two-layered model of database consumption. According to Azuma, there are two models for transmedia consumption of media mix. In the "older model," which Eiji Ōtsuka calls "narrative consumption," consumers engage with small narratives (e.g., character goods, derivative narratives, and fan works) in order to approach the "grand narrative," the "worldview" (*sekaikan*).[45] In Azuma's updated model of "database consumption," the unifying force to drive otaku consumption is no longer the grand narrative but rather the database of *moe* elements. Otaku consume small narratives not to access a fictional grand worldview but to make interactive assemblages of and to feel affective attachment to *moe* characters. As Lamarre points out, "Azuma is referring to a transformation from a narrative-centered media mix to a character-centered media mix."[46]

What I want to propose here is a third model of media mix—cybernetic consumption. Instead of the narrative-centered model of "narrative consumption" or the character-centered model of database consumption, media mix systems such as *Steins;Gate* are gearing toward a game-centered model of cybernetic consumption, whereby the unifying force is cybernetic play with informative feedback toward the true end. In this model, what drives transmedia consumption is not simply affective attachment to *moe* elements but intensive obsession (the complex) with the cybernetic procedure of steering toward the true end, in which one has to learn to improve through the repetitive consumption of various worldlines as feedback loops. In other words, the affective loop attached to *chara-moe* (in database consumption) is replaced by the cybernetic loop steering toward the true end (in cybernetic consumption).

The center of gravity, however, is not the true end itself, which represents neither a grand worldview nor *moe* attachment. Instead, pleasure comes from the difficult but rewarding journey of feedback and resets, for one is supposed to learn and improve only by repeatedly consuming as many probable worlds as possible. More importantly, this gruesome and relentless journey with cycles of trial and error leads *somewhere*—that is, the one and only true end. Although Azuma also stresses the shift toward games in media mix systems, he sees this game-ic tendency as simply an intensification of postmodern dispersal and multiplicity with proliferation of small narratives (e.g., worldlines) in the database.[47] What I want to emphasize, however, is the dialectic relation between the multiplication of worldlines and the cybernetic control toward a single true end. In order to reach the true end, one has to learn and to improve via feedback loops by going through as many worldlines as possible, but the continuously multiplying worldlines only lead to increasing informational entropy that calls for a stronger impulse for control and a greater obsession with the true end. Therefore, the transmedia consumption of a vast collection of small narratives is largely driven by the cybernetic desire to steer toward the singular true end through endless cycles of informative feedback (e.g., worldlines, derivative content, and online communication).

In sum, after Eiji Ōtsuka's model of narrative consumption (character-world model) and Azuma's model of database consumption (character-*moe*-elements model), what we are witnessing is likely the emergence of the third model of media mix, game-centered cybernetic consumption (worldlines-true-end model). In this third model, what drives and unites transmedia consumption is neither a grand worldview (sekaikan) nor the *moe* attachment (*chara-moe*) but the cybernetic mission toward the singular true end.

The *Steins;Gate* series is an illuminating case that marks the transition from character-centered database consumption to game-centered cybernetic consumption. The affective attraction to *moe* characters is still the central force in the series, because each timeline is marked by a romantic relationship with a *moe* character (a worldline is often named after a girl character, such as the "Suzuha line" or "Mayuri line"). The affective feelings toward the *moe* characters, according to fans, intensify the urgency, agony, and pleasure of going through different worldlines. However, the affective loop with *chara-moe* is noticeably displaced by the cybernetic loop toward the true end. The prominent centrality of the true-end timeline—the Steins Gate, which is chosen as the title of the whole series—marks an apparent shift from *moe* attraction toward cybernetic control.

The shift from the *chara-moe* model of database consumption to the true-end model of cybernetic consumption is underlined by the peculiar design of the leading female character, Makise Kurisu, the true love of the male protagonist who is supposed to save this one girl that matters the most to him in the Steins Gate. Based on the standard database of *moe* elements (e.g., cat ears, bells, and spiky hair), Makise Kurisu is designed with almost no *moe* traits. Neither does she have any trendy *moe* characteristics. Lacking apparent *moe* elements, Makise Kurisu can hardly be described as a *chara-moe*. In fact, she is not even clearly framed as an object of male desire, for the stories are often told from her perspective (especially in the spin-off anime, manga, and novels), giving her an almost genuine sense of subjectivity. In contrast, other female characters in the series are evidently designed with identifiable *moe* elements for otaku attachment. By anchoring the true end with the character that has the least *moe* elements, the series gestures toward a new direction that moves away from the character-centered model of media mix. Many fans also noticed that the series, unlike other franchises, was not entirely centered on *moe* attraction but was rather focused on the hard science of time travel. One reviewer commented that the anime series of *Steins;Gate* seemed to be balancing between *chara-moe* and science fiction, with the first half trying to satisfy otaku's affective attachment to *moe* elements while the second half was devoted to the heart-wrenching journey of time travel.[48] Indeed, the transmedia system of *Steins;Gate* is marked by its notable departure from the *chara-moe* model of database consumption and its movement toward a cybernetic model of informative feedback loops. As if to highlight this departure, the publishing company of the series collaborated with IBM to release a short anime miniseries, *Steins;Gate: Soumei Eichi no Cognitive Computing* (2014). The shift from *chara-moe* to cognitive computing metaphorically marked a visible transition of media mix mechanisms.

The transformation from character-centered database consumption to game-centered cybernetic consumption, more importantly, also involves a paradigm shift from visual to cybernetic pleasure. The psychological complex that structures the media mix system is shifting from affect attraction to *chara-moe* that is centered on vision to cybernetic pleasure of informative feedback control that is programmed with action. The affective economy of *chara-moe,* as Lamarre points out, is largely structured by the asymmetrical relation of the look, the "eye loop," even though this structure, which is visually formed with flattened images in anime and manga, does not generate a fixed subject positioning through a cinematic gaze.[49] Instead of a monocular scopophilia, the affective loop of *chara-moe* relies on character design as the anchor point to structure the image field that depends on looking (if not a gaze). The shift from *chara-moe* to the true end, however, shifts the center of gravity from seeing and looking to information searching and processing. Affective experience (e.g., pleasure, obsession, and agitation) no longer simply comes from the "eye loop" but is rather evoked by the endless cybernetic feedback loops of replay and reset. In the *Steins;Gate* series, for instance, the affective attraction to the leading female character, Makise Kurisu, is not so much evoked by the design of her look (which lacks *moe* elements) as it is stimulated by her cybernetic significance as the ultimate true love at the true end that can only be achieved through loops of trial and error. The affective loop of cybernetic actions also restructures the image organization in the media mix, with increasing emphasis on information fields that resemble pulldown menus. If the medium of video games, as Alexander R. Galloway argues, is fundamentally based on informatic actions, the game centered media mix has begun to shift from the regime of visual pleasure toward that of the cybernetic.[50]

The Cybernetic Pleasure of Kong (控):
Between Complex and Control

Where does this cybernetic pleasure come from? Why are players obsessed with the cybernetic procedure of reaching the one and only true end in a system that offers so many different endings? The true end in anime's media mix, as precious and challenging as it may be, is only a fiction, but it provides intense pleasure—through the mode of play—in vividly simulating and temporarily relieving the unresolvable cybernetic tension between entropy and control by providing a fictional solution in a virtual realm. Cybernetic control, as I argued earlier, can never be actualized, but it can be virtualized through the mechanism of play in the form of a fictional true end that one can finally achieve through feedback control. The pleasure of cybernetic play, therefore, derives from the fictional application of cybernetic logic in a virtual world, providing a temporary virtual solution to cybernetic struggle, a solution that is impossible in the actual structure of cybernetic systems. This temporary virtual solution can be important for millennial geeks, who, as knowledge workers, are struggling with the same cybernetic tension in their daily lives, because they are responsible for and subjected to—as producers and consumers—the same polarizing forces between information proliferation and systematic control. For these knowledge workers, the virtual realization of cybernetic control, in the form of a singular true end in a transmedia system with distributive chaos, can potentially provide both a mimetic identification and a fictional relief for their habitual struggle with the internalized cybernetic logic in their workstyle/lifestyle.

This pleasure that is evoked by the virtual realization of cybernetic control brings back the notion of the "complex." Overlapping the infrastructural with the psychological, the complex characterizes both anime's transmedia system and the geek obsession with such a system. Therefore, it is no surprise that *complex* is widespread and perceived as a key word in transnational otaku culture that constitutes and sustains anime's media mix. As I mentioned in chapter 1, the concept of the "complex" (*cong* コン in Japanese and *kong* 控 in Chinese)—which refers to a psychological state of being obsessed with something and is often expressed through compulsive information searching, collecting, and processing—is an immensely popular term in otaku communities in both Japan and China. Based on how the word is understood by otaku, the "complex" is a powerful concept to describe geek obsession with the cybernetic system of media mix in both psychic and medial terms.

Otaku's extensive navigation, consumption, and participation in the transmedia system involve cybernetic logic as both an infrastructural complex (e.g., networked complexity and transmedia connectivity) and a psychological one (e.g., obsessive information search and retrieval).

However, *complex* does not simply imply *complexity*. The Chinese version of this notion, *kong* (控), which is a homophone for the Japanese word *cong* (コン, a homophonic loanword for *complex*), ordinally means control. Overlapping complex and control, being a kong, as either a psychic state or a medial one, always involves a sense of being controlled and in control at the same time—that is, to control and be controlled by one's uncontrollable psychological complex with an uncontrollable media complex. This psychological/infrastructural condition, therefore, is situated in a curious state between complex and control, between being controlled by the complex and being in control of the complex. This peculiar state is where cybernetic pleasure is situated, because cybernetics also operates in the same tension between complex and control. The transmedia system of *Steins;Gate*, for example, operates in this tension by oscillating between the database complex of proliferating worldlines and the cybernetic control toward the true end. Pursuing the singular true end through cybernetic play, by consuming multitudes of worldlines as informative feedback, generates ambivalent feelings of both being in control (of the medial/psychic database complex) and being controlled (by the cybernetic mission). This generative state between the database complex and cybernetic control, which evokes ambivalent feelings of both being in control and being controlled, both power and powerlessness, best characterizes the pleasure (and paranoia) of being a kong—that is, being a postindustrial knowledge geek.

A Cybernetic Room-for-Play

From the hypertextual environment of anime—in both its narrative complexity and its mode of address—to the media mix system that has the cybernetic logic of gameplay at its center, anime constitutes a database complex through its intertextual and intratextual organization, transmedia operations, and modes of consumption. It is a database complex that is organized and managed for cybernetic logic that seeks to control information complexity with infinite feedback loops. In this complex, consuming the transmedial content of anime (e.g., plotlines, worldlines, spin-offs, and derivative content) is an act of cybernetic play, a mechanism of control with informative feedback to unify the expansive database of transmedia franchising. In this system, the narrative forms, modes of consumption, and transmedia expansions all epitomize the cybernetic logic for gameplay. These cybernetic play-forms are also what Gilles Deleuze describes as "ultrarapid forms of free-floating control."[51] But control is not only a technological function; it also has psychological resonance, which is why the meaning of control overlaps with the notion of the "complex" in the Chinese word *kong*. In the cybernetic complex of anime, the psychological implication of control is to be understood through the communicative action of play.

There have been many different interpretations of play: it can be an idealized, free cultural form that is separated from economic production (Johan Huizinga and Roger Caillois), an infantile mechanism to overcome trauma (Sigmund Freud), an allegory of informatic control (Galloway), or a type of post-Fordist free labor (Tiziana Terranova).[52] For Walter Benjamin, however, play represents an alternative possibility of technological innervation through sensory-reflexive activities, which has a therapeutic potential to counteract the destructive, catastrophic effects of modern industrialization. Benjamin conceptualizes play with the notion of "room-for-play" (*spiel-raum*), which is "a vast and unsuspected field of action" that is immensely expanded by technology.[53] Emphasizing "chance" (in gambling) and "repetition" (in children's play), Benjamin's theorization of play seems to anticipate cybernetics that responds to uncertainty (chance) with feedback loops (repetition). His vision of a technological "play-room," an open-ended "field of action" that is infinitely expandable, also echoes the expansive database of anime's media mix system that is centered on the logic of gameplay. Benjamin's somewhat utopian vision of play, though sometimes dismissed as naive, may offer some insight into the therapeutic function of play in the psychological complex of cybernetics. For Benjamin, repetition in play is the "transformation of a shattering experience into habit," and gambling involves a motor-sensory response in a "lightning-quick process of stimulation" at the precise temporality for not "missing chance" or arriving "too late."[54] This "shattering experience" of the "lightning-quick process of stimulation," in an uncanny manner, is almost reminiscent of the ways in which one "plays" in today's cybernetic systems: you have to be quick and repetitive to not miss any chance of important information.

The "room-for-play," though seemingly open and expansive, is full of agitation and agony, for there is a sense of "missing" and "shattering" in the center. As Galloway says: "Using the logic of supplementarity, play reconstitutes the field, not to create a new wholeness but to enforce a sort of permanent state of nonwholeness, or 'nontotalization.' Play is a sort of permanent agitation of the field, a generative motion filling in the structure itself, compensating for it, but also supplementing and sustaining it."[55] This sense of supplementary agitation is where the therapeutic potential may come from, for play is to fill in the "nonwholeness" of the database structure, like cybernetics is to supplement for the loss of Newtonian certainty.

If cybernetics is the science that teaches us how to react to the rise of entropy, uncertainty, and chaos, play is to train us, in a cognitive and neurophysiological manner, how to deal with a vastly expanding field of information that is also marked by a lack of totality in the center. The cybernetic play-room is thus a generative field of permanent agitation, which leads to affective experiences of informatics and informational culture. This cybernetic play-room is also visualized with specific aesthetics of information access and processing, or what Manovich calls "info aesthetics," which will be the focus of the next chapter.[56]

6

The Framing Field

From Superflat Windows to Facebook Walls

That extreme planarity and distribution of power allowed
the viewer to assemble an image in their minds from the
fragments they gathered scanning the image. This
movement of the gaze over an image is a key concept in
my theory of the "super flat."

—Takashi Murakami, *Superflat*

And yet, as the display screens of movies, television, and
the computer begin to grow similar to each other, a new
logic to framed visuality takes hold. The window's
metaphoric boundary is no longer the singular frame of
perspective—as beholders of multiple-screen "windows,"
we now see the world in spatially and temporally fractured
frames, through "virtual windows" that rely more on the
multiple and simultaneous than on the singular and
sequential.

—Anne Friedberg, *The Virtual Window:
From Alberti to Microsoft*

Anime's structural forms and media mix system are paired with and
reenforced by the visual field, which tends to flatten layers of images
and compresses a great number of visual elements onto a crowded
surface without compositional hierarchy or a unified perspective. This
aesthetic tendency toward a flattened, heterogeneous pictorial surface

with a density of distributed information, which has been described as either "superflat" (Takashi Murakami) or "distributive field" (Thomas Lamarre), mobilizes a viewer's gaze.[1] But ultimately, it frames the subject deeply within the techno-cultural structure of an information field. It evokes certain ways of seeing, searching, consuming, and, ultimately, being in the postindustrial environment of knowledge work with proliferating data, networks, and technological mediation of various kinds. More importantly, the rise of this visual aesthetic in anime coincided with the development and dissemination of the graphic user interface (GUI) in computer technology, ranging from Microsoft Windows to Facebook Walls, which have taken hold to establish a new logic in global visual cultures from Japanese anime to Hollywood cinema.

In this chapter, I examine the paradigm shift from Renaissance perspective to superflat vision in light of the theoretical development in interface studies. The chapter addresses the technological condition underlying the changing modes of perception by focusing on the development of computer interfaces that transformed vernacular visual structure, examining the ways in which anime echoes GUI designs by featuring a visual field of a fractured, mobilized gaze, which in turn constructs a hypermediated environment of information navigation and processing. Superflat visuality thus represents increasing mobility and a multiplicity of screens, images, and gazes through the proliferation of digital interfaces. This postperspective vision mobilized by digital interfaces implies a spatiotemporal structure of a heightened state of commodity experience in an information society. The distributive visual surfaces, though mobilizing the viewer's gaze beyond the linear perspective, constitute a framing field to contain the subject within the algorithmic structure and commodity matrix. I will examine how this framing field is developed and operated by beginning with Japanese artist Takashi Murakami's famous notion of "superflat."

Murakami's Superflat

In April 2009, Louis Vuitton released a new project with Takashi Murakami. The million-dollar collaboration between the French luxury brand and the Japanese artist produced a collection of leather goods designed by Murakami, as well as a short, animated video titled *Super-flat First Love*. The romance story in this "first love" features a multicolored panda who guides a teenage Japanese girl through a flood of "LV" monograms to meet young Louis Vuitton in nineteenth-century France. Despite the title, *Superflat First Love* is actually the sequel to Murakami's 2003 video *Superflat Monogram*, which, in a similar animation style, features the same cute panda with big, staring eyes, swimming in an ocean of the brand's multicolor monograms. And the moving images of both animated videos are deliberately flat, depthless, and floating, the signature visual style of what Murakami famously defines and promotes as "superflat."

Many have studied the distinctive visual sensibility of superflat art, which claimed to be informed by Japanese cultural traditions that connect Edo paintings to popular anime, as a radical challenge to the Western visual convention of Renaissance perspective.[2] However, Murakami's superflat campaign for Louis Vuitton, as it turns out, is nothing unique in its fetishization of the luxury brand's graphic trademarks with a depthless visual field. A simple Google search yields countless user-created Louis Vuitton desktops, wallpapers, screensavers, and even a Louis Vuitton Facebook layout. These graphics, like Murakami's superflat art, all take the brand's now-iconic multicolor monograms as the visual cue for a deliberately flat surface. Unlike Murakami's design, however, these depthless images are not for painted canvases or printed leather goods but for the screens of personal computers. As a fashion blogger comments: "Who needs skin, skateboards, or automobile bumpers when you can express your identity—or your brand obsession—by decorating your laptop?"[3] And "this paradoxical combination of in-dividuality and corporate conformity," the blogger goes on, "works on any screen." Indeed, such a depthless image with overflowing Louis Vuitton icons, like Murakami's superflat art, is the ideal format for any screen, from television to computer, from iPhone to iPad, whose ever-flattened and proliferating surfaces are saturating our entire visual environment in the digital age.

What is more stunning about these depthless images is not just their ubiquity but their unnerving combination of personal identity with brand-name commodity or, to borrow that blogger's words, "the paradoxical combination of individuality and corporate conformity."[4] When such a combination is articulated through a flattened visual field, combination becomes equation and interchangeability. In Murakami's superflat videos for Louis Vuitton, the brand's monograms are not only floating on the surface around the two-dimensional cartoon panda but are also printed on the panda's caricature body (Figure 26). This animated character is as much a consumer of the brand as it is the brand itself. And this cartoon panda, with its staring, engaging eyes, as well as its smiling, posing, and camera-ready face (it poses for cell-phone cameras on several occasions), is strikingly reminiscent of an anonymous female face that I encountered on the demo of the Louis Vuitton Facebook layout. That girl's face, like Murakami's panda, smiling and self-displaying, floats on a flat surface saturated with Louis Vuitton monograms, and that surface was metaphorically (and aptly) named the "Wall" by Facebook (before being renamed the "Timeline" but with the same visual design after 2010). If the Facebook Wall was, for a significant period of the early twenty-first century, a prevailing interface that was designed to articulate a personal identity on social media,

FIGURE 26. Louis Vuitton panda in *Superflat Monogram* (2003). Animated short video, Takashi Murakami/Kaikai Kiki Co., Ltd.

then that Wall has a striking similar visual composition as Murakami's superflat art.

Such flattened interchangeability between Murakami's superflat and the Facebook Wall, between a visual field and a computer interface, is what I want to examine in this chapter, focusing on the changing modes of visual perception and the techno-cultural conditions underneath such changes. The nonperspective mode of visualization marks Murakami's superflat art and Japanese anime and has also dominated our visual culture broadly, including cinema, television, video games, and the internet. The very ubiquity of such depthless visuality, from Murakami's superflat animation to the Facebook interface, suggests that what Murakami conceptualized as a unique Japanese artistic tradition is in fact an omnipresent visual mode in a cultural condition that is largely global. Therefore, Murakami's superflat theory, which projects superflat onto Japanese premodern and postmodern cultures as the antithesis of Western modernity, was cast into question.[5] Despite such a fixation on "Japaneseness," Murakami's notion of "superflat" still seems to be the appropriate term to describe this postperspective vision, for it describes a mode of visual perception that is indeed fundamentally different from Renaissance perspective though it may not challenge Western modernity as such.

Borrowing Murakami's notion of "superflat," this chapter takes the concept as both a critical departure and a divergence point. The purpose is to reconceptualize and delineate superflat away from Japanese visual traditions and to map it through the transforming landscape of computer technology and digital media, which, I argue, are the defining forces in changing our modes of viewing, perceiving, consuming, and being. Instead of a simple opposition between Japan and the West, between postmodernity and modernity, I will suggest that the so-called superflat should be understood as a wide-ranging visual mode that is deeply rooted in modern conditions (the mobilization of gaze) and that is further developed with (but not determined by) the techno-cultural situations of the information age. It is not merely an inheritance from premodern Japanese traditions; nor is it simply a leftover from Andy Warhol's postmodern pop art. Instead, what is articulated through the encompassing superflat visuality is a still-transforming cultural logic that is put forward by the increasing mobility and multiplicity of screens, images, information, and gaze in a digital environment that is mediated by various layers of graphic user interface. Such a postperspective vision mobilized by digital interfaces, I would further argue, implies a new spatiotemporal structure of subject position and dislocation that is ultimately propagating and propagated by a heightened state of commodity experience in an algorithmic structure (e.g., Facebook's monetization scheme). Therefore, by mapping the paradigm shift from Renaissance perspective to superflat vision, this chapter hopes to address the technocultural conditions behind the changing modes of perception and subject displacement.

What Is Superflat: Message of the Medium or Logic of the Age?

Marshall McLuhan famously says: "The medium is the message."[6] If superflat is the aesthetic articulation of the message, then the medium here is animation or, specifically, Japanese anime, whose unique visual style of remarkable flatness and negation of depth is widely claimed to be the influence and inspiration of Murakami's idea of superflat. To be fair, the notion of flatness in anime cannot be simply interpreted as completely depthless. Instead, the sense of depth in anime, according to Thomas Lamarre, is rather "a strange depth," because anime organizes its images to create depth (or lack of it) in a manner that is dramatically different from the conventional photographic or pictorial illusion of depth. Fashioning what Lamarre calls "superplanar" imagery, in which the image is densely packed with too many complex layers that all appear equal and without hierarchy, anime's "flatness" is marked by a crushed sense of "depth" that lacks a unified linear perspective.[7] Such a superflattened visual composition that disperses too many elements throughout the surface is characterized by Lamarre as a "distributed field," because the "overall tendency is toward a dehierarchization of layers of the image."[8] Unlike the perspective convention that holds a single viewpoint into a homogeneous depth, superflat imagery fashions a heterogeneous space that results in a radically different viewing experience. Instead of looking into the three-dimensional depth toward a single vanishing point, superflat imagery dispenses viewing positions and directs viewers to move their eyes to scan across the surface. Such a surface-oriented vision that mobilizes the gaze without a unified linear perspective probably best describes the superflat visuality that is celebrated by Murakami.

The superflat vision in anime is also reinforced through its overt emphasis on lateral movement that is often generated by sliding layers of images. By preferring lateral sliding over motion in depth, anime tends to flatten movements and moving visions within the two-dimensional space on the surface. This marks anime's dramatic departure from the visual convention of live-action cinema. Governed by Renaissance perspective, cinema since its very birth has largely preferred an in-depth view of motion. For instance, in the Lumière brothers' *Arrival of a Train at La Ciotat* (1897), the camera is positioned at an oblique angle to create a sensational in-depth view of a moving train. Unlike cinema's obsession with an in-depth view of motion, however, anime fashions a totally different viewing sensation of a lateral movement across the field (instead of into it), which provides viewers with an alternative sensation of speed and motion. Instead of cinema's ballistic perception penetrating the landscape with hyper-Cartesian force and precision, anime creates a sense of floating and weightlessness, as if our viewpoint is flying across the landscape.[9]

The sense of flattened movement in anime, moreover, is manifested by its unique way of creating dynamic movement within a still image, which extends the notion of superflat visuality from spatial orientation to temporal organization. Animation artist Norman McLaren famously claims: "Animation is not the art of drawings-that-move, but rather the art of movements-that-are-drawn. What happens between each frame is more important than what happens on each frame."[10] As insightful as it is, McLaren's notion of "movements-that-are-drawn" apparently is not the only way to create animation. Contrary to McLaren's famous statement, anime not only tends to move drawings (e.g., sliding layers) instead of drawing movements but also frequently creates movement precisely by "what happens on each frame" rather than "what happens between each frame." And this is especially the case in anime when heightened emotions and violent actions are portrayed by still images with exaggerated facial expressions, body gestures, and speed lines. Instead of creating a continuous stream of movement by "animating" a series of images, anime rather generates a "static movement" by using one single still frame as a moment-in-motion—it is a motion within an image rather than an animation between images. By dissecting continuous motion into a single flat moment, it returns anime to its precinematic condition. Marc Steinberg describes anime's motion within stills as "dynamic immobility," a visual style that "made it seem like the image was traversed by movement, even if it was in fact still."[11] For Steinberg, dynamic immobility functions as an intermedial reference to anime's prehistory in manga and *kamishibai* (a form of picture-based storytelling) as aesthetic precursors. And it recalls even earlier precinematic media forms in its mixed temporality—"somewhere between time-lapse photography, instantaneous photography, and the cinema."[12] Indeed, the implication of dynamic motion within a static frame is similar to Eadweard Muybridge's locomotion photography, which is arguably a reverse of the process of cinema and animation proper (though as such it is also the foundation of both). Instead of creating an "illusion" of fluid movement through projecting sequential images, superflat anime, like Muybridge's locomotion photography, dissects a continuous movement into individual stills.

Such motion-in-stills implies a dramatic transgression of time. Like instantaneous photography or frozen frames in cinema, dynamic immobility in anime creates a fractured moment, a flattened temporality that breaks linear progression into sudden timelessness. It is a mode of controlling time that Tom Gunning calls "the manufacture of the instant."[13] This process of producing the pulse of the instant reveals the technological origin for moving images: "the emergence of motion out of stillness, of continuity out of discontinuity."[14] If cinema strives to conceal its technological origin—the discontinuity of the machine—by creating seamless temporality of continuous motion, anime's dynamic immobility exposes the (often invisible) discontinuous process of motion production by flattening the machinic force of temporal discontinuity onto the visual force of spatial discontinuity—the gaps and intervals between still images. This manufacture of the instant, therefore, is a spatialization of time, a process of temporal transformation that is more multiple than singular, more simultaneous than sequential, which forms the temporal regime of the superflat vision. This temporal transgression—the flattening and layering of time—which is implied in dynamic immobile images, echoes the networked, hypertextual structure in anime narratives. Instead of a linear progression of time in a classical narrative, anime creates a nonlinear sense of time in a superflat temporality toward multiplicity and simultaneity, as time is, both visually and narratively, fractured, multiplied, and layered on the surface.

This aesthetic style of superflat has its specific lineage in Japanese TV anime, which began with the styles of limited animation of Osamu Tezuka in the 1960s and culminated in the work of the Gainax Studio in the 1990s. The dehierarchized visual field of flat compositing, the lateral movement of sliding layers, and the dynamic immobile images that use stills to convey motion, were all developed as limited cel-animated techniques that were deployed by Tezuka's Mushi Production to produce television animation such as *Astro Boy* (1963–66) in a quick, efficient, and budget-friendly fashion within the tight production schedule of TV programming. These techniques of limited animation "form the basic pattern for all anime subsequently."[15] Although later animation in Japan was no longer as limited as it was in the 1960s, the overall aesthetic tendency of limited animation remains a signature style that gives a distinctive look to TV anime, which still largely relies on flattened layers of compositing, lateral relative motion, and dynamic stills as basic techniques of animation production. The prevalence of these "flattening" techniques in TV anime, which is marked by its restrictive limitation in time and budget, highlights the relationship between superflat aesthetics and the technological conditions (or difficulties) of producing moving images in animation: arranging multiple layers of cels in front of a vertical camera (which results in dehierarchized compositing and lateral sliding) and manufacturing the instant between stillness and motion (which forms the style of dynamic immobility).[16] Anime's limited animation techniques that lead to the superflat style push the technological conditions of animation to the technical extreme. In other words, superflat is, to a certain degree, the aesthetic cultivation of the medium specificities of animation that entails its structural problems (and solutions) in compositing, movement, and temporality.

If the superflat vision is the message of anime as a distinctive medium form of animation, then that message seems to be a direct antithesis to the message of another medium: live-action cinema. For the apparatus film theorists, cinema is an ideological machine that genealogically inherits linear perspective from Renaissance paintings. The cinematic apparatus, in spite of occasional exceptions, consistently retains the convention of Cartesian perspective through various means, including single-lens camera and projection that enforces a singular point of view (Jean-Louis Baudry), as well as linear narrative and continuous editing that disavow disjunctions and maintain a unified perspective (Stephen Heath and David Bordwell).[17] Although there have been critiques of apparatus theories, the complex relationship between Renaissance perspective and photographic cinema still remains a central subject in film criticism. With its flattened space, lateral sliding, and motion in still images, the superflat imagery in anime fashions itself as a dramatic paradigm shift from a cinematic perspective. Its superplanar image and lateral movement challenge Renaissance conventions' governing of space by providing multiple—instead of singular—viewpoints, and its emphasis on the frozen moment in a single image, instead of continuous movement between images, disrupts linear cinematic temporality that is also regulated by perspective conventions. Such a paradigm shift puts forward a new way of looking and perceiving, a postcinematic vision, so to speak, which implies multiple perspectives scanning across the surface instead of a singular viewpoint looking into a distant vanishing point. And this shift of perception fashions a highly mobilized gaze. As Murakami puts it, superflat should be characterized primarily in "the way that a picture controls the speed of its observer's gaze."[18]

For Murakami, the message that is articulated by superflat—a mobilized gaze that challenges linear perspective—is distinctively Japanese.

Tracing back to ukiyo-e paintings in Japan's Edo era, superflat is celebrated by Murakami as an essential part of what could be considered Japaneseness, which is inherently postmodern but is antithetical to Western modernity. Murakami is not alone in his nationalist appropriation of superflat. According to Lamarre, there is a whole school of "otaku discourse" that seeks to establish a linear genealogy of superflat visuality that continues from the premodern culture of Edo Japan to the postmodern culture of anime and manga.[19] Not unlike apparatus film theory that is comfortably settled with a direct teleology from Renaissance paintings to cinema, the otaku discourse is based on the assumption of a direct and unquestioned genealogical continuity from Edo paintings to superflat anime. What is conveniently omitted in this discourse that directly connects premodern Edo with postmodern superflat is Japan's own technological and cultural experience of modernity, as well as all the historical and political questions associated with it. As Lamarre points out: "Superflat theory wishes above all to avoid dealing with questions about Japanese modernity and its relation to Western modernity. As such, superflat theory risks becoming yet another discourse on Japanese uniqueness (*Nihonjiron*), which celebrates Japan as always already postmodern."[20]

Of course, one can easily dismiss Murakami's celebration of superflat as nothing more than a valuable trademark—an exotic, "avant-pop" version of Japan that can be sold to a global market. As Steinberg points out, Edo exists for Murakami less as a real historical period than as a consumable "database of elements," and "the nationalist appeal to Japanese tradition—or a unique Japanese senility—is a marketing strategy, a selling point."[21] But what is at stake here is not simply dismissing Murakami's nationalistic discourse but realizing that superflat as a visual aesthetic is not distinctively Japanese. Neither is superflat's challenge to Renaissance perspective a unique message of Japanese anime. Instead, the superflat vision has become a global cultural trend and its message is being articulated across various media forms and platforms that are rapidly converging. What is described as superflat in anime is actually a prevalent visual mode that can be identified in a wide variety of media cultures across the world: in Hollywood films, computer animation, comic books, game interfaces, web design, and consumer electronics. As Andrew Darley points out, the global mainstream visual culture in the digital era "is largely given over to surface play and the production of imagery that lacks traditional depth cues."[22]

Superflat Screens and the Aesthetic of Hypermediacy

In fact, as early as the 1980s, superflat aesthetics had already manifested in many American science-fiction films. For instance, Ridley Scott's *Blade Runner* (1982), which was influenced by the dense visual style of the contemporary comic magazine *Heavy Metal* and by famous cartoonists such as Moebius (Jean Giraud), Philippe Druillet, and Angus McKie, exhibits spectacular visual complexity with a dramatically transgressed scale and perspective.[23] The film's stunning cityscape images largely echo the tightly packed superplanar imagery in anime and superflat arts. Indeed, put side by side, the superflat images in Murakami's artworks look strikingly similar to the visual density in *Blade Runner*—they are all superflattened by complex and compacted layers and visual details. Such flattened and surface-oriented spatial density, which is displayed in many 1980s science-fiction films, is what Vivian Sobchack calls "hyperspace"—a space that is "semantically described as a surface for play and dispersal."[24] Such a hyperspace could be either a "deflation of space" (e.g., the two-dimensionality and superficiality in *Tron* [1982]), or an "inflation of space" (e.g., the visual density and complexity in *Blade Runner*), or both (e.g., the "busy, eclectic, and decentered mise-en-scene" in *Liquid Sky* [1982] and *Repo Man* [1984]).[25] To a certain degree, the superflat imagery in anime can be classified in Sobchack's third category of hyperspace. It is both a deflation of space by flattening it with an excess of surface and an inflation of space by saturating it with an excess of visual complexity, and the result is what Sobchack calls "excess scenography":

> Elements of the mise-en-scene once arranged in space to represent depth now arrange themselves shallowly on and across space. . . . The

effect is a material overload that exceeds visual grasp and gives every-thing, everyone, and every activity a certain non-hierarchy equivalence.[26]

Such a hyperspace popularized by the flattened, dehierarchized spa-tial representation and arrangement in American cinema, Japanese anime, and Murakami's superflat art, to some degree, is informing and informed by the transformation of real architectural space in postmod-ern cityscapes—Hong Kong, Tokyo, and New York—that are all satu-rated with depthless surfaces of shining glass and giant digital screens. As Scott Bukatman says: "The new monument is no longer the substan-tial spatiality of the building, but the depthless surface of the screen. This is a transformation literalized in *Blade Runner* by the proliferation of walls which *are* screens."[27] Indeed, as Anne Friedberg observes, the transformation of imaginary space in cinema and television coincided with the transformation of the material reality of built space that is increasingly moving toward expansion and the multiplicity of glass, surfaces, and screens.[28] And the ultimate triumph of depthless surface in our physical space, not surprisingly, is also carried over to cyber-space. Facebook's billion-dollar Wall is probably just one indication.

From the imaginary space in *Blade Runner* to the real space of Tokyo, from anime's surface-oriented imagery to Facebook's comput-erized interfacing Wall, it seems that the visuality of superflat is not the specific message of one particular medium; rather, it points to the cultural logic of our current information age. Indeed, we should be re-minded that before Murakami coined the term, "SuperFlat" was in fact a well-advertised model name for Panasonic's flat-screen television. The sense of superflatness has become such a cultural fetish in the digital age that almost any design for electronic devices—from televi-sions to cell phones—tries to evoke a cliché imagination of flatness and slimness. Superflat is supposed to be the default design of our latest gadgets. The predominance of superflat visuality almost rend-ers its countercurrent—the increasing obsession with 3D computer graphics in cinema and video games—to seem reactionary against the very loss of depth in contemporary visual culture.

According to Sobchack, the prevalent visual flatness in our current cultural environment is a semantic response to electronic media, which is a system of simulation without the "original" and thus "has to attract spectator interest at the surface."[29] Such a reading of the "electronic simulacra" as the ontological base of visual flatness echoes Thomas Looser's interpretation of superflat as "characteristics that are tied to digital as opposed to analog," because the digital operates in a system that lacks the "interior self" (the real) and thus "can be thought of as 'flat.'"[30] Sobchack and Looser are certainly right in pointing to new media technology as the condition of superflat visions. However, their ontological reading of the digital/electronic as "simulacra" and thus "flat," though theoretically sound, seems to reductively assume a direct and unquestioned connection between the semantic depthlessness (i.e., a lack of the interior or the original) of digital media and the actual visual flatness of images. What about the technological and cultural practices that render such a connection possible? How does the simulacra nature of digital media result in widespread flatness in visual culture? What is the mediation between the semantic surface in the digital and the visual surface in the superflat?

Instead of the ontological relations between digital media and visual depthlessness, I argue that the prevalence of the superflat visuality has more to do with the discursive and material realties of information technology, which have radically mobilized and fractured our gaze from Renaissance perspective to surface-oriented visions. In her groundbreaking book *The Virtual Window,* Anne Friedberg traces the visual history from single-point perspective in Leon Battista Alberti's famous Renaissance metaphor of the "window" to the fractured and multiplied vision in Microsoft's commodified Windows system on personal computers. According to Friedberg, the centuries-long dominance of linear perspective, though constantly being challenged by various technologies, media, and art forms, still largely holds our vision to a single image in a single frame. In the current information age, however, "perspective may have met its end on the computer desktop."[31] With multiple windows coexisting and overlapping, the windows trope on the computer screen fundamentally formed a new vernacular system of visuality that is emblematic of the collapse of the Albertian perspective. Instead of a transparent window to look through into a distant vanishing point, the windows in computers overlap, obscure, and disorient—they are windows that we do not see through.[32] A transparent viewpoint with perspective depth is replaced with a dehierarchized field with information density. This virtual window of the computer age—a new logic of the "technological framing of the visual field"—is precisely the message that is being articulated in superflat. As critic Raphael Rubinstein points out, Murakami's superflat arts "owe as much to computer screens as they do to Edo screens."[33] The densely packed, overlapping, and dehierarchized superplanar images literalize the fractured frames in Microsoft's virtual windows. They articulate the very sense of visual mobility and multiplicity in the digital age that prioritizes information navigation over Cartesian penetration.

The kinship between the visual field of superflat and the Windows interface on computers is highlighted by the abundance of represented and remediated digital interfaces (or "windows") in popular anime (Figure 27), which suggests the aesthetic and technological connections between animation and computer interfaces. These animated images that mimic computer screens, according to Christopher Bolton, are also the ones that appear to be the most graphically realistic in anime, which often uses layered and flattened animation images to evoke and comment upon our mediated perception in digital culture.[34] For instance, in both *Patlabor 2* (1993) and *Ghost in the Shell* (1995), director Mamoru Oshii uses dehierarchized visual fields with dense layers of flashing data and information to vividly mimic a hypermediated vision that is filtered, enhanced, or distorted by digital censors, viewfinders, eyeglasses, screens, and monitors. The ways in which these various media screens can be imitated with such a high degree of accuracy by common techniques in anime suggests the deeply rooted techno-cultural connections between animation and digital interfaces. Not only does the multilayered compositing in animation prepare us for the multiple windows overlapped on a computer screen, but the manufactured instant between motion and still that gives an animated illusion of life also preconditions the cultural expectation of the instant response of a "click,"

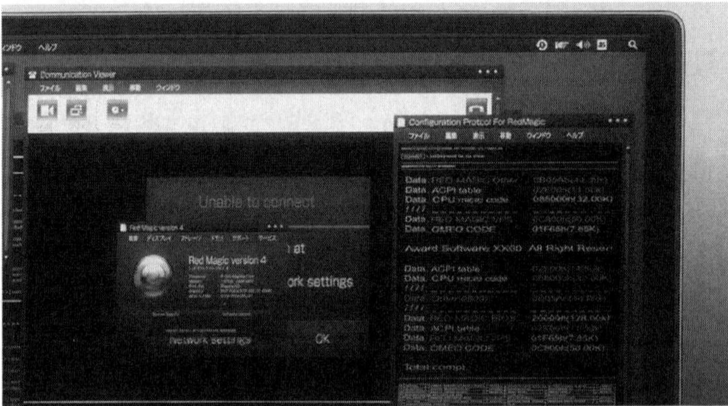

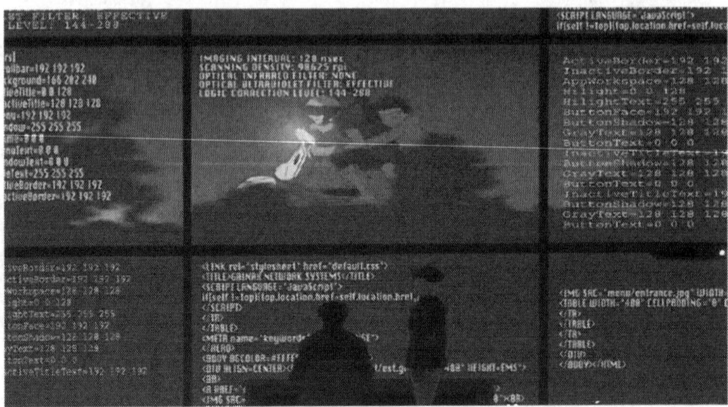

FIGURE 27. Superflat imagery is frequently used in anime to simulate informatic interfaces on digital screens. (*top*) *Valvrave the Liberator* (2013); (*middle*) *Subete ga F ni Naru* (The perfect insider, 2015); (*bottom*) *FLCL* (2000).

which transforms a computer interface from "spectral" to "live."[35] Thus, it is not surprising that the default design of a graphic user interface, which is often programmed with JavaScript, is a dynamic visual field that is largely animated (technically, aesthetically, and metaphorically).

The animated, remediated, and hypermediated interfacing effect that is visualized in the superflat imagery is, by and large, a posthuman vision. The flattened and dehierarchized images invite viewers to see the world through a networked information field with dense layers of data. In fact, cyborg vision rendered in superflat imagery is one of the most recurrent visual motifs in anime, which gained global recognition for anime as one of the most popular cultural forms to explore posthuman conditions. For instance, in *Serial Experiments Lain* (1998), an anime series that is marked by its superflat style, the title character Lain is often pictured in close-ups framed in a variety of screens—she appears on television screens, outdoor LCD screens, computer monitors, and cell phones. Since Lain is eventually revealed to be an artificial intelligence created by cyberspace, the ubiquitous imagery of Lain on layers of screens explicitly associates the omnipresence of posthuman conditions with the prevalence and proliferation of superflat visual fields in digital media. Framed in anime's superflat screen, posthuman vision is nevertheless highly mobile. Lain's flattened image moves across multiple media and appears on almost any screen. *Lain* thus equates the dehierarchized visual field with the posthuman condition of hypermediacy, mobility, and multiplicity. Like those monstrous eyes displayed in Murakami's famous work *Wink* (2001), the mobilized gaze in superflat visuality is a posthuman vision mediated and augmented by layers of digital screens.

Such a mobilized, posthuman gaze also implies a new kind of spectator who is often called a "user." As Lamarre points out, superflat images are "complexly flat," and viewing such dehierarchized, overcrowded, and remarkably disorienting images is like "orienting yourself in a densely packed distributive field—a sort of information field."[36] In other words, watching superflat anime evokes an experience that is akin to information surfing, searching, and processing. It evokes a cybernetic pleasure of information navigation that has overtaken the traditional visual pleasure of the cinematic gaze. And such a cybernetic pleasure implies a new type of viewer—"one more comfortable with scanning for information and stacked windows of data."[37] Thus, it is no surprise that the superflat style, which began in limited animation in the 1960s, culminated in Japanese anime and gained global popularity in the 1990s, when the rise of information technology—with multiwindow screens—nurtured a new generation of viewers and consumers. Indeed, if superflat imagery with densely packed layers resembles our computer screens that have increasingly been overpacked by stacks of windows, piles of web pages, and countless pop-ups, then the superflat vision with a highly mobilized gaze would certainly strike postindustrial knowledge geeks as reminiscent of their daily experience of hours of programming, gaming, web surfing, and social networking.

The visual field of superflat is often associated with a certain kind of narrative construction: the networked, hypertextual structure that I discussed in chapter 5. In fact, when the superflat style culminated in the 1990s with the success of the Gainax Studio, anime had also perfected its hypertextual, database-like narrative forms that privilege complex storylines with a crowded body of characters interacting in an ever-expanding and interlocking web of puzzles, twists, clues, references, and confusing leads. In a large number of anime series since the 1990s, both the visual (with densely packed, dehierarchized layers) and the narrative (with a networked, mazelike structure) are constructed as information fields. "This is the visual and narrative equivalent of graph theory and social network theory," to borrow from Alexander R. Galloway.[38] This visual and narrative construction of information fields with extreme density and complexity, which are designed not to be gazed at or understood but to be searched, navigated, and played with, is certainly catering to a digital generation of knowledge workers who are comfortable with, or even longing for, information overload.

The emergence of this generation of knowledge workers and consumers, who are equipped with a highly mobilized gaze and a heightened appetite for information, is a global phenomenon. The mobilized vision in anime and superflat art is also evidently present in other popular culture, including Hollywood cinema and network television.

According to Dana Polan, "cyber-age films" in Hollywood, ranging from *Pulp Fiction* (1994) to *The Matrix* (1999), often fashion a computer-screen-like style, which seduces our eyes with countless minute visual details that require "constant spectator alertness."[39] Similarly, in Hollywood's CGI films, Deborah Tudor notes a visual system that she calls "array aesthetics." Exemplified by the use of split-screens as in Mike Figgis's *Timecode* (2000) and the multilayer images resembling comic strips as in Ang Lee's *Hulk* (2003), the effect of array aesthetics "evokes computer arrays in the form of simultaneous open windows," which constitute "a new configuration of space and time."[40] Like superflat imagery, array aesthetics that resemble layers of computer windows also evoke a new type of viewer and viewing experience, catering to the digital-generation audience who is "often quite comfortable working simultaneously with an array of multimedia devices."[41] To a large degree, array aesthetics are Hollywood's own version of superflat, with their fractured and multiplied layers (arrays, windows) of audiovisual information and mobilized multimedia experiences. Galloway also notices a similar style—polyptych visual simultaneity with the windowing effect—in the American television show *24* (2001–10), which is "the great aesthetic leaps of the graphic user interface beyond the example set by the cinema."[42] Galloway characterizes this aesthetic tendency as "informatics as style"—that is, "*the distributed network as an aesthetic construction.*"[43] Indeed, both array aesthetics in Hollywood cinema and superflat in anime can be described as "informatics as style," and they imply a type of spectator who is, in Friedberg's words, a "beholder[] of multiple-screen 'windows,' . . . [who] see[s] the world in spatially and temporally fractured frames, through 'virtual windows' that rely more on the multiple and simultaneous than on the singular and sequential."[44]

Designed for the beholders of multiple windows, superflat is the visual aesthetic of hypermediacy. In their book *Remediation*, Jay David Bolter and Richard Grusin define *immediacy* and *hypermediacy* as the "double logic of remediation," which characterizes a media culture's contradictory tendencies "to erase its media in the very act of multiplying them."[45] These two logics of remediation are also associated with

different systems of aesthetics. The logic of immediacy, which pre-
scribes the tendency of a medium whose purpose is to disappear, is
expressed by the aesthetic of visual transparency that is governed by
linear perspective, because "by using projective geometry to represent
the space beyond the canvas," linear perspective dissolves the presence
of the medium and immerses the viewer in the world beyond.[46] This
logic of transparent immediacy has its aesthetic genealogy from the
Renaissance painting to cinema to virtual reality, all of which rely on
linear perspective to promise immediacy. On the other end of the spectrum is the logic of hypermediacy, which characterizes our fascination
with mediation and our desire for multiplying and intensifying the
effects of media presence. Contrary to transparent immediacy, the logic
of hypermediacy is expressed by the aesthetics of opacity, multiplicity,
and heterogeneity, which are best represented by the windows trope in
graphic user interfaces on computers:

> The multiplicity of windows and the heterogeneity of their contents
> mean that the user is repeatedly brought back into contact with the inter-
> face. . . . Where immediacy suggests a unified visual space, contemporary
> hypermediacy offers a heterogeneous space, in which representation is
> conceived of not as a window on to the world, but rather as "windowed"
> itself—with windows that open on to other representations and other
> media.[47]

The logic of hypermediacy that Bolter and Grusin identify is also the
logic of superflat, a heterogeneous and dehierarchized visual field with
mobilized and multiplied viewpoints. By associating superflat with
hypermediacy, my purpose is not to situate the aesthetic of superflat
within the genealogy of remediation but to point to an alternative possibility to theorize superflat imagery outside the familiar binary between
Japanese postmodernity and Western modernity. In fact, the logic of
hypermediacy, not unlike that of immediacy, also has its lineage in
visual forms that emerged in the techno-cultural conditions of early
modernity: illuminated manuscripts, baroque cabinets, Dutch paintings, and optical toys, all of which correspond to a modern objective of

mobility and multiplicity of observation.[48] If we understand superflat as the aesthetic of hypermediacy that has its lineage from optical toys to computer interfaces, we may realize that superflat is neither a cultural inheritance from premodern Edo nor a pop version of postmodern "cool Japan." Instead, superflat manifests a cultural logic that is deeply rooted in the modern conditions that crave visual mobility and that come to culmination in the techno-cultural situation of postindustrial informationalism, which is marked by an increasing mobility and multiplicity of screens, images, and data that are hypermediated by various layers of interfaces, a condition that cannot be simply described as "postmodern."

Decentered (and Databased) Self in the Framing Field

Renaissance perspective has been critiqued for its ideological function: constructing a unified modern subjectivity through its fixation of a singular viewpoint. The superflat vision, in contrast, with its lack of such a unified and hierarchized single point of depth, seems to challenge the system of modern subject formation with a fractured identity.[49] Thus, superflat subjectivity, with its decentered and fractured self, is often described as "postmodern."[50] Indeed, superflat's overt emphasis on surface and depthlessness is dramatically in tune with the often-inflated discourse on postmodernism, such as superficial simulacra (Jean Baudrillard), decentered subjectivity (Jacques Derrida), and "a new depthlessness" with the disappearance of history (Fredric Jameson).[51] Such discourse, as it turns out, is also extremely popular in Japan, a nation that has constantly been celebrated as essentially and uniquely postmodern. Thus, it is not surprising that language of the "postmodern" is precisely what Hiroki Azuma uses to analyze Murakami's superflat art.[52] But ironically, when Azuma charts a clean diagram illustrating a somewhat reductive genealogy that positions "postmodern" as a linear historical progression after "modern," he seems to forget that the definition of *postmodern* often involves the very loss of history as such. In fact, as Friedberg notes, the "'p' word" has been overused, inflated, and destabilized to such a degree that the debates are often infused with "many epistemic assumptions that the theorists of postmodern themselves would challenge—the ontology of history, the denotative certainty of definition."[53] Indeed, as we are increasingly being positioned, in both popular and academic discourse, in the postmodern landscape of the postmodern age, this overarching notion, with its threatening totalization of everything and everywhere, starts to lose meaning. Furthermore, when decentered superflat subjectivity is too easily coupled with the postmodern, it forecloses all other possibilities of understanding the concrete material and discursive practices that popularize such superflat vision into so-called postmodernity. In other words, by reading superflat vision simply as a symptom of the postmodern condition, we ignore the fact that this vision may also be a contributing cause of such a condition.

But if not the "'p' word," what is the best way to characterize the cultural condition of superflat subjectivity? As a highly mobilized gaze propagated by digital interfaces, the superflat vision, in fact, entails a heightened experience of networked consumption, which renders superflat a unique cultural logic of information capitalism. It is in the cultural and technological relations between a mobilized gaze and commodity experience that superflat finds its entry into postmodernity. Indeed, as Friedberg argues, the cultural condition of the postmodern can only be understood "in terms of virtual mobility of everyday life."[54] For Friedberg, the (post)modern condition—decentered and detemporalized subjectivity—is the result of increasing cultural centrality of a "mobilized 'virtual' gaze" that has always been imbued with the power of commodity experience.[55] This virtual gaze, which used to be only partially mobilized by cinema and television, is now dramatically multiplied, fractured, and dispersed by the superflat interfaces of computers, mobile phones, and the internet. It is such a highly mobilized gaze in the commodity matrix of information capitalism that forms the cultural condition behind superflat's decentered and displaced subjectivity.

Such a mobilized, virtual gaze as subject construction and dislocation for commodity experience seems to be precisely what Murakami is implying in the aptly titled *Eye Love SUPERFLAT,* which is among the artworks he provided for Louis Vuitton (2003, Figure 28). Like his previous superflat artworks, Murakami uses floating, staring, and weightless eyes as a metaphor for a mobilized gaze. That gaze, as is

FIGURE 28. Takashi Murakami, *Eye Love SUPERFLAT*, 2003. Acrylic on canvas mounted on board, 100 × 100 cm (39.4 × 39.4 inches). Copyright 2003 Takashi Murakami/Kaikai Kiki Co., Ltd. All rights reserved.

suggested by the smart homophonic pun (*eye* as *I*) in the title, is also a decentered subject. But the eyes (or "I"s) here are not just floating in an ambient space. They are happily swimming, together on the same surface, with equally afloat and weightless Louis Vuitton multicolor monograms. When the gaze is metaphorically represented by such flat and weightless but cute and seemingly innocent eyes, the gaze is not only mobilized but is also flattened and abstracted, both spatially and temporally; the superflat visuality projects the spectator into a depthless construction and dislocation of spacelessness and timelessness. Or, to borrow Friedberg's words, that floating eye in Murakami's superflat image is a mobilized virtual gaze from "elsewhere and elsewhen."[56] More importantly, when that gaze is put side by side, on the same surface, with the commodity (Louis Vuitton icons) at which it is supposed to be gazing, the look becomes the looked-at, the consumer becomes the consumed. Indeed, in Murakami's *Eye Love SUPERFLAT,* the color, size, and shape of the eyes are such a perfect match with LV icons that the eyes completely blend in with the surrounding monograms. The positions of the eyes are also organized within the monogram pattern. Upon first look, one might even mistake the eyes as round-shaped buttons sewed on Louis Vuitton leather goods. The "eyes"/"I"s in Murakami's superflat vision, therefore, are an integral part of the commodity matrix. And the gaze (the "eye"/"I," the subject), though mobilized, is also confined within that well-framed architecture of commodity experience (the perfect LV pattern). Just as Friedberg describes, "the shopper is dialectically both the observer and the observed, the transported and confined, the dioramic and the panoptic subject."[57]

The shoppers that Friedberg describes are the ones that still go to shopping malls. But that type of shopper is now replaced by virtual ones in cyberspace. In cyber malls, from Amazon to Taobao, from Google to Baidu, from Niconico to Bilibili, the mobilization of the gaze is pushed to a whole new level. Now, our vision is completely "free," and we are window-shopping every day and everywhere through the digital windows of our computer interfaces. Whenever we open our internet browsers or cell-phone apps, we are bombarded with virtual displays of all kinds of consumer goods wrapped in a flood of data and information: from new Apple gadgets to antique Atari consoles, from the latest episode of an anime series to a restored video of a 1950s B movie. To borrow a now-classic quote from the anime film *Ghost in the Shell*: "The net is vast and infinite." What a perfect depiction of our digital market with informational totality! The superflattened interchangeability between consumer identity and consumable information—as is articulated in Murakami's superflat images that resemble the Facebook interface—is now celebrated as a new cultural norm, when our personal life is reduced to a set of data that is calculated, analyzed, and then delivered back to us as personalized marketing, in which our identities are nothing more than a list of brands and commodity categories that the computer networks decide we should be interested in. Or, in broader terms, our affective attachments—the things we like and people we care about—are literalized, informationalized, and managed through layers of flattened and windowed interfaces—the Facebook Wall, the Like button, the WeChat feeds, and the *danmaku* comments—into a set of algorithmically structured data that are aptly called a "social graph" for monetization. The graph theory of digital platforms is expressed as the informatic aesthetic of superflat interfaces. Through the virtual window of computerized and networked interfaces, our gaze and subjectivity are not just flattened and decentered, they are databased and informationalized. When we look at the Net, the Net looks back and devours us. In Murakami's superflat art, the "eye"/"I" equals the LV monogram; on the Facebook Wall, the self equals data. The widespread superflat vision in the digital age may well be a manifestation of such a data-based self.

In the post-Fordist economy, the digital subjects who are mobilized, decentered, and databased on networked interfaces are not only consumers but also producers, although mostly unpaid ones offering free labor. In anime culture, the distributed visual field of the superflat style flattens the power hierarchy in culture production, encouraging a high degree of collective participation from the viewers as producers of fan culture of various kinds. In fact, the most celebrated champion of the superflat style, Gainax Studio, is well known to be established by former fans who entered the distributed field of anime by directly participating in professional media productions. Indeed, one of the key interface effects of the superflat visual field is to mobilize the viewers and to solicit their actions and participation. Superflat images are not simply to be looked at but also to be acted upon (scanning, interpreting, and playing with them in participatory fan culture), just like the graphic user interface that is supposed to solicit user actions (clicking, typing, searching, and navigating). Therefore, in the visual field of superflat, it is the evoked action more than the mobilized gaze that provides a sense of what Tara McPherson calls "volitional mobility."[58]

Evoking interfaced actions, this distributive field that invites participation, however, is a framing field of entrapment, because the superflat visual field, whose interface effect is to mediate the relationship between work and play, is a perfect aesthetic construction for the post-Fordist economy. In Murakami's superflat art, the "eye"/"I" is both looking and being looked at; on the interface of the Facebook Wall, the subject is both consuming and being consumed. Such is the logic of information capitalism, whereby all digital actions are to be enframed and exploited as informational work and commodity. If the distributive visual field in Murakami's *Eye Love SUPERFLAT* turns the "eye"/"I" into an abstracted commodity (like a button on Louis Vuitton leather goods), the distributive information field in the digital economy "turns seemingly normal human behavior into monetizable labor."[59] The viewing subject is mobilized and liberated in a decentralized field, but only to be captured, enframed, and exploited in a techno-economic matrix. This decentered and displaced but still well-structured subjectivity, as Lamarre argues, is "not a transcendental subject but a projected or projectile subject pursuing lines of sight."[60] Indeed, the distributed "eyes" are precisely such "projectile subjects" and the pursued "lines of sight" are the computerized structure and commodity matrix known as the interface, the algorithmic frames of the virtual window that entraps the subject as measurable and monetizable user stickiness. In other words, the distributive field of superflat is, in fact, a framing field that is systematized by the techno-economic force of informationalism.

This framing field is adopted and explored by many East Asian artists who embrace the superflat style under the banner of *nijigen* (*erciyuan* 二次元 in Chinese). A popular Japanese term in otaku culture, *nijigen* means two-dimensional space, and it is often interpreted as otaku's affective sexual attachment with two-dimensional virtual characters in anime's media mix. However, self-claimed nijigen aesthetics (二次元 美学) in these artists articulate a cultural sensibility that is far more informational than sexual. For these artists, *nijigen* means, first and foremost, a superflattened information field that is framed as a techno-economic matrix. The common themes in their art, which is presented in the superflat visual style that is akin to Murakami, are control, programming, signaling, processing, modeling, and standardizing—that is, the techno-rationality of informatics and cybernetics. Prominent examples of such nijigen artists who explore the framing field of superflat are Ye Linghan (叶凌瀚, China) and Agi Chen Yi-Chieh (陈怡洁, Taiwan).

A VOCALOID-loving otaku born in the 1980s, Ye Linghan belongs to China's *zhai* generation. Characterizing himself as a "right-clicking youth" (右键青年) whose relationship with the world is located in the "empty space between right clicks on the computer mouse," Ye creates his artwork with the combined media of painting, animation, computer graphics, and digital image processing.[61] His 2018 works, the *LUCY* series, were generated from randomly downloaded images from the internet that were later algorithmically processed and reassembled (Figure 29). Commenting on algorithmic control and surveillance, as well as informationalized alienation, Ye envisions "Lucy" as a post-human subject in the age of artificial intelligence when the algorithm is irrefutable "like tattoos on our bodies" (algorithmic data were literally tattooed onto Lucy's body in Ye's works).[62] This posthuman subject, Lucy, is mobilized, fractured, and multiplied: there are numerous Lucys in Ye's paintings. But these mobilized and multiplied Lucys all somehow look identical, like copied-and-pasted figures without even faces to identify or distinguish them. And they are all arranged, side by side, in a well-organized array like a sequence of numbers. In Ye's words, we are all Lucy "trapped in the networks constructed with 0s and 1s, losing our own personal references in the realm of algorithm."[63] Entrapment and control are the recurrent themes in Ye's works, such as his 2014 series *Gold. Circle. Tiger,* in which a tiger is chained by golden circles. But the gold circles—figuratively and metaphorically, chains made of gold—in Ye's superflat images are not only algorithmic structures but are also capital. His 2013 series *50% Dollar* was painted with visual motifs that are reminiscent of Gainax Studio's famous superflat images in *Evangelion* with a monstrous mecha roaring in a flattened and compressed cityscape (Figure 30). But the mecha in Ye's painting, as the title suggests, is "50% dollar." By and large, Ye's works present a powerful super-flat imagery that contains a databased self (e.g., Lucy)—the "projectile subject"—within the framing field of information capitalism.

Like Ye, Taiwanese artist Agi Chen Yi-Chieh also focuses her works on the notion of control in the framing field of superflat imagery as an algorithmic projectile—that is, a visual/informational field projected by the technological force of computer algorithms. But the superflat visual fields in Chen's artwork also demonstrate a much closer kinship with popular geek cultural elements such as anime, cartoons, and comics. The central motif in Chen's work is concentric color circles that she calls "function color" (函数色彩), which are digital vector graphics that were generated by abstracting color codes from popular animation characters with analytical tools and rendering them into geometric circles in a color matrix. This is a process that turns popular cultural icons (e.g., cartoon figures and superheroes) into a well-structured information field with standard geometric shapes on a superflat surface of data matrix. The purpose, as Chen puts it, is to generate "an informatic color spectrum of cartoon characters" and to analyze "the collective visual memory that is deeply embedded in our brains by media communication."[64] The "function," therefore, is specifically a mathematical one (as in the Chinese word 函数), which is a process of datafication and

FIGURE 29. Ye Linghan, *LUCY-E-001*, 2018–19. Acrylic on canvas, 200 × 450 cm (78.7 × 177.2 inches). Courtesy of the artist.

FIGURE 30. Ye Linghan, 50% *Dollar 001*, 2013. Watercolor on paper, 190 × 110 cm (74.75 × 43.25 inches). Courtesy of the artist.

informalization not so much of the cartoon characters as of the collective subjectivity of the geek audience who loves those favorite cultural icons. In Chen's own words: "'Function' in my works means standardizing, the geometric form displays a color structure and points toward an absent subject at the same time."[65]

This "absent subject" is prominently displayed in her work *Circle Island* (2012) as a networked subject that is programmed by the algorithmic function of the Facebook Wall. For this project, Chen set up a social group called "Circle Island" on Facebook, inviting group members to draw concentric color circles based on their favorite animation characters and to use these circles as their online avatars. Observing how Facebook members socialized with each other with these geometric circles as their new IDs, Chen created the superflat images in the *Circle Island* series (Figure 31), which she characterizes as "the database of collective memory" that is based on standardized and mathematically calculated geometric forms (i.e., the circles) as an identification system.[66] In this "database," the "function colors" (the circles) are the mathematical abstractions of the Facebook users, who used these circles

FIGURE 31. Agi Chen Yi-Chieh, *Circle Island*, 2012. Diasec-mounted digital prints, 160 × 420 cm (63 × 165.33 inches). Courtesy of the artist.

as their identification (avatars) on the interface of the Facebook Wall. The flattened interface of an algorithmically structured information field (Facebook) was thus transformed by Chen into another flattened surface of a visual field (Chen's superflat art). On the superflat surface of Chen's painting, those circles, which represent the abstracted networked subject (the empty subject), are floating around, just like the Facebook users whose avatars are circling on the superflat surface of the Facebook Wall. For Chen, therefore, superflat is a perfect visual language of mathematical function (函数), which allows her to visually transform one information field (the Facebook Wall) to another (the superflat imagery) through their shared function.

From the Window to the Wall

At the end of the twentieth century, Microsoft, a corporate Goliath in the computer world, ultimately capitalized our fractured vision into its commodified Windows.[67] In the new millennium, it is Facebook, the new Goliath of cyberspace, that has most successfully commercialized our databased gaze (and subjectivity) into a billion-dollar business, and it operates through a more-than-perfect metaphor: the Wall. On the virtual Walls of Facebook, which, not surprisingly, bear a striking visual similarity to Murakami's superflat images, the postmodern subject is not just decentered and displaced into a spaceless and timeless gaze (e.g., flattened, floating eyes in Murakami's paintings or two-dimensional, digital faces on Facebook Walls); that subjectivity itself also becomes a digitized good. On Facebook, our databased selves—the sets of data documenting our private and personal lives—are valuable digital commodities that are openly traded in the free-market economy. Despite the much-publicized controversy over Facebook's infringement of privacy, our computerized, sellable, and exploitable selves, in fact, are not alone on Facebook but are displayed and dispersed everywhere in every corner of the ever-expanding, superflattened surface of digital screens. As Zadie Smith says about Facebook: "Maybe it will be like an intensified version of the Internet I already live in . . . Or maybe the whole Internet will simply become like Facebook: falsely jolly, fake-friendly, self-promoting, slickly disingenuous."[68] After all, the Facebook Wall is just one of those stacking windows on our computer screens. Friedberg's notion of a "virtual window," from Alberti's metaphor to Microsoft's product, is basically describing the apparatus that is organizing our gaze—from linear perspective in Renaissance paintings to multiplied and fractured vision on computer screens.[69] But when that gaze becomes a mobilized virtual gaze that is captured, measured, and framed by a distributed system of computation, the virtual window—from superflat anime to the computer interface—becomes the spatiotemporal construction of a digital sweatshop of post-Fordism. And that construction, one is tempted to say, may have achieved perfection in the virtual architecture of the Facebook Wall.

The metaphorical transformation from Microsoft Windows to Facebook Wall vividly manifests a new level of paradigm shift that has changed our ways of seeing and perceiving in less than twenty years. The windows trope in Microsoft, with its mixed metaphors of having both a window (which implies looking into) and a desktop (which implies overlapping above), maps a computer space that is "both deep and flat."[70] The windows may be overlapping, obscuring, and opaque, but they still invite us to imagine a space beyond them, if not to see through them. But when the window is completely blocked and flattened into a wall, we lose all sense of visual transparency and depth, and what is left is the ultimate darkness of the surface, the surface only, and nothing beyond the surface. Now there is nothing to see through, and the mobilized gaze can only go wandering on the superficial wall, like Murakami's floating eyes, Ye's Lucy, and Chen's concentric color circles. And eventually, the floating, wandering gaze becomes nothing more than an informatic commodity experience for digital exploitation. Finally, the apparatus of the Facebook Wall is a complete superflat construction of informationalized post-Fordism—a weightless, timeless, and depthless limbo between work and play, between data and self.

To conclude this chapter, let us go back to Murakami's artwork, the "original" superflat. For his collaboration with Louis Vuitton, Murakami created two anime videos: *Superflat Monogram* (2003) and *Superflat First Love* (2009). Both have very similar visual styles and almost identical narratives. In both videos, a teenage female shopper (the girl is always introduced in front of a Louis Vuitton store) is somehow "swallowed" by the Louis Vuitton panda. Although this unnerving scene seems to suggest a dark vision of consumers' loss of identity to consumed goods, such anxiety is rather quickly dissolved by subsequent sequences featuring a cheerful journey in which the girl is led into a fantasy space flooded with loads of Louis Vuitton monograms. In the typical superflat style, the dreamland of Louis Vuitton is visualized as deliberately flat, depthless, and lacking a unitary perspective. The girl's flying motion, also in a superflat fashion, is depicted as lateral and surface oriented, giving a strong visual pleasure of floating and weightlessness (Figure 32). As delightful as they are, however, both videos seem plagued with a sense of the uncanny and discomfort. When a YouTube viewer asked about the video, "Does the animation style bother anyone else?" quite a few viewers responded, "I'm bothered." As one viewer put it: "I don't get it. The girl got sucked into a weird monster fairy thing and she's smiling and pretending nothing happened. Plus when she popped out of the box she acted like 'oh look i'm 150 years in the past. cool. This is perfectly normal.' hmm . . ."[71]

The viewers' comments suggest that those seemingly mobilizing journeys in Murakami's superflat videos, in fact, are deeply ambiguous. The ambiguity can be seen from Murakami's framing choices. The girl—a user, a consumer, and ultimately a looker (her big eyes are always highlighted)—though seemingly "freed" into a fantasy land, is often

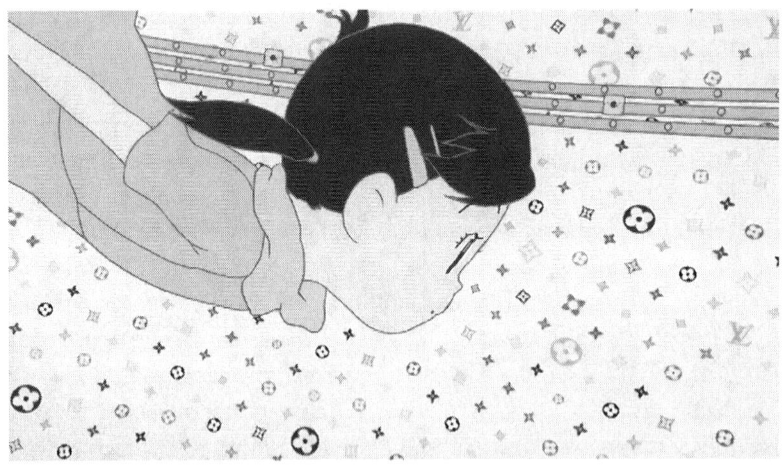

FIGURE 32. Lateral and surface-oriented flying motion with a sense of floating and weightlessness in *Superflat Monogram* (2003). Animated short video, Takashi Murakami/Kaikai Kiki Co., Ltd.

FIGURE 33. The female character, as well as her gaze, is framed within the shopping window of a Louis Vuitton store in *Superflat Monogram* (2003). Animated short video, Takashi Murakami/Kaikai Kiki Co., Ltd.

"prisoned" on the depthless surface within a certain frame—a door, a window, or a cell-phone screen (Figure 33). These frames, which are also interfaces of different sorts, are precisely the "virtual windows" that Friedberg talks about, because the "window is also a frame."[72] And these framed virtual windows, in Murakami's case, are also literalized as the shopping windows of a Louis Vuitton store. Murakami's superflat vision, therefore, provides us with a playful yet deeply disturbing scenario about our mobilized but ultimately framed subject/gaze on information networks: by looking through the superflat virtual windows (Google, Facebook, Bilibili), our vision is freed from the centuries-long governance of Renaissance perspective only to be captured and contained by another structure, another "line of sight" (albeit a digitally upgraded one), of postindustrial knowledge work, digital consumption, and algorithmic monetization. That wonderland of elsewhere and elsewhen, toward which our gaze is happily mobilized, is nothing more than the window frame of a "Garden of Louis Vuitton." Such a commodity-oriented and informationalized postperspective vision is precisely what Zadie Smith is trying to warn us about in her comments about Facebook: "Our denuded networked selves don't look more free, they just look more owned."[73]

Conclusion

I want to conclude the book by coming back to the three key elements that constitute anime geekdom: knowledge, play, and pleasure. The circulation between these three elements forms the continuous but volatile loops of cybernetic affect as the collective ethos of geek culture. The movement of anime geekdom, first of all, centers on a cultural sphere of knowledge, for it is a popular culture that is produced through, for, and about knowledge. With the hegemony of information technology, there is a profound transformation in the nature and structure of knowledge, which began to be dissociated from the hermeneutic aura of universal truth and to be codified and mass-produced as computable information and commodities that were absorbed into the daily life of cultural communication and consumption with desire, fetish, and enchantment. This is the postmodern condition that Jean-François Lyotard famously characterizes as the transformation of knowledge from "grand narratives" to "language games."[1] The popular-culturalization (or "gamification") of knowledge, which has reshaped the relationship between work and play, hinges on what Alan Liu calls "producer culture" that "governs work life and home life alike in the name of a ubiquitous new regime of knowledge."[2] In this context, knowledge as a form of cultural ubiquity, though still functioning in discursive formations, has moved away from the confinement of institutional discipline and legitimation (schools, universities, academia) and quickly entered the consumer market and popular imagination, systematically being produced and reproduced within and without culture industries. This "cultural turn" that moved knowledge from institutional power to popular culture also marks the historical transition from Michel Foucault's notion of "disciplinary society" to what Gilles Deleuze calls "control society," as knowledge transformed from a societal function of education to an individualized lifestyle of self-cultivation and lifelong learning.[3]

The emergence, development, and dissemination of anime geekdom are integral—and arguably crucial—in this historical transformation of knowledge, production, and labor. The book traces this historical development in Part I, focusing on three stories corresponding to three historical moments with major technological and social shifts: chapter 1 examines the coming of age of China's *zhai* generation in the national context of the techno-economic transformation from the industrial to the postindustrial; chapter 2 studies the sociocultural formation of anime fansub as a cosmopolitan knowledge community that was enabled by the development of transnational information networks (e.g., the web and p2p portals); chapter 3 analyzes the proliferation and transfiguration of the *danmaku* interface as an affective contact zone on a regional mediascape in the context of platformization—that is, the global expansion of platforms and platform logic as a new type of media infrastructure for sociocultural organization. This historical and cultural study illuminates the changing meaning and significance of anime geekdom in relation to the changing nature of knowledge and work in the context of China and beyond.

For Chinese zhai culture, its development and transformation from a televised fan culture to a networked cyberculture is mapped against the historical backdrop from the nation's economic reform in the 1980s to the worldwide postindustrial transition in the early twenty-first century. This cultural formation through a specific historical trajectory echoes the broader historical transformation, in both local and global terms, which is the emergence of a new type of knowledge work and a new generation of information laborer/consumer. This historical transformation is also marked by changing modes of knowledge production and consumption, which is demonstrated, in chapter 2, by the ways in which the transnational anime geekdom is organized by fansubs, the amateur subtitled videos by fan and for fans. Fansub effectively created a cosmopolitan community through collective knowledge sharing, which facilitated global cultural flow through a mode of organizing labor and production via collective voluntary communication on information networks. This is what I call "communication labor," a key production force in the digital economy. However, this form of communicative immaterial labor, as chapter 2 demonstrates, generates surplus knowledge as part of what Maurizio Lazzarato calls "mass intellectuality," which cannot be entirely actualized and valorized into the productive force of postindustrial capitalism, because it has its historical roots in struggles against work.[4] The fansubs generated endlessly proliferating content in the form of on-screen subtitles, notes, comments, jokes, and spoofs, as well as off-screen communication and coordination. This distributive cultural field is tightly controlled, disciplined, and standardized by the community itself, but this expansive knowledge sphere fails to be effectively incorporated or reformulated by the commodity space of media industries, largely and ironically due to fans' self-disciplined gesture to avoid potential conflicts with the industry's copyright ownership.

Such contradiction and excessiveness remained in this knowledge community even after anime geekdom was platformed—but not yet fully commodified—by the danmaku interface popularized by streaming platforms such as Niconico and Bilibili. The platforms, as I argue in chapter 3, do not solve these contradictory factors but only put them into contact, for contact is the core logic of platformativity as it generates informatic connections. Mediated by digital platforms, tension within the knowledge community of anime geekdom is further intensified and unveiled by its internal and external interface—that is, the intraface. I identify and characterize this platformed intraface through the danmaku interface, an affective contact zone that is marked by incoherence, rather than convergence or mix, among conflicting elements, modes, and logics within the knowledge community of anime geekdom. This affective contact zone of danmaku, which generates feelings that remain unactualized and unvalorized, points to the potential unproductivity of knowledge work, which, as Thomas Lamarre suggests, is "a strategy of refusal, a resistance to labor organized in received ways."[5] It is precisely this unproductive, "useless" knowledge that makes geek cultures "cool." Because cool, as Alan Liu tells us, is "the shadow ethos of the 'unknowing,' or unproductive knowledge" within knowledge work, which allows for a gesture of refusal toward the outward motion from inside.[6] This cool ethos of unproductivity and uselessness gives a sense of autonomy for the knowledge sphere of anime geekdom within the structure of automation in the transmedia system. The unproductive, surplus knowledge of the affective contact zone of danmaku is both a symptom and a strategy of the geek movement, an excessive energy that has to be released as useless heat through cybernetic affect. Released as such, the unproductive and useless knowledge thus has the potential to escape from the institutional and industrial control of knowledge work and to enter what Walter Benjamin calls "room-for-play."

For Benjamin, play has therapeutic, liberating, and even utopian potential, because the modes of play allow for collective, nondestructive forms of innervation of technology through cognitive, physical, and neurosomatic sensorium and behaviors, such as the mimetic imagination and performance in children's play or the gambler's play with chance and motor reflexes.[7] Benjamin's utopian view of play echoes contemporary thinkers such as Johan Huizinga and Roger Caillois, who saw play not only as a foundational building block of human civilizations but also as a cultural space of freedom that is unproductive, uncertain, and separate from the "ordinary life" of capitalist productivity.[8] Such an idealist vision that sees a division and opposition between play and work not surprisingly runs into trouble with the postmodern, post-Fordist realities of "ludic capitalism," in which "labor itself is now play, just as play becomes more and more laborious."[9] But this scenario of play-as-labor or labor-as-play obscures a significant factor: between play and labor lays the material and symbolic function of mediation. The interchange between play and work has to be mediated in technocultural forms. This function of mediation brings us back to Benjamin, who saw play as neither freedom nor work but a mediating space in between, a space he calls "room-for-play" (*spielraum*), which is a dynamic, open field full of action, movement, and imagination.[10] This "room-for-play" allows Benjamin to imagine an alternative aesthetics for technological innervation both within and against the capitalist organization of labor through nondestructive and even therapeutic forms, "a technologically mediated aesthetics of play capable of diverting the destructive, catastrophic course of history."[11]

This notion of play, as "a technologically mediated aesthetics," is the nexus connecting Part I and Part II of the book. In Part I, my historical and cultural study of anime geekdom demonstrates the centrality of play as a key factor that organized the development of this knowledge culture: Chinese zhai culture, for a significant period, was organized by computer gaming and the mode of play as the nodal points connecting the transmedia system of ACG (anime, comics, and games); in the fansub community, the transnational sphere of knowledge production was organized by fans' collective participation in "language games" through the signifying and communicative practices of translation, subtitling, interpretation, and discussion, which, according to many fans, are akin to massively multiplayer online games; on the danmaku interface, playful communication via on-screen comments is governed by a gatekeeping mechanism of knowledge tests as a threshold for membership, which demonstrates the inherent tension, rather than the often-assumed convergence, between knowledge and play in post-Fordist situations.

But why and how does play assume such a central role in the development and organization of this knowledge culture of anime geekdom? Part II of the book tackles this question by examining the ways in which the aesthetic experience of play is technologically mediated by anime. Theorizing anime as a media environment that is uniquely powerful for generating and sustaining the mode of play, I demonstrate how anime mediates this open field of "room-for-play" through certain forms (superflat), motifs (the mecha-child), and transmedial operations (the true-end model of media mix). Informed by Benjamin, I focus on how the play mechanism in anime functions as technological innervation for postindustrial knowledge work. For instance, the mecha-child motif, as I examine in chapter 4, establishes the mimetic faculty—an important mode of children's play—between the child and the mecha through their shared aesthetic forms of cuteness and animatedness. This mimetic faculty functions as technological innervation through the intimate identification and assimilation between the child and the mecha.

Another prominent mode of play that mediates technological innervation in a more effective and affective manner, as I demonstrate in chapter 5 by examining the media mix system of *Steins;Gate*, is the mechanism of cybernetic play. This mode of play is programmed by anime's media mix system centered on games, which is structured with the combination and tension between multiplying worldlines and a singular "true end." When players are persistently searching for the true end by consuming/producing proliferating worldlines as informatic feedback loops with trial and error, they are internalizing cybernetic logic into their cognitive, psychic, and neurosomatic behaviors through the mechanism of play. Cybernetics, as a techno-scientific theory influenced by contingency and probability, is marked by dialectic tension between the recognition of informational uncertainty (entropy) and the demand for performative control. This cybernetic logic is internalized into otaku sensibility in the media mix, which is pulled by the polarizing impulses between the desire for consuming more content/information/storylines (increasing informational entropy) and the obsession for pursuing the one and only true end (cybernetic control). The tension between these polarizing impulses in this internalized cybernetic logic is full of generative affect: agony, agitation, anxiousness, etc. That is what I mean by "cybernetic affect."

The mechanism of cybernetic play has increasingly replaced the previous models (narrative consumption and database consumption) of anime's media mix as a new organizational principle to structure, expand, and control the transmedia systems of anime geekdom. This change also involves a shift from visual pleasure to cybernetic pleasure. Pleasure is at the center of our understanding and theorization of technological mediation and innervation. The question of pleasure, however, is often explored (in media studies, at least) as primarily a visual experience, because visual culture such as cinema and television is still taken as the dominant media form. But as I demonstrate in this book, geek pleasure in anime culture marks a paradigm shift in media experience, from visual pleasure that is structured by the cinematic apparatus with a unified linear perspective of a singular gaze to operational, procedural pleasure that is evoked by cybernetic systems with distributive information and feedback control. Such pleasure of cybernetic operation has also begun to displace the visual pleasure even in traditional visual media. As Alexander R. Galloway observes, films and TV shows such as *24* (2001–10) increasingly feature narrative and stylistic patterns that "evoke 'informatic pleasure' over and above any sense of visual pleasure."[12]

Anime, as I demonstrate in this book, is at the frontier of this shift toward cybernetic pleasure. In Part II, my theorization of anime as a media environment for knowledge culture focuses on identifying and analyzing the themes, patterns, motifs, and styles in anime that evoke such pleasure. Beside the pleasure of cybernetic play, the affective/semantic milieu of techno-intimacy, which is evoked by the mecha-child motif, is a particularly generative field for experiencing the cybernetic logic of human–machine integration. But the pleasure of techno-intimacy is not simply about desiring cute things as substitutions or seeking an animistic spirit from a machine for companionship. Instead, techno-intimacy operates through identification and assimilation between the human and the machine, which is to say we (the children) see ourselves in the machine (the mecha), thus allowing for the reflection on and the innervation of the technological conditions of postindustrial knowledge work. Therefore, this structure of techno-intimacy, as I argue in chapter 4, should be understood in aesthetic terms rather than psychoanalytical ones, because the mimetic faculty that is needed for such human–machine identification operates through aesthetic forms (or the aesthetic–technological continuum, such as cybernetic play). And the aesthetic form that brings us to the closest identification with a cybernetic machine is probably the superflat style in anime, because it presents a visual field that resembles, and operates in the same logic as, the information field of a computer user interface. But the cybernetic pleasure that is offered by superflat visuality, which is the mobilization of the gaze through a distributed, dehierarchized visual field, is not without a price. As I argue in chapter 6, the distributive field of superflat turns out to be a framing field, as it ultimately frames the subject within the algorithmic structure and commodity matrix of information capitalism.

Knowledge, play, and pleasure: the exchange among these three elements forms the feedback loop of the cybernetic machine, which not only circulates information, capital, labor, and commodity but also releases passion, obsession, discontent, and resentment. Anime's transnational, transmedial system operates as a cybernetic machine of knowledge work, which releases its inherent contradictions and tensions as affect. This book, in many ways, is an affective mapping of anime geekdom, following the flow of affect through the disjunctions and discrepancies within this knowledge culture. Throughout the six chapters in two parts of this book, my historical and cultural study of anime fandom, as well as my theorization of anime's media environment, is marked by a recurrent motif of conflicting tendencies: between knowledge and commodity, participation and discipline (in fansub); between content and platform, liveness and spectrality (in danmaku); between subject and object, autonomousness and automation (in the mecha-child); between multiplying worldlines and the singular true end (in cybernetic play); between the distributive and the framing (in superflat). These conflicts and contradictions are where affect is generated and thus should be mapped.

Underlying these affective tensions and disjunctions in anime geekdom is the fundamental contradiction in the techno-logic of cybernetics, which is the contradiction between informational entropy and feedback control. Since cybernetic systems are the technological foundation of postindustrial knowledge work, their contradictory logic is internalized into the knowledge culture of geekdom, with anime culture as a central part. Therefore, anime geekdom, as I demonstrate throughout the book, is characterized by such polarizing impulses between the obsessive media production/consumption that breeds informational uncertainty and the persistent focus on learning through feedback that leads to cybernetic control. The true-end model in anime's media mix is a perfect example of such conflicting impulses, whereby the more storylines that a player consumes through expansive transmedia networks, the sharper the focus on the search for the singular true end through the mechanism of feedback control. The tension between these polarizing impulses is where cybernetic affect is generated.

Finally, let me conclude by reiterating what I mean by "cybernetic affect" and why it is an important concept for understanding anime geekdom. Anime and otaku culture, as well as geek fan culture in general, have often been celebrated for their open, distributive, and dehierarchized structures that encourage user participation, mobilization, and collaboration, which is supposed to decentralize the power structure from media industries to audiences, fans, and consumers. Therefore, existing studies of these cultures tend to focus on ideas like distributive fields, collaborative creativity, and collective intelligence. These notions, however, only point to one direction of the story, the direction of decentralization. But there is another direction that is also significantly present—that is the direction of recentralization. As my study in this book demonstrates, against the tendencies of multiplicity, flexibility, and distributiveness, anime culture is also marked by the opposite tendencies of singularity, standardization, and containment. Like a typical cybernetic system, the transnational, transmedial system of anime geekdom is unsettled by its intrinsic contradiction, pulling between its decentralizing desire for informational entropy (e.g., fansubs, danmaku comments, distributive visual elements in superflat, and derivative content in media mix) and its recentralizing impulse for cybernetic control (e.g., fansubbing's quality control and standardization, danmaku membership exams, the player's search for the true end, and the framing field of superflat). This cybernetic system of anime geekdom, therefore, is a machine of affect because its centralizing impulse for control is caught in a perpetual motion but can never be actualized, as it is constantly pulled away by the distributive impulse of informational uncertainty. The control impulse demands informative feedback, but more information leads to increasing entropy, which generates a stronger impulse for feedback control. And the cycle goes on.

If the anime machine is a cybernetic one, then it is a machine that runs on a permanent state of agony, agitation, and anxiety, because the two polarizing impulses in the machine are in a perpetual motion of approaching but never gratified. And that is the cybernetic affect. This brings me back to the notion of the "complex," which refers to both a psychological and an infrastructural state. Psychologically, a desire becomes a complex when it can never be fully satisfied, such as the cybernetic impulses for both control and information. Infrastructurally, a cybernetic system is a complex because it relies on loads of informative feedback to operate the control mechanism. Therefore, cybernetic affect is, by and large, a complex in both psychological and infrastructural terms. That is why the term *complex* (*cong* コン in Japanese and *kong* 控 in Chinese) becomes such a key word in transnational otaku culture.

But this notion of complex is also about control. As I discuss in chapters 1 and 5, complex is described as "kong" in Chinese zhai culture and "database complex" is thus called "database-kong." The Chinese word *kong* (控), which is a homophone for the Japanese word *cong* (コン), actually means "control." Therefore, what *kong* implies for anime geeks is this peculiar tension between the opposite impulses of complexity and control. This tension is both psychological and infrastructural. As an infrastructure, the cybernetic complex of the transmedia system of anime oscillates between entropy (distributive) and control (conjunctive). As a psychological state, the cybernetic complex of anime geeks is characterized by compulsive behaviors that oscillate between the obsession for information complexity (knowledge sharing, derivative content, and worldlines) and the longing for control (community discipline, gatekeeping, and the true end)—that is, to be both controlled and in control. This tension between complex and control is deeply affective. In what Deleuze calls "the society of control," there is something affectively attractive and even pleasurable about the ambivalence of being in control and controlled at the same time.[13] Because being a kong (having a complex), which is to control and be controlled by something, is also a gesture of commitment, attachment, and intimacy, which is a structure of feelings that oscillate between power and powerlessness, between disjunction and assimilation.

Therefore, the cybernetic affect in anime geekdom represents an affective economy of complex/control that is fundamentally contradictory. Distributive networks, as well as the decentering intrasubjectivity of knowledge work, evoke affective desire for reunification, the desire to be focused on, to be committed to, and even be controlled by something (e.g., media content, anime characters, information . . . or anything). This sense of *kong* points to the psychological and medial complex not only of anime culture but also of the postindustrial knowledge work that bounds both control and the complex in the same networks of affective economy. And that is the key lesson we learn by mapping the cybernetic affect of anime geekdom.

Acknowledgments

This book benefited greatly from the support, encouragement, and inspiration of many colleagues, friends, mentors, and students. I want to first thank my dissertation adviser, Dana Polan, whose intellect, warmth, and generosity not only inspired and fostered this project but helped me shape my scholarship more broadly. Without his continuous support and guidance, this book would not have come to its current form. I also thank my committee members, Zhang Zhen, JungBong Choi, and Robert Stam at New York University, as well as Scott Bukatman at Stanford University, whose crucial comments and feedback nurtured the early foundation of the book. I am indebted to all my teachers at NYU, Richard Allen, Robert Sklar, Bill Simon, Mitsuhiro Yoshimoto, Kristin Ross, Moya Luckett, Allen Weiss, Chris Straayer, Anna McCarthy, Dan Streible, Antonia Lant, and Howard Besser, who introduced me to the world of film and media studies and provided me with critical tools to think of media cultures through different perspectives. The project's development also benefited from the exchanges with my friends and cohort at NYU, including Shi-Yan Chao, Cindy Chen, Dominic Gavin, Paul Grant, Xiang He, Anuja Jain, Martin Johnson, Ji-hoon Kim, Sangjoon Lee, Rebecca Miller, Priya Shanker, Ying Xiao, Liang-Hua Yu, and Gregory Zinman, whose warm friendship and intellectual support accompanied me through the early stage of this journey.

I am grateful to the intellectual communities at Brown University, University of Pittsburgh, and Oregon State University, where I am fortunate to work and have worked with brilliant, generous, and thoughtful colleagues and students. At Brown, I am indebted to the support, mentorship, and inspiration of my colleagues at MCM, Ariella Azoulay, Anthony Cokes, Joan Copjec, Macarena Gómez-Barris, Bonnie Honig, Lynne Joyrich, Gertrud Koch, Kevin McLaughlin, Ellen Rooney, Rebecca Schneider, and Alexander Weheliye, who created such a stimulating and productive intellectual environment that motivated me to keep improving. Special thanks to Alex, Lynne, and Rebecca for their insightful comments and suggestions on the manuscript, which aided my revision of the book significantly. I also owe thanks to the indispensable support of Liza Hebert, Regina Longo, Susan McNeil, and Hannah Zoll. Besides my home department, the Science, Technology, and Society (STS) Program and the Pembroke Seminar provided me with additional venues to learn from a diverse range of scholarship, and I am thankful to Lukas Rieppel, Debbie Weinstein, Lingzhen Wang, Leslie Bostrom, Leela Gandhi, Evelyn Lincoln, and Suzanne Stewart-Steinberg for the vibrant discussions that broadened my approach to animation to the histories of science, technology, arts, gender, and race. The majority of the book was written when I taught at the University of Pittsburgh, where I am grateful for the warmth, friendship, encouragement, and intellectual insights of Mark Lynn Anderson, Mark Best, Don Bialostosky, Tyler Bickford, Nancy Condee, Charles Exley, Jane Feuer, Lucy Fischer, Nancy Glazener, Randall Halle, Zachary Horton, Marcia Landy, Adam Lowenstein, Colin MacCabe, Neepa Majumdar, Brenton Malin, Dana Och, Alison Patterson, David Pettersen, Kun Qian, Elizabeth Reich, Gayle Rogers, Terence Smith, Annette Vee, and Jennifer Waldron, who, at various occasions such as colloquiums, movie nights, game nights, and potluck parties, made me understand what it meant and felt to belong to a truly loving intellectual home. The Asian Studies Center provided me with generous funding and support for a vital part of my research, and I am indebted to Nicole Constable, James A. Cook, and Gabriella Lukács for their advice, discussion, and support that made me part of the community of East Asian studies at Pitt. At

Oregon State, I am thankful for the guidance, encouragement, and conversations of Jon Lewis, Sebastian Heiduschke, and Anita Helle, whose kindness and generosity helped me develop a solid early footing. I am also thankful to the exceptional graduate students whom I have the great fortune to work with: Jesse Anderson-Lehman, Daniel Beresheim, Kelsey Cameron, Kelsey Cummings, Madeline Eschenburg, Elizabeth Garcia, Cassandra Guan, Jedd Hakimi, Seungyeon Gabrielle Jung, Irina Kalinka, Mariz Kelada, Lachlan Kermode, Brittney Knotts, Théo Lepage-Richer, Alex Maxwell, Henry Osman, Rose Rowson, Kuhu Tanvir, Hei Ting Wong, Stephen Woo, and Rosa Zhang, as well as to all the undergraduate students in the anime classes that I taught at NYU, Pitt, and Brown. The discussions and exchanges with these brilliant students are informative and inspiring and they stimulated many of my thoughts and studies that built this book.

I am thankful for the communication, collaboration, and discussion with many colleagues and friends whose scholarship has profoundly influenced mine. In particular, Thomas Lamarre and Marc Steinberg inspired me greatly at numerous stages of the book's development, and my collaboration and conversations with them catalyzed many of my thoughts on the media forms and platforms of anime. Their insightful comments and critiques of the manuscript were also incredibly helpful for the improvement of the book. I thank Yomi Braester for various collaborative projects, discussions, and journeys together, which led to vibrant conversation (with the best tea) that deeply affected my studies on media cultures in and beyond China. I owe thanks to Joe Karaganis, Lawrence Liang, and Ravi Sundaram for introducing me to piracy studies through the project *Media Piracy in Emerging Economies,* which influenced my thoughts on fansubbing. I am also thankful for the helpful advice, encouragement, and exchanges from many scholars in the field: Weihong Bao, Chris Berry, Xinyu Dong, Jason Douglass, Daisy Du Yan, Victor Fan, Yuriko Furuhata, Li Guo, Dal Yong Jin, Andrew Johnston, Shuen-shing Lee, Jie Li, Ralph Litzinger, Xiao Liu, Ramon Lobato, Jean Ma, Sean Macdonald, Jason McGrath, Mihaela Mihailova, Rahul Mukherjee, Joshua Neves, Laikwan Pang, Ryan Pierson, Ying Qian, Carlos Rojas, Paul Roquet, S. V. Srinivas,

Paola Voci, Yiman Wang, Fan Yang, Guobin Yang, Alex Zahlten, Xiqing Zheng, and Ying Zhu. Special thanks to Florian Schneider for offering Marc and me the great opportunity to edit the special issue "Regional Platforms" for the journal *Asiascape* and for his thoughtful comments on an earlier version of chapter 3 on *danmaku* that was published in that special issue.

My critical studies of anime (and animation broadly) have been influenced by my creative experience, for which I owe my thanks to director Xuan Liang, who offered me the opportunity to work as a cowriter for the animated film *Big Fish & Begonia* (2016) that intrigued my thinking on anime's cultural influence on Chinese animation. I also thank Shanghai Media Group, my executive producer Helen Chen Caiyun, and my creative team, Qiang Guan, Xiaoli Tan, Leon Yan, Lei Yang, Zao Wang, Bobby Webster, and Yu Zhao, for allowing me to produce the documentary series *The Creative Future* (2012), which took me to Beijing, Tokyo, and Los Angeles to interview many animation artists and fans whose experiences and insight shaped my initial understanding of what it means to be an anime geek.

The book's final completion and production owe a great deal to the editorial support and guidance of Leah Pennywark at the University of Minnesota Press, as well as to the incisive feedback of the anonymous reviewers. I am thankful to the reviewers, editors, and colleagues who offered their time and insightful reading and comments on the manuscript.

Finally, my deepest love and gratitude to Ji Yu, the ultimate geek who inspired and accompanied the whole journey with his humor, cheers, insights, unwavering support, unconditional love, and unbelievable collection of "useless" geek knowledge.

Notes

Introduction

1. Wloszczyna and Oldenburg, "Geek Chic"; Irvine, "Suddenly, It's Hip to Be Square"; Jianxin Wang, "Cong 'yuzhai' shuo linglei 'zhai wenhua.'"

2. Terranova, *Network Culture.*

3. Studies of knowledge culture often predominantly focus on the computer cultures in California. See Katz, *Geeks*; A. Liu, *Laws of Cool*; Turner, *From Counterculture to Cyberculture*; Ensmenger, *Computer Boys Take Over.*

4. There have been increasing studies of racial identities in geek cultures. See Eglash, "Race, Sex, and Nerds"; Weheliye, "Post-Integration Blues"; Fickle, *Race Card.*

5. Collins Dictionary, "CollinsDictionary.com 'Word of the Year.'"

6. McArthur, "Digital Subculture," 61.

7. Grossman, "Geek Shall Inherit the Earth," 98.

8. Fritz, "GEEK CHIC."

9. Graser, "H'wood Learns to Speak Geek."

10. Hornaday, "Nerdy Teenage Boys Define the Zeitgeist of Summer '07," M5.

11. About the historical and cultural meanings of otaku in Japan, see Galbraith, *Otaku and the Struggle for Imagination in Japan.*

12. Okada, *Otakugaku Nyumon.*

13. Azuma, *Otaku.*

14. *Wenhui Daily*, "2008 wangluo 'reci' xin bianhua."

15. Wu, "Qiantan yiqing zhixia de 'zhai wenhua' chuanbo."

16. I borrowed the notion of a deterritorialized mediascape from Appadurai, *Modernity at Large.*

17. Wark, *Virtual Geography*, vii.

18. I borrow this notion of extraterritoriality in relation to media geography from Fan, *Extraterritoriality*.

19. Wark, *Virtual Geography*, ix.

20. Kelly, "Third Culture," 992.

21. Grossman, "Geek Shall Inherit the Earth."

22. Bourdieu, *Distinction*.

23. Bell, *Coming of Post-Industrial Society*, 20.

24. Gouldner, *Future of Intellectuals*.

25. Florida, *Rise of the Creative Class*; P. F. Drucker, *Age of Discontinuity*; A. Liu, *Laws of Cool*; Castells, *Rise of the Network Society*; Ehrenreich and Ehrenreich, "Professional-Managerial Class"; Touraine, *Post-Industrial Society*; Perkin, *Rise of Professional Society*.

26. Critics such as Alan Liu and Manuel Castells argue against the class status of knowledge workers because the claim of multicultural universalism in postindustrial capitalism is precisely to do away with both identity and class by erasing their material historicity, replacing them with either "the self vs. the net" (Castells) or "the teamwork" of new corporatism (Liu). See Castells, *Rise of the Network Society*, 1–27; A. Liu, *Laws of Cool*, 35–68.

27. Wark, *Hacker Manifesto*, 6.

28. Bourdieu, *Distinction*.

29. Hardt and Negri, *Multitude*; Virno, *Grammar of the Multitude*; Lazzarato, "Immaterial Labor."

30. Poster and Aronowitz, *Information Subject*; Turkle, *Second Self*; Jenkins, *Convergence Culture*; Lévy, *Cyberculture*; Hayles, *How We Became Posthuman*.

31. Deleuze, *Foucault*, 34.

32. Thacker, "Foreword."

33. Ensmenger, *Computer Boys Take Over*, 5.

34. Wark, *Hacker Manifesto*, 36.

35. Florida, *Rise of the Creative Class*, xxvii.

36. Eglash, "Race, Sex, and Nerds," 49.

37. Examples include Eglash, "Race, Sex, and Nerds"; Weheliye, "Post-Integration Blues"; Nugent, *American Nerd*; Phi, "NOCs"; McWan and Cramer, "Progressive Racial Representation or Strategic Whiteness?"

38. Kelly, "Third Culture."

39. Benjamin, "One-Way Street"; Benjamin, "Work of Art"; Hansen, *Cinema and Experience*, 132–46.

40. Kelly, "Third Culture"; Terranova, *Network Culture*; Castells, *Rise of the Network Society*; A. Liu, *Laws of Cool*.

41. A. Liu, *Laws of Cool*, 2.

42. Turner, *From Counterculture to Cyberculture*.

43. Paulk, "Post-National Cool."

44. Gibson, "Modern Boys and Mobile Girls."

45. About "Cool Japan" as a governmental policy and popular discourse, see Allison, "Cool Brand, Affective Activism, and Japanese Youth"; Choo, "Nationalizing 'Cool'"; Abel, "Can Cool Japan Save Post-Disaster Japan?"; Daliot-Bul, "Japan Brand Strategy."

46. McGray, "Japan's Gross National Cool."

47. About the development and expansion of anime's global market, especially its transformation from televised children's entertainment to networked global fandom among geeks, see Patten, "Anime in the United States"; Ruh, "Early Japanese Animation in the United States"; Ruh, "Transforming U.S. Anime in the 1980s"; McCarthy, "Development of the Japanese Animation Audience"; Lu, "Many Faces of Internationalization in Japanese Anime"; Ng, "Japanese Animation in Singapore"; Lent, "Vignette"; Ito, *Fandom Unbound*.

48. McArthur, "Digital Subculture."

49. Feineman, *Geek Chic*.

50. Ito, *Hanging Out, Messing Around, and Geeking Out*.

51. Napier, "World of Anime Fandom in America."

52. Feineman, *Geek Chic*, 128. The famous anime sequences in *Kill Bill* were produced by Production I.G, the Japanese animation studio that gained intentional fame through such widely claimed anime titles as *Patlabor, Ghost in the Shell*, and *Blood: The Last Vampire*.

53. *Wired*, "Geekipedia."

54. Quoted from Faiola, "Japan's Empire of Cool," A01.

55. Lamarre, *Anime Machine*, xiii.

56. For studies of media as environment (and environment as media), see Fuller, *Media Ecologies*; Peters, *Marvelous Clouds*; Hu, *Prehistory of the Cloud*; Starosielski, *Undersea Network*; Mattern, *Code and Clay*; Boczkowski and Mitchelstein, *Digital Environment*. For environmental and ecological approaches in East Asian media contexts, see Bao, *Fiery Cinema*; Roquet, *Ambient Media*; Zahlten, *End of Japanese Cinema*; Lamarre, *Anime Ecology*; Furuhata, *Climatic Media*.

57. A. Liu, *Laws of Cool*, 43.

58. A. Liu, 43.

59. I borrow the term from Chow, "Postmodern Automatons."

60. A. Liu, *Laws of Cool*, 77–78.

61. Alan Liu describes a process of internalizing the techno-logics in the aesthetics of cool, which he calls "mock- or camouflage-technology" or simply "camo-tech." It is "the construction of bodily and social pose that perfectly expressed the adjustment of technique to technology—but for *unproductive* purposes. . . . Whatever was 'really cool,' in other words, was on a different level also truly routinized and automated—like working in a machine shop,

only without the shop" (*Laws of Cool*, 101). Liu's characterization of the cool "camo-tech" is strikingly similar to Benjamin's notion of technological innervation, especially Benjamin's analysis of typewriters in *One-Way Street*. I prefer to use Benjamin's concept of innervation because it highlights the function of mediation, clashing the notion of cultural cool (Liu) with that of medium cool (McLuhan).

62. A. Liu, *Laws of Cool*, 76.

63. McLuhan, *Understanding Media*, 22–32.

64. A. Liu, *Laws of Cool*, 100–103, 176–216.

65. A. Liu, 200; Bolter and Grusin, *Remediation*. Alan Liu borrows the notion of "hypermediacy" from Bolter and Grusin to characterize cool as an ethos of information that is aware of itself as a mediation interface, a window to be looked at rather than to look through. See A. Liu, *Laws of Cool*, 183.

66. Starosielski, *Media Hot and Cold*; Furuhata, *Climatic Media*.

67. Hansen, *Cinema and Experience*, 133.

68. Choo, "Nationalizing 'Cool'"; Lam, "Japan's Quest for 'Soft Power.'"

69. Morley and Robins, "Techno-Orientalism"; Roh, Huang, and Niu, *Techno-Orientalism*. The notion of cultural cool in Euro-American contexts has always been tinted with a strong tendency of Orientalism, from the obsession with Eastern religions and philosophies in 1960s counterculture to the fascination with cool Japan in twenty-first-century cyberculture. See Chun, "Orienting Orientalism."

70. A. Liu, *Laws of Cool*, 133.

71. Iwabuchi, *Recentering Globalization*; Condry, "Anime Creativity"; Allison, *Millennial Monsters*; Allison, "Cool Brand, Affective Activism, and Japanese Youth."

72. Steinberg, *Anime's Media Mix*; Jenkins, *Convergence Culture*.

73. Steinberg, *Platform Economy*, 37.

74. Jenkins, *Convergence Culture*.

75. For how the media mix system controls fans' consumption and participation, see Steinberg, *Anime's Media Mix*, 171–203.

76. A. Liu, *Laws of Cool*, 101–2.

77. See Azuma, *Otaku*; Galbraith, *Otaku and the Struggle for Imagination in Japan*; Ito, *Fandom Unbound*.

78. Steinberg, *Anime's Media Mix*.

79. Lazzarato, "Immaterial Labor," 139.

80. Allison, "Cool Brand, Affective Activism, and Japanese Youth," 96.

81. Lamarre, *Anime Machine*, xiv; For more on how anime organizes a transmedia ecology, see Lamarre, *Anime Ecology*.

82. Lamarre, *Anime Machine*.

83. McLuhan, *Understanding Media*, 22–23.

84. Denson, *Discorrelated Images*.

85. Manovich, *Language of New Media*, 286–333; Levitt, *Animatic Apparatus*.

86. Suan, *Anime's Identity*, 17–21.

87. Suan, *Anime's Identity*.

88. Iwabuchi, *Recentering Globalization*, 24–29.

89. My study of geek feelings focuses on the affective relationship between otaku culture and cybernetic systems, which is methodologically different from the predominant approach centered on the psychoanalysis of male otaku's sexual desire and erotic fantasies, such as in Tamaki, *Beautiful Fighting Girl*; Galbraith, *Otaku and the Struggle for Imagination in Japan*.

90. Wiener, *Cybernetics*, 127–29.

91. Wiener, *Human Use of Human Beings*, 26–27.

92. Seigworth and Gregg, "Inventory of Shimmers," 1. I borrow the notion of affect-as-medium from Bao, *Fiery Cinema*.

93. Massumi, *Parables for the Virtual*.

94. Anne Allison provides illuminating studies of how the generation and circulation of affective immaterial labor in the transmedia otaku culture are associated with unproductivity in both the biological and social senses among Japanese youth. Allison, "Cool Brand, Affective Activism, and Japanese Youth."

95. A. Liu, *Laws of Cool*, 236.

96. Levitt, *Animatic Apparatus*, 4.

97. Ngai, *Ugly Feelings*, 31.

98. Ngai, 91.

99. Chow, "Postmodern Automatons," 62, quoted in Ngai, *Ugly Feelings*, 99.

100. Ngai, *Ugly Feelings*, 97.

101. Eisenstein, *Eisenstein on Disney*.

102. Lamarre, "Otaku Movement," 359.

103. Tronti, "Strategy of Refusal." I borrowed Mario Tronti's notion from Lamarre, "Otaku Movement."

104. Chow, "Postmodern Automatons," 68.

105. Chen, *Asia as Method*, 212.

106. Patterson, *Open World Empire*, 58.

107. Chen, *Asia as Method*, 3.

108. Galloway, "Postscript."

1. Knowledge Is Power

1. *Time*, "TIME 100 Competition."

2. Chiang, "China's Movie Industry."

3. Aldama, "From Made in China to Created in China."

4. Ying, "Guo Jingming bu shi zuojia."

5. *Nanfang ribao,* "Han Han lao le."

6. On the one-child generation, see Fong, *Only Hope.*

7. Zhang, "'80 hou.'"

8. China's historical aspiration and transformation toward information capitalism in the reform era of the 1980s is well examined by X. Liu, *Information Fantasies.*

9. "Knowledge is power" (知识就是力量) is also the title of a popular science magazine published by China Science and Technology Press, which is the same publisher that published the Chinese translation of the comic series *Astro Boy* in the 1980s.

10. Before anime's popularization in China in the 1980s, there were occasional artistic and cultural exchanges between Japanese anime and Chinese animation. See Du, *Animated Encounters.*

11. The "three-period" scheme was first raised by Chen and Teng, "Riben dongman zai zhongguo dalu chuanbo fenxi."

12. Hong, *Internationalization of Television in China.*

13. The Chinese government's restriction of broadcasting anime on television was partly a strategy to promote China's domestic animation production. About the history and culture of Chinese animation production, see Macdonald, *Animation in China.*

14. "Guanyu fazhan woguo yingshi donghua chanye de ruogan yijian" [Several suggestions about the development of the animation industry in our country], State Administration of Radio, Film, and Television (SARFT, renamed as National Radio and Television Administration in 2018), April 2004.

15. "Guanyu jinyibu guifan dianshi donghuapian bochu guanli de tongzhi" [Further regulations of TV animation broadcasting], SARFT, October 2006.

16. Lull, *China Turned On,* 5.

17. On China's economic reforms, see Chang, *China under Deng Xiaoping;* White, *Riding the Tiger.*

18. Lardy, *Foreign Trade and Economic Reform in China,* 1.

19. Lull, *China Turned On,* 17.

20. *China Radio and Television Yearbook,* 1981–1991, China Broadcasting & TV Press.

21. Hong, *Internationalization of Television in China,* 73–74.

22. C. Li, *China,* 55.

23. Lull, *China Turned On,* 171–75.

24. T. Zhang, *Dianshi kanke.*

25. C. Li, *China,* 52.

26. Hadade, "Atongmu zai zhongguo de qianshijinshen."

27. Huang, "Zhong ri guanxi fazhan 30 nian."

28. National Bureau of Statistics of China.

29. See Wei, "'Manhua zhi shen.'"

30. Cultural proximity was often taken as the key factor in the regional popularity of Japanese media in East Asia. See Choi, "Of the East Asian Cultural Sphere"; Katzenstein and Shiraishi, *Beyond Japan*; Iwabuchi, *Recentering Globalization*.

31. Huang, "Zhong ri guanxi fazhan 30 nian."

32. Anime Song Lyrics, "Astro Boy (1963) Opening Theme"; Follow Lyrics, "阿童木之歌 歌词."

33. Liu, *Information Fantasies*.

34. Iwabuchi, *Recentering Globalization*.

35. Leung, "Romancing the Everyday," 73.

36. Hong, *Internationalization of Television in China*, 83.

37. Fang, "Jiyi suipian."

38. Kusakawa, *Terebi anime 20 nen shi*, 30–32, quoted in Steinberg, *Anime's Media Mix*, ix.

39. Steinberg, *Anime's Media Mix*, 39.

40. Steinberg, ix.

41. Hong, *Internationalization of Television in China*, 84.

42. Lull, *China Turned On*, 152.

43. Fang, "Jiyi suipian," RB05.

44. Allison, *Millennial Monsters*, 51–62.

45. Schodt, "Mighty Atom."

46. Joel Andreas traces this policy to an earlier era of socialist nation-building that gave rise to a new ruling class of technocrats in China. See Andreas, *Rise of the Red Engineers*.

47. Deng, *Deng Xiaoping wenxuan*, 120.

48. This tendency to associate anime and manga with science education continues today. For instance, one of China's first manga magazines was called *Popular Science Comics* (科普画王), published by *Science and Technology Daily*, the official newspaper of the Ministry of Science and Technology of China. The editorial mission stated in the launching issue in 1995 presented the magazine as "a mediator between the arts of comics and the popularization of science" by introducing the "newest comic works and latest science knowledge."

49. X. Zhang, "Intellectual Politics in Post-Tiananmen China"; Jing Wang, *High Culture Fever*.

50. Guo and Zhang, "Zhongguo qingshaonian yu donghua chuangbo de shizheng yanjiu."

51. About China's higher education and its relation to the only-child generation, see J. Jiang, "Higher Education in China"; Fong, *Only Hope*.

52. About the economic transition and China's effort to cultivate creative labor, see Song, Fang, and Johnston, "China's Path towards New Growth";

World Bank, "China 2030"; Rossiter, "Creative Industries in Beijing"; Keane, "Unbundling Precarious Creativity in China"; Fung, "Redefining Creative Labor"; Zweig and Wang, "Can China Bring Back the Best?"

53. Steinberg, *Anime's Media Mix*, 71.

54. XYM, "Fuxing yu luan ma."

55. China Internet Network Information Center, "Internet Statistics."

56. *Statistical Report on Internet Development in China.*

57. Beech, "New Radicals"; G. Yang, "Historical Imagination in the Study of Chinese Digital Civil Society," 23.

58. B. Jiang, "Lun 8ohou wenxue de wenhua beijing."

59. Deleuze, "Postscript on the Societies of Control"; Galloway, *Protocol*; Chun, *Control and Freedom.*

60. Lamarre, *Anime Ecology.*

61. Lamarre.

62. Zhongguo jiaoyu zaixian, "2018nian quanguo gaokao luqulv 81.13%."

63. *Nanfang dushi bao*, "Guangzhou chuxian 'yuzhaizu.'"

64. *Nanfang dushi bao.*

65. P. Jiang, "Ye tan woguo de 'zhainan zhainv' xianxiang."

66. *Ziben shichang*, "Nishi qiangran fali, zhongguo de 'zhai jingji' shidai."

67. GroupM Knowledge Center, "Jujiao 'zhaishidai.'"

68. GroupM Knowledge Center.

69. *Diyi caijing ribao*, "Jinrong weiji cuire 'zhai yi zu.'"

70. Cheng, "Ni hui bei 'zhai jingji' shidai taotai ma."

71. Sohu, "'Zhai jinji' bei pingwei niandu reci."

72. Loo, "Report."

73. Sina Tech, "Maopuwang datui jike gainian."

2. Fansub

1. Ito, introduction, xxiii.

2. Gibson, "Modern Boys and Mobile Girls."

3. Williams, *Television*, 25.

4. Lazzarato, "Immaterial Labor."

5. For more on fansub, see Díaz Cintas and Munoz Sanchez, "Fansubs"; Hatcher, "Of Otaku and Fansubs"; Lee, "Participatory Media Fandom."

6. On fansub culture in China, see J. Li, "Pirate Cosmopolitanism and the Undercurrents of Flow"; Meng, "Underdetermined Globalization."

7. Hatcher, "Of Otaku and Fansubs"; Leonard, "Progress against the Law"; Leonard, "Celebrating Two Decades of Unlawful Progress"; Condry, "Dark Energy"; Denison, "Anime Fandom and the Liminal Spaces between Fan Creativity and Piracy"; Ito, "Contributors versus Leechers."

8. J. Li, "Pirate Cosmopolitanism and the Undercurrents of Flow."

9. Lyotard, *Postmodern Condition.*

10. Gouldner, *Future of Intellectuals.*

11. I borrow the term *transduction* from biology, in which it refers to either a cellular mechanism to convert one form of signal to another or a genetic operation that delivers viral or bacterial DNA from one cell to another. These models of biological transduction, I believe, are useful analogies for understanding the transnational production and distribution of fansub, as both center on the transboundary trafficking and mediation of information of a certain kind (a cellular signal, a genetic sequence, or an animated audiovisual text).

12. Hookway, *Interface.*

13. Stam, *Subversive Pleasures,* 75.

14. Terranova, *Network Culture,* 78.

15. McPherson, "Reload," 207.

16. As I argued in the introduction, anime geekdom is as much a subculture as it is an intraculture, because of its ambivalent position of an "outsider inside" that is both marginal and mainstream, both particular and omnipresent, both localized and global. This chapter highlights these ambivalences by demonstrating that fansub, on one hand, is genuinely and purposely different and distanced from the corporate-controlled global media market, but that, on the other hand, it is also part of the broader systems of informational knowledge work within postindustrial capitalism.

17. After the 2010s, fansubbing in Euro-American contexts began to decline, largely due to the tightened copyright regulation and the rising dominance of video-streaming platforms such as Netflix and Crunchyroll. But Chinese fansubs continue to flourish today and migrated from peer-to-peer networks to video-streaming platforms such as Bilibili and AcFun. I will discuss the movement of anime geekdom to digital platforms in chapter 3.

18. Hebdige, *Subculture,* 118–19.

19. Bakhtin, *Speech Genres and Other Late Essays*; Voloshinov, *Marxism and the Philosophy of Language.* There is a long-standing dispute over whether Voloshinov or Bakhtin authored *Marxism and the Philosophy of Language.* For the sake of clarity and convenience, I attribute the authorship of this work to Voloshinov but consider it a key text that represents Bakhtinian ideas of language, because Voloshinov is a core member of the Bakhtin Circle in Russia that centered on Bakhtin's work and thoughts in the early twentieth century. For an analysis of Bakhtin's theories in the context of film and media studies, see Stam, *Subversive Pleasures.*

20. Voloshinov, *Marxism and the Philosophy of Language,* 14.

21. Stam, *Subversive Pleasures,* 40.

22. Metz, *Film Language*; Debord, *Society of the Spectacle.*

23. Stam, *Subversive Pleasures,* 57.

24. Voloshinov, *Marxism and the Philosophy of Language,* 15.

25. Voloshinov, 20.

26. Bakhtin, "Problem of Speech Genre."

27. Nornes, "For an Abusive Subtitling."

28. P. E. Lewis, "Measure of Translation Effects," 41, quoted in Nornes, "For an Abusive Subtitling," 18.

29. Nornes, "For an Abusive Subtitling," 18.

30. Nornes, 18.

31. Nornes, 29.

32. Cubbison, "Anime Fans, DVDs, and the Authentic Text"; Leonard, "Progress against the Law"; Díaz Cintas and Munoz Sanchez, "Fansubs."

33. Hatcher, "Of Otaku and Fansubs."

34. Hatcher, "Of Otakus and Fansubs [Appendix]."

35. "Fansubs Suck!," Anime News Network Forum, February 3, 2003, https://www.animenewsnetwork.com/bbs/phpBB2/viewtopic.php?t=1315.

36. Lamarre, "Otaku Movement," 390.

37. A. Liu, *Laws of Cool.*

38. Derrida, "Structure, Sign, and Play," 289.

39. Bakhtin, "Problem of the Text," 106.

40. Díaz Cintas and Munoz Sanchez, "Fansubs"; Nornes, "For an Abusive Subtitling."

41. Bakhtin, "Problem of Speech Genre."

42. Bertschy, "Interview with the Fansubber."

43. Bertschy.

44. Lévy, *Collective Intelligence.*

45. Lévy.

46. Jenkins, *Fans, Bloggers, and Gamers,* 134.

47. McPherson, "Reload," 207.

48. On these legal battles, see Storm.mg, "Zimuzu bei zhua la!"; Manxiaozhi, "Zimuzu hui xiaowang ma?"

49. Lévy, *Collective Intelligence.*

50. Galloway, *Interface Effect,* 40–41.

51. Galloway, 42.

52. Tofusensei, "History of Live-Evil."

53. Yiduimutou, "Zimuzu shi zenme zuodao zheme kuai fabu xinpian de?" [How can fansubbing groups release new videos so fast?]. Zhihu.com, November 14, 2017. https://www.zhihu.com/question/68131737.

54. About the networked condition of immediacy and simultaneity, see Terranova, *Network Culture,* 39–72; Tomlinson, *Culture of Speed,* 72–93.

55. Harvey, *Condition of Postmodernity.*

56. Galloway, *Protocol*; Terranova, *Network Culture*, 63–71.

57. Terranova, *Network Culture*, 69–70.

58. Tomlinson, *Culture of Speed*, 1.

59. Tomlinson, 1–13.

60. Tomlinson, 9.

61. Landa, "Niche Market, Global Scale."

62. Tomlinson, *Culture of Speed*, 9.

63. Tomlinson, 9.

64. Castells, *Rise of the Network Society*.

65. Leaver, "FlashForward or FlashBack?"

66. Wang and Zhu, "Mapping Film Piracy in China."

67. Landa, "Niche Market, Global Scale."

68. Appadurai, *Modernity at Large*.

69. greenkabbage, "Re: Where Are You Guys From?," Live-Evil forum, May 5, 2004, http://forum.live-evil.org/index.php/topic=305.15.

70. Jenkins, "Pop Cosmopolitanism."

71. Lévy, *Collective Intelligence*.

72. Terranova, *Network Culture*, 74.

73. Terranova, 78.

74. Terranova, 79.

75. Lazzarato, "Immaterial Labor," 133.

76. Lazzarato, 139.

77. Lazzarato, 137.

78. Lazzarato, 139.

79. Lazzarato, 139.

80. Ownerizer, "Re: Fansubs Suck!," Anime News Network Forum, February 5, 2003, https://www.animenewsnetwork.com/bbs/phpBB2/.

81. See Ansatsu Senjutsu Tokushu Butai, "FAQ."

82. Kamigami Fansubbing Group, "Zhushen zimuzu zhaoren qishi" [Recruitment announcement by Kamigami Fansubbing Group], subs.kami gami.org, March 8, 2022, https://subs.kamigami.org/28.html.

83. Bertschy, "Interview with the Fansubber."

84. Leonard, "Progress against the Law"; Leonard, "Celebrating Two Decades of Unlawful Progress"; Hatcher, "Of Otaku and Fansubs."

85. Miller, *Well-Tempered Self*.

86. Jenkins, *Convergence Culture*, 53.

87. Lamarre, "Otaku Movement," 374.

88. Lamarre, 375.

89. Lamarre, 372.

90. Bakhtin, *Dialogic Imagination*.

3. *Danmaku*

1. This techno-cultural transportation of anime fandom from p2p networks to video-streaming platforms was partly due to the forced shutdown of numerous BitTorrent sites by the Chinese government in antipiracy campaigns.

2. Van Dijck, *Culture of Connectivity*, 5.

3. About Niconico and its interface, see Sasaki, *Niconico doga ga mirai wo tsukuru*; Johnson, "Polyphonic/Pseudo-synchronic."

4. Steinberg, "Converging Contents and Platforms."

5. Van Dijck, *Culture of Connectivity*.

6. Condry, *Soul of Anime*.

7. Hands, "Introduction."

8. Wang and Lobato, "Chinese Video Streaming Services."

9. L. Li, *Zoning China*.

10. Bodle, "Assessing Social Network Sites as International Platforms," 15.

11. Van Dijck, *Culture of Connectivity*, 29.

12. In Japan, the interface is simply described as コメン (*komen*, "comment"). And the word *danmaku* is used to describe a certain interface effect in which layers of comments fly over the screen at an overwhelming scale or speed, resembling danmaku games in which the entire screen is covered with waves of bullets. In China, however, *danmaku* (*danmu*) is used more generally to describe both the interface and the comments on it. In this chapter, I use the word *danmaku* to refer to the interface.

13. Johnson, "Polyphonic/Pseudo-synchronic."

14. On the adoption, development, and function of the danmaku interface in Chinese digital culture, see Xu, "Postmodern Aesthetic of Chinese Online Comment Cultures"; Dwyer, "Hecklevision, Barrage Cinema, and Bullet Screens"; Y. Yang, "Danmaku Interface on Bilibili"; Zhang and Cassany, "Making Sense of Danmu"; Cao, "Bullet Screens (Danmu)"; Y. Yang, "Danmaku Subtitling."

15. Tencent Technology, "Weixin shang dianshi!"

16. Jenkins, Ford, and Green, *Spreadable Media*.

17. About the politics of platforms, see Jin, *Digital Platforms, Imperialism, and Political Culture*; Gillespie, "Politics of 'Platforms.'"

18. Steinberg, "Converging Contents and Platforms," 99.

19. Bolter and Gromala, *Windows and Mirrors*, 35.

20. Jay David Bolter and Richard Grusin describe this tension between immediacy and hypermediacy as the "double logic of remediation." See Bolter and Grusin, *Remediation*.

21. Friedberg, *Virtual Window*.

22. Chun, *Programmed Visions*, 59.

23. Chun, 59.

24. Chun, 64.

25. Chun, 59.

26. Shaviro, *Post-Cinematic Affect,* 5.

27. About the computational concept, see Bogost and Montfort, "Platform Studies"; Ballon and Van Heesvelde, "ICT Platforms and Regulatory Concerns in Europe."

28. For the economic definition of *platform,* see Rochet and Tirole, "Platform Competition in Two-Sided Markets"; Gawer, "Bridging Differing Perspectives on Technological Platforms."

29. Steinberg, "Converging Contents and Platforms," 96.

30. Gillespie, "Politics of 'Platforms.'"

31. Gillespie, 315.

32. Hands, "Platform Communism," 3.

33. Van Dijck, *Culture of Connectivity,* 174.

34. Terranova, *Network Culture,* 16.

35. Terranova, 17.

36. Steinberg, "Converging Contents and Platforms," 103.

37. Murugesan, "Understanding Web 2.0," 36.

38. Helmond, "Platformization of the Web," 4.

39. Baldwin and Woodard, "Architecture of Platforms."

40. Gawer, "Bridging Differing Perspectives on Technological Platforms," 1,243.

41. Steinberg, "Converging Contents and Platforms."

42. Lessig, *Remix*; Navas, *Remix Theory.*

43. Manovich, *Software Takes Command,* 46.

44. O'Reilly, "What Is Web 2.0."

45. Benslimane, Dustdar, and Sheth, "Services Mashups."

46. Hookway, *Interface,* ix.

47. Galloway, *Interface Effect,* 40.

48. Pratt, *Imperial Eyes,* 7.

49. Jin, *Digital Platforms, Imperialism, and Political Culture.*

50. Shaviro, *Post-Cinematic Affect,* 4.

51. J. Drucker, "Humanities Approaches to Interface Theory," 3.

52. Steinberg, "Converging Contents and Platforms," 100.

53. Jeong, *Cinematic Interfaces,* 10.

54. In fact, many users at Bilibili and AcFun indicate that they often watch the same video at least twice: once with the danmaku effect (to read the comments) and once without (to concentrate on the video).

55. Such conflation between reading and watching, according to Daniel Johnson, is one of the key characteristics of danmaku, because the "'counter-transparent,' image-oriented writing" of those on-screen comments is "part of a shift between denotational and pictorial forms of text production that

troubles the distinction between reading and other modes of vision." Johnson, "Polyphonic/Pseudo-synchronic," 297.

56. Qin, "Theaters in China Screen Movies, and Viewers' Text Messages."

57. Tencent Technology, "95 Hou de danmu shejiao."

58. Zhou and Zhang, "Jiyu shouzhong diaocha de danmu dianying tiyan yingxiao fang'an de pingjia yu celue yanjiu."

59. Tencent Technology, "95 Hou de danmu shejiao."

60. *Xin wenhua bao*, "Kan dianying or gao shejiao."

61. Zhong, "Rang danmu fei."

62. *Zongguo qingnian bao*, "Danmu hui ba dianying 'wan hao'?"

63. *Xinjing bao*, "Zai danmu mianqian, dianying haowu zunyan keyan."

64. Xiao, "Danmu dianying."

65. Van Dijck, *Culture of Connectivity*, 120.

66. Galloway, *Interface Effect*, 40.

67. Jianchajun, "Ruhe zai dianyingyuan kan yichang danmu dianying."

68. *Zongguo qingnian bao*, "Danmu hui ba dianying 'wan hao'?"

69. Johnson, "Polyphonic/Pseudo-synchronic," 299.

70. Hamano, *Aakitekucha no seitaikei*.

71. Steinberg, "Converging Contents and Platforms," 104.

72. Hamano, *Aakitekucha no seitaikei*.

73. This is why Chun describes interface as "spectral," "daemonic," and "ghostly" in *Programmed Visions*, 59–95.

74. McPherson, "Reload," 202.

75. Jane Feuer argues that liveness should be seen as an ideology of television instead of the medium's ontology. See Feuer, "Concept of Live Television."

76. Chun, *Programmed Visions*, 68.

77. Chun, 68.

78. Chun, 89.

79. On Niconico, the limit is one thousand for each video. On Bilibili and AcFun, the limit is determined by the video length. A thirty-minute video allows a maximum of three thousand comments.

80. Xiao10286, "Geren zhengli: Shubaibu B-zhan fanju lei danmu (baokuo suoyou lishi danmu)" [Personal collection: Danmaku comments for hundreds of videos at b-site (including all the historical danmaku)], Baidu Tieba, March 25, 2015, http://tieba.baidu.com/p/3658868673.

81. Hamano, *Aakitekucha no seitaikei*; Johnson, "Polyphonic/Pseudo-synchronic."

82. Lévy, *Collective Intelligence*.

83. Hainanji, "B-zhan kaoshi zuichu you duo nan?" [How difficult were the early danmaku exams on Bilibili?], Zhihu.com, October 18, 2020, https://www.zhihu.com/question/389088073.

84. Chan, "Bilibili guanyu jingyan dengji de zhidu."

85. Geyeyehenzhai, "B zhan tuichu 'yinghe huiyuan' kaoshi."

86. Hookway, *Interface.*

87. Lévy, *Collective Intelligence,* 16.

88. Tinajiadezhuji, "Danmu liyi."

89. Geyeyehenzhai, "B zhan tuichu 'yinghe huiyuan' kaoshi."

90. Lamarre, "Regional TV."

91. Lamarre, 94.

92. Lamarre, 122.

93. Massumi, *Parables for the Virtual,* 35.

4. The Mecha-Child

1. On anime as a transmedia environment or ecology, see Lamarre, *Anime Ecology*; Steinberg, *Anime's Media Mix*; Zahlten, "Between Two Funerals"; Roquet, "From Animation to Augmentation."

2. Turkle, *Second Self.*

3. In this chapter, I use *mecha* as more a motif than a genre, referring to technological beings broadly, though some of the anime examples that I examine belong to the mecha subgenre.

4. Tatsumi, *Full Metal Apache,* 47.

5. On the relationship between cyberpunk and anime, see S. T. Brown, *Tokyo Cyberpunk*; Tatsumi, *Full Metal Apache*; Sato, "How Information Technology Has (Not) Changed Feminism and Japanism"; Park, "Stylistic Crossings."

6. On the representation of the feminine in Lang's *Metropolis,* see Doane, "Technophilia."

7. Wood, *Hollywood from Vietnam to Reagan,* 75–76.

8. Napier, *Anime from "Akira" to "Howl's Moving Castle,"* 40–48.

9. See Bakhtin, *Dialogic Imagination.*

10. Heuser, *Virtual Geographies,* xviii.

11. Bukatman, *Blade Runner,* 50.

12. Doherty, *Teenagers and Teenpics*; J. Lewis, *Road to Romance and Ruin.*

13. Ruh, "Robots from Takkun's Head," 147.

14. For a psychoanalytical reading of the maternal–mecha-child relationship in *Evangelion,* see Lunning, "Between the Child and the Mecha."

15. Freud, "Uncanny."

16. Bukatman, *Poetics of Slumberland,* 140.

17. Wells, *Understanding Animation,* 19.

18. Many scholars study how anime tackles youth problems. See Allison, *Millennial Monsters*; Napier, *Anime from "Akira" to "Howl's Moving Castle"*; Ruh, "Robots from Takkun's Head."

19. Allison, *Millennial Monsters,* 57.

20. Allison, 63.

21. Lamarre, *Anime Machine*, 117.

22. Anno quoted in Samuels, "Let's Die Together."

23. Scott, "Death of Adulthood in American Culture."

24. Zeng, "Meng wenhua weihe liuxing."

25. Goldfarb, "Is It Time for More Adult Supervision at Facebook?"; Stewart, "Ruth Porat May Be Just What Investors Think Google Needs."

26. Scott, "Death of Adulthood in American Culture."

27. Ogata, *Designing the Creative Child*.

28. Ogata, xvi.

29. Ogata, xv.

30. Okada, *Otakugaku Nyumon*.

31. Jung, *Archetypes and the Collective Unconscious*, 167.

32. Jung, 174.

33. Nietzsche, *Thus Spoke Zarathustra*, 27.

34. Cavell, *Pursuits of Happiness*, 262.

35. Allison, "Cool Brand, Affective Activism, and Japanese Youth," 101.

36. Ogata, *Designing the Creative Child*.

37. Allison, *Millennial Monsters*.

38. Allison, 90–91.

39. Allison, 190.

40. Such psychoanalytical readings can be found in Allison, *Millennial Monsters*, 9–14; Lamarre, *Anime Machine*, 243–44.

41. Kinsella, "Cuties in Japan."

42. Allison, *Millennial Monsters*, 18.

43. Ngai, *Our Aesthetic Categories*, 53–109.

44. Ngai, 60.

45. Ngai, 88.

46. Ngai, 65–66.

47. In fact, the combination of tenderness and abuse characterizes most cartoon characters that are considered cute, including Mickey Mouse, Porky Pig, and Tom and Jerry. Animation as a cultural form thrives on abusive cuteness.

48. Gunning, "Cinema of Attraction."

49. Ngai, *Our Aesthetic Categories*, 66.

50. Thomas Lamarre describes Rei Ayanami's body as "quintessentially soulful," which is probably another way to say her vulnerable body makes her cuteness affectively demanding and communicative. See Lamarre, *Anime Machine*, 204.

51. Ngai, *Our Aesthetic Categories*, 91.

52. Ngai, 67.

53. Benjamin, *Walter Benjamin,* vol. 2, pt. 1, 114–19, 278–79; quoted in Ngai, *Our Aesthetic Categories,* 74–75.

54. Ngai, *Our Aesthetic Categories,* 75.

55. Turkle, *Second Self,* 13.

56. Turkle, 22.

57. Allison, *Millennial Monsters,* 13–14.

58. Baudelaire, "Philosophy of Toys," 20–21.

59. Ngai, *Our Aesthetic Categories,* 66.

60. Ngai, 93.

61. I must admit that when I was a child, I liked to tear apart my toys too, but rarely to search for the soul—I would look for the mechanical parts inside to play with them.

62. Benjamin, *Walter Benjamin,* vol. 2, pt. 2, 545.

63. Baudelaire, "Philosophy of Toys," 20.

64. Ngai, *Ugly Feelings,* 89–125.

65. Bukatman, *Poetics of Slumberland,* 20–23.

66. Ngai, *Ugly Feelings,* 113–14.

67. Steinberg, *Anime's Media Mix,* 28.

68. Gunning, "Animating the Instant," 48.

69. Turkle, *Second Self,* 16.

70. Benjamin, *Walter Benjamin,* vol. 2, pt. 2, 545.

71. Benjamin, 545.

72. Hansen, *Cinema and Experience,* 147.

73. Benjamin, *Walter Benjamin,* vol. 2, pt. 2, 720.

74. Benjamin, *Walter Benjamin,* vol. 1, 450.

75. Hansen, *Cinema and Experience,* 150.

76. Hansen, 80.

77. Allison, *Millennial Monsters,* 104–6.

78. Informed by Donna Haraway's "A Cyborg Manifesto," many argue that anime's representation of powerful female cyborgs has feminist potential toward renewed gender identities. However, it is difficult to ignore the excessively sexualized female bodies, as well as the recurrent motif of the Oedipal scenario, in many anime, both of which assume a male gaze and subjectivity. For a feminist reading of female cyborgs in anime, see Napier, *Anime from "Akira" to "Howl's Moving Castle"*; Park, "Stylistic Crossings." For counter arguments, see Sato, "How Information Technology Has (Not) Changed Feminism and Japanism."

79. On shojo culture in Japan, see Kinsella, "Cuties in Japan"; Shamoon, "Situating the Shojo in Shojo Mango"; Kotani, "Metamorphosis of the Japanese Girl."

80. Cuteness itself has a tendency of sexualization, which is an erotic regulation and recognition of child sexuality. See Ngai, *Our Aesthetic Categories*, 60.

81. On how the figure of mecha-shojo addresses sexual desires of male otaku, see Tamaki, *Beautiful Fighting Girl*.

82. Lamarre, *Anime Machine*, 235.

83. Analysis of such anxiety expressed in anime can be found in Napier, "When the Machines Stop"; Bolton, "Mecha's Blind Spot."

84. Asada, "Infantile Capitalism and Japan's Postmodernism."

85. Jameson, *Postmodernism*, 367.

86. Ngai, *Our Aesthetic Categories*, 68–69.

87. Scott, "Death of Adulthood in American Culture."

88. Asada, "Infantile Capitalism and Japan's Postmodernism," 275.

89. Asada, 276–77.

90. Galloway, *Interface Effect*, 85.

91. Galloway, 86.

92. Galloway, 91.

93. Azuma, *Otaku*.

5. Cybernetic Play

1. Canbuno, "Donghua weihu ruci xiyin women?—Jiedu donghua zhong lingni pengfudaxiao de 'NETA'" [Why are we attracted to anime?—Interpreting "NETA" that makes you laugh], bigfun, March 31, 2020, https://www.bigfunapp.cn/post/244690.

2. Tsurumaki Kazuya quoted in Ruh, "Robots from Takkun's Head," 141.

3. Comics by William Haefeli, in *New Yorker*, March 23, 2009, 53.

4. Von Trier quoted in M. Brown, "Lookey Here," quoted in Elsaesser, "Mind-Game Film," 13.

5. See Buckland, *Puzzle Films*; Elsaesser, "Mind-Game Film"; Bordwell, "Film Futures"; Branigan, "Nearly True"; Staiger, "Complex Narratives"; Cameron, *Modular Narratives in Contemporary Cinema*; Shaviro, *Post-Cinematic Affect*.

6. Buckland, *Hollywood Puzzle Films*, 3.

7. Nelson, *Literary Machines*, 2.

8. Landow, *Hypertext 2.0*. Many film scholars notice hypertextual tendencies in puzzle films and characterized them as "hypertext cinema." See Polan, *Pulp Fiction*, 35–37; Booth, "Intermediality in Film and Internet"; Levy, "Hypertext Cinema Jumbles Storytelling."

9. For a criticism of this poststructuralist impulse in hypertext from the perspectives of media history and theory, see Moulthrop, "You Say You Want a Revolution?"

10. Quoted in Graham, "Anecdotes from Mr. Hideaki Anno," 40; Sadamoto, *Neon Genesis Evangelion*, 171.

11. A. Liu, *Laws of Cool*, 103.

12. Sanders, "Virtual Ephemeralities."

13. Lamarre, "Multiplanar Image," 137.

14. Nelson, *Literary Machines*.

15. On the database as a cultural form, see Manovich, *Language of New Media*, 218–43; Kinder, "Designing a Database Cinema"; Vesna, *Database Aesthetics*; Azuma, *Otaku*.

16. Sun, "Playing the Shell Game," 17.

17. Elsaesser, "Mind-Game Film," 35.

18. Polan, *Pulp Fiction*, 18.

19. Polan, 35.

20. Steinberg, *Anime's Media Mix*, 151–52.

21. Steinberg, 160.

22. Manovich, *Language of New Media*, 218–43.

23. Manovich, 235.

24. Lamarre, *Anime Ecology*.

25. Lamarre, 288–89.

26. Lamarre, 287–310.

27. Azuma, *Gēmu-teki riarizumu no tanjō*.

28. On game-centered media mix in Japanese media studies, see Picard and Pelletier-Gagnon, "Geemu and Media Mix."

29. See Steins;Gate Wiki, "List of Known Worldlines."

30. I borrow the notion of "metamodel" from Thomas Lamarre, who borrowed it from Félix Guattari, in Lamarre, *Anime Ecology*, 293–95.

31. Azuma, *Otaku*.

32. To be fair, Manovich also sees the rise of the database as a postmodern phenomenon, a departure from the modern linear perspective. But for him, postmodernity itself is technologically determined—that is, a "computerized society." Manovich, *Language of New Media*, 219.

33. Azuma, *Otaku*, 25–38. On narrative consumption, see Ōtsuka, "World and Variation."

34. Azuma, *Gēmu-teki riarizumu no tanjō*.

35. Siliconera, "STEINS;GATE ELITE Producer."

36. Wiener, *Human Use of Human Beings*, 8.

37. Wiener, 25.

38. Wiener, 27.

39. Wiener, *Cybernetics*, 113.

40. Siliconera, "STEINS;GATE ELITE Producer."

41. Wright quoted in McGowan and McCullaugh, *Entertainment in the Cyber Zone*, 71.

42. Dahlen, "What Dark Souls Is Really All About."

43. Dahlen.

44. Galloway, *Gaming*, 26.

45. Azuma, *Otaku*; Ōtsuka, "World and Variation."

46. Lamarre, *Anime Machine*, 272.

47. Azuma, *Gēmu-teki riarizumu no tanjō*.

48. Spaziani, "Review."

49. Lamarre, *Anime Machine*, 277–99.

50. Galloway, *Gaming*.

51. Deleuze, "Postscript on the Societies of Control."

52. Huizinga, *Homo Ludens*; Caillois, *Man, Play, and Games*; Freud, *Beyond the Pleasure Principle*; Galloway, *Gaming*; Terranova, "Free Labor."

53. Benjamin, *Walter Benjamin*, vol. 3, 117.

54. Benjamin, *Walter Benjamin*, vol. 2, pt. 1, 120, 297–98, quoted in Hansen, *Cinema and Experience*, 184, 186.

55. Galloway, *Gaming*, 26–27.

56. Manovich, *Language of New Media*, 217.

6. The Framing Field

1. Murakami, *Superflat*; Lamarre, *Anime Machine*.

2. Darling, "Plumbing the Depths of Superflatness"; Looser, "Superflat and the Layers of Images and History"; Dare, "Grinding Superflat"; Rubinstein, "In the Realm of the Superflat."

3. Scafidi, "Screen Scene."

4. Scafidi.

5. For a critique of Murakami's superflat theory in relation to the notion of modernity in Japan and the West, see Lamarre, *Anime Machine*, 116.

6. McLuhan, *Understanding Media*.

7. Lamarre, "Multiplanar Image," 121.

8. Lamarre, *Anime Machine*, 126.

9. Lamarre, "Multiplanar Image," 120–23.

10. Sifianos, "Definition of Animation," 62.

11. Steinberg, *Anime's Media Mix*, 31.

12. Steinberg, 29.

13. Gunning, "Animating the Instant."

14. Gunning, 49.

15. Steinberg, *Anime's Media Mix*, 17.

16. Lamarre emphasizes the multilayered condition as a problem of compositing for animation in *The Anime Machine*; Gunning considers managing

the stillness–motion relationship to be the primary condition of animation in "Animating the Instant."

17. Baudry, "Ideological Effects of the Basic Cinematographic Apparatus"; Heath, "Narrative Space"; Bordwell, *Narration in the Fiction Film*. These critiques of cinematic apparatus, narrative, and perspective are part of the so-called grand theories. See Rosen, *Narrative, Apparatus, Ideology*.

18. Murakami, *Superflat*, 9.

19. Lamarre, "Otaku Movement."

20. Lamarre, *Anime Machine*, 114.

21. Steinberg, "Otaku Consumption, Superflat Art, and the Return to Edo," 467.

22. Darley, *Visual Digital Culture*, 124.

23. Bukatman, *Terminal Identity*, 132–34.

24. Sobchack, *Screening Space*, 228.

25. Sobchack, 255–72.

26. Sobchack, 271.

27. Bukatman, *Terminal Identity*, 132.

28. Friedberg, *Virtual Window*, 101–39.

29. Sobchack, "Toward a Phenomenology of Cinematic and Electronic Presence," 56–58.

30. Looser, "Superflat and the Layers of Images and History," 97–98.

31. Friedberg, *Virtual Window*, 2.

32. Friedberg, 229.

33. Rubinstein, "In the Realm of the Superflat," 115.

34. Bolton, "Mecha's Blind Spot."

35. The illusion of "liveness" in computer interfaces is critically analyzed by Chun, *Programmed Visions*.

36. Lamarre, "Multiplanar Image," 137.

37. Lamarre, 138.

38. Galloway, *Interface Effect*, 117.

39. Polan, *Pulp Fiction*, 38.

40. Tudor, "Eye of the Frog," 96.

41. Tudor, 102.

42. Galloway, *Interface Effect*, 115.

43. Galloway, 117.

44. Friedberg, *Virtual Window*, 243.

45. Bolter and Grusin, *Remediation*, 5.

46. Bolter and Grusin, 24–25.

47. Bolter and Grusin, 33–34.

48. Bolter and Grusin, 31–44.

49. Like superflat, computer interfaces, according to Friedberg, also produce a fractured subjectivity. The computer user is a decentered self, who, by shuffling between multiple windows, "has a fractured but multiple identity." Friedberg, *Virtual Window,* 235.

50. Examples include Steinberg, "Otaku Consumption, Superflat Art, and the Return to Edo"; Azuma, *Otaku*; and Murakami's own theorization in *Superflat.*

51. Baudrillard, *Simulacra and Simulation*; Derrida, *Writing and Difference*; Jameson, *Postmodernism.*

52. Azuma, *Otaku.*

53. Friedberg, *Window Shopping,* 10–11.

54. Friedberg, *Virtual Window,* 245.

55. Friedberg, *Window Shopping.*

56. Friedberg.

57. Friedberg, 115.

58. McPherson, "Reload."

59. Galloway, *Interface Effect,* 136.

60. Lamarre, *Anime Machine,* 128.

61. T. Wei, "'Youjian'qingnian Ye Linghan."

62. Target, "Ye Linghan."

63. Yishuyuntu, "Zai o he 1 gouheng de shijie, women doushi Lucy."

64. Y.-C. Chen, "Chen yijie."

65. Y.-C. Chen, "Artwork."

66. Y.-C. Chen, "Chen yijie."

67. Friedberg, *Virtual Window,* 3.

68. Smith, "Generation Why?"

69. Friedberg, *Virtual Window.*

70. Friedberg, 227.

71. Originally from users' comments on the YouTube post of Murakami's video "Superflat First Love by Takashi Murakami for Louis Vuitton," accessed in 2019. This video is no longer available due to a copyright claim by Kaikai Kiki Co., Ltd.

72. Friedberg, *Virtual Window,* 1.

73. Smith, "Generation Why?"

Conclusion

1. Lyotard, *Postmodern Condition.*

2. A. Liu, *Laws of Cool,* 77.

3. Deleuze, "Postscript on the Societies of Control."

4. Lazzarato, "Immaterial Labor."

5. Lamarre, "Otaku Movement," 371.

6. A. Liu, *Laws of Cool*, 78.

7. See Hansen, "Play-Form of Second Nature," 183–204.

8. Both Huizinga and Caillois define the first characteristic of play as "free." See Huizinga, *Homo Ludens*; Caillois, *Man, Play, and Games*.

9. Galloway, *Interface Effect*, 29.

10. Benjamin, *Walter Benjamin*, vol. 3, 117.

11. Hansen, "Play-Form of Second Nature," 196.

12. Galloway, *Interface Effect*, 112.

13. Deleuze, "Postscript on the Societies of Control"; Galloway, *Protocol*; Chun, *Control and Freedom*.

Bibliography

Abel, Jonathan E. "Can Cool Japan Save Post-Disaster Japan? On the Possibilities and Impossibilities of a Cool Japanology." *International Journal of Japanese Sociology* 20, no. 1 (2011): 59–72.

Aldama, Zigor. "From Made in China to Created in China, in the Space of Just 10 Years." *South China Morning Post,* December 17, 2017.

Allison, Anne. "The Cool Brand, Affective Activism, and Japanese Youth." *Theory, Culture & Society* 26, no. 2–3 (March 1, 2009): 89–111.

Allison, Anne. *Millennial Monsters: Japanese Toys and the Global Imagination.* Berkeley: University of California Press, 2006.

Andreas, Joel. *Rise of the Red Engineers: The Cultural Revolution and the Origins of China's New Class.* Stanford, Calif.: Stanford University Press, 2009.

Anime Song Lyrics. "Astro Boy (1963) Opening Theme." https://www.anime songlyrics.com/astro-boy-1963/tetsuwan-atomu.

Ansatsu Senjutsu Tokushu Butai. "FAQ: What Are the Steps Involved in a Release?" ANBU. http://anbudom.net/faq/#release.

Appadurai, Arjun. *Modernity at Large: Cultural Dimensions of Globalization.* Minneapolis: University of Minnesota Press, 1996

Asada, Akira. "Infantile Capitalism and Japan's Postmodernism: A Fairy Tale." In *Postmodernism and Japan,* edited by Masao Miyoshi and Harry Harootunian, 273–78. Durham, N.C.: Duke University Press, 1989.

Azuma, Hiroki. *Gēmu-teki riarizumu no tanjō* [The birth of game-ic realism: The animalizing postmodern 2]. Tokyo: Kōdansha, 2007.

Azuma, Hiroki. *Otaku: Japan's Database Animals.* Translated by Jonathan E. Abel. Minneapolis: University of Minnesota Press, 2009.

Bakhtin, Mikhail Mikhaïlovich. *The Dialogic Imagination: Four Essays.* Austin: University of Texas Press, 2004.

Bakhtin, Mikhail Mikhaĭlovich. "The Problem of Speech Genre." In *Speech Genres and Other Late Essays*, edited by Michael Holquist and Caryl Emerson, translated by Vern W. McGee, 60–102. Austin: University of Texas Press, 1986.

Bakhtin, Mikhail Mikhaĭlovich. "The Problem of the Text." In *Speech Genres and Other Late Essays*, edited by Michael Holquist and Caryl Emerson, translated by Vern W. McGee, 103–31. Austin: University of Texas Press, 1986.

Bakhtin, Mikhail Mikhaĭlovich. *Speech Genres and Other Late Essays*. Edited by Michael Holquist and Caryl Emerson. Translated by Vern W. McGee. Austin: University of Texas Press, 1986.

Baldwin, Carliss Y., and C. Jason Woodard. "The Architecture of Platforms: A Unified View." In *Platforms, Markets, and Innovation*, edited by Annabelle Gawer. 19–44, Cheltenham, U.K.: Edward Elgar Publishing, 2011.

Ballon, Pieter, and Eric Van Heesvelde. "ICT Platforms and Regulatory Concerns in Europe." *Telecommunications Policy* 35, no. 8 (2011): 702–14.

Bao, Weihong. *Fiery Cinema: The Emergence of an Affective Medium in China, 1915–1945*. Minneapolis: University of Minnesota Press, 2015.

Baudelaire, Charles. "The Philosophy of Toys." In *On Dolls*, edited by Kenneth Gross, 11–21. London: Notting Hill Editions, 2018.

Baudrillard, Jean. *Simulacra and Simulation*. Translated by Sheila Glaser. Ann Arbor: University of Michigan Press, 1994.

Baudry, Jean-Louis. "Ideological Effects of the Basic Cinematographic Apparatus." Translated by Alan Williams. *Film Quarterly* 28, no. 2 (1974): 39–47.

Beech, Hannah. "The New Radicals." *Time*, February 2, 2004.

Bell, Daniel. *The Coming of Post-Industrial Society: A Venture in Social Forecasting*. New York: Basic Books, 1976.

Benjamin, Walter. "One-Way Street." In *Walter Benjamin: Selected Writings*. Vol. 1, *1913–1926*, edited by Marcus Bullock and Michael W. Jennings, 444–88. Cambridge, Mass.: Belknap Press, 2004.

Benjamin, Walter. *Walter Benjamin: Selected Writings*. Vol. 1, *1913–1926*, edited by Marcus Bullock and Michael W. Jennings. Cambridge, Mass.: Belknap Press, 2004.

Benjamin, Walter. *Walter Benjamin: Selected Writings*. Vol. 2, Part 1, *1927–1930*, edited by Michael W. Jennings, Howard Eiland, and Gary Smith. Cambridge, Mass.: Belknap Press, 2005.

Benjamin, Walter. *Walter Benjamin: Selected Writings*. Vol. 2, Part 2, *1931–1934*, edited by Michael W. Jennings, Gary Smith, and Howard Eiland. Cambridge, Mass.: Belknap Press, 2005.

Benjamin, Walter. *Walter Benjamin: Selected Writings*. Vol. 3, *1935–1938*, edited by Howard Eiland and Michael W. Jennings. Cambridge, Mass.: Belknap Press, 2006.

Benjamin, Walter. "The Work of Art in the Age of Its Technological Reproducibility: Second Version." In *Walter Benjamin: Selected Writings*. Vol. 3, *1935–1938*, edited by Howard Eiland and Michael W. Jennings, 101–33. Cambridge, Mass.: Belknap Press, 2006.

Benslimane, Djamal, Schahram Dustdar, and Amit Sheth. "Services Mashups: The New Generation of Web Applications." *IEEE Internet Computing* 12, no. 5 (September 2008): 13–15.

Bertschy, Zac. "Interview with the Fansubber." Anime News Network, March 11, 2008. http://www.animenewsnetwork.com/feature/2008-03-11.

Boczkowski, Pablo J., and Eugenia Mitchelstein. *The Digital Environment: How We Live, Learn, Work, and Play Now*. Cambridge, Mass.: MIT Press, 2021.

Bodle, Robert. "Assessing Social Network Sites as International Platforms." *Journal of International Communication* 16, no. 2 (January 1, 2010): 9–24.

Bogost, Ian, and Nick Montfort. "Platform Studies: Frequently Questioned Answers." *Digital Arts and Culture 2009*, December 12, 2009. http://eschol arship.org/uc/item/01rok9br.

Bolter, J. David, and Diane Gromala. *Windows and Mirrors: Interaction Design, Digital Art, and the Myth of Transparency*. Cambridge, Mass.: MIT Press, 2003.

Bolter, J. David, and Richard Grusin. *Remediation: Understanding New Media*. Cambridge, Mass.: MIT Press, 1999.

Bolton, Christopher. "The Mecha's Blind Spot: *Patlabor 2* and the Phenomenology of Anime." *Science Fiction Studies* 29, no. 3 (November 2002): 453–74.

Booth, Paul. "Intermediality in Film and Internet: *Donnie Darko* and Issues of Narrative Substantiality." *Journal of Narrative Theory* 38, no. 3 (2009): 398–415.

Bordwell, David. "Film Futures." *SubStance* 31, no. 1 (2002): 88–104.

Bordwell, David. *Narration in the Fiction Film*. Madison: University of Wisconsin Press, 1985.

Bourdieu, Pierre. *Distinction: A Social Critique of the Judgement of Taste*. Cambridge, Mass.: Harvard University Press, 1984.

Branigan, Edward. "Nearly True: Forking Plots, Forking Interpretations—A Response to David Bordwell's 'Film Futures.'" *SubStance* 31, no. 1 (2002): 105–14.

Brown, Mark. "Lookey Here: Lars von Trier Is at It Again." *Guardian*, December 8, 2006.

Brown, Steven T. *Tokyo Cyberpunk: Posthumanism in Japanese Visual Culture*. New York: Palgrave Macmillan, 2010.

Buckland, Warren, ed. *Hollywood Puzzle Films*. New York: Routledge, 2014.

Buckland, Warren, ed. *Puzzle Films: Complex Storytelling in Contemporary Cinema*. Oxford: Wiley-Blackwell, 2009.

Bukatman, Scott. *Blade Runner*. London: British Film Institute, 1997.

Bukatman, Scott. *The Poetics of Slumberland: Animated Spirits and the Animating Spirit*. Berkeley: University of California Press, 2012.

Bukatman, Scott. *Terminal Identity: The Virtual Subject in Postmodern Science Fiction*. Durham, N.C.: Duke University Press, 1993.

Caillois, Roger. *Man, Play, and Games*. Urbana: University of Illinois Press, 2001.

Cameron, Allan. *Modular Narratives in Contemporary Cinema*. New York: Palgrave Macmillan, 2008.

Cao, Xuenan. "Bullet Screens (Danmu): Texting, Online Streaming, and the Spectacle of Social Inequality on Chinese Social Networks." *Theory, Culture & Society* 38, no. 3 (2021): 29–49.

Castells, Manuel. *The Information Age: Economy, Society, and Culture*. Vol. 1, *The Rise of the Network Society*. Cambridge, Mass.: Blackwell, 2000.

Cavell, Stanley. *Pursuits of Happiness: The Hollywood Comedy of Remarriage*. Cambridge, Mass.: Harvard University Press, 1984.

Chan, Baiheling. "Bilibili guanyu jingyan dengji de zhidu" [About the rules in Bilibili membership levels]. Bilibili, July 9, 2019. http://www.bilibili.com/read/cv339659.

Chang, David Wen-Wei. *China under Deng Xiaoping: Political and Economic Reform*. New York: Palgrave Macmillan, 1991.

Chen, Kuan-Hsing. *Asia as Method: Toward Deimperialization*. Durham, N.C.: Duke University Press, 2010.

Chen, Yi-Chieh (Agi). "Artwork: 函數色彩/Function Color." *Agi Chen* (blog), February 14, 2010. http://agiagiagi.blogspot.com/2010/02/blog-post.html.

Chen, Yi-Chieh. "Chen yijie: Bianmaodao" [Yi-Chieh Chen: Programming island]. Artron.net, July 6, 2015. https://news.artron.net/20150706/n756543.html.

Chen, Qiang, and Yingying Teng. "Riben dongman zai zhongguo dalu chuanbo fenxi" [Analyzing the spread of Japanese anime in mainland China]. *Xiandai Chuanbo* [Modern communication] 141, no. 4 (2006): 78–81.

Cheng, Wu. "Ni hui bei 'zhai jingji' shidai taotai ma" [Will you be phased out in the age of 'zhai economy'?]. *Zhonghua gongshang shibao*, May 18, 2009, sec. 7.

Chiang, Jeongwen. "China's Movie Industry: All That Glitters Isn't Gold." *Forbes Asia*, August 24, 2014.

China Internet Network Information Center. "Internet Statistics." Accessed July 20, 2023. https://www.cnnic.com.cn/IDR/.

Choi, JungBong. "Of the East Asian Cultural Sphere: Theorizing Cultural Regionalization." *China Review* 10, no. 2 (2010): 109–36.

Choo, Kukhee. "Nationalizing 'Cool': Japan's Global Promotion of the Content Industry." In *Popular Culture and the State in East and Southeast Asia,* edited by Nissim Otmazgin and Eyal Ben-Ari, 85–105. New York: Routledge, 2011.

Chow, Rey. "Postmodern Automatons." In *Writing Diaspora: Tactics of Intervention in Contemporary Cultural Studies,* 55–72. Bloomington: Indiana University Press, 1993.

Chun, Wendy Hui Kyong. *Control and Freedom: Power and Paranoia in the Age of Fiber Optics.* Cambridge, Mass.: MIT Press, 2006.

Chun, Wendy Hui Kyong. "Orienting Orientalism, or How to Map Cyberspace." In *Asian America.Net: Ethnicity, Nationalism, and Cyberspace,* edited by Rachel C. Lee and Sau-ling Cynthia Wong, 3–36. New York: Routledge, 2013.

Chun, Wendy Hui Kyong. *Programmed Visions: Software and Memory.* Cambridge, Mass.: MIT Press, 2011.

Collins Dictionary. "CollinsDictionary.com 'Word of the Year': The Changing Face of Words." *Language Lovers* (blog). December 16, 2013. https://blog.collinsdictionary.com/language-lovers/collinsdictionary-com-word-of-the-year-the-changing-face-of-words/.

Condry, Ian. "Anime Creativity: Characters and Premises in the Quest for Cool Japan." *Theory, Culture & Society* 26, no. 2–3 (2009): 139–63.

Condry, Ian. "Dark Energy: What Fansubs Reveal about the Copyright Wars." *Mechademia* 5 (2010): 193–208.

Condry, Ian. *The Soul of Anime: Collaborative Creativity and Japan's Media Success Story.* Durham, N.C.: Duke University Press, 2013.

Cubbison, Laurie. "Anime Fans, DVDs, and the Authentic Text." *Velvet Light Trap* 56, no. 1 (2005): 45–57.

Dahlen, Chris. "What Dark Souls Is Really All About." Kotaku, January 9, 2012. https://kotaku.com/what-dark-souls-is-really-all-about-5874599.

Daliot-Bul, Michal. "Japan Brand Strategy: The Taming of 'Cool Japan' and the Challenges of Cultural Planning in a Postmodern Age." *Social Science Japan Journal* 12, no. 2 (2009): 247–66.

Dare, Kevin. "Grinding Superflat: The Options." *Concrete* 39, no. 9 (September 2005): 28.

Darley, Andrew. *Visual Digital Culture: Surface Play and Spectacle in New Media Genres.* London: Routledge, 2000.

Darling, Michael. "Plumbing the Depths of Superflatness." *Art Journal* 60, no. 3 (Autumn 2001): 77–89.

Debord, Guy. *Society of the Spectacle.* Detroit: Black & Red, 1977.

Deleuze, Gilles. *Foucault.* Translated by Sean Hand. Minneapolis: University of Minnesota Press, 1988.

Deleuze, Gilles. "Postscript on the Societies of Control." *October* 59 (1992): 3–7.

Deng, Xiaoping. *Deng Xiaoping wenxuan* [Selected writings of Deng Xiaoping]. Vol. 3. Beijing: Renmin Chubanshe, 1993.

Denison, Rayna. "Anime Fandom and the Liminal Spaces between Fan Creativity and Piracy." *International Journal of Cultural Studies* 14, no. 5 (2011): 449–66.

Denson, Shane. *Discorrelated Images*. Durham, N.C.: Duke University Press, 2020.

Derrida, Jacques. "Structure, Sign, and Play in the Discourse of the Human Sciences." In *Writing and Difference,* translated by Alan Bass, 278–93. Chicago: University of Chicago Press, 1978.

Derrida, Jacques. *Writing and Difference*. Translated by Alan Bass. Chicago: University of Chicago Press, 1978.

Díaz Cintas, J., and P. Munoz Sanchez. "Fansubs: Audiovisual Translation in an Amateur Environment." *Journal of Specialised Translation* 6 (2006): 37–52.

Diyi caijing ribao. "Jinrong weiji cuire 'zhai yi zu,' fengtou nishi guanzhu 'zhai jingji'" [Otaku gained momentum amid economic recession, ventral capitals pay attention to 'zhai economy']. March 11, 2009, sec. C2.

Doane, Mary Ann. "Technophilia: Technology, Representation, and the Feminine." In *Cybersexualities: A Reader in Feminist Theory, Cyborgs, and Cyberspace,* edited by Jenny Wolmark, 20–33. Edinburgh: Edinburgh University Press, 1999.

Doherty, Thomas Patrick. *Teenagers and Teenpics: The Juvenilization of American Movies in the 1950s*. Boston: Unwin Hyman, 1988.

Drucker, Johanna. "Humanities Approaches to Interface Theory." *Culture Machine* 12 (2011). https://www.culturemachine.net/the-digital-humanities -beyond-computing/.

Drucker, Peter Ferdinand. *The Age of Discontinuity: Guidelines to Our Changing Society*. New York: Harper and Row, 1969.

Du, Daisy Yan. *Animated Encounters: Transnational Movements of Chinese Animation, 1940s–1970s*. Honolulu: University of Hawaii Press, 2019.

Dwyer, Tessa. "Hecklevision, Barrage Cinema, and Bullet Screens: An Intercultural Analysis." *Participations: Journal of Audience & Reception Studies* 14, no. 2 (2017): 571–89.

Eglash, Ron. "Race, Sex, and Nerds: From Black Geeks to Asian American Hipsters." *Social Text* 20, no. 2 (71) (Summer 2002): 49–64.

Ehrenreich, Barbara, and John Ehrenreich. "The Professional-Managerial Class." In *Between Labor and Capital,* edited by Pat Walker, 5–45. Boston: South End Press, 1979.

Eisenstein, Sergei. *Eisenstein on Disney*. London: Methuen, 1988.

Elsaesser, Thomas. "The Mind-Game Film." In *Puzzle Films: Complex Storytelling in Contemporary Cinema,* edited by Warren Buckland, 13–41. Oxford: Wiley-Blackwell, 2009.

Ensmenger, Nathan L. *The Computer Boys Take Over: Computers, Programmers, and the Politics of Technical Expertise.* Cambridge, Mass.: MIT Press, 2012.

Faiola, Anthony. "Japan's Empire of Cool: Country's Culture Becomes Its Biggest Export." *Washington Post,* December 27, 2003.

Fan, Victor. *Extraterritoriality: Locating Hong Kong Cinema and Media.* Edinburgh: Edinburgh University Press, 2019.

Fang, Yimin. "Jiyi suipian: Yu Atongmu yiqi chengzhang" [Fragments of memory: Growing up with Astro Boy]. *Nanfang dushi bao* [Southern metropolis daily], October 25, 2009.

Feineman, Neil. *Geek Chic: The Ultimate Guide to Geek Culture.* Berkeley, Calif.: Gingko Press, 2005.

Feuer, Jane. "The Concept of Live Television: Ontology as Ideology." In *Regarding Television: Critical Approaches—An Anthology,* edited by E. Ann Kaplan, 12–22. Frederick, Md..: University Publications of America, 1983.

Fickle, Tara. *The Race Card: From Gaming Technologies to Model Minorities.* New York: New York University Press, 2019.

Florida, Richard L. *The Rise of the Creative Class: And How It's Transforming Work, Leisure, Community, and Everyday Life.* New York: Basic Books, 2002.

Follow Lyrics. "阿童木之歌 歌词." https://zh.followlyrics.com/lyrics/270448/a -tong-mu-zhi-ge.

Fong, Vanessa L. *Only Hope: Coming of Age under China's One-Child Policy.* Stanford, Calif.: Stanford University Press, 2004.

Freud, Sigmund. *Beyond the Pleasure Principle.* London: International Psychoanalytical Press, 1922.

Freud, Sigmund. "The Uncanny." In *Standard Edition of the Complete Psychological Works of Sigmund Freud.* Vol. 17, *(1917–1919): An Infantile Neurosis and Other Works,* translated by James Strachey, 217–56. London: Hogarth Press, 1955.

Friedberg, Anne. *The Virtual Window: From Alberti to Microsoft.* Cambridge, Mass.: MIT Press, 2006.

Friedberg, Anne. *Window Shopping: Cinema and the Postmodern.* Berkeley: University of California Press, 1994.

Fritz, Ben. "Geek Chic . . . but 'Netsters Wary of Showbiz Wooing." *Variety,* August 4, 2004.

Fuller, Matthew. *Media Ecologies: Materialist Energies in Art and Technoculture.* Cambridge, Mass.: MIT Press, 2005.

Fung, Anthony. "Redefining Creative Labor: East Asian Comparisons." In *Precarious Creativity: Global Media, Local Labor,* edited by Michael Curtin and Kevin Sanson, 200–14. Berkeley: University of California Press, 2016.

Furuhata, Yuriko. *Climatic Media: Transpacific Experiments in Atmospheric Control.* Durham, N.C.: Duke University Press, 2022.

Galbraith, Patrick W. *Otaku and the Struggle for Imagination in Japan.* Illustrated ed. Durham, N.C.: Duke University Press, 2019.

Galloway, Alexander R. *Gaming: Essays on Algorithmic Culture.* Minneapolis: University of Minnesota Press, 2006.

Galloway, Alexander R. *The Interface Effect.* Cambridge: Polity, 2012.

Galloway, Alexander R. "Postscript: We Are the Gold Farmers." In *The Interface Effect,* 120–43. Cambridge: Polity, 2012.

Galloway, Alexander R. *Protocol: How Control Exists after Decentralization.* Cambridge, Mass.: MIT Press, 2004.

Gawer, Annabelle. "Bridging Differing Perspectives on Technological Platforms: Toward an Integrative Framework." *Research Policy* 43, no. 7 (2014): 1,239–49.

Geyeyehenzhai. "B zhan tuichu 'yinghe huiyuan' kaoshi" [Bilibili released the "hardcore membership" exam]. Bilibili, April 2, 2022. https://www.bilibili .com/read/cv15950181.

Gibson, William. "Modern Boys and Mobile Girls." *Observer* 1 (2001).

Gillespie, Tarleton. "The Politics of 'Platforms.'" *New Media & Society* 12, no. 3 (2010): 347–64.

Goldfarb, Jeffrey. "Is It Time for More Adult Supervision at Facebook?" *New York Times,* June 8, 2018.

Gouldner, Alvin Ward. *The Future of Intellectuals and the Rise of the New Class.* Oxford: Oxford University Press, 1982.

Graham, Miyako. "Anecdotes from Mr. Hideaki Anno." *Protoculture Addicts* 43 (1996): 40–41.

Graser, Marc. "H'wood Learns to Speak Geek." *Daily Variety,* July 28, 2008, 1–22.

Grossman, Lev. "The Geek Shall Inherit the Earth." *Time,* October 3, 2005.

GroupM Knowledge Center. "Jujiao 'zhaishidai': Zhongguo zhainan zhainv yanjiu baogao" [Focus on the zhai generation: Report on Chinese otaku]. *Zhongguo guanggao* [China advertising] 6 (2008).

Gunning, Tom. "Animating the Instant: The Secret Symmetry between Animation and Photography." In *Animating Film Theory,* edited by Karen Beckman, 37–53. Durham, N.C.: Duke University Press, 2014.

Gunning, Tom. "The Cinema of Attractions: Early Cinema, Its Spectator, and the Avant-Garde." *Wide Angle* 8, no. 3–4 (1986): 63–70.

Guo, Hong, and Guoliang Zhang. "Zhongguo qingshaonian yu donghua chuangbo de shizheng yanjiu: Yi Beijing Shanghai de Donghua Chuanshou Zhuangkuang Weil" [Positive research on animation audiences in Beijing and Shanghai]. *Xinwen Daxue* [Journalism quarterly] 4 (Winter 2003): 30–35.

Hadade. "Atongmu zai zhongguo de qianshijinshen" [The life of Astro Boy in China]. November 26, 2010. http://www.hahade.com/zhuanti/atongmu -china.html.

Hamano, Satoshi. *Aakitekucha no seitaikei: Jōhō Kankyō Wa Ikani Sekkei Sarete Kita Ka* [Ecosystems of architecture: How do information environments come to be planned?]. Tokyo: NTT Shuppan, 2008.

Hands, Joss. "Introduction: Politics, Power, and 'Platformativity.'" *Culture Machine* 14 (2013): https://www.culturemachine.net/platform-politics/.

Hands, Joss. "Platform Communism." *Culture Machine* 14 (2013): https://www.culturemachine.net/platform-politics/.

Hansen, Miriam. *Cinema and Experience: Siegfried Kracauer, Walter Benjamin, and Theodor W. Adorno.* Berkeley: University of California Press, 2011.

Hansen, Miriam. "Play-Form of Second Nature." In *Cinema and Experience: Siegfried Kracauer, Walter Benjamin, and Theodor W. Adorno,* 183–204. Berkeley: University of California Press, 2011.

Haraway, Donna J. "A Cyborg Manifesto: Science, Technology, and Socialist-Feminism in the Late Twentieth Century." In *Simians, Cyborgs, and Women: The Reinvention of Nature,* 149–81. New York: Routledge, 1991.

Hardt, Michael, and Antonio Negri. *Multitude: War and Democracy in the Age of Empire.* New York: Penguin Books, 2005.

Harvey, David. *The Condition of Postmodernity: An Enquiry into the Origins of Cultural Change.* Cambridge, Mass.: Wiley-Blackwell, 1989.

Hatcher, Jordan S. "Of Otaku and Fansubs: A Critical Look at Anime Online in Light of Current Issues in Copyright Law." *Script-Ed* 2, no. 4 (2005): 514–42.

Hatcher, Jordan S. "Of Otaku and Fansubs: A Critical Look at Anime Online in Light of Current Issues in Copyright Law [Appendix]." *Script-Ed* 2, no. 4 (2005): https://script-ed.org/archive/volume-2/issue-24-415-548/.

Hayles, N. Katherine. *How We Became Posthuman: Virtual Bodies in Cybernetics, Literature, and Informatics.* Chicago: University of Chicago Press, 1999.

Heath, Stephen. "Narrative Space." *Screen* 17, no. 3 (1976): 68–112.

Hebdige, Dick. *Subculture. The Meaning of Style.* New York: Routledge, 1988.

Helmond, Anne. "The Platformization of the Web: Making Web Data Platform Ready." *Social Media + Society* 1, no. 2 (2015): 1–11.

Heuser, Sabine. *Virtual Geographies: Cyberpunk at the Intersection of the Postmodern and Science Fiction.* New York: Rodopi, 2003.

Hong, Junhao. *The Internationalization of Television in China: The Evolution of Ideology, Society, and Media since the Reform.* Westport, Conn.: Praeger, 1998.

Hookway, Branden. *Interface.* Cambridge, Mass.: MIT Press, 2014.

Hornaday, Ann. "Nerdy Teenage Boys Define the Zeitgeist of Summer '07." *Washington Post,* September 9, 2007.

Hu, Tung-Hui. *A Prehistory of the Cloud.* Illustrated ed. Cambridge, Mass.: MIT Press, 2016.

Huang, Dahui. "Zhong ri guanxi fazhan 30 nian" [Thirty years of development in the Sino–Japan relationship]. *Jiaoyu yu Yanjiu* 11 (2008).

Huizinga, Johan. *Homo Ludens: A Study of the Play-Element in Culture.* Boston: Beacon Press, 1955.

Irvine, Martha. "Suddenly, It's Hip to Be Square." *Associated Press,* July 19, 2005.

Ito, Mizuko. "Contributors versus Leechers: Fansubbing Ethics and a Hybrid Public Culture." In *Fandom Unbound: Otaku Culture in a Connected World,* edited by Mizuko Ito, 179–204. New Haven, Conn.: Yale University Press, 2012.

Ito, Mizuko, ed. *Fandom Unbound: Otaku Culture in a Connected World.* New Haven, Conn.: Yale University Press, 2012.

Ito, Mizuko, ed. *Hanging Out, Messing Around, and Geeking Out: Kids Living and Learning with New Media.* Cambridge, Mass.: MIT Press, 2010.

Ito, Mizuko. Introduction to *Fandom Unbound: Otaku Culture in a Connected World,* edited by Mizuko Ito. New Haven, Conn.: Yale University Press, 2012.

Iwabuchi, Kōichi. *Recentering Globalization: Popular Culture and Japanese Transnationalism.* Durham, N.C.: Duke University Press, 2002.

Jameson, Fredric. *Postmodernism, or The Cultural Logic of Late Capitalism.* Durham, N.C.: Duke University Press, 1991.

Jenkins, Henry. *Convergence Culture: Where Old and New Media Collide.* New York: New York University Press, 2006.

Jenkins, Henry. *Fans, Bloggers, and Gamers: Media Consumers in a Digital Age.* New York: New York University Press, 2006.

Jenkins, Henry. "Pop Cosmopolitanism: Mapping Cultural Flows in an Age of Media Convergence." In *Fans, Bloggers, and Gamers: Media Consumers in a Digital Age,* 152–72. New York: New York University Press, 2006.

Jenkins, Henry, Sam Ford, and Joshua Green. *Spreadable Media: Creating Value and Meaning in a Networked Culture.* New York: New York University Press, 2013.

Jeong, Seung-hoon. *Cinematic Interfaces: Film Theory after New Media.* New York: Routledge, 2013.

Jianchajun. "Ruhe zai dianyingyuan kan yichang danmu dianying" [How to watch a danmaku cinema in movie theatre]. Douban, August 6, 2014. https://movie.douban.com/review/6803291/.

Jiang, Bing. "Lun 80hou wenxue de wenhua beijing" [The cultural background of post-80s literature]. *Wenyi Pinglun* 1 (2005).

Jiang, Jin. "Higher Education in China." *Oxford Research Encyclopedia of Education,* December 19, 2017.

Jiang, Ping. "Ye tan woguo de 'zhainan zhainv' xianxiang: Yige kongjian she-huixue de fenxi shijiao" [Another look at the otaku phenomenon in our country: From the perspective of spatial sociology]. *Zongguo Qingnian Yan-jiu* [China youth study] 8 (2009): 81–83.

Jin, Dal Yong. *Digital Platforms, Imperialism, and Political Culture.* New York: Routledge, 2015.

Johnson, Daniel. "Polyphonic/Pseudo-synchronic: Animated Writing in the Comment Feed of Nicovideo." *Japanese Studies* 33, no. 3 (2013): 297–313.

Jung, Carl G. *The Archetypes and the Collective Unconscious.* Translated by R. F. C. Hull. Princeton, N.J.: Princeton University Press, 1981.

Katz, Jon. *Geeks: How Two Lost Boys Rode the Internet out of Idaho.* New York: Villard, 2000.

Katzenstein, Peter J., and Takashi Shiraishi, eds. *Beyond Japan: The Dynamics of East Asian Regionalism.* Ithaca, N.Y.: Cornell University Press, 2006.

Keane, Michael. "Unbundling Precarious Creativity in China: 'Knowing-How' and 'Knowing-To.'" In *Precarious Creativity: Global Media, Local Labor,* edited by Michael Curtin and Kevin Sanson, 215–30. Berkeley: University of California Press, 2016.

Kelly, Kevin. "The Third Culture." *Science* 279, no. 5,353 (February 13, 1998): 992–93.

Kinder, Marsha. "Designing a Database Cinema." In *Future Cinema: The Cinematic Imaginary after Film,* edited by Jeffrey Shaw and Peter Weibel, 346–53. Cambridge, Mass.: MIT Press, 2003.

Kinsella, Sharon. "Cuties in Japan." In *Women, Media, and Consumption in Japan,* edited by Lise Skov and Brian Moeran, 220–54. Honolulu: University of Hawaii Press, 1995.

Kotani, Mari. "Metamorphosis of the Japanese Girl: The Girl, the Hyper-Girl, and the Battling Beauty." *Mechademia* 1 (2006): 162–69.

Kusakawa, Sho. *Terebi anime 20 nen shi* [A twenty-year history of television anime]. Tokyo: Rippu Shobo, 1981.

Lam, Peng Er. "Japan's Quest for 'Soft Power': Attraction and Limitation." *East Asia* 24, no. 4 (2007): 349–63.

Lamarre, Thomas. *The Anime Ecology: A Genealogy of Television, Animation, and Game Media.* Minneapolis: University of Minnesota Press, 2018.

Lamarre, Thomas. *The Anime Machine: A Media Theory of Animation.* Minneapolis: University of Minnesota Press, 2009.

Lamarre, Thomas. "The Multiplanar Image." *Mechademia* 1 (2006): 120–43.

Lamarre, Thomas. "Otaku Movement." In *Japan after Japan: Social and Cultural Life from the Recessionary 1990s to the Present,* edited by Tomiko Yoda and Harry D. Harootunian, 358–94. Durham, N.C.: Duke University Press, 2006.

Lamarre, Thomas. "Regional TV: Affective Media Geographies." *Asiascape: Digital Asia* 2, no. 1–2 (2015): 93–126.

Landa, Amanda. "Niche Market, Global Scale: Simulcasting Anime Online." *Flow,* July 2, 2010. http://flowtv.org.

Landow, George P. *Hypertext 2.0.* Baltimore: Johns Hopkins University Press, 1997.

Lardy, Nicholas R. *Foreign Trade and Economic Reform in China, 1978–1990.* Cambridge: Cambridge University Press, 1993.

Lazzarato, Maurizio. "Immaterial Labor." In *Radical Thought in Italy: A Potential Politics,* edited by Paolo Virno and Michael Hardt, 133–47. Minneapolis: University of Minnesota Press, 1996.

Leaver, Tama. "FlashForward or FlashBack: Television Distribution in 2010?" *Flow,* January 9, 2010. http://flowtv.org.

Lee, Hye-Kyung. "Participatory Media Fandom: A Case Study of Anime Fansubbing." *Media, Culture & Society* 33, no. 8 (2011): 1,131–47.

Lent, John A. "Vignette: Anime and Manga in Parts of Asia and Latin America." In *Animation in Asia and the Pacific,* edited by John A. Lent, 73–84. Bloomington: Indiana University Press, 2001.

Leonard, Sean. "Celebrating Two Decades of Unlawful Progress: Fan Distribution, Proselytization Commons, and the Explosive Growth of Japanese Animation." *UCLA Entertainment Law Review* 12 (2004): 189–212.

Leonard, Sean. "Progress against the Law: Anime and Fandom, with the Key to the Globalization of Culture." *International Journal of Cultural Studies* 8, no. 3 (2005): 281–305.

Lessig, Lawrence. *Remix: Making Art and Commerce Thrive in the Hybrid Economy.* New York: Penguin, 2008.

Leung, Lisa Yuk Ming. "Romancing the Everyday: Hong Kong Women Watching Japanese Dorama." *Japanese Studies* 22, no. 1 (2002): 65–75.

Levitt, Deborah. *The Animatic Apparatus: Animation, Vitality, and the Futures of the Image.* Winchester, U.K.: Zero Books, 2018.

Lévy, Pierre. *Collective Intelligence: Mankind's Emerging World in Cyberspace.* Cambridge, Mass.: Perseus Books, 1997.

Lévy, Pierre. *Cyberculture.* Translated by Robert Bononno. Minneapolis: University of Minnesota Press, 2001.

Levy, Shawn. "Hypertext Cinema Jumbles Storytelling the Way a Video Game Does." *Newhouse News Service,* August 17, 1999, 1.

Lewis, Jon. *The Road to Romance and Ruin: Teen Films and Youth Culture.* New York: Routledge, 1992.

Lewis, Philip E. "The Measure of Translation Effects." In *Difference in Translation,* edited by Joseph F. Graham, 31–62. Ithaca, N.Y.: Cornell University Press, 1985.

Li, Conghua. *China: The Consumer Revolution.* New York: John Wiley & Sons Asia, 1998.

Li, Jinying. "Pirate Cosmopolitanism and the Undercurrents of Flow: Fansubbing Television on China's P2P Networks." In *Transnational Convergence of East Asian Pop Culture,* edited by Seok-Kyeong Hong and Dal Yong Jin, 127–46. New York: Routledge, 2021.

Li, Luzhou. *Zoning China: Online Video, Popular Culture, and the State.* Cambridge, Mass.: MIT Press, 2019.

Liu, Alan. *The Laws of Cool: Knowledge Work and the Culture of Information.* Chicago: University of Chicago Press, 2004.

Liu, Xiao. *Information Fantasies: Precarious Mediation in Postsocialist China.* Minneapolis: University of Minnesota Press, 2019.

Loo, Egan. "Report: 2007 Japanese Otaku Market Is 187 Billion Yen." Anime News Network, December 18, 2007. https://www.animenewsnetwork.com.

Looser, Thomas. "Superflat and the Layers of Images and History in 1990s Japan." *Mechademia* 1 (2006): 92–109.

Lu, Amy Shirong. "The Many Faces of Internationalization in Japanese Anime." *Animation: An Interdisciplinary Journal* 3 (2008): 169–87.

Lull, James. *China Turned On: Television, Reform, and Resistance.* New York: Routledge, 1991.

Lunning, Frenchy. "Between the Child and the Mecha." *Mechademia* 2 (2007): 268–82.

Lyotard, Jean-Francois. *The Postmodern Condition: A Report on Knowledge.* Translated by Geoff Bennington and Brian Massumi. Minneapolis: University of Minnesota Press, 1984.

Macdonald, Sean. *Animation in China: History, Aesthetics, Media.* New York: Routledge, 2015.

Manovich, Lev. *The Language of New Media.* Cambridge, Mass.: MIT Press, 2002.

Manovich, Lev. *Software Takes Command.* London: Bloomsbury Academic, 2013.

Manxiaozhi. "Zimuzu hui xiaowang ma?" [Will fansubbing groups disappear?]. Wangyi [NetEase], March 12, 2022. https://www.163.com.

Massumi, Brian. *Parables for the Virtual: Movement, Affect, Sensation.* Durham, N.C.: Duke University Press, 2002.

Mattern, Shannon. *Code and Clay, Data and Dirt: Five Thousand Years of Urban Media.* Minneapolis: University of Minnesota Press, 2017.

McArthur, J. A. "Digital Subculture: A Geek Meaning of Style." *Journal of Communication Inquiry* 33, no. 1 (January 1, 2009): 58–70.

McCarthy, Helen. "The Development of the Japanese Animation Audience in the United Kingdom and France." In *Animation in Asia and the Pacific,* edited by John A. Lent, 73–84. Bloomington: Indiana University Press, 2001.

McGowan, Chris, and Jim McCullaugh. *Entertainment in the Cyber Zone*. New York: Random House, 1995.

McGray, Douglas. "Japan's Gross National Cool." *Foreign Policy* 130 (June 2002): 44–54.

McLuhan, Marshall. *Understanding Media: The Extensions of Man*. Cambridge, Mass.: MIT Press, 1994.

McPherson, Tara. "Reload: Liveness, Mobility, and the Web." In *New Media, Old Media: A History and Theory Reader*, edited by Wendy Hui Kyong Chun and Thomas Keenan, 199–208. New York: Routledge, 2006.

McWan, Blessy, and Linsay M. Cramer. "Progressive Racial Representation or Strategic Whiteness? Raj and Priya Koothrappali in *The Big Bang Theory*." *Southern Communication Journal* 87, no. 4 (2022): 312–23.

Meng, Bingchun. "Underdetermined Globalization: Media Consumption via P2P Networks." *International Journal of Communication* 6 (2012): 467–83.

Metz, Christian. *Film Language: A Semiotics of the Cinema*. Chicago: University of Chicago Press, 1991.

Miller, Toby. *The Well-Tempered Self: Citizenship, Culture, and the Postmodern Subject*. Baltimore: Johns Hopkins University Press, 1993.

Morley, David, and Kevin Robins. "Techno-Orientalism: Japan Panic." In *Spaces of Identity: Global Media, Electronic Landscapes and Cultural Boundaries*, 147–73. New York: Routledge, 1995.

Moulthrop, Stuart. "You Say You Want a Revolution? Hypertext and the Laws of Media." *Postmodern Culture* 1, no. 3 (1991).

Murakami, Takashi. *Superflat*. San Francisco: Last Gasp, 2003.

Murugesan, S. "Understanding Web 2.0." *IT Professional* 9, no. 4 (July 2007): 34–41.

Nanfang dushi bao [Southern metropolis daily]. "Guangzhou chuxian 'yuzhaizu'" ['Otaku' appears in Guangzhou]. March 14, 2008.

Nanfang ribao [South Daily]. "Han Han lao le, 90 hou zuozhe zai zuo shenme?" [Han Han is old, but what is the post-90s generation doing?]. April 9, 2009.

Napier, Susan J. *Anime from "Akira" to "Howl's Moving Castle": Experiencing Contemporary Japanese Animation*. Rev. ed. New York: Palgrave Macmillan, 2005.

Napier, Susan J. "When the Machines Stop: Fantasy, Reality, and Terminal Identity in *Neon Genesis Evangelion* and *Serial Experiments Lain*." *Science Fiction Studies* 29, no. 3 (2002): 418–35.

Napier, Susan J. "The World of Anime Fandom in America." *Mechademia* 1 (2006): 47–63.

National Bureau of Statistics of China. Accessed July 20, 2023. https://data .stats.gov.cn/.

Navas, Eduardo. *Remix Theory: The Aesthetics of Sampling*. New York: Springer, 2012.

Nelson, Theodor H. *Literary Machines*. Sausalito, Calif.: Mindful Press, 1992.

Ng, Wai-ming. "Japanese Animation in Singapore: A Historical and Comparative Study." *Animation Journal* 9, no. 1 (2001): 47–60.

Ngai, Sianne. *Our Aesthetic Categories: Zany, Cute, Interesting*. Cambridge, Mass.: Harvard University Press, 2012.

Ngai, Sianne. *Ugly Feelings*. Cambridge, Mass.: Harvard University Press, 2005.

Nietzsche, Friedrich. *Thus Spoke Zarathustra: A Book for All and None*. Translated by Walter Kaufmann. New York: Modern Library, 1995.

Nornes, Abé Mark. "For an Abusive Subtitling." *Film Quarterly* 52, no. 3 (Spring 1999): 17–34.

Nugent, Benjamin. *American Nerd: The Story of My People*. New York: Scribner, 2008.

Ogata, Amy F. *Designing the Creative Child: Playthings and Places in Midcentury America*. Minneapolis: University of Minnesota Press, 2013.

Okada, Toshio. *Otakugaku Nyumon* [Introduction to otakuology]. Tokyo: Ota Publishing, 1996.

O'Reilly, Tim. "What Is Web 2.0: Design Patterns and Business Models for the Next Generation of Software," O'Reilly, September 30, 2005. http://www.oreilly.com/pub/a//web2/archive/what-is-web-20.html.

Ōtsuka, Eiji. "World and Variation: The Reproduction and Consumption of Narrative." Translated by and with an introduction by Marc Steinberg. *Mechademia* 5 (2010): 99–116.

Park, Jane Chi Hyun. "Stylistic Crossings: Cyberpunk Impulses in Anime." *World Literature Today* 79, no. 3/4 (2005): 60–63.

Patten, Fred. "Anime in the United States." In *Watching Anime, Reading Manga: 25 Years of Essays and Reviews*, 52–73. Berkeley, Calif.: Stone Bridge Press, 2004.

Patterson, Christopher B. *Open World Empire: Race, Erotics, and the Global Rise of Video Games*. New York: New York University Press, 2020.

Paulk, Charles. "Post-National Cool: William Gibson's Japan." *Science Fiction Studies* 38, no. 3 (2011): 478–500.

Perkin, Harold James. *The Rise of Professional Society: England Since 1880*. New York: Routledge Press, 1989.

Peters, John Durham. *The Marvelous Clouds: Toward a Philosophy of Elemental Media*. Chicago: University of Chicago Press, 2015.

Phi, Bao. "NOCs (Nerds of Color)." *Star Tribune*, January 20, 2010. https://www.startribune.com/nocs-nerds-of-color/82188702/.

Picard, Martin, and Jérémie Pelletier-Gagnon, eds. "Geemu and Media Mix: Theoretical Approaches to Japanese Video Games." Special issue, *Kinephanos* 5, no. 1 (December 2015).

Polan, Dana B. *Pulp Fiction.* London: BFI, 2000.

Poster, Mark, and Stanley Aronowitz. *Information Subject.* London: Routledge, 2001.

Pratt, Mary Louise. *Imperial Eyes: Travel Writing and Transculturation.* London: Routledge, 2007.

Qin, Amy. "Theaters in China Screen Movies, and Viewers' Text Messages," *New York Times,* August 25, 2014.

Rochet, Jean-Charles, and Jean Tirole. "Platform Competition in Two-Sided Markets." *Journal of the European Economic Association* 1, no. 4 (2003): 990–1,029.

Roh, David S., Betsy Huang, and Greta A. Niu, eds. *Techno-Orientalism: Imagining Asia in Speculative Fiction, History, and Media.* New Brunswick, N.J.: Rutgers University Press, 2015.

Roquet, Paul. *Ambient Media: Japanese Atmospheres of Self.* Minneapolis: University of Minnesota Press, 2016.

Roquet, Paul. "From Animation to Augmentation: Dennō Coil and the Composited Self." *Animation* 11, no. 3 (2016): 228–45.

Rosen, Philip, ed. *Narrative, Apparatus, Ideology: A Film Theory Reader.* New York: Columbia University Press, 1986.

Rossiter, Ned. "Creative Industries in Beijing: Initial Thoughts." *Leonardo* 39, no. 4 (2006): 367–70.

Rubinstein, Raphael. "In the Realm of the Superflat." *Art in America* 89, no. 6 (June 2001): 110.

Ruh, Brian. "Early Japanese Animation in the United States: Changing Tetsuwan Atomu to Astro Boy." In *The Japanification of Children's Popular Culture: From Godzilla to Miyazaki,* edited by Mark I. West, 209–26. Lanham, Md.: Scarecrow Press, 2009.

Ruh, Brian. "The Robots from Takkun's Head: Cyborg Adolescence in *FLCL.*" In *Robot Ghosts and Wired Dreams: Japanese Science Fiction from Origins to Anime,* edited by Christopher Bolton, Istvan Csicsery-Ronay Jr., and Takayuki Tatsumi, 139–59. Minneapolis: University of Minnesota Press, 2007.

Ruh, Brian. "Transforming U.S. Anime in the 1980s: Localization and Longevity." *Mechademia* 5 (2010): 31–49.

Sadamoto, Yoshiyuki. *Neon Genesis Evangelion,* vol. 1. 2nd ed. San Francisco: VIZ Media, 2004.

Samuels, David. "Let's Die Together." *Atlantic,* May 1, 2007. https://www.the atlantic.com.

Sanders, Leonard. "Virtual Ephemeralities: Idoru and Evangelion, Popular Visual Cultures in Japan." In *On Verbal/Visual Representation: Word & Image Interactions 4,* edited by Martin Heusser et al., 137–49. Amsterdam: Rodopi, 2005.

Sasaki, Toshinao. *Niconico doga ga mirai wo tsukuru: Dwango monogatari* [Niconico video is creating the future: The Dwango story]. Tokyo: Ascii Media Works, 2009.

Sato, Kumiko. "How Information Technology Has (Not) Changed Feminism and Japanism: Cyberpunk in the Japanese Context." *Comparative Literature Studies* 41, no. 3 (2004): 335–55.

Scafidi, Susan. "Screen Scene." *Counterfeit Chic* (blog), November 17, 2008. http://www.counterfeitchic.com/culture_of_the_copy/.

Schodt, Frederik L. "Mighty Atom, TV Star." In *The Astro Boy Essays: Osamu Tezuka, Mighty Atom, and the Manga/Anime Revolution,* 55–75. Berkeley, Calif.: Stone Bridge Press, 2007.

Scott, A. O. "The Death of Adulthood in American Culture." *New York Times,* September 11, 2014. http://www.nytimes.com.

Seigworth, Gregory J., and Melissa Gregg. "An Inventory of Shimmers." In *The Affect Theory Reader,* edited by Melissa Gregg and Gregory J. Seigworth, 1–25. Durham, N.C.: Duke University Press, 2010.

Shamoon, Deborah. "Situating the Shojo in Shojo Mango: Teenage Girls, Romance Comics, and Contemporary Japanese Culture." In *Japanese Visual Culture: Explorations in the World of Manga and Anime,* edited by Mark W. MacWilliams, 137–54. New York: M. E. Sharpe, 2008.

Shaviro, Steven. *Post-Cinematic Affect.* Winchester, U.K.: Zero Books, 2010.

Sifianos, Georges. "The Definition of Animation: A Letter from Norman McLaren." *Animation Journal* 3, no. 2 (1995): 62–66.

Siliconera. "STEINS;GATE ELITE Producer on Stringing Together Its Worldlines and a Science Adventure Teaser." February 28, 2019. https://www.siliconera.com.

Sina Tech. "Maopuwang datui jike gainian" [Mop.com promoted the concept of geek]. May 24, 2006. http://tech.sina.com.cn/i/2006-05-24/1956954653.shtml.

Smith, Zadie. "Generation Why?" *New York Review of Books,* November 25, 2010. https://www.nybooks.com.

Sobchack, Vivian Carol. *Screening Space: The American Science Fiction Film.* New Brunswick, N.J.: Rutgers University Press, 1997.

Sobchack, Vivian Carol. "Toward a Phenomenology of Cinematic and Electronic Presence: The Scene of the Screen." *Post Script* 10, no. 1 (Fall 1990): 50–59.

Sohu. "'Zhai jinji' bei pingwei niandu reci" ["Zhai economy" was chosen as the word of the year]. March 8, 2021. https://www.sohu.com/a/454694296_100184288.

Song, Ligang, Cai Fang, and Lauren Johnston. "China's Path towards New Growth: Drivers of Human Capital, Innovation, and Technological Change."

In *China's New Sources of Economic Growth,* edited by Ligang Song, Cai Fang, Lauren Johnston, and Ross Garnaut, 2:1–20. Canberra, Australia: ANU Press, 2017.

Spaziani, Scott. "Review: *Steins;Gate.*" Otaku In Review, February 15, 2012. https://otakuinreview.com/2012/02/15/review-steinsgate/.

Staiger, Janet. "Complex Narratives, An Introduction." *Film Criticism* 31, no. 1/2 (2006): 2–4.

Stam, Robert. *Subversive Pleasures: Bakhtin, Cultural Criticism, and Film.* Baltimore: Johns Hopkins University Press, 1992.

Starosielski, Nicole. *Media Hot and Cold.* Durham, N.C.: Duke University Press, 2022.

Starosielski, Nicole. *The Undersea Network.* Durham, N.C.: Duke University Press, 2015.

Statistical Report on Internet Development in China. China Internet Network Information Center, 1997–2002.

Steinberg, Marc. *Anime's Media Mix: Franchising Toys and Characters in Japan.* Minneapolis: University of Minnesota Press, 2012.

Steinberg, Marc. "Converging Contents and Platforms: Niconico Video and Japan's Media Mix Ecology." In *Asian Video Cultures: In the Penumbra of the Global,* edited by Joshua Neves and Bhaskar Sarkar, 91–113. Durham, N.C.: Duke University Press, 2017.

Steinberg, Marc. "Otaku Consumption, Superflat Art, and the Return to Edo." *Japan Forum* 16, no. 3 (2004): 449–71.

Steinberg, Marc. *The Platform Economy: How Japan Transformed the Consumer Internet.* Minneapolis: University of Minnesota Press, 2019.

Steins;Gate Wiki. "List of Known Worldlines." https://steins-gate.fandom.com/wiki/List_of_Known_World_Lines.

Stewart, James B. "Ruth Porat May Be Just What Investors Think Google Needs." *New York Times,* July 23, 2015.

Storm.mg. "Zimuzu bei zhua la!" [Fansubbing groups were arrested!]. *Fen chuanmei* [The storm media], October 7, 2016. https://www.storm.mg.

Suan, Stevie. *Anime's Identity: Performativity and Form beyond Japan.* Minneapolis: University of Minnesota Press, 2021.

Sun, Kevin. "Playing the Shell Game." *AsianWeek* 17, no. 35 (April 26, 1996).

Tamaki, Saito. *Beautiful Fighting Girl.* Translated by J. Keith Vincent and Dawn Lawson. Minneapolis: University of Minnesota Press, 2011.

Target. "Ye Linghan: Hulian shidai de yishu chuangzuo" [Ye Linghan: Art creation in the age of connectivity]. Sohu, September 12, 2018. https://www.sohu.com/a/253513106_662707.

Tatsumi, Takayuki. *Full Metal Apache: Transactions between Cyberpunk Japan and Avant-Pop America.* Durham, N.C.: Duke University Press, 2006.

Tencent Technology. "95 Hou de danmu shejiao" [Danmaku socialization among the post-95 generation]. Tech.qq, August 20, 2014. http://tech.qq.com/a/20140820/007842.htm.

Tencent Technology. "Weixin shang dianshi!" [WeChat on television!]. Tech.qq, September 4, 2014. http://tech.qq.com/a/20140904/032857.htm.

Terranova, Tiziana. "Free Labor: Producing Culture for the Digital Economy." *Social Text* 18, no. 2 (63) (2000): 33–58.

Terranova, Tiziana. *Network Culture: Politics for the Information Age.* Ann Arbor, Mich.: Pluto Press, 2004.

Thacker, Eugene. "Foreword: Protocol Is as Protocol Does." In *Protocol: How Control Exists after Decentralization,* by Alexander R. Galloway. Cambridge, Mass.: MIT Press, 2004.

Time. "TIME 100 Competition: The 2010 TIME 100 Poll." December 21, 2010.

Tinajiadezhuji. "Danmu liyi: Hai jide bei b-zhan huiyuan kaoshi zhibei de kongju ma?" [Danmaku courtesy: Do you still remember the fears of being controlled by the Bilibili membership exams?]. Bilibili, November 6, 2018. http://www.bilibili.com/read/cv1470684.

Tofusensei. "History of Live-EviL." Live-evil.org. January 25, 2008. http://www.live-evil.org/history-of-live-evil.

Tomlinson, John. *The Culture of Speed: The Coming of Immediacy.* London: SAGE, 2007.

Touraine, Alain. *The Post-Industrial Society: Tomorrow's Social History—Classes, Conflicts, and Culture in the Programmed Society.* Translated by Leonard F. X. Mayhew. London: Wildwood House, 1974.

Tronti, Mario. "The Strategy of Refusal." In *Workers and Capital,* translated by David Broder, 241–62. New York: Verso Books, 2019.

Tudor, Deborah. "The Eye of the Frog: Questions of Space in Films Using Digital Processes." *Cinema Journal* 48, no. 1 (2008): 90–110.

Turkle, Sherry. *The Second Self: Computers and the Human Spirit.* New York: Simon & Schuster, 1984.

Turner, Fred. *From Counterculture to Cyberculture: Stewart Brand, the Whole Earth Network, and the Rise of Digital Utopianism.* Chicago: University of Chicago Press, 2008.

Van Dijck, José. *The Culture of Connectivity: A Critical History of Social Media.* Oxford: Oxford University Press, 2013.

Vesna, Victoria, ed. *Database Aesthetics: Art in the Age of Information Overflow.* Minneapolis: University of Minnesota Press, 2007.

Virno, Paolo. *A Grammar of the Multitude: For an Analysis of Contemporary Forms of Life.* Translated by Isabella Bertoletti, James Cascaito, and Andrea Casson. London: Semiotext, 2004.

Voloshinov, Valentin. *Marxism and the Philosophy of Language*. Translated by Ladislav Matejka and I. R. Titunik. Cambridge, Mass.: Harvard University Press, 1986.

Wang, Jianxin. "Cong 'yuzhai' shuo linglei 'zhai wenhua'" [From "otaku" to "zhai culture"]. *Nanfang Ribao* [Southern daily], November 1, 2009.

Wang, Jing. *High Culture Fever: Politics, Aesthetics, and Ideology in Deng's China*. Berkeley: University of California Press, 1996.

Wang, Shujen, and Jonathan J. H. Zhu. "Mapping Film Piracy in China." *Theory, Culture & Society* 20, no. 4 (2003): 97–125.

Wang, Wilfred Yang, and Ramon Lobato. "Chinese Video Streaming Services in the Context of Global Platform Studies." *Chinese Journal of Communication* 12, no. 3 (2019): 356–57.

Wark, McKenzie. *A Hacker Manifesto*. Cambridge, Mass.: Harvard University Press, 2004.

Wark, McKenzie. *Virtual Geography: Living with Global Media Events*. Bloomington: Indiana University Press, 1994.

Weheliye, Alexander G. "Post-Integration Blues: Black Geeks and Afro-diasporic Humanism." In *Contemporary African American Literature: The Living Canon*, edited by Lovalerie King and Shirley Moody-Turner, 213–34. Bloomington: Indiana University Press, 2013.

Wei, Tan. "'Youjian'qingnian Ye Linghan" [The right-clicking youth Ye Linghan]. Artron, October 2, 2019. https://news.artron.net/20191002/n1062000 .html.

Wei, Xaoyun. "'Manhua zhi shen' Shouzhong Zhichong de zhongguo qingjie" [The "god of anime" Osamu Tezuka and his China complex]. People.cn, August 22, 2006. http://people.com.cn.

Wells, Paul. *Understanding Animation*. London: Routledge, 1998.

Wenhui Daily. "2008 wangluo 'reci' xin bianhua: You shehui hanyi de ci jiancheng zhuliu" [New changes in the internet buzzwords of 2008: Words with social meanings become the mainstream]. December 9, 2008.

White, Gordon. *Riding the Tiger: The Politics of Economic Reform in Post-Mao China*. Stanford, Calif.: Stanford University Press, 1993.

Wiener, Norbert. *Cybernetics: Or the Control and Communication in the Animal and the Machine*. 2nd ed. Cambridge, Mass.: MIT Press, 1961.

Wiener, Norbert. *The Human Use of Human Beings: Cybernetics and Society*. New York: Da Capo Press, 1988.

Williams, Raymond. *Television: Technology and Cultural Form*. New York: Routledge, 1974.

Wired. "Geekipedia." Special issue, September 2007.

Wloszczyna, Susan, and Ann Oldenburg. "Geek Chic." *USA Today*, October 23, 2003. http://www.usatoday.com.

Wood, Robin. *Hollywood from Vietnam to Reagan.* New York: Columbia University Press, 1986.

World Bank. "China 2030: Building a Modern, Harmonious, and Creative Society." World Bank, March 23, 2013. http://documents.worldbank.org.

Wu, Xiaohui. "Qiantan yiqing zhixia de 'zhai wenhua' chuanbo" [On the spread of "zhai culture" in the pandemic]. *Xinwen Chuanbo* [Journalism and communication] 7 (2020): 837–40.

Xiao, Yang. "Danmu dianying: Lanpian de yanwudan haishi yingshi de xin shangji" [Danmaku cinema: A mask for terrible movies or a new business opportunity for film market]. *Beijing qingnian bao* [Beijing youth daily], August 9, 2014.

Xinjing bao [Beijing news]. "Zai danmu mianqian, dianying haowu zunyan keyan" [In front of danmaku, cinema lost all its dignity]. August 7, 2014.

Xin wenhua bao. "Kan dianying or gao shejiao" [Watch films or social networking]. August 12, 2014. http://enews.xwh.cn.

Xu, Yizhou. "The Postmodern Aesthetic of Chinese Online Comment Cultures." *Communication and the Public* 1, no. 4 (2016): 436–51.

XYM. "Fuxing yu luan ma: Lianai yu naoju" [Urusei and Ranma: Love and farce]. *Dianzi youxi ruanjian* [Electronic game software] 3 (1995): 76–77.

Yang, Guobin. "Historical Imagination in the Study of Chinese Digital Civil Society." In *China's Information and Communications Technology Revolution: Social Changes and State Responses,* edited by Xiaoling Zhang and Yongnian Zheng, 17–33. New York: Routledge, 2009.

Yang, Yuhong. "The Danmaku Interface on Bilibili and the Recontextualised Translation Practice: A Semiotic Technology Perspective." *Social Semiotics* 30, no. 2 (2020): 254–73.

Yang, Yuhong. "Danmaku Subtitling: An Exploratory Study of a New Grassroots Translation Practice on Chinese Video-Sharing Websites." *Translation Studies* 14, no. 1, (2021): 1–17.

Ying, Xiao. "Guo Jingming bu shi zuojia, Han Han shi shehui pipingjia" [Guo Jingming is not a writer, and Han Han is a social critic]. *Liaoning ribao,* December 23, 2009.

Yishuyuntu, Y. T. "Zai 0 he 1 gouheng de shijie, women doushi Lucy" [In the world constructed with 0 and 1, we are all Lucy]. Ifeng, July 29, 2019. https://ishare.ifeng.com/c/s/7ohpm5FQiqt.

Zahlten, Alexander. "Between Two Funerals: Zombie Temporality and Media Ecology in Japan." *Positions: Asia Critique* 29, no. 2 (2021): 291–317.

Zahlten, Alexander. *The End of Japanese Cinema: Industrial Genres, National Times, and Media Ecologies.* Durham, N.C.: Duke University Press, 2017.

Zeng, Yuli. "Meng wenhua weihe liuxing: Erciyuan, zhiyuxi yu chengren de 'ertong hua'" [Why is *moe* culture popular: Two-dimensionality, healing,

and the "infantilization" of adulthood]. *Paper,* November 3, 2017. https://
www.thepaper.cn/.

Zhang, Leticia-Tian, and Daniel Cassany. "Making Sense of Danmu: Coherence in Massive Anonymous Chats on Bilibili.Com." *Discourse Studies* 22, no. 4 (2020): 483–502.

Zhang, Tongdao. *Dianshi Kanke: Diaocha Zhongguo Dianshi Shouzhong* [Television viewers: A study on Chinese television viewership]. Anhui, China: Anhui Education Press, 2003.

Zhang, Xudong. "Intellectual Politics in Post-Tiananmen China: An Introduction." *Social Text* 55 (1998): 1–8.

Zhang, Yiwu. "'80 hou,' xunzhao chaoyue pingyong de kongjian" [The post-80s: Looking for a space beyond mediocrity], *21 Shiji Jingji Baodao* [21st century business herald], September 24, 2007.

Zhong, Shuting. "Rang danmu fei: Cong yiming B-zhan yonghu jiaodu kan danmu dianying" [Let danmaku fly: Look at danmaku cinema from the perspective of a b-site user]. Ifanr, August 21, 2014. http://www.ifanr.com/44 4836/.

Zhongguo jiaoyu zaixian. "2018nian quanguo gaokao luqulv 81.13%" [National college entrance admission rate in 2018 is 81.13%]. February 26, 2019. https://gaokao.eol.cn/news/.

Zhou, Jing, and Lin Zhang. "Jiyu shouzhong diaocha de danmu dianying tiyan yingxiao fang'an de pingjia yu celue yanjiu" [A study of danmaku cinema: Audience survey and marketing strategy]. *Zhongguo Dianying Shichang* [Chinese film market] 1 (2016): 17–21.

Ziben shichang. "Nishi qiangran fali, zhongguo de 'zhai jingji' shidai" [China in the age of "zhai economy"]. October 2009.

Zongguo qingnian bao [China youth daily]. "Danmu hui ba dianying 'wan hao'?" [Can danmaku 'play well' in cinema?]. August 19, 2014.

Zweig, David, and Huiyao Wang. "Can China Bring Back the Best? The Communist Party Organizes China's Search for Talent." *China Quarterly* 215 (2013): 590–615.

Index

Page references in italics refer to illustrations.

JINYING LI is assistant professor of modern culture and media at Brown University.